S0-BJN-307

DATE DUE

The
Emergence
of Society

The Emergence of Society

A PREHISTORY OF THE ESTABLISHMENT

BY John E. Pfeiffer

McGRAW-HILL BOOK COMPANY

New York   St. Louis   San Francisco
Düsseldorf   Mexico   Toronto

Book design by Stanley Drate.

Map drawings by Vantage Art Inc.
Drawings by Mona Marks.

1 2 3 4 5 6 7 8 9 DO DO 7 8 9 7

Library of Congress Cataloging in Publication Data

Pfeiffer, John E. 1915–
The emergence of society.

Bibliography: p.
Includes index.
1. Man, Prehistoric.   2. Social evolution.
3. Society, Primitive.   I. Title.
GN74.1.P33   301.2   76-27308
ISBN 0-07-049759-1 Trade Ed.
ISBN 0-07-049758-3 Text Ed.

To Andy and Marianne
and Joan and Bill

Contents

The human press/An explosion of culture/
The abandonment of hunting-gathering and the rise
of farming and cities/Pristine states and independent
origins/Taming the male/Population pressure and
the passing of equality/Innocent beginnings/
revolutionary results

Primate evolution/The move from forests to savannas/
The origins of meat-eating, sharing and home bases/
The oldest butchering site/Migrations out of Africa and
the earliest hearths/Neanderthal man and beliefs in
an afterlife/The coming of modern man and art/
The last hunter-gatherers/A Kalahari Christmas

Illustrations

Paintings and Reconstructions

Acknowledgments

THIS book began taking shape in August 1969, when I spent a few days with Robert McC. Adams of the University of Chicago's Oriental Institute at his cabin in the Rockies. In between chores—he was busy clearing his land at the time—he gave me an idea of what a study of the origins of agriculture and the first cities would entail, of what books to read and people and sites to visit.

Adams was a charter member of my unofficial "board of consultants," investigators I have turned to on many occasions for information and advice. My first invitation to join an archeological expedition came from his colleague at the Institute, Robert Braidwood, a pioneer in studies of early farming villages in the Near East. Other charter members include Lewis Binford of the University of New Mexico, Robert Carneiro of the American Museum of Natural History, Michael Coe of Yale University, Kent Flannery of the University of Michigan, Eric Higgs of Cambridge University, Donald Lathrap of the University of Illinois, Richard MacNeish of the Peabody Foundation for Archaeology, John Murra of Cornell University, William Sanders of Pennsylvania State University, Paul Wheatley of the University of Chicago, and Howard Winters of New York University.

The following investigators explained their work to me in the field during visits to sites over a period of four years: Greece—Higgs. Guatemala—Dennis Puleston, University of Minnesota. Hawaii—Marshall Sahlins, University of Chicago. Iran—Harvey Weiss, Yale University; Henry Wright, University of Michigan. Iraq—McGuire Gibson, University of Chicago; Julian Reade,

London; Jürgen Schmidt, German Archaeological Institute in Baghdad. Mexico—Richard Blanton, Purdue University; Flannery; David Grove, University of Illinois; Susan Lees, Hunter College; Joyce Marcus, University of Michigan; James Neely, University of Texas; Jeffrey Parsons, University of Michigan; Sanders. New Guinea—Jocelyn Powell, University of Papua and New Guinea. New Zealand—Wilfred Shawcross, Australian National University. Peru—Lathrap, MacNeish; Thomas Patterson, Temple University. Taiwan—Kwang-chih Chang, Yale University. Tasmania—Rhys Jones, Australian National University. Turkey—Braidwood. United States—Charles Bareis, University of Illinois; Binford; James Brown and Gail Houart, Northwestern University; William Longacre and Jefferson Reid, University of Arizona; Robert Salzer, Beloit College.

Individuals mentioned in the book reviewed sections dealing with their work. In addition, Coe and Warwick Bray of the Institute of Archaeology in London received first drafts of chapters and suggested changes in the interests of accuracy and proper emphasis. Their comments have resulted in many changes; any errors that remain are my fault.

The following provided information not yet published, checked sections for accuracy, answered questions, and generally kept me posted: Albert Ammerman, Stanford University; James Anderson, Cahokia Mounds State Park; Pedro Armillas, University of Illinois, Chicago Circle; David and Nancy Asch, Northwestern University; Eduard M. van Zinderen Bakker, University of the Orange Free State; Ofer Bar-Yosef, Hebrew University of Jerusalem; Daniel Bates, Hunter College; Donn Bayard, University of Otago, New Zealand; Peter Bellwood, Australian National University; Robert Bettarel, York College; Michael Bisson, McGill University; Ester Boserup, Danish Delegation, United Nations; Jeffrey Brain, Harvard University; Keith Brandt, University of Wisconsin; Bennet Bronson, Field Museum of Natural History, Chicago; Karl Butzer, University of Chicago; Edward Calnek, University of Rochester; Halet Cambel, Istanbul University; Vern Carroll, University of Michigan; Richard Cassels, University of Auckland; Napoleon Chagnon, Pennsylvania State University; William Chmurny, State University of New York College, Potsdam; Desmond Clark, University of California, Berkeley; Clemency

Coggins, Harvard University; Mark Cohen, State University of New York College, Plattsburgh; Michael Cole, Rockefeller University; Della Cook, Indiana University; Pat Coursey, Tropical Products Institute, London; George Cowgill, Brandeis University; Carole Crumley, University of Missouri.

Also Bruce Dahlin, Catholic University of America; Patricia Daly, Columbia University; Hilary Deacon, University of Stellenbosch; Robin Dennell, University of Sheffield; Jan De Wet, University of Illinois; William DiVale, York College; Genevieve Dollfuss, French Archaeological Delegation in Iran; Theodore Downing, University of Arizona; Patricia Draper, University of New Mexico; Robert Drennan, Peabody Foundation for Archaeology; Robert Dyson, University of Pennsylvania; Timothy Earle, University of California, Los Angeles; James Ebert, University of New Mexico; John Eisenberg, Smithsonian Institution; Carol and Melvin Ember, Hunter College; Brian Fagan, University of California, Santa Barbara; Walter Fairservis, Vassar College; Kenneth Farnsworth, Northwestern University; Louise Firouz, Teheran; Richard Ford, University of Michigan; Melvin Fowler, University of Wisconsin, Milwaukee; Derek Freeman, Australian National University; Walton Galinat, University of Massachusetts, Waltham; Howard Scott Gentry, United States Department of Agriculture; Ian Glover, Institute of Archaeology, London; Jack Golson, Australian National University; Chester Gorman, University of Pennsylvania; Richard Gould, University of Hawaii; Michaed Gregg, University of Wisconsin, Milwaukee; James Griffin, University of Michigan; Daniel Gross, Hunter College.

Also Robert Hall, University of Illinois, Chicago Circle; Christopher Hamlin, University of Pennsylvania; Norman Hammond, Cambridge University; Margaret Hardin, Loyola University of Chicago; Thomas Harding, University of California, Santa Barbara; Jack Harlan, University of Illinois; Michael Harner, New School for Social Research; Henry Harpending, University of New Mexico; David Harris, University College London; Eric Havelock, New Milford, Conn.; Charles Higham, University of Otago; Robert Hitchcock, University of New Mexico; Ping-ti Ho, University of Chicago; Michael A. Hoffman, University of Virginia; Robert Hommon, Bishop Museum, Honolulu; Frank Hole, Rice University; Gail Houart, Northwestern University;

Alan Howard, University of Hawaii; Nancy Howell, University of Toronto; Eva Hunt, Boston University; Karl Hutterer, University of Michigan; Fumiko Ikawa-Smith, McGill University; Glynn Isaac, University of California, Berkeley; Michael Jarman, Cambridge University; Gregory Johnson, Hunter College; Christopher Jones, University of Pennsylvania; William Judge, University of New Mexico; Marion Kelly, Bishop Museum, Honolulu; Diana Kirkbride, British School of Archaeology in Iraq; Anne and Michael Kirkby, University of Bristol; Richard Klein, University of Chicago; Philip Kohl, Wellesley College; Conrad Kottak, University of Michigan; Stephen Kowalewski, Lehman College; Carl Lamberg-Karlovsky, Harvard University; Richard Lee, University of Toronto; David Lewis, Australian National University; Michael Logan, East Carolina University; Jose Luis Lorenzo, Department of Prehistory, Mexico; Thomas Lynch, Cornell University.

Also Abdullah Masry, Department of Antiquities, Saudi Arabia; Margaret Mead, American Museum of Natural History; Heinrich Mendelssohn, Tel-Aviv University; Dorothy Menzel, University of California, Berkeley; Sarunas Milisauskas, State University of New York, Buffalo; René Millon, University of Rochester; Marion Mochon, University of Wisconsin, Parkside; Michael Moseley, Field Museum of Natural History; Hallum Movius, Harvard University; Patrick Munson, Indiana University; Toni Nelken-Terner, University of the Sorbonne; Robert Netting, University of Arizona; Hans Nissen, Free University of Berlin; Joan Oates, Cambridge University; Arturo Oliveros, Department of Prehistory, Mexico; Leo Oppenheim, University of Chicago; Hamilton Parker, University of Otago; Richard Pearson, University of British Columbia; Christopher Peebles, University of Michigan; Dexter Perkins, Columbia University; Jean Perrot, French Archaeological Delegation in Iran; Nicolas Peterson, Australian National University; Warren Peterson, University of Illinois; Barbara Pickersgill, University of Reading; Jane Wheeler Pires-Ferreira, George Washington University; Fred Plog, State University of New York, Binghamton; James Porter, Loyola University of Chicago; Gregory Possehl, University of Pennsylvania; Tatiana Proskouriakoff, Harvard University; Olga Puleston, University of Minnesota; Nanette Pyne, University of Washington.

Also Roy Rappaport, University of Michigan; William Rathje,

University of Arizona; Evelyn Rattray, Mexico City; Richard Redding, University of Michigan; Charles Redman, State University of New York, Binghamton; Charles Reed, University of Illinois, Chicago Circle; Colin and Jane Renfrew, University of Southampton; James Rock, Klamath National Park, California; Robert Rodden, University of California, Berkeley; Ralph Rowlett, University of Missouri; Jeremy Sabloff, University of Utah; Isa Salman, Directorate General of Antiquities, Baghdad; Earl Saxon, University of Durham; Robert Schacht, University of Maryland; Charles Scheffer, Temple University; Carmel Schrire, Rutgers University; Thayer Scudder, California Institute of Technology; Thurstan Shaw, Cambridge; Kathleen Shawcross, Department of Internal Affairs, New Zealand; Gale Sieveking, British Museum; Gurdip Singh, Australian National University; William Skinner, Stanford University; Carol Smith, Duke University; Philip Smith, University of Montreal; Wilhelm Solheim, University of Hawaii; Michael Spence, University of Western Ontario; David Starbuck, Yale University; Ledyard Stebbins, University of California, Davis; David Stronach, British Institute of Archaeology, Teheran; Derek Sturdy, Cambridge University.

Also Joseph Tainter, University of New Mexico; Eitan Tchernov, Hebrew University of Jerusalem; David Thomas, American Museum of Natural History; Harold Thomas, Harvard University; Charles Tilly, University of Michigan; Ruth Tringham, Harvard University; Robert Vierra, Northwestern University; Bernard Wailes, University of Pennsylvania; Patty Jo Watson, Washington University; David Webster, Pennsylvania State University; Fred Wendorf, Southern Methodist University; Theodore Wertime, Smithsonian Institution; Polly Wiesner, University of Michigan; Johannes Wilbert, University of California, Los Angeles; Gordon Willey, Harvard University; Stephen Williams, Harvard University; Edwin Wilmsen, University of Michigan; Elizabeth Wing, University of Florida; Marcus Winter, University of Michigan; John Wilson, Hightstown, N.J.; Martin Wobst, University of Massachusetts, Amherst; Gary Wright, State University of New York, Albany; Vero Wynne-Edwards, University of Aberdeen; Richard Yarnell, University of North Carolina; Douglas Yen, Bishop Museum, Honolulu; Cuyler Young, Royal Ontario Museum; Melinda Zeder, University of Michigan; Daniel Zohary,

Hebrew University of Jerusalem. A number of these also assisted in gathering photographs and other art.

Richard Krause of the University of Alabama; Warren Kornberg of the National Science Foundation; Cyr Descamps, Richard Shutler deserve thanks for special efforts in providing photographs.

I have received assistance, financial and otherwise, from foundations. Visits to nearly a hundred sites were made possible by a grant from the Carnegie Corporation of New York and by the active interest of Margaret Mahoney. Lita Osmundsen of the Wenner-Gren Foundation for Anthropological Research has contributed in a number of ways—with suggestions based on her wide knowledge of anthropology and anthropologists, with her understanding of a writer's problems, and with solid encouragement when most needed.

Lois White of the Australian National University has served throughout as an invaluable intermediary, keeping information flowing between my office in Pennsylvania and hers in Canberra.

Susan Gamer, Orren Alperstein, and Cathy Clark handled a large part of the correspondence and research required to check chapter sections and obtain illustrative material. Rita Chesterton did the typing of drafts and Barbara Honal of the final copy; they met their deadlines, which is more than I did. Special thanks are due to Bob Mitchell, art director, and to Peggy Conroy, for her work in coordinating the complex problems of scheduling.

I owe a great deal to Jeannette Hopkins, who edited this book as well as *The Emergence of Man*. There is so much to be done after the interviews and reading, after the digesting and organizing of research findings, after the first draft effort, to present information colorfully and clean of jargon—matters of style, clarity, economy of expression. Her contributions at this stage, when most books are considered completed, have been appreciable, and I acknowledge them with many thanks. She was also responsible for the supervision of research on illustrations.

Introduction:
The Uses of Society

Whatever the future, man is moving into it faster and faster, swept up in a revolution which started ten thousand years ago when all the world was a wilderness and he was a wild animal living essentially as his ancestors had lived for millions of years—foraging within his home ranges, exploiting other wild species, moving on when local abundances dwindled. Stone-age man, the hunter and gatherer, is known by his camping grounds, by sealed deposits excavated in rock shelters, caves and open-air sites. The transformation, the first stage of the revolution, is also clear in the prehistoric record. There are constructions, walls of stone and clay bricks in standard sizes, plaster and windows and niches, neatly fitting joints, prefabricated clay slabs, sockets for doors. The people who built them were no longer nomads. They had come to stay. They had invented a new kind of place, and more significant, a new world view whose impact they could not have foreseen.

Ten thousand years ago man's earliest life-style, his original traditions, and his ethics began to crumble. The rule among foragers, hunter-gatherers, had always been to stay small; they lived in small bands, huddled at night around isolated camp fires, rarely saw strangers. The new people stayed small also, at first, their earliest communities clusters of houses sheltering a few related families. When the families became larger, they tended to split into two communities. As the land filled up, however, the process went into reverse. Slowly, then at an accelerating rate, people streamed by the hundreds into a few centers of trade and ceremony and bustling marketplaces. They were creating new environments which in turn attracted others, a new glamor and new opportunities to explore activities beyond hunting and gathering and cultivating the land. The first towns and cities appeared not long after the first villages; they were the first masses and the first neighbors who were not kinfolk.

Crowding separated people as they had never been separated before. The hunter-gatherers' world had been a world of equals. Braggarts had been ridiculed until they fell silent. Would-be hoarders had been made to feel so uncomfortable, so resented, that valued possessions quickly became gifts and passed like hot potatoes from person to person and band to band. Now for the first time there were places for big men and elites, pomp and circumstance, arrogance and the accumulation and display of wealth. The emergence of complex society, the most radical development in human evolution since the emergence of the family of man from ancestral apes some 15,000,000 years ago, is one of science's deepest mysteries. It must have been a response to the threat of extinction. Nothing less could have brought about the abandonment of a way of life that had endured for ages.

Hunting-gathering had been an effective adaptation to the wilderness, permitting man to spread from the African woodlands and savannas where he arose, and to find living space on all continents and in all climates. It offered more leisure, more easy and spontaneous living, than any system devised since. The full story of its passing is not known. One theory holds overpopulation, famine, and the threat of famine probably responsible. World populations had been increasing very slowly but steadily, and the pressure was on. Ten thousand years ago in a few scattered areas of the Near East and perhaps elsewhere the old reliable methods of obtaining food were beginning to fail. In a sense, nature itself was failing. The wilderness could no longer provide enough food; there were too many people.

Perhaps the world could have been made forever safe for hunting-gathering then and there, if man had been able to change his breeding habits, if populations had stopped rising. He multiplied instead and, in the process, changed nature. He settled down, developed farms and irrigation systems, and multiplied even faster. The last ten millenniums have been a struggle to keep in balance, a race between rising population and increasingly sophisticated use of the land, with population always running ahead.

The striving for control in a world of uncontrolled growth offers clues to the origins of complex society. There are basic connections, yet to be explored in depth, between population pressure and emerging elites and hierarchies. With the coming of large communities, families no longer cultivated the land for themselves and their immediate needs alone, but for strangers and for the future. They worked all day instead of a few hours a day, as hunter-gatherers had done. There were schedules, quotas, overseers, and punishments for slacking off.

People could never justify their efforts merely because of the need to survive. They needed special reasons for working long and hard against their better judgment, reasons over and above necessity. They may have begun accounting for and validating necessity by establishing new beliefs, artificial environments for sustaining those beliefs, and a work ethics sanctioning and glorifying the task of organizing institutions for survival. Religion was central in the shaping of early cities and city-states. People did not work primarily for their own ends. They obeyed the commands of gods as communicated by kings who, in due course, became gods themselves. Entire societies, audiences and actors alike, participated in the grandest of ceremonies, moving to the rhythms of dance and music and chants, dwarfed and overawed and bewitched by the scale of things—the acre-wide plazas and high platforms, the temples and palaces, the monuments and sculptures and brilliantly painted friezes.

Science as well as art was mobilized in the service of belief. Predicted eclipses, predicted sunrises at summer and winter solstices were taken as evidence that king and priests, the star performers in the pageants, were not only close to the gods but had a voice in the running of celestial affairs. It was theater and more than theater, illusion and more than illusion, because nothing is as real as illusion believed collectively. The animal and human sacrifices were real, and so was the need to hold people together by loyalties wider than the loyalties of blood and kin.

Conflict existed even in the simplest, most flexible and informal societies, even among small bands of hunter-gatherers where, in times of mounting tension, individuals could always move away to another band. Conflict reached new levels of intensity among groups which had to stay put, having committed themselves to property and mass living. Proximity created a source of tension, a gulf separating people who had once been closer. In hunter-gatherer times men and women had usually lived together as equals. For reasons unknown sexism arrived with settling and farming, with the emergence of complex society.

Trade as well as religion was mobilized to keep conflict under control. Elites exchanged valuable gifts. Communities refrained from making products they needed and made other products in quantities far beyond their needs, simply to have things to trade with neighboring communities—all for the sake of maintaining goodwill and law and order. Yet war was chronic. Man was still in the process of taming himself, changing from a wild to a domesticated species, a transformation still in progress.

In the continuing effort to achieve peace, deciphering the elusive record of times past is as important as marches and petitions and top-level diplomacy. Research on evolving societies, in itself a significant example of evolution in action, is expanding and attracting students who a decade or so ago would have gone in for such "hard" sciences as physics, chemistry, and biology. There are clues everywhere, in relic patches of mountain and desert and jungle wilderness so isolated that they can be reached only after days of walking, and close at hand in backyards and in the shadows of skyscrapers. From artifacts uncovered in ruins throughout the world, from regional surveys and the analysis of ancient settlement patterns, from observations of contemporary peoples in cities and hinterland tribes, investigators are gradually reconstructing the emergence of gods and power.

Prehistory has attracted its share of pseudoscientists. In no area of research does the easy answer come easier or do more damage. Travelers who cannot believe that the ancestors of native peoples built cities in the high Andes, pyramids along the Mississippi, temples on remote Pacific islands, come back with "proof" that it was all the work of the Chinese or the Lost Tribes of Israel or, most recently, visitors from outer space. Statements foolish enough to arouse universal embarrassment apparently embarrass no one. Amateur philosophers do not hesitate to discuss the nature of man, the most complex problem known, with the unabashed self-confidence of a quack proclaiming his cure for cancer. So essays appear describing man as naked or killer or sexy ape, essays in which hackneyed heredity-versus-environment arguments are dusted off and offered—and widely accepted—as stunning new insights.

The gullibility is what hurts, what discourages, the readiness to swear by nonsense. Pseudoscience dishonors the struggle for perspective, the effort to reach for humility and understanding in the teeth of increasing complexity. The only certainty is that there are no revelations, no final answers. There are only hypotheses, fragile and deliberate "falsehoods," oversimplified versions of reality offered for testing in the hope that they may advance knowledge a few steps before they, in turn, are disproved. In continuing to probe the mystery of his beginnings, man learns more about the mystery of his possible futures. He becomes better at predicting and planning.

The revolution that has brought about the change from hunter-gatherer to city dweller is in its early stages. The greatest problems remain to be solved. Man the postponer supreme has postponed the task of limiting his numbers—a task which seems to run counter to his strongest instincts—for the better part of ten thousand years, primarily because of a succession of advances in agriculture. He is beginning to realize that this delaying action must come to an end.

Taking the pressure off, achieving zero population growth, will demand changes at the top of the social pyramid. The function, the existence, of elites hangs in the balance. They probably ceased serving evolutionary purposes a millennium or two ago. People who have not been admitted into elites have greater expectations than ever. Leisure, prestige, and authority will have to be shared more widely, and that calls for new kinds of hierarchy, or perhaps for something better than hierarchies. We have so far managed to muddle through despite the corruption of power and a scorn for commoners, strangers, and other excluded majorities so deep that they are treated as inferior species. The question is whether such abuses can be eliminated without eliminating centralized

Photo by Jerry Irwin

Courtesy of Nikon, Inc.

control itself, whether the disease can be cured without killing the patient.

Control, however efficient, is never enough for survival. There must be some slack in the system, a reserve of flexibility so that people can adapt to unpredictable changes which are certain to arise, assuming they cope successfully with overpopulation, war and violence in cities. This is where "useless" activities come in, doing silly things and things not so silly as long as they have never been done before—walking tightropes between skyscrapers, trying to do backward double somersaults on skis, training fourteen hours a day to break Olympic records, flying to the moon, searching for subatomic particles, theorizing about the origins of life and the universe (and the origins of society), wrapping buildings and mountains in cellophane, avant-garde movements in all the arts.

Play, exploration, and daredeviltry are preparation for evolution yet to come. The spirit of experiment and challenge contributes to the creation of an enormous repertoire of possibilities, possible inventions and actions and concepts, possible worlds. Only a tiny fraction of all man's adventures will ever pay off, but there is no way of telling beforehand which fraction. Sooner or later we will face emergencies many times more critical and complex than those we face now. If we survive them, as we probably will, it will be because our ability to control and organize is stimulated by the innovations of those who cannot help driving themselves to the limit and beyond.

Pioneers of evolution: the role of play, exploration, daredeviltry

1

Man, A New Kind
of Evolution

*The human press/An explosion of cultures/
The abandonment of hunting-gathering and the
rise of farming and cities/Pristine states and independent
origins/Taming the male/Population pressure and the
passing of equality/Innocent beginnings,
revolutionary results*

O NE of the last camping grounds of Africa's last remaining
hunter-gatherers is a pinpoint in immensity—a circle of low grass
huts in a sandy plain as large as France. Outside the circle the
Kalahari Desert extends in all directions to the horizon and
beyond, marked by lines of parallel dunes running for miles
roughly east-west, and in the basins between the dunes stretches
of grassland and thorn bushes and scattered trees and dried-up
river beds.

Inside the circle some thirty Bushmen, at home in the late
afternoon, sit around their hearth fires, back to back, shoulder to
shoulder, thigh against thigh, forming what one observer has
called "the human press." Food passes from hand to hand. Two

27

Richard Lee (University of Toronto) / Anthro-Photo

The human press: Bushman hunter-gatherers in a communal circle, Kalahari desert, southern Africa

men several hearths apart talk without raising their voices. A child cries, and a woman is there within arm's reach to pick it up and console it. Laughter starts near one fire and passes in a wave through the group. In its closeness, in the soft swift movements and sounds among its members, the group behaves almost like a flock of birds.

People in cities have created another kind of closeness, a less intimate human press. For them the wilderness has become an abstraction, something far away, vaguely romantic and dwindling. Their out-of-doors is geometric, marked off, a grid system of long avenues whose buildings hide horizons. They live in small brightly lit places, bounded by walls and sharp corners, among noises most of which are made by machines, within shouting distance of hundreds of persons, most of them strangers.

In all evolution there is no transformation, no "quantum leap," to compare with this one. Never before has the life-style of a species, its way of adapting, changed so utterly and so swiftly. For some fifteen million years members of the family of man foraged as animals among animals. The pace of events since then has been explosive. The entire sequence from the first farming villages, the first sharp break with hunting-gathering, to a world dominated by cities, to the even more highly urbanized future which, before the end of the twentieth century, will see the coming of supermetropolises made up of several hundred million persons each—all this has been packed into an instant on the evolutionary time scale, a mere 10,000 years.

Times have changed, but not basic problems. The world was a wilderness 10,000 years ago, without farms or cities or roads. Yet people were dealing with shortages of food and fuel, overcrowding, famine and the threat of famine, violence. They were not moving gladly into the future. They struggled to preserve the hunting-gathering way of life, no doubt bemoaning the mediocrity of their leaders and longing for a return to the good old days.

Life was relatively simple before the change. It was a good life, better in many respects than anything that has evolved since. There were fewer people in the whole world than there are now in New York City, and they were all hunter-gatherers. They had spread out of Africa, out of the wide savanna lands where they arose. They had learned to survive and multiply in tundras, semideserts, and tropical rain forests, in the thin air of mountain valleys two to three miles high, during long subzero winters near the edges of advancing glaciers.

This strange new breed of primate seemed to have found its place in the scheme of things, living on what nature offered, as small-band, small-time nomads in balance with other wild species. But that balance would soon be upset. After ages of moving about in search of food, migrating when local resources were depleted, and following herds and exploring new terrain, people tended increasingly to stay put, spending more and more of their time in a single familiar area. They came together in larger and larger groups, as if attracted and drawn in toward a center. Man had been a highly social animal from the beginning, but this was socialization on an unprecedented scale.

Settling down left its mark in the archeological record. In the Near East there are wide desert plains with dozens of small hills and some not so small. All look like natural features. But they are not natural. The hills were built up over generations from the debris of successive occupations. They are prehistoric mounds, time capsules of a sort, each containing relics of vanished settlers.

Global views: the world as it was during the last ice age, about 20,000 years ago (upper view), and as it is today

George Buctel

Man was losing the old freedom to pack up and move. The evidence is there inside the mounds: walls of stone and hardened mud, sun-baked bricks, storage and garbage pits, pottery, ovens, kitchen areas. The mounds also include remains of domesticated species, fossil bones and plant fragments and the sharp imprints of seeds in clay, indicators of farming on the rise. Plots of land had to be cleared and kept clear, fenced off and weeded, protected from birds and other competing plant-eaters. It was a new kind of commitment to places.

The earliest states appeared at about the same time, roughly 3500 B.C. to 3000 B.C. in Egypt and Sumer, southernmost Mesopotamia; later, states arose in the Indian subcontinent, in China, Africa, Mesoamerica and South America. These were "pristine" or primary states, systems developed in response to forces arising from within, independently of other states, a direct consequence of their own internal problems and efforts to adapt.

The emphasis on independent systems, independent origins, is new. Until recently most investigators thought in terms of a single origin. They regarded Egypt, Sumer or the Near East in general as the "hearth" or "cradle" of civilization. They assumed that everything originated in this region and spread to other lands. Their view implied that the rest of the world was backward, that other people were inferior for having failed to discover or invent civilization.

This assumption has fewer champions than it once had. But it is perpetuated, among other places, in the pages of a recent world history published, ironically, under the auspices of the United Nations. It explains that the Chinese had to learn metallurgy from the West, where it was invented; that their writing came from the West, from Sumer; and that some of their rituals and religious practices "may be due to Western influence." Such arrogance dies hard—the belief that civilization began in a special place with special individuals, a favored spot, a Garden of Eden. The weight of accumulating evidence suggests that there were no Edens, or that there were many Edens.

Prehistoric people did not change because they were more intelligent than their neighbors, more resourceful or more creative. The great challenge is to understand what happened to them—and what is happening to us, for we are in the throes of responding to the same forces that changed them. Increasing social complexity is not new in man. It is an old mammalian custom. Among primates it can be traced back at least sixty to seventy million years to the earliest forerunners of monkeys and apes and human beings.

Most primates of that era, small creatures resembling today's mouse lemur or huge-eyed tarsier, lived in the simplest possible groupings, a mother and her offspring. As John Eisenberg of the Smithsonian Institution indicates, complete dependence on a lone female represents the minimum social unit. The mother's fertilizing encounter was brief and with an anonymous male. She nursed her young and defended them from predators until they were old enough to forage for themselves.

The main thrust of evolution since then has been toward more inclusiveness. That meant socializing or "taming" the male to become a responsible, full-time member of the group, in the interests of superior defenses and more effective reproduction. The breaking-in process continues. It has not yet been worked out to the complete satisfaction of all parties concerned. In rare cases, the male was built into the basic female-offspring unit; more often, one or more males lived together with a number of females and offspring.

Change was gradual. Relatively few males had the required genetic makeup, the temperament, to be less of a rugged individualist and more of a social creature, or the ability to learn new behavior patterns readily. Those who did outlived their less sociable brethren and passed their genes on to more offspring. Most surviving males were domesticated after a fashion. Among more advanced monkeys and apes, a still more elaborate group emerged —the troop, an association of many males and females and their young.

Taming the male continues to be a problem. It is enormously complicated by the inexorable growth of population. In the beginning human beings were a minority breed scattered in bands or troops over African savannas. Prehistory since then has been a record of population fluctuations, local booms and declines. But on a worldwide long-run basis, and exceedingly slowly until recent times, populations kept rising. In response, man did what no other species had ever done. He created new environments which could support far greater populations than the wilderness, and succeeded too well. He found himself swept up in a round of changes as populations continued to climb, each change producing new conditions which demanded further change. It was a new kind of spiralling, accelerating evolution.

Population growth was one of the main forces that brought the hunting-gathering way of life to an end. It shattered traditions, unspoken rules, established over thousands of millenniums. Violence, a problem even in small-band times, increased. Judging by today's hunter-gatherers, people were quite aware of the disruptive effects of fighting and evolved ways of avoiding it. One way was to stay small. Band size may vary from a dozen to several persons. But it tends to hover around the "magic number" of twenty-five, a figure that holds for Bushmen, Australian aborigines, and other present-day hunter-gatherers, and, according to estimates based on the areas of excavated living sites, for their prehistoric ancestors as well. Staying small keeps conflict at a low level; so does moving away, an option frequently used when tempers began to run high.

These options became less available with mounting population pressure. The magic number changed, too. As the countryside became more thickly settled, conflict was more of a problem. The risk of fighting between villages increased, so that a village had to be large enough to defend itself. On the other hand, its size was limited. The more people living close together, the greater the number of conflicts among them, the greater the risks of internal dissension and falling apart. The first villages may have included 50 to 200 persons, but the magic number probably worked out to about 100 persons, with the tendency to split into two villages increasing sharply over that level. (This makes an interesting comparison with the sizes of groups of savanna-dwelling African baboons which tend to split when they reach more than about 100 members.)

Much of the casualness and informality had gone out of life. A village is a system with built-in tensions, in uneasy and dynamic balance between opposing forces. Energy, time, and discipline and organization are necessary to keep such a system in running order. There were elaborate rituals, each step designed to bypass conflict at all costs, and when they failed, other rituals regulated fighting. People sought to maintain law and order, even as they met in frequent and violent armed conflict. They struggled to remain at peace while preparing for battles that had always been inevitable. The paraphernalia of control became more and more elaborate, detailed and complicated as populations continued to rise, and as the size and number of communities continued to increase.

The most elaborate controls were associated with cities, which one investigator describes as "places where unexpected things happened." They were glamorous places, often with wide avenues leading "downtown" to massive and brightly painted buildings, high massive walls and pyramids and towers. People from the surrounding countryside and beyond came for worship and adventure. They came to gape, to be impressed and overawed, to see things rarely seen—ceremonial spectacles conducted on lofty platforms, ceramics and textiles and other craft objects in the marketplace, strange-looking people in strange clothes.

Viewed from a more analytical standpoint, cities were religious and administrative centers, centers occupying the top positions in hierarchies of smaller centers, towns and villages, and hamlets. Most early cities were small; one working definition classifies "urban centers" as any settlement covering more than 125 acres or so. Populations usually ranged from 10,000 to 40,000, although at least 125,000 persons are believed to have lived in Teotihuacan in Mexico.

Cities represent only one aspect of early control systems, a focus on highly concentrated populations. "State," pristine or otherwise, refers to the entire region organized around a religious-administrative center, usually but not necessarily a city. In recent studies it has been defined in terms of administrative levels and the flow of information from level to level. "Civilization" applies mainly to a people's world view as expressed in art, science and religion. It became a loaded word in imperial-colonial times, implying *we* as civilized and *they* as uncivilized, so its usefulness is somewhat limited.

People played new roles in their new societies. It is an old notion that human nature cannot be changed, whatever that means. But human behavior certainly can be. Back in hunter-gatherer times all people in nomadic bands were equal, or at least as close to equal as they have ever been. Among modern hunter-gatherers the opinion of the best hunter carries extra weight in determining where to seek big game, interpreting tracks, planning tactics. The best storyteller holds the center of the stage around the fire at night when the hunt is done, and the best healer is consulted most frequently in times of sickness. There is no single leader, no man for all seasons and for all decisions.

Equality passed with the passing of the band, another shattered tradition. There was an explosion of differences, a swift rise of special people with special privileges, proto-elites and elites, perhaps the sort observed among tribal societies of the present or recent past, among other places, in New Guinea, the Pacific islands, Africa and the Amazonian jungles of South America. Marshall Sahlins of the University of Chicago describes various levels or degrees of leadership. There is the "petty chieftain," often the oldest man in the community: "[He] is usually spokesman of his group and master of its ceremonies, with otherwise little influence, few functions and no privileges. One word from him and everyone does as he pleases." His central role in disputes and on other occasions is to sense which way the wind is blowing, and then give voice to the consensus.

The so-called big man has considerable influence, although it tends to be local and precarious. His position is not official, in the sense of being supported by ancient tribal traditions. He is a self-made leader, a natural organizer who rises to the top on the strength of his personal qualities. As an outstanding fighter or farmer or rainmaker, he gains the support of kinsmen and other followers. The big man remains big as long as he can hold his support and, in a group which includes would-be and not-yet big men, that may not be very long.

There may have been big-man societies before the coming of agriculture. They probably existed 15,000 or more years ago in southwestern France, in the countryside around the present village of Les Eyzies, a region rich in prehistorical sites. Abundant game and water and great limestone rock shelters and caves attracted unusually high concentrations of hunter-gatherers, conditions that might have called for informal leadership.

At higher levels leadership becomes more of an institution. The leader may or may not have outstanding personal qualities; the office itself assumes special importance. He may be a chief or a paramount chief heading a coalition of lesser chiefs. Such men appeared most widely among settled communities, almost always among agriculturalists. A notable exception occurred along the 2,000-mile coastline from northwestern California to southeastern Alaska. As recently as the early 1900s Indians without agriculture were living here in large permanent villages with ample food close at hand in local forests and salmon-rich waters. They had elaborate ceremonies, a characteristic art style, and chiefs and nobles whose wealth and prestige were measured in furs, canoes, copper, slaves, and other possessions signifying high status.

Kings headed states and empires, such as those that arose earliest in Sumer, Egypt, the Indus Valley and China. There were various grades of kingship—kings who were heroes or messiahs or crusaders, but still human beings; slightly superhuman kings regarded as intermediaries or middlemen between their subjects and the gods; and divine kings, full-fledged gods in their own right, who were living for a time among mortals.

The process which led to such people, such institutions, was largely hit-or-miss. That has been the rule during the long course of biological evolution, the passing-on of inherited or genetic traits from generation to generation which dominates among non-human species. Fossil evidence suggests that about 100 to 1,000 species have become extinct for every present-day survivor. The several million existing species are a small and select group, the residue of vast numbers of species that did not make it.

Today's societies, an estimated 6,000 of them, represent a comparable residue. Cultural evolution, evolution by tradition, also involved many extinctions and few survivals. Traces of extinct societies lie buried in all lands. Village clusters vanished after enduring for hundreds of years, as seen in archeological layers rich in hearths and tools and pottery—and then an abrupt break in the record, nothing but sterile soil empty of artifacts. Investigators have found entire cities which dwindled from tens of thousands of persons to hundreds within a few centuries. The death rate for prehistoric societies could easily have been as high as the death rate for species.

The suspicion of high social death rates is reinforced by present-day efforts to adapt. Planners are continually launching grand projects without foreseeing the consequences. More than a decade ago, for example, the World Health Organization sprayed the thatched-roof huts of Borneo villages with DDT. It was part of a major drive to wipe out malaria and one result, the desired result, was the eradication of malaria-carrying mosquitoes and a sharp drop in the frequency and severity of the disease. Spraying also produced some unexpected and unwelcome results. Cockroaches in the huts ate DDT-containing foods and were in turn eaten by lizards. The lizards concentrated the powerful drug in their bodies to such a level that lizard-eating cats were poisoned and died off. In the absence of cats, rat populations soared and so did populations of lice, fleas, and other rat-infesting organisms, thus increasing the risks of such conditions as typhus and plague.

Health authorities moved to combat the new threat. Planes of Britain's Royal Air Force parachuted fresh supplies of cats into isolated villages, and doctors prepared for possible epidemics by stockpiling quantities of antibiotics and vaccines. There were other effects, such as increased numbers of caterpillars which destroyed thatched roofs. Strategies for avoiding similar complications in the future have yet to be devised.

In Egypt, a host of troubles has followed completion of the billion-dollar Aswan Dam, one of the greatest construction feats of the twentieth century—and one of the saddest examples of ecological mismanagement. The dam is doing many of the things it was built to do: it is generating electricity, preventing severe floods along the Nile, and providing irrigation waters for about a million acres of land that once was desert and now yields up to three crop harvests per year.

But it has created new problems, among them a serious health emergency. In pre-dam days irrigation canals had contained snails carrying bilharzia, a lingering and weakening parasitic disease, but the canals dried up periodically and the snails died. Now that that the canals are full all the time, snails are flourishing, and the disease has increased tenfold. Meanwhile crop yields have been declining in certain areas. Salts which reduce soil fertility are accumulating, and the only countermeasure is to build a network of special canals to drain irrigated lands. More than a hundred scientists are engaged in an effort to deal with these and other difficulties.

Even people with the highest technical skills act on the basis of insufficient knowledge, insufficient foresight. Acting in ignorance seems to be a chronic part of the human condition. It has kept men off balance ever since the world became too crowded for hunting-gathering. There are still pockets of stability, however, places where crowding has never been a problem, where poor nutrition, disease, infanticide, drugs that produce abortion, fighting, and sex taboos keep populations from soaring.

The Tsembaga, 200 farmers in the highlands of New Guinea, have evolved an effective system of checks and balances on some 2,000 rugged acres of dense forest and grassland, only about half suitable for cultivation. They live predominantly on taro, manioc, sweet potatoes and other vegetables. They also keep pigs, not to eat but primarily for sacrificing to their ancestors. Roy Rappaport of the University of Michigan spent more than a year with the Tsembaga, studying how their system works to insure survival. He found that pigs compete with people for food, being fed manioc and sweet potatoes. Upon occasion they break into cultivated gardens and devour more than their quota of the crops. As pig populations rise, tensions also rise. The animals break into gardens more frequently and require more food and care, which is

Courtesy of Roy A. Rappaport, University of Michigan

woman's work. The situation comes to a head by a consensus of grumbling. Tired women complain when they come home in the evening and, when their complaining becomes sufficiently intense

A self-adjusting system: Tsembaga pig-killing festival controls pig population, highland New Guinea (lower left and below)

and persistent, their husbands begin agitating publicly for a "kaiki," an elaborate pig-killing festival followed by ritual warfare between the Tsembaga and their neighbors. The result is a sharp decline in pig populations, less work for women and less grumbling, and peace until pig pressure builds up again, in ten to twenty years.

Self-adjusting, self-adapting systems tend to be extremely complicated. A small change in pig populations, crop yields or any one of a dozen other factors might seriously affect the well-being of the group. Computers are being used to help analyze such problems. Steven Shantzis and William Behrens at the Massachusetts Institute of Technology fed information about the Tsembaga into the memory circuits of a high-speed electronic computer, together with a program or set of instructions originally developed for the investigation of business cycles. This stimulation model indicated what might happen if better medical care increased the annual human population growth rate from 1.3 to 1.5 percent. The machine calculated the effects over a period of half a century, only a fraction of a second in actual computing time. Its tentative answer: the land could support the extra people, providing that pig-killing festivals and warfare took place more frequently, say, every eight or nine years.

That is close to the limit. If the human growth rate were further increased to 2.0 percent a year, the pig population would drop to zero within a century and within another forty years four out of every five people would starve. Other simulated measures, such as preventing warfare or providing superior diets, produced similar results, thus supporting what experience in the real world has amply demonstrated. Improved living conditions, however well intended, can be disastrous unless they are part of a whole complex of adjustments, among them birth control and new ways of using the land.

Archeology is another way of learning about efforts to achieve equilibrium, peace. The process can be followed time-lapse fashion, step by step over hundreds and thousands of years. It all started so simply, so innocently. No one seemed to be doing anything much out of the ordinary. There were no big decisions to switch from hunting-gathering to farming. Major changes were probably as unwelcome then as they are now. Then as now, the tradition was probably never to make basic changes, but to make small makeshift compromise-changes which would cause as little disruption as possible and help postpone really important changes forever or at least for a generation or two. It was revolution without revolutionaries, the most effective kind. No antisocial individuals were abroad calling for an end to nomadism. Staying put was merely the best, usually the only, possible course under prevailing circumstances.

The people who changed the world beyond recall were struggling not to change. First it was a matter of doing more hunting-gathering, settling down and exploiting wild species more intensively; then the use of cultivated plants as supplementary items in the diet; and finally complete dependence on domestication and widespread irrigation systems. It is all recorded in the living sites of prehistory, in patterns of artifacts. People concentrated in larger groups, and one of the chief reasons was that population kept increasing.

Power and arrogance appeared on the grand scale. They were as necessary as growing more food. People were trying to establish order and security, and they knew of no better way than to create elites and absolute, divine authority invested in men on earth. Survival would have been impossible in those times without power and arrogance, however dangerous they have become since. The latest and most turbulent phase of human evolution was under way.

	20,000 B.C.–10,000 B.C.	10,000 B.C.–8,000 B.C.	8000 B.C.–6000 B.C.
WORLDWIDE	End of ice age, melting glaciers, seas rise 250–500 feet	Population about 10,000,000	
NEAR EAST	Earliest domestication of dog, Iraq, before 10,000 B.C. Possible domestication of gazelle, Palestine, 15,000 B.C. or earlier Early hunter–gather village, Palestine, 10,000 B.C.	Domesticated sheep, Iraq, 8900 B.C.	First farming villages, wheat, barley, sheep, goats, 7500 B.C. Sophisticated house construction, Iran, 7000 B.C. Obsidian trade under way, 7000 B.C. Earliest excavated nomad site, Iran, 6000 B.C.
INDUS VALLEY			
FAR EAST			Earliest known pottery, Japan, 7500 B.C. First signs of plant tending, gardening, Thailand, 7000 B.C.
AFRICA	Possible domestication of Barbary sheep, North Africa, 15,000 B.C. or earlier		End of Sahara drought, 7500 B.C.
EUROPE	Height of cave art in France and Spain	End of cave-art period	First farming village, Greece, 6000 B.C. Ireland first settled, 6000 B.C.
THE PACIFIC AREA			First cultivated gardens, New Guinea, before 6000 B.C.
MESOAMERICA	First hunter-gatherer band arrives in Mexico's Tehuacan Valley, before 10,000 B.C.		Probable first steps in domesticating corn, Mexico, 7000 B.C.
SOUTH AMERICA		Man reaches southernmost tip, 9000 B.C.	First domesticated plant, bean, Peru, 7500 B.C.
NORTH AMERICA	Man reaches Pennsylvania, 12,000 B.C.	Settling of New World Arctic, 9000 B.C.	

World time chart: some major events marking the

6000 B.C.–4000 B.C.	4000 B.C.–2000 B.C.	2000 B.C.–BIRTH OF CHRIST	BIRTH OF CHRIST –A.D. 1000	A.D. 1000–PRESENT
	Population about 100,000,000			Population, nearly 4,500,000,000
First irrigation, 5500 B.C. First steps toward writing, seals on clay, 5000 B.C.–4000 B.C.	First city, Uruk, 3500 B.C. Earliest known writing, Uruk, 3500 B.C. Population "implosion" at Uruk, 3100 B.C.	Moses leads Hebrews out of Egypt, 1300 B.C.	Romans destroy Jerusalem, 70 Birth of Mohammed, 570	Crusades, 1096–1270
Earliest domesticated animals, sheep, goat, pig, humped cattle, dog, 5500 B.C. Earliest farming villages, 4000 B.C.	First Indus cities, first Indus writing, 2500 B.C.	End of Indus cities, 1750 B.C.		
First farming villages, China, 5000 B.C. Origin of writing, China, 4000 B.C.	Earliest traces of rice, China, 3000 B.C. Established farming villages, Thailand, 4000 B.C. Earliest bronze artifacts, Thailand, about 3600 B.C.	First cities, China, 1800 B.C. Buddha, 560 B.C.–483 B.C. Confucius, 551 B.C.–479 B.C. Great wall finished, 200 B.C.	First Southeast Asia city, Vietnam, 100 Monumental architecture, Java, 700–850	Angkor Wat, Cambodia, 1200
First farming villages, Egypt, 4500 B.C. Herders in Sahara, 5000 B.C.	Hierakonpolis, Egypt's southern capital, 3200 B.C. Writing, Egypt, 3000 B.C. Full-scale yam cultivation, West Africa, 3000 B.C. Drought returns to Sahara, 2500 B.C.	Village clusters, perhaps with paramount chiefs, southwestern Sahara, 700 B.C. Terra-cotta figurines and iron smelting, West Africa, after 500 B.C.	Chariot trade routes across Sahara, 500 First cities, West Africa, 500 Height of agriculture, iron age, Congo to Cape Town, 100–400	Domestication, iron, widespread in Southern Africa, 1000 Zimbabwe, 1000–1400 A "pristine" state reaches its peak, Madagascar, 1895
First megalithic tombs, 4500 B.C.	Stone temples on Malta, 3500 B.C. Building starts at Stonehenge, 2700 B.C. Olives and grapes domesticated, Greece, 2500 B.C. First European city, Greece, 2000 B.C.	Peak period at Stonehenge: 2000 B.C.–1500 B.C. End of megalithic period, 1500 B.C. First Olympic games, 776 B.C. Romans invade England, 55 B.C.	Nero and the burning of Rome, 64 Vandals sack Rome, 455 Charlemagne proclaimed Holy Roman Emperor, 800	Spread of Black Death, 1349 First universities, 1100–1150 Leonardo da Vinci, 1452–1519
First agricultural drainage ditches, New Guinea, about 4000 B.C.	First irrigation, New Guinea, 3000 B.C. Voyages start into open Pacific, 3000 B.C.	"Lapita" people reach Fiji, Tonga, and Samoa Islands, about 1200 B.C.	Voyagers reach the Marquesas and Hawaii, about 300; Easter Island, 400; Hawaii, 500; New Zealand, 750	States or near-states arise in Polynesia perhaps by 1500
Corn, beans, squash, prickly pear, chili peppers in Tehuacan gardens, 5000 B.C.	First farming villages, Tehuacan and Oaxaca, 2000 B.C.	First public building, Oaxaca, 1500 B.C. Collapse of San Lorenzo, 900 B.C. Olmec culture, 1200 B.C.–400 B.C. Beginnings of Tikal, Monte Alban, 500 B.C. Beginnings of Teotihuacan, 400 B.C.	Monte Alban peak, 400; collapse, 600 Teotihuacan peak, 600; collapse, 750 Tikal peak, 700; collapse, 800	Aztecs, 1300–1519
Guinea pig domesticated, Ayacucho, 5000 B.C. Ancestors of llama and alpaca being domesticated in Andes, 4000 B.C.	First farming villages, 2000 B.C.	Chavin culture, 1200 B.C.–500 B.C.	Beginnings of Tiahuanaco, 100 Rise of Huari empire, 700	Huari collapse, 1100 Tiahuanaco collapse, 1200 Inca empire, 1430–1532
Vanishing of mammoths, mastodons and other big game, 5000 B.C.	Earliest domesticated squash, Kentucky, 2500 B.C. Earliest corn in Southwest, 2000 B.C. Two-acre fish weir in Boston, 2000 B.C.	Irrigation, farming villages, in Southwest, 300 B.C. First native domesticated plants, sunflower, sumpweed, 1500 B.C. Beginnings of mound-building in Midwest, 1000 B.C.	Irrigation, farming villages established in Southwest, 100–300 End of Hopewell mound–building, 500 Pueblos appear in Southwest, 900 Beginnings of first city, Cahokia, 900 Leif Ericson lands on eastern coast, 1000	Chaco Canyon pueblos: 900–1300 Broken K pueblo, 1150–1275 Cahokia peak, 1200 Grasshopper pueblo, 1275–1400 Cahokia collapse, 1300 U.S. bicentennial, 1976

rise of power and elites, organized by regions

2

Living with Nature, the Wisdom of Hunter-Gatherers

Primate evolution/ The move from forests to savannas/
The origins of meat-eating, sharing and home bases/
The oldest butchering site/ Migrations out of
Africa and the earliest hearths/ Neanderthal
man and belief in an afterlife/ The coming of modern
man and art/ The last hunter-gatherers/
A Kalahari Christmas

F OR all but a fraction of their time on earth, hominids, members of the family of man, have lived as hunter-gatherers. Their record includes 15,000,000 years of foraging in wildernesses, and 10,000 years for everything else from the first farms to superhighways, megaton nuclear weapons, and the United Nations. They learned a great deal during those first 15,000,000 years. They developed language, increasingly sophisticated ways of surviving, the beginnings of religion and art. Still their story represents a staggering degree of conservatism. The essential techniques of obtaining food did not change for tens of thousands of generations, and traditions formed over such spans were deep-rooted and enduring.

45

Hunting-gathering had far more than habit to recommend it. It persisted not simply by the sheer power of inertia, the resistance to change of any kind, but for a number of positive reasons. The human species was in harmony with nature, one among many wild species living together as parasites of sunlight in cycles of birth and decay. Prey as well as predator, consumed as well as consumer, humans were part of the chain of being as they have never been since. Settling down and congregating in larger and larger groups had serious disadvantages.

Hominids had to change, however. They arose at the margins of things, in transition zones where diverse landscapes merged imperceptibly with one another. Tropical and subtropical forests, forests so dense that creatures beneath the treetops lived mostly in shadow, stretched across entire continents from the west coast of Africa to the East Indies. Life was brighter moving away from the edges of the dense forests into woodlands with more sunlight, with trees fewer and further between, and into woodland glades near the shores of seasonally flooded lakes and rivers—and brightest of all past the woodland edges out into the glare of savanna land, grassy plains extending wide and open for miles and miles.

Most apes remained exclusively in the forests. But some of them, often groups of three or four subadult males who had not yet attained positions of status in their troops, foraged back and forth between zones, moving out of the shadows into woodlands and then into the shadows again. They ventured into savanna grasslands on rare occasions, perhaps only during I-dare-you games, at least in the beginning. The bright sunlight and the openness were strange. Trees were fewest there and risks greatest from the attacks of lions, wild dogs and other predators. Eventually some apes became seriously committed to areas outside the deep forests, perhaps to escape the crowds among the trees. They found new living space in the savannas and abundant food, including meat on the hoof. They found ways of fitting in with the established order of things. Lions hunted mainly at night, wild dogs in the evening and early morning. That left the daylight hours for primate predators.

The first hominid was a creature in transition, moving in and out of transition zones, then as now a breed on the make, in the

San Diego Zoo Photo

**Chimpanzees, closest living relative of man: mother and child (above);
upright and on the lookout (below)**

San Diego Zoo Photo by Ron Garrison

process of becoming something radically different. It looked far more like an ape than a human, something like today's chimpanzees in the Congo, three and a half feet tall, weighing perhaps forty to forty-five pounds, slender and elusive, probably nesting in trees. Even with far more evidence than is available now, it would be impossible to specify the point at which the hominid evolved from an advanced ape, as impossible as specifying the moment when twilight ends and night begins. But such creatures may have been at large on African savannas fifteen million years ago.

The behavior of present-day forest-dwelling chimpanzees serves as one basis for speculations about the behavior of early hominids. There is something very special about killing and eating animals. Eating fruit, buds, insects, and blossoms, the predominant diet of chimpanzees in the wild and probably of our earliest ancestors, is a rather innocent and uncomplicated activity. Such items can be chewed and swallowed quickly, in a tree or grove of trees where fellow chimpanzees are similarly preoccupied, busily and enthusiastically cramming themselves with the same foods. It is basically each individual for himself.

Hunting can also be an individual enterprise, but it is far more efficient for two or more individuals to work together. The odds that they will make a kill are about two or three times greater than for a lone hunter. Chimpanzees know of this strategy, and occasionally several will close in on a prey from different directions. The pressure for such behavior, however, is not intense. Chimpanzees in the forest eat meat now and then only; they do not need it to survive.

For early people on the savanna, getting meat was a matter of life or death. Meat was an estimated one-third or more of their diet. They would have soon become extinct if they had not observed and anticipated the movements of prey together, and together planned appropriate strategies. Cooperation could not be a casual, sometime thing. Cooperation was vital after the prey was killed, as well. Meat comes in large packages compared to fruits and other customary forest fare, providing a sizable chunk of food concentrated in one place, a focus of intense attraction. Among chimpanzees, the individual with the carcass, which weighs about ten pounds or so on the average, is under pressure

Worzel meditating:
showing whites of eyes,
rare among chimp,
common among humans

Chimpanzees sharing
carcass of a monkey,
Gombi Reserve,
Tanzania

Courtesy of Geza Teleki, Pennsylvania State University

to give some of the meat to other members of the troop. As in the case of cooperative hunting, the pressure is rather mild; sharing may occur or not, usually not.

Early hominids had to share. Sharing played a critical role in the socializing or taming of large vigorous males, the most active hunters among man as among chimpanzees. That put a premium on self-control, on inhibition of "natural" impulses. Evolution favored males who could save most of the meat at a kill site for later distribution—and, in general, individuals capable of devising and abiding by rules, participating in some sort of system for dividing the spoils. Bands composed of such individuals endured; less socialized bands failed to make it.

Many things were happening all at once, in a web of interacting and mutually reinforcing developments. People depended more on stone tools, at first perhaps to cut through thick hides or get at bone marrow, and later for defense and offense. Carrying tools and large portions of meat favored an upright stance and two-footed gait, which in turn freed the hands for further use and making of tools. And through it all, like a benign tumor at the head end of the spine, the brain continued to expand.

The increasing complexity of life on African savanna favored an increasingly complex nervous system, a larger memory and a greater capacity for weighing and choosing among an increasing number of alternative actions. This process had major repercussions. The bigger a primate's brain, the more slowly it matures. Mothers were compelled to devote themselves to their infants for longer and longer periods. Monkey infants depend completely on their mothers for about a year, ape infants for more than two years. The hominid infant of millions of years ago, however, was helpless for an estimated four to five years. It was even more helpless than the infants of other primates because, unlike them, it could not cling to its mother as she moved about. It watched her go away and had to learn to bring her back by crying.

One result was a different kind of home life. Although chimpanzees may sleep in the same trees night after night, they forage in a single group and leave the trees together in the morning. Among early hominids, however, home became a more permanent place. Mothers with infants and young children, and probably all females, stayed behind with a large male or two for protection.

Since plant foods could usually be gathered near home base, gathering became woman's work chiefly, while men went on the hunt, perhaps overnight or for several nights.

This arrangement, itself partly the product of increasing brain size and infant dependency, may have put a premium on further expansion of the brain because it increased the need for language. Hunters must have had some way of spelling out their plans in detail, particularly in dealing with the future. They must have had some way of letting the folks at home know where they intended to go, for how long, when they expected to return, and what to do in case they did not return on schedule. The ability to

Prehuman tool use: chimpanzee wielding stick

Photo by Linda and Tony Pfeiffer, Rutgers University-Lion Country Safari
Chimpanzee Rehabilitation Project, West Palm Beach, Florida

convey such information would also have encouraged longer trips and more ambitious exploration.

Meat-eating, cooperative hunting and sharing, tool use and an upright gait, larger brains and home bases and language—such developments were interrelated and evolved together. All the oldest remains of early hominids have been found in Africa, indicating that they spent most of their formative years there, and one of the world's most remarkable archeological sites is in the parched badlands of Kenya, ten sun-baked miles east of Lake Turkana (formerly Lake Rudolf), not far from a long, low rocky hill known as Fever Tree Ridge. It is dead, eroded, cracked-earth country. About the only things that move are sands blown by desert winds and investigators on the lookout for traces of early man.

Ages ago, before the erosion set in, this was a green and abundant world, a thousand-square-mile delta floodplain where a great river breaks into a maze of branching streams. In a clearing near a grove of trees along a stream a strange creature appears. It looks like an ape, but no ape ever walked that way, no bent-knee shuffle, but erect and striding like a human. It stands only four feet tall, about the size of an eight-year-old child, but its purposes are not childlike.

There is red meat for the taking—a partly dismembered hippopotamus. The creature walks back into the trees, toward the stream, and returns with companions. They have pebbles in their hands, and, squatting near the carcass, they use hammerstones to strike chips from the sides of the pebbles, forming sharp edges. Then they fall to it—hacking away at the joints, slicing off hunks of meat, shattering long bones for the marrow inside. After an hour or so they go away, with large portions of meat slung over their shoulders.

Time passes, thousands and thousands of years. A gentle fall of silt followed by rains of volcanic ash and further floods and volcanoes. Traces of the feast are buried under hundreds of feet of rock, sealed in layers of sediments, like a flower pressed between the pages of a book. Ages later the rock crumbles away and an archeologist, Glynn Isaac of the University of California, reconstructs the original event from the exposed clues. He has recovered a mass of broken bones from the site, an area about twenty feet across, and all but a few of them are hippopotamus bones. Scattered among the debris were more than a hundred artifacts, including a half dozen pebble choppers. The site itself yielded no signs of the meat-eaters, but their fossilized remains have been found in similar deposits throughout the general area. They are early hominids.

The most significant thing about the site is its age, which has been determined by a "radioactive clock" technique. The radioactive potassium in volcanic rock disintegrates at a regular rate, so many atoms per second, and leaves a residue of the inert gas argon. The older the rock, the more potassium atoms break down and the more gas accumulates. Measurements of the gas in rock samples collected during Isaac's excavations indicate that his is the oldest known archeological site. The hippopotamus meat was eaten 2,600,000 years ago, give or take a quarter of a million years.

One or two million years ago hominids began to spread out of Africa. No satisfactory explanation exists for the migrations, why they took place when they did or, for that matter, why they took place at all. They would, however, have been impossible if this had not already become one of the most adaptable of species. Darwin describes people who went about almost naked in frigid conditions at the southernmost tip of South America. Similar ruggedness helped their Old World ancestors to cope with cold climates to the north. Fire may also have helped. The oldest known home fires burned in the north, in Europe and Asia. Their traces, roughly circular areas found in caves and containing ashes and charred bones and heat-cracked rocks, are a million to half a million years old.

The hearth, the fireside, marked the end of a life dictated by the rising and setting of the sun. It created special settings in thousands of sheltered places throughout the world, circles of warmth and light on the coldest, darkest nights, a longer day for work and play and the sharing of ideas. The hominids who built the fires were about a foot and a half taller than the first near-ape members of the family of man, twice as heavy, equipped with a brain about four times bigger (already within the range of present-day brain sizes), and considerably more human. They had advanced most of the way toward the earliest types of *Homo sapiens*, who appeared 250,000 to 300,000 years ago.

The pace of evolution seems to have accelerated from this point on. One important sign was the appearance some 75,000 years ago of Neanderthal people, much-maligned human beings. The name has become associated with ungainly heavy-browed brutishness, and that image is likely to endure. For the record, however, it is a case of mistaken identity. It is based on a study more than half a century old, on the analysis of fossil bones found in southern France—the skeleton of an elderly man with extensive arthritis. Investigators failed to recognize the disease, interpreting abnormal bone thicknesses and curvatures as signs of a bent-over, heavy-footed "simian" gait.

Neanderthal people were stocky and rugged. Their brain was not as advanced as the brain of modern man. But, like modern humans, they were full-fledged members of the species *Homo sapiens* with remarkable abilities to adapt, surviving through long ice-age winters in western Europe. A British-American study confirms their human status: "There is no valid reason for the assumption that the posture of Neanderthal man . . . differed significantly from that of present-day man . . . If he could be reincarnated and placed in a New York subway—provided that he were bathed, shaved and dressed in modern clothing—it is doubtful whether he would attract more attention than some of its other denizens."

The Neanderthals were the first people to bury their dead, with flint tools, heavy stone slabs, and ibex horns or bear skulls arranged in ritual patterns around the deceased—and sometimes with flowers, as indicated by concentrations of flowering-plant pollens found in a grave north of Baghdad. They probably believed in an afterlife, judging by the presence of charred bones suggesting supplies of roasted meat for a journey to parts unknown. Such remains point to ceremonies and a concern with new kinds of questions involving the nature of death, the world of the dead, and the world of the living. One feels that the Neanderthals were groping for insights they could never attain, sensing ideas and aspirations beyond their abilities to express. In any case, there was a burst of "expression" toward the end of the Neanderthal times, with the emergence perhaps 40,000 or more years ago of fully modern people.

Their tool kits became more and more diverse. Instead of several types of flint burins or engravers, used to make differently shaped grooves or slots, a hunter-gatherer of western Europe might have two dozen or more types, indicating mounting sophistication, a multiplication of special requirements and special purposes. There were also tools made of bone, which tended to be rare and crude in Neanderthal tool kits, including harpoons and tiny awls and eyed needles. Heavier concentrations of large animal remains, notably reindeer, on excavated living floors and a sharp rise in the number and size of sites attest to an increase in cooperative big-game hunting conducted by large groups, perhaps members of tribes or confederacies.

A sudden increase in self-awareness was reflected in a sudden appearance of numerous ornaments such as necklaces of pierced teeth and fish vertebrae, shell beads, and ivory bracelets. None of these have been found at Neanderthal sites. This change may have something to do with increasing populations and another magic number involving the size of hunter-gatherer tribes, people speaking the same language. Again, as in the case of twenty-five persons for bands, actual numbers may vary over a wide range. But among Australian aborigines, Andaman Islanders in the Bay of Bengal, Shoshoni Indians of the American Great Plains and other hunter-gatherers, tribal counts tend to cluster at about 500 persons.

The possible connection between this figure and the wearing of ornaments is that 500 may not be far from the number of individuals a person can be expected to recognize on a first-name basis. Beyond that the strain becomes greater on man's powers of memory (one reason for the architect's rule of thumb that an elementary school should not exceed 500 pupils if the principal expects to know them all by name and the decision of some churches to split into smaller groups when membership exceeds 500). When populations rise much above that level, people may need markers to identify themselves as friend or foe.

Such markers had better be easy to see. A recent study of "stylistic behavior" in present-day Yugoslavia, by Martin Wobst of the University of Massachusetts, revealed that men of different ethnic and religious groups wear "items that are visible over long distances, such as from one mountain side to another, or over some distance along the road . . . [and] that allow you to decipher a stylistic message before you get into the gun range of your enemy." The only items that meet these specifications of long-range visibility nowadays are cloaks, coats, and hats or head-dresses. Allowing for the fact that lethal ranges were considerably shorter in prehistoric times, the ornaments worn by hunter-gatherers may indicate the growing importance of similar loyalties and allegiances.

The post-Neanderthal period also saw the emergence, full-blown, of art. It was a spectacular emergence, reaching a peak around 15,000 years ago in the paintings and engravings on the walls of Lascaux and other caves in the Les Eyzies region of southwestern France, as well as in Spain. The pattern, more varied and specialized tools, larger groups and large-scale hunting, and the appearance of ornaments and fine arts, is evidence for rising social complexity, new levels of organization and the increasing use of symbols. There is good reason to believe that this period saw a significant advance in the evolution of language. Investigators have not yet come up with theories about the nature of the change, or with ways of checking the theories archeologically, but new word and sentence structures probably permitted more precise, compact and rapid communication and expression.

A modern-style brain had evolved—our brain, with all that implies. Hunting-gathering ultimately required the highest order of intelligence, sufficiently high to deal with everything that has developed since, and with plenty to spare. Knowing which plants out of hundreds make the best foods and medicines, observing the habits of solitary and herd animals, particularly the stereotyped, predictable habits which are their undoing, deducing from signs in wind and weather where potential prey will appear, devising traps and pitfalls and ambushes—these and a thousand other activities for survival demanded the same powers that have produced in contemporary society the new art, the new poetry, satellites, computers, guided missiles, rudimentary world governments.

The innate inferiority of people who went about nearly naked and had few possessions has been taken for granted, an attitude preserved in the reports of colonial administrators. One British district officer of the 1920s dismissed the Hadza, Africans living in an isolated Tanzanian valley about 250 miles south of the equator, as "a black apelike tribe," "a wild man," "a creature of the bush . . . incapable of becoming anything esle." Such ignor-

Modern man: artist's interpretation of Cro-Magnon sculptor and cave painters

ance accounts in part for the scarcity of serious scientific studies of surviving hunter-gatherers.

Twenty years ago, James Woodburn, a student at Cambridge University and now at the London School of Economics, set out to find out about these people for himself. He went against the advice of his professors who preferred that he conduct a more conventional study of an agricultural or pastoral community. Some local administrators were even skeptical that hunter-gatherers existed in the area. But Woodburn went into the bush anyway, found the Hadza, and spent almost three years with them.

The Hadza had adapted effectively to a bush environment no one wanted. They were living well on their land, and they were living the way they preferred to live. Their food was mostly roots, tubers, including a relative of the sweet potato, berries, honey and the fruit of baobab tree. They were by no means overjoyed about such fare, regarding much of it as unpalatable (with some justification), and were hungry for more "real food," meaning more meat, which was less abundant. But they had all they needed, if not all they wanted. Thorough medical examinations indicated a well-balanced diet with no signs of common tropical diseases resulting from protein and vitamin deficiencies. Furthermore, the food quest was hardly time-consuming, requiring only about two hours a day.

Studies currently under way elsewhere support Woodburn's findings. Hunter-gatherers in the Australian bush, the Kalahari Desert, the rain forests of the Philippines and other areas also get along well and enjoy considerable leisure. Not that their world is idyllic. Death comes mysteriously, often striking early. They have little more than hope and their beliefs when it comes to combatting serious illness, and half the infants born die before the end of their first year. On the other hand, those who survive may attain a ripe old age; about one out of every ten persons lives past sixty.

Richard Lee of the University of Toronto set aside one month out of an extended stay among the Kalahari Bushmen for a detailed study of diets. In one group, male hunters and female gatherers provided themselves and nonworking dependents (old persons and children, about a third of the group) with a good diet, two-thirds nuts and vegetables and one-third meat. They worked one to three days a week to fill their stomachs and spent the rest of the time talking and visiting relatives. Lee points out that the record "assumes an added significance because this security of life was observed during the third year of one of the most severe droughts in South Africa's history." Fewer than seven inches of rain fell that year and the drought struck hard at neighboring farmers who survived only by joining Bushman women in collecting wild plants. Even during the drought, there was enough for all. Farmers outside the area, with no Bushmen to rely on, needed famine relief from the United Nations.

Hunter-gatherers know their land in incredible detail. They know in their mind's eye, without conscious thought, the appearance of several hundred square miles of territory, often flat semi-desert spaces with no markers detectable to strangers. They know their territory so well, so precisely, that they can meet one another at a specified place as reliably as two New Yorkers meeting on the southeast corner of Fifth Avenue and Fifty-seventh Street. Their minds contain atlases of maps. For the benefit of inquiring anthropologists they can make maps showing the locations of

"Mental maps," indicating how well Eskimos know their land: remarkably accurate map produced by Eskimo hunters from memory, (outlined area) compared here to a map of the actual coastline in the Cumberland Sound–Frobisher Bay region of Baffin Island, Northwest Territories, Canada

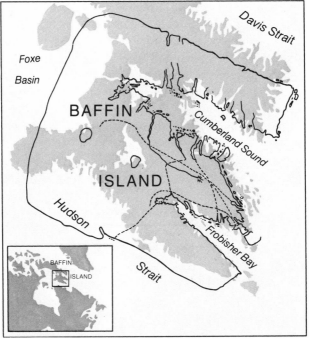

rivers, streams, lakes, ponds, bays, islands—maps that compare amazingly, feature by feature, with official surveyor's maps.

But that is only part, the beginning, of what they know. Their lives depend on seeing and holding in memory the subtlest signs of things growing. In her book about the Kalahari, *The Harmless People*, Elizabeth Marshall Thomas tells how one Bushman walked unerringly to a spot in a wide plain "with no bush or tree to mark place," and stopped to point out a blade of grass with barely visible filament of vine wrapped around it. He had come across that vine months before during the rainy season when it was green. Now things were dry and water scarce and he was thirsty. So he dug at the spot, exposed a succulent root about two feet down, and quenched his thirst with its milky juices.

The Australian aborigines are capable of similar feats. Richard Gould of the University of Hawaii, who has lived with them for long periods in the Western Desert, estimates that the average hunter knows the locations of more than 400 places with water. The list includes perhaps half a dozen "native wells" or permanent water holes, a larger number of water holes which may be used for limited periods and are dry the rest of the year, and a great many more obscure sources such as pools hidden in rock clefts and rainwater trapped in the crotches of trees.

An encyclopedia could be written about tracking knowledge or, rather, the very small fraction of tracking knowledge that has been imparted to investigators. Eskimos can tell from patterns in the snow what sort of animal passed, how long ago, whether male or female or juvenile, whether male or pregnant female, and so on. It is rumored that they are even trying to deduce from snowmobile tracks the identities of the drivers. Like all hunter-gatherers, they notice everything that may some day under unpredictable circumstances mean survival, and push their observing power to the limit.

The measure of a way of life, as of a human relationship, is how well it stands up in a crisis. Judging by that standard, the hunting-gathering way of life must rate high. It has not been infallible. It did not work for Eskimos, who as recently as early this century starved to death in their camps, immobilized by fierce gales and blizzards or waiting along traditional migration routes for caribou that never came. But far more often than not, and throughout the long course of prehistory, it has seen people through emergency after emergency.

Successful adaptations involve a deep and intimate knowledge of people as well as land. Prehistoric hunter-gatherers were as wise about their own strengths and weaknesses as they were about what the wilderness had to offer, and for the same reason. They had to be. For one thing, they had to deal with violence. Even after millenniums of selection for self-control, violence still represented something imminent, something to guard against, chiefly in the male of the species. It was the familiar problem, the problem of all primates, all mammals—how to transform males into peaceable members of society.

As already indicated, part of the solution was to stay small, but that is not always possible or desirable. There are forces which draw people together for a time. Several hundred Bushmen may congregate to conduct traditional healing and initiation cere- monies, arrange marriages, exchange trade items and information and general gossip. They provide extra food for the occasion, but as a rule their patience is exhausted before the food supply. Tension mounts, and they usually disperse into small bands after a week or two. Dispersing is not possible during the dry season when a number of bands must live near the few permanent water holes, so people locate their camps as far from one another as possible and try not to cross paths too often.

Staying small is not enough by itself. If the same Bushmen had to live together in the same bands for indefinite periods, conflict would be considerably more frequent. Individuals often move from band to band. The people know very well what they are doing: "We like to get together, but we fear fights." And even then violence flares up. Lee has records of eighteen killings, and all but three of them occurred in larger-than-average groups of forty or more individuals. Other records show that most hunter- gatherers engaged in some sort of fighting at least one every two years. So, although staying small by no means guarantees peace, it does help reduce the frequency of conflict.

Staying small applies to individuals as well as to bands. The desire for status, the tendency to lord it over others, seems to be strong—another chronic problem, with males again the chief troublemakers. There is an even stronger ethics of humility. The rules against appearing greedy and acquisitive apply to the hunt and the sharing of meat. A male must lean over backward to avoid giving the impression that he wants or expects special privileges. This may result in some highly complicated maneuvers.

According to one study, among the Algonkin Indians of Canada, "There is a specific etiquette outlined for sharing moose. . . . The person that kills the moose usually gives it to someone else. That person then distributes it and is obliged to give himself a smaller part. When two fellows are hunting, each one tries to jockey the other into killing the moose. Some men who are very skilled hunters make the situation a real chess game, not to let the moose get away and yet have the other one kill him."

A hunter who has made a kill had better not walk into camp boasting of his success. Even if it were a buffalo in its prime, occasion for a gala celebration, he would be wise to play it cool and, if possible, say nothing at all. Even a remark as neutral as "I have shot an animal" will arouse a swift response of "Only one?" or words to that effect. Beneath the joke and others like it, between the lines, is a mild rebuke against even the hint of a show of arrogance.

Once Lee himself went through a less gentle experience of this sort in the Kalahari. It was Christmas time and, to show his appreciation for the Bushman's cooperation during the year, he planned a special feast and bought a magnificent ox from neighboring cattle-raisers. Although it weighed some 1,200 pounds, more than enough to feed all the expected guests from miles around, he was subjected to a steady barrage of pointed comments about the scrawniness of the beast and his poor judgment. What upset him even more, the procedure being new to him, was the grim forecast that everyone would go hungry and be so frustrated that serious fighting might break out.

It was an elaborate put-down, perfectly acted out. The Bushmen knew that they would have a grand feast and they did. Later, Lee was somewhat mollified to learn that it was nothing personal, that they would have treated an equally proud Bushman in the same way: "When a young man kills much meat he comes to think of the rest of us as his servants or inferiors. We can't accept this. We refuse one who boasts, for some day his pride will make him

Christmas ox roast: Richard Lee serving as host in the Kalahari, southern Africa

kill somebody. So we always speak of his meat as worthless. This way we cool his heart and make him gentle."

The peace and survival of the band, the tribe, depend on keeping violence and arrogance within bounds. Violence and arrogance are closely related. A man convinced of his superiority is likely to harm others, particularly in times of stress. Hunter-gatherers live by the principle that the only way to get along together is in a society of equals. Accumulating wealth in any form is unheard of. Social pressure is so intense that an individual with a valuable object feels ill at ease and guilty for having something that others want. He gives it away with a sigh of relief, a passion that exceeds generosity. A Bushman who received a sweater from a visitor gave it to his son a few weeks later. Within a month it had passed to the brother of the son's wife, and when last seen it was being worn by a cousin in a band twenty miles away.

Giving goes on continually in elaborate networks, which Bushmen call "paths for things." Polly Wiesner of the University of Michigan recently returned from the Kalahari with records of a maze of such paths involving dozens of persons and more than 2,000 articles—blankets, beadwork, knives, eyeglasses, safety pins, sandals, arrows, bags. Articles move from relative to relative, from A to B to C to D and so on, along paths with many links that extend for distances of 300 or more miles. A Bushman may know as many as ten individuals along "giving" paths that lead away from him, and ten more individuals along "receiving" paths that lead to him. He may keep a gift for weeks or months, but sooner or later he passes it on.

These networks of circulating gifts are a form of insurance, the most ancient form known. They create and continually replenish goodwill over wide regions. A person is sure of being welcome somewhere when help is needed, when that person is sick or old or short of food, or simply wants a change of scenery. Training to give starts a few months after birth, Wiesner explains: "By this time parents and grandparents have put beads around a child's arms, legs, neck and waist. Between the ages of six months and a year one of the grandparents cuts off the beads, replaces them with new beads, putting the original beads in the child's hand and having him give them to some other relative."

Millions of years in the making, such traditions were not given up easily. The enormous paradox of evolution is that things manage to evolve at all. The most formidable of forces favor rigid conservatism, a deep-seated clinging to the status quo. Resistance to change amounts almost to an instinct, a reflex. It is bitter and often based on the best of reasons. Yet it is always overcome by even stronger tendencies. Despite the forces lined up against change, change occurs. This phenomenon is seen in all its grand complexity with the reluctant but accelerating abandonment of the hunting-gathering way of life.

3

Cultivating the Land, Changing Nature

*Shortages of food and land/Population pressure,
melting glaciers and rising seas/The effort to
save hunting-gathering/Gardens and slash-and-burn
agriculture/The domestication of animals/
Settling down and the first population booms*

MAN moved conservatively toward the most radical development in his evolutionary record. The shift from hunting-gathering to agriculture came swiftly compared to the pace of things during the preceding ten million years. But measured in terms of a generation or a lifetime change came slowly. At any given time nothing much was happening. Big decisions tended to be rare. Revolution was a process of tiny changes, none of which seemed to make much difference, as people fought to prevent or at least postpone major changes, while the pressure to change built up.

Hunter-gatherers, confronted by local scarcities of food and fuel, were shocked and then took stopgap measures. As soon as the trouble simmered down, they forgot—until the next crisis. And crises seemed to be more and more frequent. People knew very well what was happening, but they behaved almost as if they did not know, as if by forgetting the trouble would go away. Their way of life was failing, mainly because the world was becoming overcrowded.

A prehistoric meeting, a place for decision, some time between 15,000 B.C. and 10,000 B.C. and somewhere along the eastern shore of the Mediterranean. First item on the agenda is the current meat shortage. No one is going hungry. But for a number of years gazelles, the main source of meat, have been getting scarcer, and now people are asking why and discussing what to do about it. They agree that too many animals are being killed, that herds should be less heavily "harvested" until they have a chance to replenish their numbers.

After some debate, a temporary measure is agreed on. For the next two seasons only a restricted number of adult male gazelles are to be killed. Some of the people grumble, recalling less restrictive times when they had fewer rules and taboos to contend with. They do not believe the shortage of food is their fault and, in the absence of leaders to blame, attribute it to evil spirits. And they do some poaching. The new policy works, however, so well in fact that the gazelle populations rise again and the conservation rule is cancelled earlier than expected.

A few years later the problem recurs. This time the rule stays in effect longer, and people concentrate more than ever before on other species. For the first time women sow some seeds to extend the natural range of wild cereals, again, a stopgap measure. Once more there are gazelle steaks for all, although fewer than in the old days, and they are rather more difficult to get. Wild plants are plentiful and although the restricted-hunting rule has become permanent, people hardly notice and no longer grumble. It is business as usual, almost—at least for the time being.

Many such emergencies must have arisen in communities throughout the world. They were ultimately solved by splitting. Bands broke up to relieve subsistence pressure, less food for the group or more mouths to feed with the same amount of food. Many leave-takings must have occurred, as families of nomads moved away from friends and relatives and home territories into new lands further on, just over the next ridge into the next valley.

Imagine the first shock of discovery, the first suspicion that there might not be enough land for everyone. Imagine a group of people taking the old ancestral option of moving on. They pack up and say good-byes, climb over a high pass, look down with great expectations into the next valley—and see smoke rising from the hearth fires of settlers who have gotten there first.

That sort of thing must have happened more and more frequently. The population flood was out of control, largely because of man's impressive ability to adapt. Most other species stayed put within bounded evolutionary niches, jungle or savanna or desert or tundra, their numbers limited and regulated by food supplies. Man, originally a creature of the savanna, moved on and spread everywhere, postponing subsistence crises, but not indefinitely. Populations increased despite the existence of powerful counterforces. Natural causes such as disease and accidents killed one out of every two infants before the end of the first year of life—about the rate for present-day hunter-gatherers and chimpanzee troops—and took a heavy further toll during childhood and later years. Over and above that, people applied extra controls of their own. They made every effort to limit their numbers by resorting to abortion, infanticide (in some cases, putting to death twenty percent or more of their newborn offspring), and other measures.

And still the flood rose, although very slowly for a long while. According to one calculation, the annual rate of growth of prehistoric people was only about 0.001 per thousand, which means that on the average it required some ten centuries for a population of 1,000 persons to increase by one additional member. (Today the world's average growth rate is about 20,000 times greater, and the same increase occurs within three weeks instead of a thousand years.)

This extremely small growth rate, compounded over millions of years, provided a driving force for band-splitting and the spread of humankind over the earth. Assume that the world's total hominid population five million years ago consisted of about 25,000 individuals, a sheer but plausible guess considering that our ancestors may still have been very much of a minority species confined to parts of Africa. At an annual growth rate of 0.001 per thousand that figure would have increased to about 10,000,000 persons by 10,000 B.C., several hundred thousand bands foraging in the wildernesses of Europe, Asia, Australia and the Americas, as well as Africa.

To be sure, a population of 10,000,000, some two to five square miles of land for every individual, can hardly be regarded as jam-packed by modern standards. But crowding is a relative thing and, taking into account the state of the art of obtaining food in those days, two to five square miles per person was not nearly as ample as it may appear. Yields of wild plants and animals were such that on the average it required one square mile to feed a person. The best lands were already well exploited. The world was filling up.

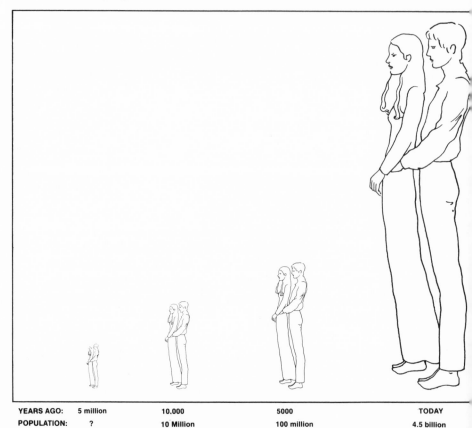

| YEARS AGO: | 5 million | 10,000 | 5000 | TODAY |
| POPULATION: | ? | 10 Million | 100 million | 4.5 billion |

Five million years of population growth

There was less land as well as more people. Land had been decreasing ever since the height of the last ice age 20,000 or so years ago, when so much water was locked up in polar ice caps and glaciers that ocean levels stood 250 to 500 feet lower than they stand today. Hunter-gatherers exploited herds roaming over the exposed continental shelf, a system of gently sloping plains that form a lip or rim up to 800 miles wide around the ocean basins.

Then, as the glaciers started melting, released waters poured back into the seas, ocean levels rose, and year after year successively higher tides inched further up the slopes of the shelf. Within a few millenniums most of the shelf lay underseas. A great glacial flood submerged millions of square miles that had once been dry land, with shorelines sometimes disappearing at a rate of a mile or more per century. An area about the size of Africa, nearly a fifth of the earth's land surface including some fine hunting-gathering territory, vanished beneath the waves. As far as human living space is concerned, the world had become an appreciably smaller place.

Slowly rising seas and slowly rising populations represent a kind of pace-setting system or background pressure, broad forces on a worldwide scale that brought about the agricultural revolution. At a given time in a given area, a complex of local factors was at work—decreasing rainfall, increasing erosion, declining soil fertility, epidemics of plant and animal disease, and so on. Prehistoric people adapted to new conditions by drawing on a vast store of knowledge about plants and animals. There is no valid way of figuring out just how much they knew or how early. They no doubt knew a great deal more than they have been credited with.

Belittling ancestors seems to be as tempting as belittling present-day tribesmen. Investigators once believed that agriculture was discovered some 10,000 years ago when someone observed seeds sprouting in a refuse heap near camp, had a flash of insight, and started the first garden. This so-called Eureka theory had a number of distinguished adherents, including Darwin himself. But it underrates hunter-gatherers. It assumes that they had exploited wild plants for several million years without learning what happens when seeds are placed in the ground.

The first representatives of *Homo sapiens* may have known that bit of information 300,000 years ago. The Neanderthals, who endured long glacial winters and stored their meat by freezing and buried their dead with food for the afterlife, almost certainly knew it 75,000 years ago. What about other basic insights— that plants grow better if they are watered, manured, weeds removed, or animals kept away by fences and scarecrows? How far back were living things brought into the home? More than 30,000 years ago people were decorating the walls near cave entrances with paintings and engravings presumably to make home more attractive. Could they have set flowering plants or cut flowers in bowls on convenient ledges for the same purpose? And how early did they keep pets?

The basic elements of agriculture were known long before agriculture was established. But domestication makes no sense at all in a normal hunting-gathering context. Wiesner tells of one man in the Kalahari who cleared a plot of land, put a fence around it, sowed corn, and obtained a good crop. At harvest time his relatives came, and all the corn was consumed in a week. In the winter they tore down his fence for firewood. This premature venture had a sad ending. Next year he refused to share his crop and was forced to leave the band.

People responding to subsistence pressure, however, were able to modify the hunting-gathering way of life bit by bit. At first it was simply a matter of doing what had already been done, only more so, hunting-gathering on a more and more intensive scale. Resources were exploited to the hilt, with the focus sometimes on a few food staples and sometimes on a wide variety of wild plants and animals in season. Increasing use of domesticated plants as dietary supplements, and ultimately heavy dependence, came later.

As the ancient custom of moving on, of walking away from subsistence problems, became more difficult or downright impossible, people turned inward in the sense of concentrating more and more on their home territories. Often the situation called chiefly for putting their "useless" knowledge to work. Such knowledge must have been considerable, judging by their unique capacity for becoming curious about something and sticking with it for extended periods and retaining curiosity late in life. They could hardly have avoided learning, because many important species practically forced themselves upon the human forager. Grasses grew everywhere. The wild ancestors of wheat, barley, corn, rice and other cereals originated under conditions that prepared or preadapted them for close association with man, during dinosaur times some 100,000,000 years before he appeared on earth.

Ledyard Stebbins at the University of California in Davis suggest that the first grasses had rugged beginnings. They gained precarious rootholds in second-best places, places generally unfavorable for flowering plants which dominated the earth at the time—high on the exposed slopes of mountains, perhaps in central Asia, in the Himalayas, and Tien Shan ranges of western China. The good earth may be unstable in such settings. Waters tumble fast and turbulent down mountain slopes, cutting deep channels; landslides are common. The grasses early evolved seeds which took root and grew rapidly in loose, shifting soils and which, borne by high winds millions of years later, invaded the lowlands, flourishing wherever earth was churned up, agitated, deposited and redeposited—in delta regions, seasonally flooded plains, lands grooved and furrowed by glaciers or trampled by the hooves of herds on the move. And still later the seeds found new places to grow, places created by the most recent disturber of the soil, man.

People left their marks on the landscape practically from the beginning. They cleared land around campsites, scooped out places for hearths and sleeping areas, dug pits for refuse disposal and holes for posts to support tents and huts (often made of grass). They could hardly have been more effective if they had acted with foresight to provide niches for the spread of grass. The grasses moved in naturally, becoming part of the everyday environment and part of man's diet.

Other plants joined the ranks of camp followers. Among them were species like yams and manioc and sweet potatoes, which evolved at least as long ago as the grasses in forest regions which had long and alternating wet and dry seasons. During rainy periods they are shrubs and creeping or climbing vines, but when the rain stops they literally go underground. Nearly all their substance flows down into swelling roots and tubers packed with up to 700 or 800 pounds of high-calorie food and lying dormant until the next rains. These buried storage organs probably served as primate fare long before the coming of human beings. African baboons have been observed digging holes as much as two feet deep to get at tubers, and one of man's earliest tools, the digging stick, may have been used for the same purpose. Such plants, like grasses, are adapted to disturbed soils. The odds are that hunter-gatherers helped spread them over campgrounds by casually tossing away bits of stem and root which can propagate themselves asexually or vegetatively, growing where they fall into complete plants.

Root crops leave no enduring remains like the hard, charred seeds of cereals. Indirect evidence of their presence comes from David Davis of Brandeis University, who studied small obsidian flakes found at sites along the Pacific coast of Mesoamerica, which may have been teeth in graters used to grind manioc tubers to a pulp before cooking. He made a grater with flakes knocked off a piece of obsidian and driven into a balsa-wood board. After four hours of determined manioc mashing, he examined the flakes under a microscope. They showed characteristic "pockets" along the edges where tiny chips had broken off, a wear pattern which matches markings found on flakes from prehistoric living floors and hints that people may have been eating manioc, presumably domesticated.

Humans evolved in intimate association with entire constellations of wild species and must have experimented with them often, particularly in new territories. Thayer Scudder of the California Institute of Technology provides a modern and tragic example of what may have happened occasionally under analogous conditions in the past. In 1958 an often-fatal illness struck African villagers in the Zambesi River Valley, not long after completion of a large dam had forced them to move into unfamiliar downriver country.

The first deaths occurred early in September. Victims complained of severe stomach pains, and death when it came, came quickly, always within two days or so and often in a matter of hours. The cause of the outbreak has never been identified. But there was a food shortage at the time and all the fatal cases were women and children, the regular plant collectors, circumstantial evidence which led a team of physicians to the following conclusions: "This condition was due to a powerful poison, probably of vegetable origin, innocent in appearance and not unpalatable."

Many people must have died mysteriously in remote times before dangerous plants were positively identified; and, of course, the process of trial-and-error learning did not stop there. In their search for new plants, and foods that can be used as a last resort when famine threatens, people have developed elaborate and time-consuming ways of grinding, soaking and boiling plants to remove poisons and bitter tastes. The poisons themselves may be used on arrowheads and darts, to stun and paralyze fish, and in milder form as medicines and drugs, including substances that produce dream states and hallucinations.

Man's association with animals, notably with his fellow mammals, has been as close and ancient as his association with plants. Many of today's domesticated species, including sheep and goats and cattle, are the descendants of creatures which, like humans themselves, gradually adapted from a life among trees to life on the plains during times of dwindling forests and spreading savannas. They probably moved into open country more than twenty million years ago, some time before the first hominids. In the course of establishing places for themselves as grazers and browsers on the savanna, they helped prepare the way for the later coming of humans. They represented an important food supply, the lure of meat on the hoof, a major factor in adapting to savanna lands.

Man became increasingly effective as a predator, especially a predator of large herd animals. Quantities of bone unearthed at kill and butchering sites furnish evidence for the rise of organized "mass production" hunting, often concentrated chiefly on a single species. People stampeded herds into marshy places, dead-end ravines and steep-sided streambeds, and lay in ambush at strategic points along migration routes. In many areas cooperative hunting reached a peak when glaciers of the last ice age were melting and seas rising, from about 20,000 to 12,000 years ago.

It was a great period for hunter-gatherers in southwestern France; for example, in the countryside around Les Eyzies, a golden age. One of the richest regions for archeological research, it contains scores of important living sites and art caves. It was a prehistoric crossroads, providing abundant game for tens of thousands of years. Reindeer bones make up more than ninety percent of animal remains found at some sites. Nevertheless, there were signs of subsistence pressure.

Some of the most magnificent cave paintings, polychrome portrayals of bulls and horses and deer, were produced at a time when the herds were beginning to dwindle, and may have been part of secret fertility rituals designed to restore past abundances. Prehistoric art flourished as never before during the region's heyday, especially toward the end of the period. It was a time of soaring populations, reflected in a sharp increase in the number of sites as well as in the sizes of individual sites.

People came to rely less on big game and more on a variety of other species. Fish were increasingly exploited; salmon in particular became abundant as the seas rose. Before the glaciers retreated, and when seas were low, swift white-water rivers plunged roaring and turbulent across the exposed slopes of coastal plains into the ocean deeps. Even salmon could not swim upstream against such currents. But they could when glaciers melted and ocean waters covered the slopes and rivers slowed down as they entered warm, shallow seas.

Salmon, shad, and other fish that migrate upstream to spawn inland emerged in many rivers and streams throughout the world. New species appeared nearer the coasts as well as inland. While only a few species of mussels and other mollusks might cling in clusters to rocks in swift rivers, dozens of species thrived in relatively sluggish postglacial waters, in swamps and lagoons and tidal salt marshes, which also contained fish and served as stopping places for migratory birds. The sheer bulk of living things may have increased a hundredfold, including people who moved in to take advantage of the situation.

They were hunter-gatherers still, but hunter-gatherers on the verge of agriculture. The transition started as early as 9000 B.C. or so in the Near East and as late as A.D. 500 in the eastern United States and in southern Africa, and includes some of the earliest evidence of domestication. Early moves toward agriculture were probably made on a small-scale family basis. In many regions the first farmers or protofarmers seem to have been gardeners. Faced with food shortages or the threat of shortages, people turned more and more to their own backyards. They created new

Clearing the land for crops, highland New Guinea: burning tree litter on a new garden; Tsembaga garden at about six months

abundances, new concentrations of plants which were still wild but not quite as wild as before, because now they depended increasingly on man's needs and preferences.

A first step was to push the wilderness a little further back, probably by so-called slash-and-burn techniques, cutting down small trees and undergrowth and setting fire to the debris—a simple way of changing the environment with rather complicated effects. In crowded times like ours forest fires are catastrophes. But for most of the past they helped rejuvenate the soil, actually serving as a kind of fertilizer. Started by lightning or man himself, they left ashy residues rich in phosphorus and other minerals and a scorched earth freed for the time being of insects and weeds. Also, because fire tends to break up the soil, it has a mild "plowing" effect.

Things burst into fresh growth after the earth cooled down. Many seeds are not only fire-resistant but have adapted so completely that they will sprout only after a period of intense heat. As a result, young shoots of grasses and ferns, bushes and trees spring up, representing plant food in its tenderest and most palatable form. Originally people took advantage of this fact by creating open burned-off areas to attract deer and other game animals, an old hunting strategy—and only later, with the coming of chronic subsistence pressure, to provide space for gardens.

Again, it was a matter of putting traditional knowledge to new uses, clearing the land around the home, or perhaps simply adding to and extending areas already cleared. It is quite possible that gardens existed long before food supplies ever became a problem, gardens containing a few fruit and nut trees and other edible species but devoted primarily to species used in the making of clothes and nets, cosmetics, ritual items, drugs and other products. When pressure arose, prehistoric gardeners responded with an increasing emphasis on food plants.

Previously, people, mainly women and children, had gone out on daily excursions to places where such plants grew, returning with choice items for the next few meals. Now they also brought seeds and tubers and whole plants for their gardens rather than for immediate eating, all of which resulted in further settling down, less time spent on long walks and more time spent tending plants nearer home. Chores included watering shoots when rain was scarce, pruning dead leaves and twigs, weeding and fencing off areas to keep animals out.

Excavated sites provide no direct evidence for the gardening origins of agriculture. Early gardens involved relatively little meddling with landscape; terraces, plow furrows and irrigation ditches came later. So archeologists can only offer possibilities that seem plausible. In the recent words of one investigator, however, it is time to go "beyond arguments of plausibility" and seek proof one way or the other. Perhaps markers can be found in the forests that now cover previously occupied sites, in individual plants or complexes of plants which would not exist if people had not disturbed the earth and grown things long ago. Or perhaps vanished prehistoric gardens have left traces in the soil, substances detectable by chemical tests.

But until appropriate archeological techniques are developed, the present provides the most revealing clues to the past. There are gardens in Africa, South America and Southeast Asia with a wide variety of plants growing in apparent disorder, miniature versions or imitations of the tropical rain forests surrounding them, and so much like the forests that it is not always easy to tell the difference. A number of years ago, during a brief visit to a Peruvian village in the Amazon Basin, I walked through such a garden time after time without noticing anything special. Then one day I saw a boy carefully pulling out weeds in an area which looked to me like nothing but weeds, and I realized that every one of the more than thirty different species left growing was there for a very definite purpose—as a source of dye, medicine, poison, perfume, food, seasoning, fiber, and so on.

House gardens may well have served as the agricultural experiment stations of prehistory, special places where plants were relocated for intensive close-at-hand observation and ultimately discarded or encouraged depending on their value to man. As the demand for more food continued, a few plants which showed promise as highly productive and nutritious food sources were chosen and grown on larger burned-off areas, in some cases not for single families, but for a number of families, or even the community as a whole. Further selection occurred at an accelerated rate on early farmlands, usually unconsciously. People did not realize that they were selecting "regimented" varieties of cereal grasses, strains that tended to ripen at about the same time. Yet that was one result of going into the fields to harvest those plants that had already ripened fully, and not bothering to go back for the late ripeners. Similar practices favored other changes which may show up in the archeological record, such as larger seeds and differences in seed shapes and stems.

The relationship between men and animals changed during this transition period. Some people had probably already modified traditional methods of stampeding, ambushing and rushing in for the kill among panic-stricken herds. In a recently published Cambridge University report, Derek Sturdy indicates the sort of activities that may represent a step toward full-scale domestication. He observed how Lapps exploit reindeer in western Greenland today, a system that requires frequent contact but slight interference with herds, which are usually free to wander through ranges of more than 300 square miles.

The critical area is a corridor of five square miles, a narrow neck of land between two fjords where herds pass on their way to summer feeding grounds. Roundups work by remote control. The deer are allowed "to see or smell a man in a given position so that they will move away . . . in a desired direction," that is, into a corral between high cliffs and a deer fence where a number of animals are slaughtered—mainly individuals weakened by age or disease, the chief prey of most predators, and young males. The herds then move into open ranges again for the rest of the year.

Not hunting, and not domestication, which includes keeping animals in restricted pasturelands and selecting for tameness, high milk production and other characteristics, this broad startegy does involve a kind of cropping or harvesting season with appreciable yields, since the size of a herd can generally be maintained even if as much as twenty-five to thirty percent of its members are killed annually. People may have used some such system in the Les Eyzies region 10,000 to 15,000 years ago, perhaps altering traditional reindeer migration routes in a region whose little valleys and rivers and limestone cliffs offer many natural corrals. Recent work, as yet unpublished, indicates that similar techniques may have been developed thousands of years earlier in North Africa and Israel.

It could hardly have been an extraordinary step from this sort of herd management to outright domestication, raising part of a herd close to home and feeding and fattening animals with fodder from local fields. In a few generations selection brought about physical changes which may help investigators to distinguish wild from domesticated species. Changes in behavior have been far more dramatic. Several years ago in Iran I saw two wild sheep in a play-chase down a steep mountainside, leaping and dodging from rock to rock at full speed, marvelously sure-footed—and then thought of the dull, sluggish tamed creatures munching away on modern farms.

The last stage in the development of early agriculture is marked by the appearance between about 6000 B.C. and A.D. 500 of established farming villages and a heavy reliance on domesticated species. It was essentially a point-of-no-return stage for hunting-gathering, the end of stopgaps and the stopgap attitude. During earlier periods people rarely believed they were doing anything radical. In local communities scattered over the world they made decisions in a spirit of cooperation, pulling together until the crisis blew over, like citizens of the industrialized West who grew a few vegetables in backyard "victory" gardens during their world wars.

Acceptance of change came as gradually as the changes themselves, as younger generations took for granted new living conditions their parents had considered only temporary. Many factors worked against a return to hunting-gathering, and one of the most important seems to have been the very act of settling down. After millions of years of wandering freely from valley to valley, taking up life in new foraging grounds whenever the old grounds became less productive or overcrowded, moving out of the home valley became increasingly difficult. Most of the moving was now done within the valley, exploiting resource zones seasonally. With the coming of villages travel within the valley itself diminished.

The course of subsequent evolution would have been much slower if that were the whole story. If population had continued to increase at the average 0.001-per-thousand rate of all previous prehistory, this might still be a rural world. Reduced mobility had an unexpected and unpredictable effect, providing another example of the fact that people never know all the consequences of their behavior. Itself the result of increasing population, reduced mobility resulted in further and faster increases. Once again people unwittingly aggravated the problem they were trying to solve, the subsistence-pressure problem.

The same thing is happening today, in a few isolated communities, as the last of the hunter-gatherers settle down. The Eskimo settlement of Anaktuvuk in the Brooks Range of north central Alaska, about 150 miles inland from the Arctic Ocean, is now an official village complete with landing strip, elementary school, post office and zip code. But until 1950 its founders were fully mobile hunters (not hunter-gatherers, since they lived on a diet consisting almost entirely of caribou meat).

Field research by Lewis Binford and his associates of the University of New Mexico shows that between this date and 1964, birthrates nearly doubled and the population rose from 76 to 128 persons. David Harris of University College London reports a similar study based on statistics for a group of aborigines living in northern Australia. Between 1910 and 1940, mothers averaged one baby every 4.5 years. But after the people settled at a mission in 1948, the average birth interval fell to 3.3 years, and by 1960 the population had risen more than ten percent. Such changes have been observed among the Bushmen. Nancy Howell of the University of Toronto points out that Kalahari women living in hunter-gatherer bands tend to have a baby every three years. An increasing number of these women are living in settled communities now, however, and among them the spacing between births may be two and a half years or so.

Certain investigators have suggested that settled women have fewer miscarriages than women on the move, or more pregnancies since they tend not to nurse their infants as long, and milk production may inhibit ovulation, the release of eggs from the ovaries. According to another suggestion, settled menfolk hunt for briefer periods and are home more of the time. Detailed analysis indicates that none of these theories can account for the full effect.

Howell recently suggested a more promising theory. It is based on the work of Rose Frisch of the Harvard Center for Population Studies, who has discovered that fatness and fertility are related. The timing of a girl's adolescent growth spurt depends on her weight, not her age. Ovulation depends on maintaining fat levels above a certain minimum, and Howell believes this may be the key point in accounting for sharp population increases among groups shifting from hunting-gathering to a settled life. A Bushman woman needs an extra 1,000 calories a day to nurse her child and, after it is weaned, she must build up fat reserves before she can produce ova again. Under Kalahari conditions, that may take longer than it does in settled communities where food supplies are more abundant.

This change could easily be enough to account for the population booms that followed the establishment of settled villages. Not only were more babies being born, but probably fewer of them died after birth, largely because of reduced infanticide and better nutrition with the coming of agriculture. Other factors such as a presumed rise in epidemic diseases helped reduce the average rate of population increase. But the net effect was more problems, more people, and continuing pressure on the land. Man found himself caught in a trap, a subsistence trap resulting from his own ability to adapt and devise new ways of coping with emergencies.

He had developed new subsistence techniques that could support populations forty or more times greater than the old techniques. He had, for better or worse, achieved a new abundance. More people were alive than ever before. Going back to hunter-gatherer life-styles would have starved most of them to death. They were locked into a new life-style—and there was, and is, no going back.

4
Conflict and Control, Elites in the Making

The coming of elites/ The arithmetic of violence/
The role of trade in reducing conflict/ Ritual
warfare/"Chiefdom" archeology/ The struggle for
security/ The appearance of divine kings

A DIRT road off the main highway in the northern arm of Mexico's Valley of Oaxaca leads to a ruined church and an ancient graveyard, and to a much older site nearby, a small man-made mound about twenty-five feet high overlooking three terraces and a river. There is nothing to see on the top of the mound now. But a single house once stood there above people working in the fields and above their houses. It was the residence of a local overseer.

Susan Lees of Hunter College in New York took me to this site a few summers ago as part of an afternoon introduction to the archeology of power. Our next stop was a bigger site on a hill less than a mile and a half away. We climbed the hill, past the remains of plazas and a dozen mounds, to the top and to the edge

83

Courtesy of Richard Blanton, Purdue University

A seat of power: Monte Alban, valley of Oaxaca, central Mexico; main plaza area, 270 meters long

of a 300-foot cliff. Looking down, we could see every village and farm in that part of the valley, including the place with the little mound and ruined church.

Our last stop, the climax of the afternoon, took us to the geographical center of the valley—and to the central area of the valley's highest and biggest site, Monte Alban, one of the great cities of prehistoric Mesoamerica. We drove up a long winding road which ends near the heart of the city, the seventeen-acre main plaza with courtyards and painted tombs and ceremonial buildings including stone pyramids. At the top of the staircase of the highest pyramid, more than 1,500 feet above the surrounding landscape, we had a panoramic view of the entire valley, eastern and western arms as well as northern arm, rivers and rolling hills and encircling mountains in the far distance.

These sites visited successively, from lowest and smallest to highest and largest, represent the broad outlines of a story which Lees and other investigators would like to be able to spell out in detail. More than two millenniums ago, after at least 10,000 years of human occupation, first by hunter-gatherers and then by farmers, life in the Valley of Oaxaca changed radically and swiftly. Within a century or two, houses appeared where there had never been houses before, on sites chosen for the same reason that a king chooses a throne located strategically above his subjects. Hilltop sites were in line with the established ritual of height as a symbol of dominance, and climbing and looking up as symbols of deference. The most formidable sites, surrounded by thick walls, also served as fortresses to be defended in times of trouble.

Hierarchies of places, indicating hierarchies of duties and status, followed the establishment of agriculture. They appeared earlier in the Near East than in the Valley of Oaxaca (about 4000 B.C.), in India, China, Southeast Asia and Europe (2500 B.C. to 1500 B.C.), and in West Africa and the Peruvian highlands (about 2500 B.C. to 2000 B.C.); during roughly the same period in other regions of Mesoamerica (from 1200 B.C. to A.D. 100); and rather later in some parts of the United States.

And behind the walls, secure and protected in the grandest rooms and the highest places, like queen bees in a hive, lived a new kind of human being, a new species almost, a class of elites ranking far above the common run of mankind. No change in prehistory is more difficult or more important to comprehend than this explosion of differences which was so intimately related to the coming of complex societies. Now that people were living closer together than they had ever lived before, something had appeared to separate them once more, an enormous and widening distance between the chosen few and their numerous inferiors. It was an ancient theme, even then. Tensions, individuals drawn together and pulled apart, existed even in simpler hunter-gatherer times, even millions of years ago in early hominid and prehominid times. Conflict is at the root of things and accounts in part for the emergence of power.

Hunter-gatherer bands have many admirable qualities. They are close to one another and to their land in a way that no one will ever be again. They share and live together more nearly as equals than most people and they enjoy an enviable degree of leisure. But they were never noble savages. There is nothing to the notion that our ancestors were grand and free before the coming of civilization and that everything since then, including ourselves, has been a comedown. This patronizes and demeans hunter-gatherers. It is a more respectable form of racism than hatred and scorn, but racism nonetheless, and unnecessarily complicating. There are no noble people, or thrifty or harmless or evil or fierce people—only people, human beings, and that is enough of a problem.

The Bushmen have their share of violence, even with a most permissive upbringing in infancy and childhood, and even with their stress on staying small. People are so close in camp, the human press is so strong, that quarrels among children are never allowed to develop into something serious, and children on the verge of fighting are separated gently and without fuss. Yet when they grow up, tensions appear which separation cannot relieve completely. Neither can ritual, the most potent and prevalent of social pacifiers.

The aborigines of central Australia have a range of rituals graded according to the severity of the grievance. Nicolas Peterson of the Australian National University, who has spent considerable time living with them, describes how two men recently settled a quarrel about the sharing of food: "The men stood about a hundred yards apart and started yelling at each other, calling each other names, daring each other to fight. Then each threw a boomerang at the other in turn, hard and close, but not intended to hit and not difficult to dodge. Finally, they rushed at one another fiercely, as if for a fight to the death. Instead they rushed into one another's arms, hugging and weeping." A more serious conflict, say over the stealing of a wife, may start the same way. But it may end with two men kneeling close together and the offender receiving a slash with a knife, just deep enough to draw blood, the mark of blood vengeance.

Settling down is a goad, inevitably aggravating and intensifying tension, because it involves more people and less chance to get away from it all. Robert Carneiro of the American Museum of Natural History offers some straightforward calculations as a basis for gauging how conflict might mount under such conditions. He indicates that since it takes two to make a quarrel, the number of quarrels can be expected to increase with the number of possible two-person combinations, which, in turn, increases at something close to the square of the population.

For example, 300 different pairs of potentially disagreeing individuals are possible in a band made up of 25 persons, nearly 20,000 pairs in a 200-person village, and about 50,000,000 pairs in a town of 10,000. These figures cannot be taken too literally, of course, but they provide a rough theoretical index of how steeply conflict levels may rise with increasing numbers and how important it is to have more policing, more rules and tighter controls. One might think that family ties, kinship ties, would act to reduce the amount of conflict. But it has never worked that way. Violence is far more common among relatives than among nonkin.

Carneiro's theory works out in practice. Patricia Draper of the University of New Mexico has studied some fifty Bushmen who recently shifted from hunting-gathering to agriculture and are living mainly on corn, sorghum, squash, sheep, goats and other domesticated species. Increasing conflict shows up at an early age:

> In hunter-gatherer bands children confine their play to the immediate camp area, and adults are always nearby to nip fights in the bud. But the children of Bushmen farmers have other places to go. They may visit other villages and drive animals to pasture, where they are unsupervised and fights tend to build up in intensity. Generally one sees more agressive horseplay, pushing and name-calling, and more crying.

There are also more outright fights among adults. Emotions rose toward the danger point during one violent argument about whether or not a man's wife had given food to persons who were not relatives, and Draper retreated into her Land Rover just in case poison arrows started flying about. The argument simmered down before things got out of hand. But such incidents are far more common among villagers, usually male villagers, than among the dwindling few who still live by hunting and gathering (probably about 2,000 persons).

Richard Lee/Anthro Photo

Changing times in the Kalahari: hunter-gatherers as they have lived for thousands of years (above); and (below) with settled villages, domesticated animals, fences, and Western clothes

Marjorie Shostak/Anthro Photo

The shift has brought further changes in life-style, including a brand-new settlement geometry and a brand-new "architecture." Think of the hunter-gatherer's camp out in the bush with its circle of grass huts, not to live in but to store tools and skins, and all the people talking and working outside together. This pattern has no place in Bushman farming villages. Round mud-walled houses, with thatched roofs and ample space for eating and sleeping in addition to storage, have replaced many of the grass huts. Furthermore, the houses tend to be lined up in rows and each house is surrounded by a log fence five to six feet high.

The fences, originally built to keep out domesticated animals, particularly goats, tend to keep out people as well, creating private areas that never existed before, because they were not needed in open bush country. And behind the fences and the walls are more possessions. Settled Bushmen own more things than their nomadic brethren, who must travel light. Some villagers own more than others—more blankets, finer clothing and jewelry, trunks with locks, and so on—another sharp and significant break with old egalitarian traditions. It is the end of gift-giving networks.

The coming of haves and have-nots contributes one more source of tension to already tense situations calling for new and more effective controls. The evolution of increasingly elaborate controls demonstrates how difficult it is for people to live together and how much energy, how much struggle, is required to maintain social equilibrium. Among the salmon-fishing Northwest Coast Indians, chiefs periodically sponsored festivals or "potlatches," occasions for giving away everything from food, blankets, clothing and baskets to copper ornaments and canoes. The custom probably originated as a method of equalizing people, a leveling device, but it developed highly aggressive and competitive aspects. Men indulged in orgies of ostentatious giving, determined at all costs to outdo and shame their rivals.

Mexican Indians had similar share-the-wealth customs, also corrupted upon occasion. The system had been working effectively in one Oaxaca village, the richest men sponsoring annual fiestas and other religious ceremonies. Then late last century a Señor Lopez, a wealthy farmer, made a deal with local priests to select a farmer who could not afford the honor, could not refuse it, and had to put up his land as security for a loan—from Señor Lopez, naturally. Eventually a few families, mostly Lopezes, owned more than ninety percent of the village farmlands, a state of affairs which was not readjusted until the Mexican Revolution.

Present-day groups practice other anticonflict customs. Napoleon Chagnon of Pennsylvania State University has spent some four years among the Yąnomamö Indians in southern Venezuela and northern Brazil, who represent a group that has just made the

Napoleon Chagnon (Pennsylvania State University) / Anthro-Photo

Ritual aggression among the Yąnomamö in the dense jungles of southern Venezuela and northern Brazil: line of spears; side-slapping duel; archer

transition from hunting-gathering to agriculture in a tropical context and is having growing pains. They subsist mainly on the bananalike plantain, cassava roots and other garden produce, are organized into villages, and cannot avoid living in a chronic state of warfare. But, like the rest of us, they try hard to keep the peace.

These people have established an unusual kind of trading relationship. One village specializes in making vine hammocks, another in hallucinogenic drugs, still another in clay pots or bamboo arrowheads, and so on. But no village specializes because it has any sort of edge on the rest, because it has access to natural resources which are not found elsewhere. The resources are available to all villages. Theirs is essentially an artificial system for the sole purpose of creating items to trade, creating mutual needs and close ties. Similar systems have evolved among Pacific islanders and many other peoples.

Life for the Yạnomamö is a succession of conflicts. It involves everything from relatively innocuous chest-pounding and side-slapping duels, which may help let off steam but only for a while, to increasingly bloody behavior such as club fights, spear fights, treacherous feasts and ambushes, and all-out warfare. Alliances are continually being made and broken. Fighting tends to be especially severe in central parts of the Yạnomamö countryside. When tensions build up, people living on the outskirts can always avoid trouble by moving into remote jungle areas. But people at the center, hemmed in by settlements on all sides, cannot get as far away and must fight more and more intensely.

The Yạnomamö are facing a problem familiar enough to most of their contemporaries in other lands: their population is increasing faster than their ability to organize themselves. Apparently a local head man and kinship ties can hold things together as long as the group includes fewer than 80 to 85 persons, but beyond that the odds that a village will split in two increase rapidly, with most divisions occurring in the 100-to-125 range. One region which contained a single village 150 years ago now contains fifteen villages.

One agricultural society north of the Yạnomamö has had a bit more time to evolve. The Warao people, who originally lived in a swamp-lagoon setting in the Orinoco River delta of Venezuela, have been studied in great detail by Johannes Wilbert of the University of California in Los Angeles. In 1926 a major flood, and a backup of salt water which wiped out the fish in their home territory, drove a group of the people away. Some tried to make a go of it in a refugee village further upstream.

The new setting called for a period of adjustment, the bringing in of new plants and new techniques. The Warao settlers paddled a dugout canoe to a village about fifty miles away where they picked up a load of more than 200 pounds of ocumo, a high-starch root crop, most of which they ate when they returned home. But they planted some of the cuttings right outside their house, without even bothering to clear the land. Later they brought in some sugarcane and two fruit trees, including one calabash tree, an especially important addition since its fruit is made into sacred rattles to communicate with the spirit world. They also adopted harpoons and other equipment to catch big deep-water fish in the river.

The group has flourished. Since the flood, a better and more varied diet and the move away from the original malaria-infested swamp-lagoon environment have stimulated a local population boom from some 50 persons in the early 1940s to nearly 200 by 1953, when Wilbert first arrived as a graduate student. Aggressiveness and incidents of violence and hostility also increased as among the Bushmen and other groups. A fighting ritual helps to maintain peace. About every four or five months tension builds up to a point where action must be taken, something like the consensus by grumbling which Rappaport observed in New Guinea. One man, the official "insulter," triggers the event, placing a wood carving representing a phallus-vagina on a path leading from the village to one of the neighboring villages. Excitement mounts rapidly. "I was caught up in a fight like this," Wilbert reports, "and wondered whether to go away until it blew over. But I stayed through it all."

It was a fabulous spectacle. The men of each side lined up opposite one another, looking fierce and brandishing rectangular shields. They started coming at each other, menacing, closer and closer and with much shouting. I thought fighting would break out in earnest. But then the opposing lines just barely touched shields, and went back to their original positions.

At that stage the violence was confined to the insulter and the opponent selected to confront him. The two men had a serious but nonfatal duel. The only real bodily contact took place among the women of both villages, who had a hair-pulling and scratching fight of their own. After two hours or so, the offended villagers departed in a friendly spirit.

By ritual warfare or the real thing, people are attempting, often desperately, to eliminate or reduce conflict. In at least one case on record, an outsider has been invited to rule over them in the interests of peace. More than half a century ago members of an East African tribe petitioned a neighboring tribe for a man to serve as their chief and help them stop fighting among themselves.

The archeological record suggests that people faced similar problems in times past and attempted similar solutions. It is less detailed than the record of living societies, of course, but tends to cover longer periods, providing the only evidence for origins and early developments. The evolution of control measures and institutions, the change from transitory local leaders with limited authority over a few hundred individuals, at most, to kings with absolute dominion over tens of thousands, seems to have been a kind of sudden-release phenomenon. The process gained headway slowly, and then all at once picked up momentum.

Big men and chiefs and coalitions of chiefs probably appeared here and there in hunter-gatherer days, for example, perhaps 15,000 years ago among the reindeer hunters and cave painters of southern France and in northern Russia where high-status individuals have been found buried with abundant ornaments. But not until the rise of settled living and agriculture did such people come into their own.

At a site in southern Jordan, a 7000 B.C. occupation level is made up entirely of small houses averaging some 120 square feet, the size of a small twentieth-century bedroom. In the level immediately above a different pattern appears, representing the same settlement no more than a few generations later, the beginnings of a range of hierarchy of house sizes. The village now consisted mostly of small houses distributed around a slightly raised central area, a section reserved for houses three to four times larger than the rest, with large hearths and plastered walls

Courtesy of British Tourist Authority

30,000,000 man-hours of labor: Stonehenge, Salisbury Plain, England

and floors. These special houses may have belonged to people better off than their neighbors. Other sites yield more direct traces of wealthy families, far more substantial residences with thicker and better constructed walls, more rooms, extra-fine pottery, and a variety of luxury items. The oversized houses may have belonged to the community rather than to individuals, however, serving as public buildings where people met and made decisions and participated in rituals.

More intensive research, a combination of approaches, is required to document by digging the coming of chiefdoms. The most direct and spectacular evidence is the existence of large stone monuments. Stonehenge on England's Salisbury Plain certainly represents a massing of power. Power was required to get it built in the first place, sufficient power to mobilize more than 30,000,000 man-hours of labor. But Stonehenge represents a great deal more. The need for a new monument larger than anything previously constructed in the region implied a highly organized reaching-out process, a determined extension of controls; the creation of a greater and more impressive ceremonial center designed to attract more people from further away than ever before; the establishment of a system of beliefs to sanction future plans. In short, the building of Stonehenge and all such monuments implied a need for still more power.

Stonehenge also implied the emergence of new allegiances or, rather, the possibility of new allegiances. Increasingly complex societies were marked by efforts to broaden, to generalize, the notion of family to include more and more people. Clans and other kinds of kinship groups evolved, and with them clannishness, which brought a measure of increased solidarity among members in good standing and, at the same time, frequently gave rise to a heightened distrust of similarly organized outsiders. The earliest monumental architecture, as well as extensive irrigation systems and other large-scale public works projects, involved specialists at both ends of the social scale, elites and skilled workers in the process of forming wider loyalties over and above those of family and kin.

"Chiefdom archeology" also calls for research on the way people disposed of their dead, especially their distinguished dead.

Moundville reconstruction: a prehistoric American center near Tuscaloosa, Alabama, as it looked half a millennium ago

Christopher Peebles of the University of Michigan has made a detailed study of mortuary practices at one of the largest prehistoric ceremonial centers in the eastern United States, a 300-acre complex of twenty mounds surrounding a central plaza, known appropriately enough as Moundville and located on a bluff of the Black Warrior River about fifteen miles south of Tuscaloosa, Alabama. He conducted a computer-aided investigation of 719 burials accompanied by 157 varieties of grave goods ranging from pottery and objects of copper to woodpecker bills, garfish snouts, stone pipes and shells. The objective was to find out which items usually occurred together, and what the associations indicated about the status of the people they had been buried with.

This so-called cluster analysis revealed two broad types of special burial. Prestigious "dress and office" items such as copper symbol badges, shell beads, and ceremonial stone celts—items generally made of rare, imported materials and requiring considerable time and skill to produce—tended to be buried with individuals of all ages, suggesting inherited status, status acquired by birth and hence attached automatically to all family members. The inference of inherited status is reinforced by the fact that some infants and children, individuals obviously too young to have accomplished great things and made names for themselves, were also buried in high style.

Other clusters of grave goods, rather less glamorous, represent the second type of special burial. "Although some of the artifacts show remarkable skill in execution," Peebles points out, "the time invested in them is not comparable to the time invested in the dress-and-office artifacts." Plain and decorated water bottles, bone awls, flint projectile points and plain stone pipes have been found, usually made of local materials. They seem to reflect social positions that are not inherited and hence not open to people of all ages, the artifacts of self-made individuals who achieved status on their own.

The growth of power is regional as well as local, in countrysides surrounding major centers as well as in the centers themselves. The prehistory of Moundville, for example, will never be reconstructed on the basis of excavations at Moundville alone. It was the largest of seventeen Black Warrior Valley sites, including hamlets only a fraction of an acre in size, villages with and with-

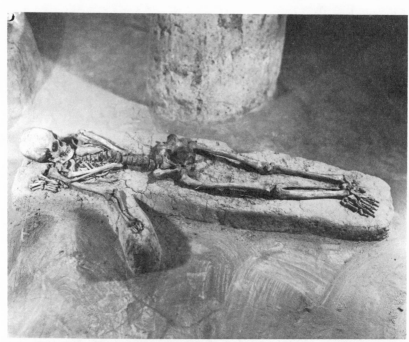

Courtesy of Richard Krause, University of Alabama

Status as revealed by Moundville burials: low status or poverty, female buried without grave goods (upper left); moderate wealth, male with goods, probably acquired by own efforts (lower left); great wealth, child buried with goods, presumably inherited (above)

out mounds, and four smaller subcenters within a radius of two miles. The valley included a hierarchy of places and, together with the evidence from burials and large public works, that implies a hierarchy of duties and social positions.

Moundville provided important services to other settlements, and depended on them for survival. For one thing, the center needed more food than its own farmers and hunters could supply. Fertile farmlands and forests with abundant game, mainly white-tailed deer and turkeys, were close at hand, but were insufficient to feed an estimated 2,000 to 3,000 persons. Outlying hamlets and villages undoubtedly provided extra food, perhaps distributed through middlemen at the subcenters. In return Moundville provided ceremonial facilities, a refuge in case of enemy raids, and a launching point for raids of its own.

Moundville-type systems appeared all over the world, despite internal and external conflicts. They were temporary solutions to subsistence problems, old and continuing problems such as food scarcities and threatened food shortages. From the start agriculture was never as reliable as hunting-gathering, that is, as hunting-gathering was before populations became too large. Farming always represented a gamble with high stakes. It increased the people-carrying capacity of the land considerably, and also the danger of widespread famine. Insect pests, disease, and the vagaries of the weather probably led to crop failures two to four times every decade or so.

Village life was often a tightrope affair, proceeding on the edge of failure. People had never before existed under such insecure conditions. For parents and their children it must have been something like living in a high-risk flood area along the Mississippi, knowing that sooner or later the river will rise over the levees again and inundate the valley. One cannot feel afraid constantly, day in and day out. But the sense of imminent catastrophe, imminent chaos, is always there.

The prehistoric counterstrategy was essentially to establish a steady, ample and predictable flow of food in the face of widely fluctuating and unpredictable local conditions, a formidable task. That meant, first of all, building up abundant reserves. Just as important, since stored surpluses inevitably dwindle and may go bad, it also meant having on hand whenever possible goods that could, in a pinch, be exchanged for food with people in other communities. Herds represented living storehouses, money in the bank. Meat on the hoof brought a higher barter price in the form of grain and other plant foods. The products of craftsmen, such as pottery and jewelry and ceremonial items, could also be converted into food when necessary.

Reducing uncertainty was the heart of the problem. People had to give up things and give things away, work long and regular hours for other people as well as for themselves, work today to guard against emergencies that might arise tomorrow. That represented a large order then, as it does now. The sharing was not so bad, since that was part of a tradition established during less populous hunter-gatherer times. But working long and hard and regularly was something else again. It ran directly counter to that tradition, and working for the future was even less congenial, considering the old days when the wilderness offered all the food needed, right now.

In the beginning, people following hunter-gathering customs and imbued with the old hunter-gatherer psychology, worked in their fields to produce only enough food to meet their own needs, and no more. In fact, Sahlins emphasizes that they often produced rather less than enough. Underproduction may have been the rule, as a not inconsiderable number of villagers made a practice of sponging off friends and relatives and settled for getting along on substandard diets.

Ways had to be developed to overcome the traditional inertia, first locally and later on a regional basis. There must have been calls for volunteers in villages scattered over wide areas, appeals to work for the common good, and then more organized procedures if volunteers were few, and the setting up of formal rules requiring work—measures which may have been applied one after the other in a sequence of increasing urgency, or all at once. In certain ways, the basic techniques may have resembled those army recruiters use today. Older people, who had lived through many food shortages and knew how much was at stake, were presumably prominent among the persuaders.

Something more than exhortation and compulsion would be necessary, incentives, material and otherwise. Perhaps the forerunners of country fairs originated in such a context with animals and crop plants on display, and prizes awarded. The effect must have been to create a greater respect for hard work, an ethics of providing and providence. If you contribute to surpluses for the future, you will be rewarded. Your children will lead long and healthy lives, evil spirits will stay away from your door, and your ancestors and the gods will look upon you with favor.

Was all this consciously planned? Did people know what they were doing? At one level, at least, they undoubtedly did. They must have arrived at many important decisions after due deliberation, for example, when it came to recruiting and rewarding workers on the land. But they almost certainly did not convene and decide by consensus to establish a new ethics. That was probably left to individuals who felt and voiced the implications of what was happening, and influenced behavior in a rather more subtle manner. In this sense, in the sense that most effects of the furthest-reaching innovations cannot be foreseen, people never know what they are doing.

People organized themselves and acted. Special houses appeared in prehistoric villages, houses larger than the rest, not for living but for meeting, places for decision. Opportunities for cooperation increased. So did opportunities for conflict. As Carneiro has indicated, doubling the size of a community more than doubles the need for organizing, looking ahead, and scheduling. Activities which had once been relatively secondary in the conduct of affairs, accessory to the main event, assumed greater and greater importance in their own right.

Consider the practical side of a major festival, say, week-long ceremonies honoring a rain god held in a large village or town. It was no great problem to take care of people coming in from the countryside. Presumably they stayed with relatives. But at some later stage providing food and lodging and other services must have called for more formal arrangements on a larger scale. Sharp and temporary increases in demand during religious holidays may well have required planning at least as intricate as that required to meet the demands of permanent local populations. Within a brief period visitors would have to be supplied with room and board, quantities of gifts and souvenirs and relics.

Modern occasions like football games, rock festivals, grand operas, high masses, revival meetings, Christmas celebrations pose related problems. All such events involve the spontaneous enthusiasm and beliefs of performers, participants, and audiences. But the superstructure of minor things that become major things sometimes threatens to take over completely—parking privileges, concessions, publicity calculated to lure more participants. The study of present-day institutions may provide hints to the shaping of prehistoric institutions.

Every institution, every set of rules designed to create and maintain order, increased the risk of disorder. So people built centers on hilltops offering panoramic views of the countryside, and built massive outer walls and ditches as defenses against enemies from neighboring regions. There were also centers within centers, ceremonial and administrative precincts surrounded by inner walls with narrow, easy-to-guard entrances, which in some cases may have been erected to protect resident elites more from internal revolts than from outside invasion.

Certainly the process of getting more and more work out of more and more people had its limits. The need for such things as defense walls and irrigation networks may have been obvious. But elaborate arsenals, palaces, temples and tombs called for increas-

	BAND	TRIBE	CHIEFDOM	STATE	TYPE OF SOCIETY
LOCAL GROUP AUTONOMY					
EGALITARIAN STATUS					
EPHEMERAL, INFORMAL LEADERSHIP					
UNSCHEDULED AD HOC RITUAL					
RECIPROCAL OR BARTER ECONOMY					
	UNRANKED DESCENT GROUPS				
	PAN-TRIBAL ASSOCIATIONS, FRATERNAL ORDERS				
	CALENDRIC REGULARLY SCHEDULED RITUALS				SOME INSTITUTIONS, IN ORDER OF APPEARANCE
		RANKED DESCENT GROUPS			
		CENTRAL ACCUMULATION AND REDISTRIBUTIVE ECONOMY			
		HEREDITARY LEADERSHIP			
		ELITE ENDOGAMY			
		FULL-TIME CRAFT SPECIALIZATION			
			STRATIFICATION		
			KINGSHIP		
			TRUE LAW		
			BUREAUCRACY		
			MILITARY DRAFT		
			TAXATION		
PRESENT-DAY AND RECENT EXAMPLE	KALAHARI BUSHMAN SOUTH AFRICA AUSTRALIAN ABORIGINES ESKIMOS SHOSHONI U.S.A. HADZA EAST AFRICA	NEW GUINEA HIGHLANDERS SOUTHWESTERN PUEBLOS, U.S.A.	HAWAII TLINGIT INDIANS NORTHWEST PACIFIC COAST	FRANCE ENGLAND INDIA U.S.A.	
ARCHEOLOGICAL EXAMPLES	EARLY INDIANS OF U.S.A. AND MEXICO (10,000-6000 B.C.) Near East (10,000 B.C.)	VALLEY OF OAXACA, MEXICO (1500-1000 B.C.) Near East (8000-6000 B.C.)	GULF COAST OLMEC OF MEXICO (1000 B.C.) Near East (5300 B.C.) MISSISSIPPIAN OF MID-WEST U.S.A. (1200 A.D.)	CLASSIC MESO-AMERICA SUMER SHANG CHINA IMPERIAL ROME	

Mona Marks. From Flannery, 1973

The coming of complexity: stages in social evolution

ingly elaborate justifications. A significant role of religion was to provide what Paul Wheatley of the University of Chicago calls "validation" for the more ambitious plans of those in authority.

Hierarchies were evolving, hierarchies of control. According to a definition proposed by Henry Wright of the University of Michigan, the state is a system with at least three administrative levels. The lowest ranking administrators are overseers and foremen who supervise the work of farmers and laborers, most of the people. At the next highest level are individuals designated to oversee the overseers. Usually operating away from the action in public offices, they keep track of schedules. They serve the policymakers at the top of the social pyramid. This is a minimum or "atomic" system, the simplest of which can be called a state in Wright's definition. A mark of its emergence in prehistoric times was the multiplication of middlemen, the most exalted middleman being the paramount chief or king serving as intermediary between his people and the gods. Considerable effort went into the making of the absolute ruler. People had to believe in the existence of such a being; the ruler also had to believe it.

The need for belief must have been strong. It was the need for a living symbol of permanence. People may not hesitate to overthrow or kill a petty chieftain or big man. He is one of their own. But they may think twice before removing a man of distinction. The higher his status, the more impressive his credentials, the safer he is. If prestige thus acquires selective value as a form of life insurance, being a god or near-god should represent the safest position of all. Even divinity does not guarantee 100 percent protection; people under pressure have managed to do away with gods on earth. The absolute leader, however, was a step in the right direction. At a certain stage of human evolution his coming was part of the price paid for stability.

5

New Ways of Detecting Change in Times Past

*New techniques for reconstructing prehistoric society/
Surface finds as clues to what lies underground/
The evidence from bones/ Translating the "language"
of pottery/ The mysterious roads of Chaco
Canyon/ Hexagonal settlement patterns/
On-site computers*

ARCHEOLOGISTS are notoriously critical of one another, at least an order of magnitude more so than scientists in other disciplines, sometimes with good reason. It is easy to miss important clues, to lose information that can never be retrieved. An excavated site is a site destroyed. Thinking of all that has been lost in the Near East, Mortimer Wheeler of the British Academy has called it "the land of archeological sin." To which Kent Flannery of the University of Michigan replies: "Such a statement could only have been made by a man who had never worked in Mesoamerica."

Mistakes are made everywhere. But they are less common than they were in the old days of "museum" archeology when investigators, actually looters with doctor's degrees, were more interested in finding objects of art than in reconstructing the life of the past. Careful excavators work slowly. Often the only traces of pre-historic houses are post holes, places where wooden supports for walls and roofs were driven into the ground. The posts themselves have long since rotted to dust. All that remains are columns of soil slightly looser and slightly darker than the surrounding soil. Sometimes the evidence is invisible. Color differences do not exist, and the excavator must go by feel, sensing the looseness by scraping gently with the tip of a trowel.

An expert at identifying plant remains spends hours at a microscope focusing on individual grains, or bits of root and stem and husk which may be no bigger than pinheads, looking for distinguishing shapes and textures, identifying the species whenever possible, recording the results for more sophisticated analysis later on. If he has strong eyes, he can examine about a fifteenth of an ounce of plant material a day, a tiny fraction of the day's collection.

Some 90,000 pieces of animal bone, 45,000 seeds and other plant parts, some 30,000 flint and obsidian tools and several hundred thousand chips, 25,000 sherds or pottery fragments, and an assortment of ornaments, spindle whorls, figurines, burials, impressions of mats and baskets on patches of asphalt, mud-brick walls, storage bins and building debris—this is what Frank Hole of Rice University, Flannery, James Neely of the University of Texas, their wives and other associates recovered during one three-month digging season at one site known as Ali Kosh on a desolate sandy plain in western Iran.

So material continues to accumulate season after season from hundreds of sites throughout the world, and work continues to pile up at hundreds of archeological laboratories back home. There is more than enough to keep people busy for decades. The laboratory work is piling up faster than the material itself. It takes at least six months of study to analyze items unearthed during a single month of excavating, and the "at least" means that it often takes a good deal longer.

Studies on a large scale, studies of maps and aerial photographs, cover extensive regions and countrysides. The elements analyzed are not individual artifacts but sites or, rather, complexes of sites, varying in size from an acre or two to several hundred acres. The emphasis is on broad relationships, settlement patterns. The investigator is concerned with such things as the distances between sites and their distribution over the landscape, factors which may hint at the structure of prehistoric societies.

In all cases, microscopic or bird's-eye view, the search is for enduring patterns of times past. Some of the patterns are relatively easy to detect; others are much more subtle and can be detected only with the aid of special statistical techniques. The patterns consist basically of changes in the soil, in plant and animal species, in rooms and buildings, in settlements and the trails linking settlements, in practically everything that prehistoric people touched. Wherever they moved into an area they left marks that say "we were here."

With mounting pressure to use land, sites have often been found in the wake of bulldozers moving earth for new houses or industrial developments. While laws provide for construction delays, archeologists work in haste on so-called salvage projects to learn what they can before the bulldozers start rolling again. Since a site may cover many acres, limited funds as well as construction worker impatient to get on with it dictate that only the most promising areas be selected for excavation.

More than a decade ago Binford pioneered a strategy for dealing with such problems, and for surveying in general. At Hatchery West, a river-terrace site in southern Illinois, after a light plowing, he and his associates marked off the fields into 416 six-by-six-meter squares and walked over the area picking up all artifacts and other remains—pottery sherds, flint tools, grinding stones, shells, chipping debris and so on, a total of nearly 8,000 items. Among other things, they found low sherd densities (1 to 5 per square) often marked buried houses, while high densities (16 to 20 per square) marked middens or refuse dumps.

The excavation revealed a type of house previously unknown in the midwest. Built 1,000 to 15,000 years ago, these houses were keyhole-shaped, round half-sunken rooms, probably winter quarters, with long narrow extensions, that may have provided storage space. But the most intriguing thing about the dig, and others conducted elsewhere using the same approach, is the persistence of archeological patterns. The Hatchery West fields, plowed for years, had long served as hunting grounds for artifact collectors, and still items on the surface provided clues to what lay buried underneath.

Animal bones represent an increasingly rich source of information, but require long and often tedious sorting-out sessions in the field laboratory, usually a tent or shack. Most specimens, more than 77,000 out of the 90,000 found at Ali Kosh, are too shattered to be of much use. The rest are numbered and identified as precisely as possible—by site location (layer and grid square), species, type of bone, condition of bone (burned, diseased, worked), age, sex, and so on. With such basic data, investigators can proceed to more detailed analyses. They may deduce the nature of prehistoric environments as Eitan Tchernov of the Hebrew University of Jerusalem did on the basis of bird bones found at a Jordan Valley site. In one layer 56.5 percent of the birds were meadow and grassland dwellers, 31.8 percent rock dwellers, 7.5 percent tree dwellers, and 4.2 percent water and swamp dwellers, providing a rough indication of the types of landscape and their relative proportions. Apparently rainfall increased later, because the percentage of water and swamp birds more than doubled in the layer immediately above this one.

Research currently under way points to future developments along similar lines, for instance, the wider use of rodent remains as landscape markers. One of the world's most widespread genera is the field mouse, which exists in a variety of species and subspecies adapted to open meadows, woodlands, rocky slopes, bushy field margins and other settings. Richard Redding of the University of Michigan is looking for characteristic skeletal changes that go with different adaptations, changes in the size and shape of bones which might be recovered at archeological sites.

He suggests that remains of a less familiar rodent, the Indian gerbil, provide an almost certain sign of prehistoric irrigation in certain regions of the Near East. This species lives on shoots and grass seeds. It needs abundant all-year-round supplies, which do not exist in that part of the world, with the six-month growing season typical of many areas. The most prevalent locations with permanent vegetation are the banks of irrigation canals. This is where gerbils are found today, and gerbil bones are prominent among the 90,000 specimens recovered from Ali Kosh where other evidence supports the possibility of irrigation.

Bone studies provide clues to domestication. Techniques have been developed for detecting changes that come with the taming of wild animals. Often there is a decrease in size, presumably because smaller animals need less food and thus have a better chance for surviving and multiplying on the limited diets available in early farming villages. The foot and leg bones of domesticated cattle and pigs may be less than half as large as the corresponding bones of their wild relatives, although the difference is not always that clear-cut. In some sites the change can be observed in stages by comparing specimens from early and more recent levels.

Charles Reed of the University of Illinois has noted a more precise change in the goat. The horns of certain wild goats are shaped rather like scimitars, curving back to form a pair of sharp-pointed prongs. During the early stages of domestication the horns tend to flatten out, the cross section shifting from a roughly four-cornered to an oval or lens-shaped pattern. Later the cross section becomes even flatter, and still later the horns begin to show a corkscrew twist which becomes more and more pronounced. These changes are seen in excavated horn cores, the horn bones that remain after the outer sheath has disintegrated. No one know why the process of taming should produce such effects, or similar effects in some sheep. Ideally, investigators would find equally clear-cut markers for every species, but that goal has yet to be attained.

If there are enough bones in good condition, the proportion of animals killed at different ages can be estimated by studying tooth eruption and tooth wear as well as "fusion lines," places where cartilage has calcified and hardened when bones stop growing. If a high proportion of young animals and fully grown animals was being killed, the odds are that people were harvesting them from domesticated herds.

The search continues for other ways of detecting domestication. Most tests depend on examining the appearance of bone, external markings and changes in size and shape. Some investigators believe they have found internal changes which cannot be seen by the naked eye. In 1968, Isabella Drew, Dexter Perkins, and Patricia Daly of Columbia University announced that by examining thin sections of bone under a light-polarizing microscope, which produces different color patterns for different crystal formations, they could distinguish wild from domesticated animals.

The patterns were predominantly red and magenta for specimens of bone from wild species, strong blue and yellow colors in specimens from tamed animals. Patterns showed up most clearly in thin section obtained from the joint regions of weight-bearing bones. These investigators reported that the difference may be related to the fact that the bones of tame species are less rugged than those of wild species, because animals living with man do not eat as well or get as much exercise.

Preliminary tests suggested similar changes in human bones, apparently tending to support the notion that when man settled down and domesticated other species, he also domesticated himself, or at least made a modest step in that direction. Thin sections from the foot bone of a Neanderthal individual who lived some 50,000 years ago showed the red-magenta colors typical of untamed species in general, while the blue and yellow colors appeared in sections from modern-type man, who presumably leads a softer life. These findings have aroused some debate. In a recent study Melinda Zeder of the University of Michigan was unable to repeat the Columbia results, so the matter remains up in the air, pending further research. But prospects are nevertheless promising that chemical analysis involving the crystalline microstructure of bone can provide important information about the use of animals in prehistoric times.

Bone can serve as a stress gauge, a sensitive indicator when investigators suspect that people are not eating as well as they should. Della Cook of Indiana University has measured the long bones of two prehistoric populations of children recovered from burial mounds on bluffs overlooking the Mississippi and Illinois rivers. One population dates to about A.D. 100 to A.D. 250 when Indians in the Midwest were living primarily by hunting, gathering, and fishing; the other population lived around A.D. 800 to A.D. 900 when people were beginning to use corn as a dietary staple.

Judging by the lengths of arm and leg bones at different ages from birth to five years old, the hunter-gatherer children had better balanced diets. The introduction of corn, which provided plenty of calories but not enough protein, was marked by a lower growth rate, so in some cases a price had to be paid for supporting increased numbers of people. In the later group dental caries are also more frequent, reflecting the high carbohydrate content of the diet.

This is only one of a series of bone studies which Cook and other investigators are conducting and which emphasize populations and population trends. Their approach makes it possible to identify the one disease out of two dozen or more diseases most likely to have produced certain types of bone damage, and to arrive at a more precise picture of how health patterns and diseases themselves may have changed with changing diets. A great deal more is being done, all of it requiring detailed examinations of bone specimens as part of the effort to determine such things as longevity, possible causes of fractures, the extent of physical stress, the nature of prehistoric diets, and so on.

Another rich and abundant source of information about prehistoric life and tradition is the study of pottery. Pottery-making, like domestication itself, had roots in the remote past. It became increasingly important with settling down and the rise of agriculture, but some of the basic methods were known at least 10,000 years before that. Man's first artificial material consisted of clay mixed with ground-up bone and other tempering substances to improve its working qualities and then hardened by firing. Hunter-gatherers in southern Russia and elsewhere used it chiefly to make so-called Venus figurines, miniature statues of women often found in special pits under house floors and perhaps serving as fertility symbols. For containers people may have used gourds and bowls made of stone and wood. (Traces of a wooden bowl more than 400,000 years old have been reported from a site on the French Riviera.)

In some areas pottery was developed long before the beginnings of agriculture. But it appeared on a larger and larger scale in response to new necessities and purposes connected with farming. There was a demand for a material not found in nature, a composite heat-treated material that could be molded by hand into made-to-order shapes. Studies of the material and the products help solve immediate problems of digging and, when the digging is done, long-term problems concerning the daily lives of prehistoric people.

A representative excavation may yield 30,000 sherds, although

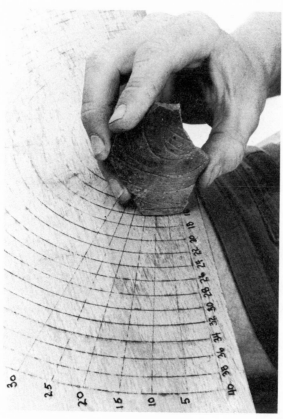

Measuring original
dimension from small
fragment of pottery:
sherd from a satellite
of Cahokia on
diameter board
gauging original
mouth of a dish

Pottery vessels
(below) reconstructed
from "diagnostic"
sherds: typical rim
sherds of early
Amazon Basin

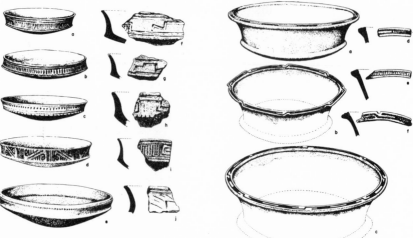

Courtesy of Donald W. Lathrap. Photo by David Minor, University of Illinois, Urbana

the number ranges from several hundred to several million depending on the richness of the site and the time spent digging. From that mass of debris the archeologist attempts to reconstruct an inventory of vessels used for each occupation level. It is something like trying to put together a complete set of china from a twenty-foot pile of thoroughly shattered and mixed china objects, accumulated from hundreds of houses over a period of several generations or more. If the archeologist is lucky, he has unearthed a few vessels intact or nearly intact, as well as a number of broken vessels which could be restored because the pieces happened to be lying close together. He may fit some pieces together to restore half a vessel or, more usually, only a small section, a task which requires hours of work with pieces spread out on a table and a special talent for jigsaw puzzles several orders of magnitude trickier than the most complex available in stores.

Experience also helps. In the words of Donald Lathrap of the University of Illinois: "I never see a sherd. I see a whole vessel." That comes from examining hundreds of thousands of sherds and hundreds of vessels. His archeological region is one of the most difficult in the world, the Amazon Basin of central Peru, near the eastern slopes of the Andes. Finding sites in such densely overgrown territory demands tramping through miles of jungle and the cooperation of Indian farmers who know the locations of many sherd concentrations.

In the course of studying the region's prehistory for more than a decade, Lathrap has excavated more than 44,000 sherds covering eight main occupation intervales from about 2000 B.C. to A.D. 500, examining every single sherd at least five times, often for up to ten minutes and under the microscope. "Diagnostic" sherds, the pieces most useful in identifying and reconstructing vessels (mainly rim sherds as well as base sherds and decorated zones, all of which make up about a fifth of the total collection), call for extra attention. He has examined every one of them twenty or more times.

His first step in the laboratory is a rough sorting-out, making eight piles of sherds, one for each interval. He tries to decide how many types of vessel are represented in each pile. After that, the real work starts, the objective being to prepare precise drawings of each type of vessel. In line with established practice, the study includes figuring out the diameters of vessel mouths by measuring the arcs of all rim sherds, recording the angles of all sherds showing a sharp change in curvature, and using a lapidary saw designed for working precious stones to cut rim sherds and obtain sharply defined profiles as further clues to vessel shape.

Even then the work is not finished. Every study is preliminary, since new results will modify or radically change interpretations. For example, after going through his 44,000-sherd collection, Lathrap refined the analysis considerably by examining some 40,000 additional sherds which he and his students unearthed during later excavations, as well as 25,000 to 30,000 related sherds in the collections of other archeologists. Such work helps set up time scales for prehistoric events. Often sites can be dated by a "radioactive clock" which works on the same general principle as the one mentioned in Chapter 2 (see page 53) but depends on a radioactive form of carbon, not potassium. This substance, known as carbon 14, is present in all organic materials and disintegrates at a known and steady rate. The older a specimen of organic material, say, some charcoal or shell or wood, the less carbon 14 it contains.

Recent and continuing studies show that most of the so-called radiocarbon dates cited in archeological reports will have to be corrected. It had originally been assumed that the concentration of carbon 14 in the earth's atmosphere remained constant during the past. This turns out not to be the case. Calculated dates for the period from 4000 B.C. to 5000 B.C. may be as much as a thousand years too low, too recent, while smaller but still important discrepancies exist for more recent times. The extent of discrepancies for earlier times is being investigated. (Since relative sequences are generally not affected, however, most archeologists use the uncorrected dates, a policy followed in this book.)

Once an investigator has established a carbon-14 sequence that holds for sites in his territory and has identified the characteristic types of pottery that go with each occupation level, he can use the sherds alone for dating new sites. This is an important alternative if the sites fail to yield suitable organic specimens for radiocarbon dating. A high, lustrous black polish, part of a diamond or zigzag decoration just below the rim, a buff surface with red or gray blotches, traces of a red coating or "slip" or refined clay applied before firing, a piece of squat globular spout—such fragmentary clues may be enough to indicate roughly when a site was occupied.

Often sherds provide more precise dates than radioactive clocks alone. If clearly defined pottery differences exist within successive occupation levels, it may be possible to break a period defined by radiocarbon dates into a number of subperiods. The work is roughly equivalent to using a camera or microscope with higher resolution to obtain sharper and more detailed images, and it calls for an especially intensive analysis. Distinguishing pottery types and styles is an exercise in resolution throughout, an example of a process fundamental to all science and all thinking, the process of classifying and comparing.

Pottery may be classified on the basis of many different characteristics—kind of clay, tempering material, wall thickness, color, shape, firing method, size, surface finish, bottom form, neck form, appendages such as lugs and handles, decorative techniques, location of decoration, design motifs and so on. There are forty to fifty such general features or attributes, and many types of each. The variety of decorations, stylistic elements and themes and variations on themes is practically infinite.

Finding specific features or sets of features which distinguish the pottery of different subperiods represents a high point in the search for pattern. A feature may be any detail which, however small or for whatever reason, varies through time clearly enough to serve as a marker for change. One expert in the art of pottery analysis, Dorothy Menzel of the University of California, notes such things as the decreasing width of white bands outlined in black, increasingly abstract representations of feline heads, and changes in the design of arms or handles to define subperiods within a 500-year span of Peruvian prehistory. The subperiods may be thirty to fifty years long, a degree of precision beyond that generally possible with the carbon-14 technique. But that is about the limit. In those days it apparently took a generation or two for a new style or fashion to become established, to "take" and show up as a trend in the record.

Sherds also provide information about changes in life-style, in the way people organize themselves. The appearance in one region of vessels typical of another region implies some form of contact. The nature of the contact, anything from ordinary trade to outright conquest, may be gauged by noting whether the new vessels appear in the record gradually or suddenly, and whether they are simply one of many types used or the dominant type.

The drive is continually toward more detailed, more precise information. Pottery may be traced to a locality by chemical analysis, or by microscopic studies of thin sherd sections like those prepared for distinguishing between the bones of wild and domesticated animals. Current research includes efforts to identify the work of individual potters, which would help greatly in deducing the movements of goods and people from community to community. James Hill and his associates at the University of California in Los Angeles went to Mexico, bought seventy-five pots made by five craftsmen, proceeded to smash the pots into some 2,500 pieces, mixed the pieces together, and demonstrated that sherds representing individuals could be identified with an accuracy of eighty-five to ninety percent.

After spending more than a year in a Mexican village where potters have been making characteristic thin-walled green-glazed vessels for several generations, Margaret Hardin of Loyola University of Chicago can identify the products of workers by thickness and spacing of painted lines, the size of design elements, the way the centers of certain flowers are drawn, and other details. She can tell which potters communicate most intensively with one another. The same principles could be applied to studies of prehistoric vessels.

Despite all the research already done, we have hardly begun to learn what can be learned from pieces of hardened clay. They are sources of clues to family size, population change and migration, the rise of elites, the establishment of mass-production systems, tightening political controls, and the relative power of priests and soldiers.

"We are trying to reconstruct history in the absence of written records," Menzel emphasizes. "People expressed political opinions and other ideas esthetically in their ceramics. Each pot is a commentary, a composition in which design elements and representations serve the purpose of phrases and sentences. Studying a pottery style is like studying a language, with dialects and slang expressions and idioms. We can learn to read that language, but only if we make a complete analysis of its grammar, vocabulary and syntax." Excavated objects such as stone tools, soil and rock samples, pollen grains and other items are all being studied with as much attention to detail as seeds, bones, and sherds.

Other investigators are concerned less with such individual finds than with entire sites. They are commited to a form of analysis in the large. One such study draws on a branch of mathematics known as graph theory. Involving higher geometry and algebra, and with a special attraction for algebraists, it deals with relationships and connections among points which are completely abstract elements. They can represent anything the investigator is interested in, from intangibles like hypotheses and arguments and measurements to furniture in a room, pieces on a chessboard or the corners of a cube. In a number of recent applications the points have represented cities connected by highways, railroads, and telephone lines. One effort has been to evaluate regional communication networks and the relative accessibility of various centers.

Graph theory is emerging as a method to study accessibility and related problems in archeology. Norman Hammond of Cambridge University in England undertook a pioneer analysis several years ago. He took a map of sixteen major ceremonial and residential plazas at a Maya site in British Honduras and translated it into an abstract graph or network diagram. The points represented plazas and the lines represented the pathways between them. Then he calculated a special "central accessibility" index to measure the relative seclusion of each plaza, obtaining a picture of how the area was organized into public and private sections.

Increasingly sophisticated use of aerial photography and advanced electronic gear indicates wider connections and relationships. The past seventy-five years have seen notable progress in "aerial archeology," high-altitude studies designed to distinguish man-made patterns from background landscapes. Cameras and infrared sensors mounted in airplanes have detected features which cannot be noticed on the ground—surface marks indicating buried road, falls, ditches and houses—entire villages such as those recently located deep in the waters of Lake Neuchatel in Switzerland, and ancient cities and their surroundings.

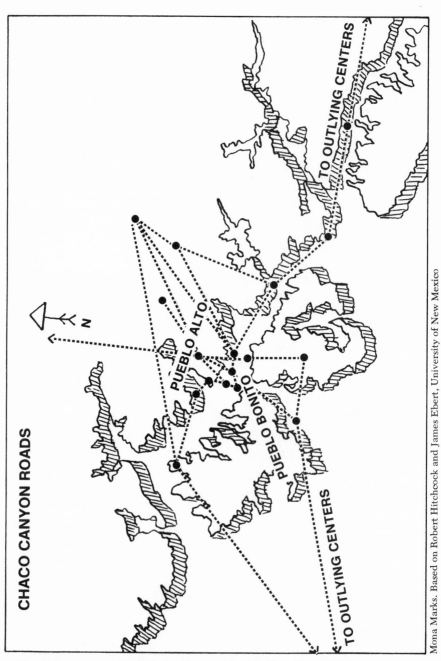

Graph-theory network analysis: diagram showing locations of main crossroads, prehistoric road systems, Chaco Canyon, New Mexico

The extraordinary prehistoric roads of Chaco Canyon in north-western New Mexico have been investigated using such techniques. Twenty miles long and up to three-quarters of a mile across, the canyon is eroded and barren now, but it was a thriving area a thousand years ago, when 10,000 to 20,000 people lived there in a dozen pueblo centers with adobe houses of three or four stories and in scores of smaller communities.

For some time archeologists and others had known that there were ancient roads in the canyon. No one suspected the extent of the system because it is practically impossible to see anything at ground level. In many cases the sole traces are the faintest of shadow lines which appear only if the light is just right, striking them at an angle when the sun is low on the horizon, early in the morning or toward the end of the day, and even then you are likely to miss the lines completely without the help of an experienced observer. In all, perhaps five miles of road sections are visible, most of them just barely, from the ground.

It is a different story aloft. An intensive research drive is under way at the National Park Service's Chaco Center in Albuquerque. Investigators there have examined and reexamined many hundreds of aerial photographs taken from the late 1920s on at altitudes as low as forty feet and as high as nine miles, from balloons and regular survey planes and Army antimissile jets. Some roads were spotted directly through stereo viewers. Others could be identified only through electronic eyes, television cameras focused on aerial photographs and connected with special edge-enhancing circuitry which senses and amplifies light-dark contrasts too subtle for the naked eye to detect. This equipment looks something like a cross between a giant television set and a space-center control panel. Originally developed to analyze satellite photographs of the moon and planets, it has played a major role in helping to identify more than 300 miles of roads. And, according to one estimate, the prehistoric total probably includes at least 200 additional miles. The system is remarkable in its extent, and in a number of other ways.

The roads frequently run straight toward and up and over obstacles any modern engineer would avoid, up the face of a 200-foot cliff by precarious footholds hewn out of solid rock, across the top of the mesa and down the other side. They show a stubborn and determined recognition of the fact that a straight line is the shortest distance between two points. The main roads are wide, usually thirty feet across, or two and a half superhighway lanes. They connect Chaco Canyon pueblo centers with sites at least sixty-five miles away.

What were the Indians using this impressive network for? They had no wheeled vehicles or animals for transport. In an effort to make sense of the situation James Ebert and Robert Hitchcock of the University of New Mexico, like Hammond in his study of Maya plaza locations, turned to graph theory. They translated a map of major Chaco Canyon roads into an abstract network diagram indicating intersection points and distances between them, and analyzed the pattern mathematically, comparing it with patterns of modern roads constructed for various purposes. Their preliminary report suggests that the Chaco Canyon system reflects the presence of merchant-traders operating a private monopoly.

Such work is a kind of code-cracking. It depends on discovering a variety of patterns and interpreting or "reading" them to obtain information about elusive plans and activities. It depends on the fact that however widely modern man differs from his remote ancestors, and the differences are enormous, similarities exist which are strong enough so that contemporary behavior may provide valid insights into prehistoric behavior.

Given a choice, people now as then will travel so far and no farther for things they want. A supplier of farm tools finds most of his customers within a certain radius or market circle, and most customers living at greater distances patronize other suppliers. A region in which people, good farmlands and raw materials are evenly distributed will be filled with market circles that just touch one another. When all customers are served, the so-called packing effect takes over and squeezed-together circles become hexagons as in a honeycomb. Under ideal conditions competing suppliers tend to space themselves in a hexagonal lattice or network.

Central place theory, Szechuan, China, with basic hexagonal structure: map of market towns, with roads connecting standard to larger market towns; abstraction from map

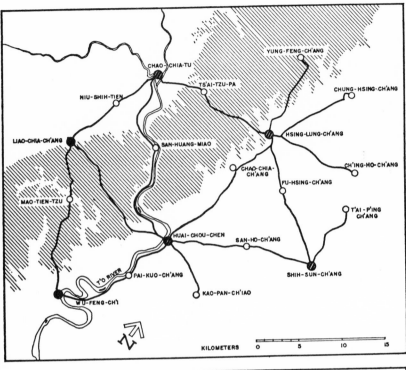

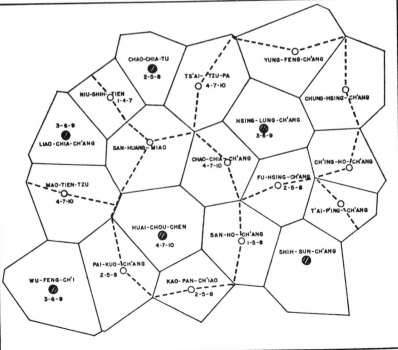

This general principle applies also to the spacing of trees and other plants competing for light and good earth, or birds within a small flock competing for feeding territory. Almost half a century ago Walter Christaller, a German geographer, used it as the starting point for a study of market distribution in a modern urban setting, a study which is finding increased application in archeology. Christaller extended the concept to include many suppliers offering many goods and services. The spacing is influenced by the minimum number of persons it takes to support a particular business. For one region in southern Canada a community of only 20 persons or so was enough to support a small general store; some 350 persons were required for a bank or beauty parlor; between 900 and 1,000 persons for a lawyer's office, funeral home and new-car dealer; and about 21,000 persons for a piano tuner, hearing-aid center, furrier and daily newspaper (a weekly newspaper required about 900 persons).

Christaller considered these and other factors in formulating his "central place" theory, which predicts the appearance of hierarchies of communities of hexagonal patterns. A village will tend to be located at a point equally distant from six surrounding hamlets, a town at a point equally distant from six villages, and a city at a point equally distant from six towns— the whole marketing-region pattern forming a complex of nested hexagons.

In a pioneer study William Skinner of Stanford University, who lived with a peasant family in China's Szechwan Province during 1949–50, showed that at least one real landscape accords with the model of nested hexagons. Starting with a map of modern market towns and larger centers, he prepared successively more abstract diagrams that revealed the underlying hexagonal pattern. He has also traced similar patterns back more than 700 years.

We do not live in a world of hexagons only. They tend to be found in regions where resources and services are evenly distributed. But linear patterns take shape along rivers, irrigation canals and trade routes, and clusters of diverse types appear under other conditions. The main point is that settlement patterns provide information about social organization, in our times and in the remote past.

Prehistoric studies demand considerable effort and the coordination of a number of searching methods. To start with, you have to find your sites. That means poring over maps and aerial photographs, covering wide regions on foot, accumulating bag after bag of sherds, used to locate, date, and estimate the sizes of sites, and plotting them all on new maps—more than 450 sites for a survey of a 1,000-square-mile region in southeastern Iraq, some 2,000 sites for a region of about the same area in the Valley of Mexico, and so on.

Looking for meaningful distributions comes next. Certain patterns leap out from the site maps; others can be seen only after careful inspection. Still others, beyond naked-eye detection, must be extracted by analysis. They may not emerge until site-to-site distances and other variables have been measured and the region subjected to mathematical study. Patterns, combined with information from excavations, can be interpreted as evidence of alliances, kinship groupings, trade relationships, resource location, domination or conquest. Chapter 7 includes an account of the use of central place theory in detecting the emergence of a state some 6,000 years ago in the Near East.

Future studies of evolutionary social patterns will depend on the combined talents of investigators in many branches of science, an approach originally put into practice more than a generation ago at Jarmo, an 8,500-year-old site on top of a steep cliff in the Zagros Mountains of northern Iraq. Jarmo is no grand museum site, no place for looting; no more than 150 people lived there in houses made of mud. Robert Braidwood, of the University of Chicago, selected it from a list of potential sites known to the Iraqi government's Antiquities Service, sites that promised to furnish information about the origins of agriculture. It yielded a mass of material, bones and charred plant remains as well as stone artifacts, providing evidence of one of the world's earliest communities of full-time or nearly full-time farmers. Even more significant, what is known about Jarmo comes from the findings of archeologists, geologists, zoologists, botanists, and other specialists working together on the spot.

This so-called multidisciplinary approach, first tested in the Near East, was actually pioneered in the early 1900s in Turkestan. It has become something rather more elaborate in America's Middle West. In the lower Illinois River Valley about forty-five miles from St. Louis is Kampsville, a town almost entirely taken

Jarmo, Iraq: site on edge of eroded hill; close-up of house excavation

Photos by Robert J. Braidwood, courtesy of the Oriental Institute, University of Chicago

over by people concerned with prehistory. Stuart Struever of Northwestern University directs the operation, which includes a small museum, dormitories for students and investigators, a field school, a mess hall, lecture rooms, and a dozen laboratories.

Digging activities have concentrated on the nearby Koster site, a rich source of Indian remains extending more than forty feet deep and covering the period from about 7000 B.C. to A.D. 1200. During the past seven seasons work crews have excavated more than 6,000 square feet of territory in squares six feet on a side, going down in successive "slices" or units about three inches deep and collecting everything in sight, plus soil samples containing pollen and other material which requires microscopic analysis.

Details about the contents of each square, the equivalent of some two million words of information, are stored in the memory files of a large computer located more than 700 miles away in Maryland—and connected with a typewriter terminal in one of the Kampsville laboratories. The terminal permits two-way communication with the computer. Information about any one of some 60,000 excavated units can be retrieved in typed form within a minute or so, and new information can be added daily.

Computers will be needed increasingly to help in organizing masses of detail, and organized detail is the ultimate source of all our insights. The presentation, the arrangement, of observations and measurements is in itself a form of patterning. What it adds up to is a process of translating messages or fragments of messages from the past. Meaning can be found in everything from individual sherds to entire valleys, by direct inspection or under the microscope or with the aid of mathematical formulas and equations, and always based on accumulating experience, familiarity with the material and the terrain—and, beyond that, a feel for the past, and intuition.

6

The Rise of Farming in the Near East

The Fertile Crescent/The significance of microliths, grinding stones and sickle sheen/ Gazelle herds in Israel/An experiment in harvesting, prehistoric style/The buildings at the "Treasure Island" site/Architecture as a sign of social change/The earliest irrigation canals

THE earliest known farms, cities and states appeared in the Near East. More than 5,500,000 square miles of land and sea, it has long been a major crossroad. Three continents meet here, three worlds, Europe and Africa and Asia, and three climatic zones, the westerlies with their low-pressure systems to the north, arid tropical and subtropical conditions in the center and much of the south, and to the extreme south monsoons and heavy summer rains. People first passed this way two million or so years ago when pioneer bands moved out of Africa along the Mediterranean coast, through Iraq and Iran and south of the Himalayas into Southeast Asia—and later, across Turkey and the Dardanelles into Bulgaria and Greece and the rest of Europe.

127

The question of who did what first no longer seems quite as urgent or relevant as it did in the old imperial days when breaking away from hunting-gathering was considered a mark of racial superiority instead of evolutionary necessity. Furthermore, there are hints of early developments elsewhere. The Near East, nevertheless, is the classical proving ground where archeologists test new techniques and ideas.

Our notions about the rise of agriculture are based on accumulating information, much of it obtained during the past decade or so. Some 200 sites representing perhaps a tenth of all known sites have been excavated with varying degrees of thoroughness, from a few weeks of relatively casual digging to large-scale efforts lasting for years. Many of the sites are located in a great sickle-shaped arc of land about 50 to 175 miles wide, which extends from southern Israel and Jordan along the eastern shores of the Mediterranean, curves due east across Turkey, and sweeps south along the Zagros Mountains past the Persian Gulf. Known as the "Fertile Crescent," it once supported abundant wildlife

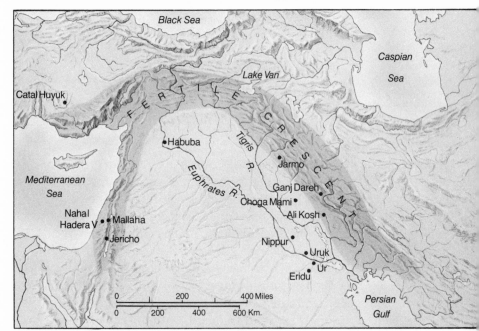

Beginnings in the Near East: the Fertile Crescent, scene of early efforts at herd management and of the settling of many early farming villages

including wild sheep, goats, cattle and pigs, as well as wild grasses such as wheat and barley. It played a central role in the development of agriculture. In a getting-close stage from about 15,000 B.C. to 9000 B.C., people, still hunter-gatherers, exploited wild species more intensively. From 9000 B.C. or so to 6000 B.C. came the earliest reliable records of domestication. Farming was established from about 6000 B.C. to 5000 B.C., when domesticated species became a primary source of food, no longer simply dietary supplements.

One of the region's best hunting grounds had been the coastal plain of Israel and Lebanon, and inland along green wooded valleys into the foothills of mountains running parallel to the coast. Ofer Bar-Yosef of the Hebrew University of Jerusalem found that the people who lived in the area invented special types of tools for killing and butchering herd animals, with an emphasis on large numbers of miniature artifacts or "microliths." Their most characteristic products were neatly worked flint blades only half an inch to an inch long, rows of which were inserted into grooved shafts and handles to form long knives, spear and arrow points, and other composite tools.

Around 10,000 B.C. or earlier, a number of families set up base camps further inland, following the valleys east into open woodlands which were abundant although not as abundant as their home territory, with less rain and presumably less game. They ate less meat, the proportion of microliths and hunting tools dropping by about fifteen percent. Grinding tools, mainly mortars and pestles, increased fourfold. Some of the grinding tools show traces of red ocher, suggesting that they served to pulverize the natural pigment which has a long prehistory of use as an ingredient of paint to decorate the body and ceremonial objects. But most of the grinding tools are ocher-free and worn far more than they could have been from the working of such soft material. They were no doubt used to grind the seeds of grasses which flourished in open woodlands.

Blades have been found with "sickle sheen," a smooth lustrous wear often produced by cutting the silica-containing stalks of wheat and other cereal grasses. Sites yielding these tools may also have bell-shaped pits, wider at the base than at the top and identical to pits used today in Near Eastern villages for storing grain.

Some of the pits were lined with plaster, probably to keep out insects and moisture.

People were apparently eating more cereal products than they had previously. Since their tool kit was still predominantly a hunter-gatherer's tool kit, however, it would be stretching things to refer to them as farmers. There is no firm evidence that grasses, or any other kind of plant for that matter, had been domesticated. Prehistoric wheat seeds preserved by charring near an oven or hearth tend to have the narrow, wrinkled appearance characteristic of modern wild-wheat seeds.

Eric Higgs of Cambridge University has developed "catchment analysis," a special method of surveying, to learn more about the ways of prehistoric people. He follows in their footsteps, walking over the territory surrounding their sites and noting types of terrain. He speaks with workers, allows for erosion and changes in climate, and tries to figure out what the land offered in times past. This method may have come naturally to Higgs who lives close to the land as a matter of habit, works on notoriously low budgets, and saves money by camping on the site in a tent or convenient cave.

The technique is to start at the site and take half a dozen or so walks in as many different directions. Each walk lasts about two hours one way, covering about six miles on level ground, for a site believed to have been occupied by hunter-gatherers, and one hour for a farming site. According to research on existing communities, these are the approximate limits for routine ventures in search of food and raw material. Higgs then produces a catchment map of the land with clues to past subsistence patterns. For comparison, similar studies have been made of present-day villages and herders.

In one survey Higgs and his associates hiked over territories surrounding early-stage sites in Israel where cereal grains have been found, areas ranging from some 16,000 acres to more than 26,000 acres. Marshes and rough grazing lands, the sort most suitable for wild species, made up seventy-five to eighty-five percent of the territories. Land suitable for farming was scarce, often located toward the outer limits of the exploited area. Such observations, taken together with the lack of definite evidence for plant domestication, suggest a hunting-gathering economy including some wild grains.

Animals, particularly gazelles, whose remains are abundant at many early sites, could have been tamed. "It would be easy to domesticate gazelles," says Heinrich Mendelssohn of Tel-Aviv University who has observed them closely at his Wildlife Research Center and elsewhere, "but not starting with adults—and not with males. You would start with infant females, hand-reared from birth, as close to birth as possible. Reared in this way they would have become imprinted with a lifelong attachment not just to the people they knew but to human beings in general.

"Males form a similar attachment, but it does not last," Mendelssohn continues. "When they mature at the age of a year and a half or so, they may become aggressive suddenly and attack people, especially those they know well. The male deer is now ready for mating. He considers these people, male or female, as if they were rival males, and his fighting urge is directed against them. So you would have to let wild males mate with domesticated females."

Mendelssohn has observed a number of such attacks, and he speaks from firsthand experience. He was once gored in the leg by a male gazelle which had been timid until the day before the accident. Gazelles, by the way, avoid staying close to one another, and would probably fight viciously if kept in pens like sheep, goats, and other "contact" animals. Domesticated, imprinted gazelles would have to be allowed to wander in wide, parklike ranges.

In an as yet unpublished study, Earl Saxon, formerly a Higgs student at Cambridge and now at the University of Durham, suggests that some such system was practiced in prehistoric Israel. He spent six weeks along a thirty-mile stretch of coast between Tel Aviv and Haifa investigating some seventy hunter-gatherer sites dating from 16,000 B.C. to 13,000 B.C. Catchment surveys of a sample of twenty-eight of these sites show they were all located in strategic positions for exploiting herds on the coastal plain, for example on ridges providing good lookouts and along passes through which the animals migrated.

The people were clearly concentrating on gazelles. One of the sites Saxon discovered during his study lies near a ruined Roman bridge and the remains of "a more recent empire," a deserted World War II British military base. Known as Nahal Hadera V, it yielded nearly 1,300 identifiable animal bones, and some 960 of them were gazelle bones, about a third representing animals two years of age or younger. Apparently ancient Israelis were managing gazelle herds very much as present-day Greenlanders manage reindeer herds, letting the free-roaming animals feed themselves on their own grazing grounds, and killing selectively and seasonally. Furthermore, Saxon believes that herd management had been going on for a long time, at least 30,000 years ago and probably much earlier.

The big push toward domestication came later. Saxon reports that all his coastal-plain sites were abandoned by about 15,000 years ago, and for the best of reasons. The coastal plains had all but disappeared. Runoff waters from melting polar glaciers raised worldwide sea levels, reducing the width of the plains in some previously occupied areas from about ten miles to less than a mile. From this point on, pressure increased to exploit other animals

A hunter-gatherer's village, Mallaha, Israel; circular wall with mortar in top center

Courtesy of Jean Perrot, photo copyright Mission Archéologique Française en Iran

and to focus increasingly on plants, particularly inland in the hills where there were abundant stands of wild wheat and barley.

Animal and plant remains in countries bordering the eastern Mediterranean show that land was used far more extensively than ever before. Knowledge gained over many generations was applied to mobilize their food resources, exploiting practically everything edible, big and small game, acorns and pistachio nuts, seeds, fruits, lentils and other legumes, fish and water fowl. It was all part of a steady settling-down process. Now more and more people had food for all seasons, and close at hand. Migratory fish and birds would appear in the spring when herds of antelope and other animals had scattered to rear their young. A sign of the times is the nearly inland village of Mallaha, about twenty-five miles from the Mediterranean coast, not far from the Sea of Galilee, where Jean Perrot of the French Archeological Mission has excavated about half an acre of the site he calls "a paradise for prehistoric settlers."

Like most good sites, it was in a rich and varied area, where a number of environments came together—marshlands and a lake and mountains and valleys. People arrived here around 10,000 B.C. with tool kits including microliths, grinding stones and bladelets with sickle sheen. They prepared to stay put. They built round houses on stone foundations, the largest unearthed to date about twenty-five feet in diameter, and dug many plaster-lined storage pits. They established a community of one or two hundred individuals, and remained for at least a thousand years and perhaps twice as long, forty to eighty generations.

People were settling down not only in Israel and surrounding lands but, on an increasing scale, throughout the Near East. It was a prelude to the rise of agriculture around 9000 B.C. Domestication involved a new direction in man's relationship to his fellow species, a way of tinkering with evolution which was probably an unconscious innovation. Simply by undertaking new chores he became an unwitting agent of natural selection.

Gathering wild grass seeds must have been relatively inefficient. A field of wild wheat consists predominantly of plants with seeds that scatter easily when brushed against or when the wind blows, because they are attached to the stalk by brittle stems. The plant seeds itself that way. There are also less efficient wheat varieties,

genetic sports or mutants with stems so tough that only a relatively few seeds fall off. Man harvested a disproportionately high
number of seeds from tough-stemmed plants and scattered many
seeds from brittle-stem plants, thus helping nature by weeding
out some of the inefficient self-seeders—that is, as long as he ate
all he collected.

But all that changed with sowing. Daniel Zohary of Hebrew
University points out that people began working against nature,
and in their own favor, as soon as they decided not to consume
their entire harvest and to put some of it back into the ground
later on. The seeds they saved for sowing included an extra-high
proportion from the tough-stem mutants, and these plants eventually dominated the natural self-seeding variety within a decade
under good conditions and generally within a century or two.
These early farmers now collected perhaps twice as much seed
for the same time and effort. They created totally dependent
"unnatural" species, mutants like hybrid corn and other modern
crops, which became highly ineffective self-seeders and would
have dwindled rapidly without seasonal assists from man.

The puzzle is why people started to sow seeds at all. Wild
cereal grasses grew in such enormous stands throughout much of
the Near East, and are still plentiful in a few areas, that no one
need have bothered to do any sowing at all. Jack Harlan, of the
University of Illinois, decided to test natural abundances a number of years ago. He saw "vast seas of primitive wild wheats"
covering the slopes of a mountain in southeastern Turkey, and
set out to gather as much grain as he could with his bare hands.
In five trials he averaged 4.5 pounds per hour, but found it a bit
rough on his uncallused "urbanized" hands. Using a prehistoric-
type sickle with a flint blade, he boosted his hourly harvest by
nearly a pound. His conclusion: "A family group . . . working
slowly upslope as the season progressed, could easily harvest wild
cereals over a three-week span or more and, without even working
hard, could gather more grain than the family could consume in
a year." His estimate is based on the annual requirements of a
family of four, about one metric ton of 2,204 pounds.

People living in lush areas like those found in Turkey or the
open woodlands of Israel and Lebanon would hardly have gone
to the trouble of spreading seeds when there were already dense

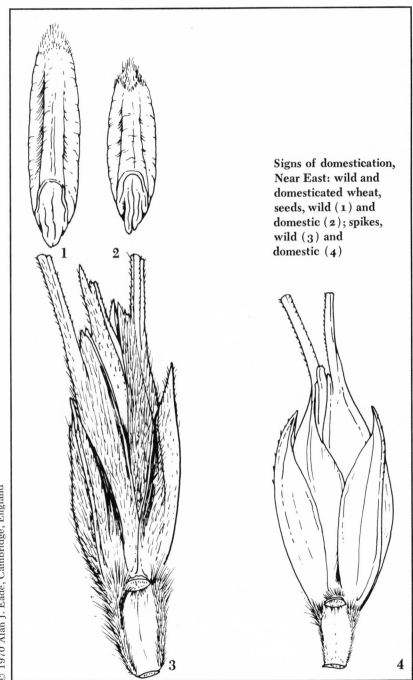

Signs of domestication, Near East: wild and domesticated wheat, seeds, wild (1) and domestic (2); spikes, wild (3) and domestic (4)

stands of wild wheat and barley. Sowing would have been far more appropriate if subsistence pressure had forced some families to move away into less favorable marginal areas. They might well have brought wild seeds with them and started the process of deliberate planting. Tough-stem plants, larger seeds and other desirable features resulted.

Something like this apparently happened at Ali Kosh, the Iranian site mentioned in the preceding chapter. Investigators spilled baskets of soil into water, scooped off the lightweight matter that floated to the surface, and passed it on to a colleague, Hans Helbaek of the Danish National Museum. Of the 45,000 seeds and assorted plant fragments which he separated painstakingly from millions of particles under the microscope, more than 31,000 came from the lowest and oldest deposits dating to the period from 7500 B.C. to 6750 B.C., and of these, 1,100 were domesticated species.

Domesticated wheat was identified by its charred seeds, which are plumper and shorter than wild-wheat seeds, and by spikelets or tiny ears with shorter and more tightly attached stems. The wheat had been domesticated earlier and elsewhere, not in the Ali Kosh lowlands but in an upland area not far from some grass-rich mountain valley, perhaps by people who, according to Helbaek, had "only faintly developed agricultural attitudes but with a long tradition of plant collecting behind them." It was possibly their second move within a relatively brief period. They may have brought wild wheat to a less abundant place outside the valley, planted the seeds for a few years, and then moved down from the mountains into the plains. The settlers had a varied diet. Besides wheat, they ate a type of barley which may or may not have been domesticated, as well as wild plants such as oats, capers and alfalfa. There are traces of high-protein legumes—lentils, peas and other plants whose seeds come in pods and which were domesticated in the Near East at about the same time as the cereal grasses.

A dozen typically flattened horn cores show that these farmers tamed local wild goats, which can still be found in mountains to

Early farming village, Ganj Dareh, Iran: wild sheep skulls in niche of possible shrine (above); subfloor cubicles (below)

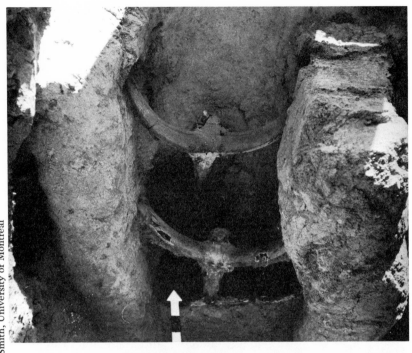

the north. They domesticated sheep, brought in from elsewhere, as indicated by the hornless skull of a female found in a small room. (Female sheep tend to lose their horns in captivity.) Remains of animals generally believed to have been domesticated earliest come from the Near East, from caves in northern Iraq, the dog dating back to about 12,000 B.C. and the sheep to 9000 B.C. Pigs also seem to have been domesticated first in the Near East, perhaps a few centuries after 7000 B.C., judging by the reduced size of bones and molar teeth unearthed in a prehistoric village of eastern Turkey.

Another important site, a small conical mound known as Ganj Dareh or "Treasure Island," lies about a hundred miles north of Ali Kosh and some three-quarters of a mile higher in a small valley in the Zagros Mountains. Philip Smith of the University of Montreal came across it accidentally one summer afternoon in 1965 when his car had a flat. After changing the tire he scanned the countryside through binoculars, as any good archeologist would, in search of caves and mounds—and spotted Ganj Dareh half a mile from the road. Returning to inspect it a few weeks later, he found flints, bones, charcoal and traces of brick walls, promising even more interesting features underneath.

Four digging seasons have confirmed his impressions. The mound contained small quantities of simple but unmistakable pottery, from large storage jars nearly three feet high to two-inch vessels, possibly toys. There were many clay animal and human figurines, generally regarded as ceremonial items. But some of them may also have been toys, judging by similar objects which children make in present-day villages and which often include female statuettes described by one investigator as "very explicit." Among other features were rare two-story houses, each probably with a "basement" for storage and an upper floor (originally interpreted as two separate occupation levels), and goat or sheep hoofprints on clay bricks, a mark of domestication since wild animals are not likely to wander about in or near a village.

The most spectacular thing about Ganj Dareh is what it tells us about prehistoric construction methods. Because its architecture dates back to about 7300 B.C., it is one of the world's earliest settlements with buildings and domestication. Yet a number of its structural features are neither crude nor primitive, as only an experienced excavator can appreciate fully. The features imply generations of learning and tradition, knowledge passed on by word of mouth and example from masters to apprentices. "The people showed remarkable sophistication in their use of clay," Smith reports. "They used standardized straw-tempered bricks, sometimes nearly a yard long; slotted mortise-and-tenon arrangements to provide tight-fitting joints between bricks in highly stressed parts of walls; prefabricated clay slabs which were about half an inch thick and a yard square, had beveled edges, and were slid into place to form cubicle partitions; a unique wall-building technique in which alternating layers of mud and fine plaster were built up in strips, a bit like modern cinder blocks; round or oval "port holes" in the walls of some rooms or storage places and clay plugs with finger-holes to seal them; and at least one structure which I can't figure out—a tall, thick clay column about a yard in diameter with a capping of cobblestones."

Many structural features unearthed at early sites are still in use. A particularly striking example comes from the village of Jarmo, which was occupied from 6750 B.C. to 6500 B.C. As the first prehistoric site chosen specifically to throw light on the origins of agriculture, it was a classical case of deciding what to look for and where to look, and then going out and finding it. Playing his hunch of the moment that major developments occurred in mountain villages adjacent to the Fertile Crescent, Braidwood selected Jarmo in 1948 and dug there for three seasons.

Among the tens of thousands of artifacts which he and his associates recovered—sickle blades, mortars and pestles, houses, the remains of domesticated plants and animals—are certain neatly ground stones with conical holes at the top, which turn out to be sockets for doors to swing on. Almost identical fixtures are found today, nine millenniums later, in rural Near Eastern settlements.

There is something amazingly persistent about architectural detail, at least at the village or hamlet level. Once people learn how to make something efficiently, a type of brick or wall or storage pit, or an entire house, the design may last century after century, as one of the last hangovers from the even more enduring conservatism of remoter prehistoric times. Such patterns are frozen habits.

For all the conservatism, however, architecture will change under the impact of sufficiently powerful forces. Flannery, one of the investigators at Ali Kosh, notes a tendency for early settlers in the Near East to live in clusters of small huts with about eight to nine square feet of floor space, enough for only one person or perhaps for a mother and child. This is the arrangement found at Mallaha. In other villages the residential unit consists of rectangular houses with forty to forty-five square feet of floor space, generally large enough to hold families of at least three to five persons. Various arrangements may occur at different occupation levels of the same site, with a change from small to large dwellings. The transition has been reported at a site in Syria between 8000 B.C. and 7500 B.C., and somewhat later at a site in Jordan.

Flannery believes that the small-hut pattern may represent a situation where several men lived together, each with several wives. The wives probably occupied the small huts (generally circular), while the menfolk lived separately in a large communal "long house" (generally rectangular), a pattern perhaps reflecting the importance of all-male groups organized to do the hunting. This pattern exists in many African villages today, and in many ancient settlements of Near Eastern hunter-gatherers on the verge of becoming farmers. Larger dwellings may have appeared in increasing numbers as agriculture became increasingly important, indicating a change from many wives to one wife, rather less emphasis on hunting, and the establishment of family units each having its own land and storage facilities.

Around 7750 B.C. people settled at Jericho near the Dead Sea, a ten-acre oasis site in the desert country with a still-gushing spring whose waters today are piped across the desert to irrigate fields. They built small circular dwellings, suggesting a one-man-with-many-wives system, and a surrounding wall nearly twenty feet high (the original ancestor of the walls which, according to biblical accounts, tumbled down at Joshua's command more than six thousand years later). Within a millennium or so an even more massive wall protected the settlement, which now consisted of large rectangular houses, indicating that defense requirements

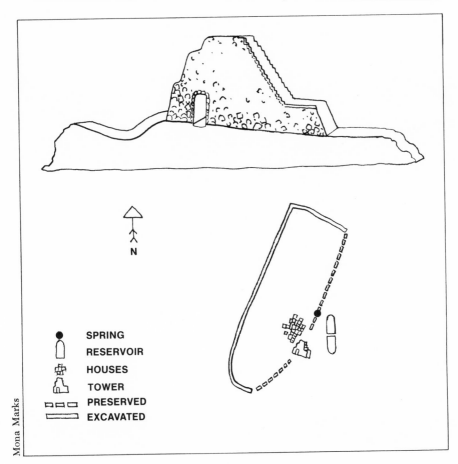

N

SPRING
RESERVOIR
HOUSES
TOWER
PRESERVED
EXCAVATED

Mona Marks

Early walls of Jericho

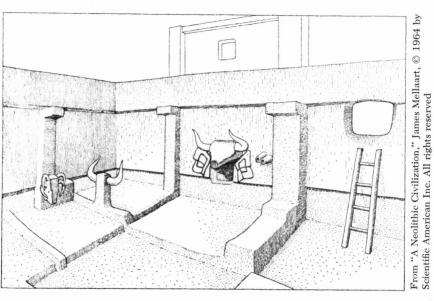

Shrine of the bulls: reconstruction at Catal Hüyük, Turkey

may have speeded organization along family and property lines in a world that depended increasingly on agriculture. The shape of a house thus had implications for the role of status and conflict in social evolution.

Not long ago some investigators challenged the accuracy of Jericho's dating, arrived at by carbon-14 methods, finding it difficult to believe that such impressive architecture could have existed so early. The dating seems to be correct, however, and the site may have served as one of the world's first trade centers. Another remarkable settlement, Catal Hüyük in the mountains of southern Turkey, flourished in 6000 B.C. or earlier. Also believed to be a trade center, perhaps specializing in obsidian from nearby mountain sources, it eventually covered more than thirty acres and included ceremonial buildings, beautifully worked flint daggers, statuettes in clay and limestone, and wall paintings of hunters.

There is no way of knowing when people in the Near East stopped regarding cultivation as a temporary, stopgap measure and began taking it for granted as the basis of their food supply.

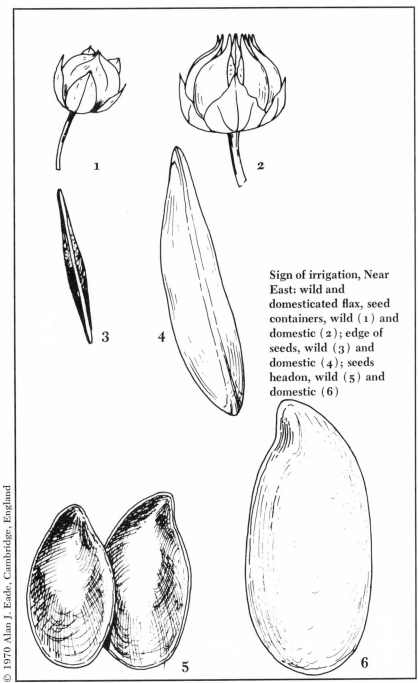

Sign of irrigation, Near East: wild and domesticated flax, seed containers, wild (1) and domestic (2); edge of seeds, wild (3) and domestic (4); seeds headon, wild (5) and domestic (6)

But in certain places a point of no return seems to have been reached between 6000 B.C. and 5000 B.C., the stage of established agriculture. By that time it was no longer a matter of planting seeds in a few gardens, keeping a few animals, while depending primarily on wild species. As domestication increased it brought unceasing pressure for greater and greater production.

A major source of pressure was overflow population, in some regions mountain people coming down to the plains, often young people joining their relatives or eager to start a new life on their own, if the ways of modern migrants are any criterion. They came to Ali Kosh and nearby settlements. The newcomers needed more food, and the first known use of irrigation was a result. Settlers were drawing on old experience. It did not require a genius or a burst of insight to know that water may help plants grow better, or to dig ditches and tap water flowing down from the mountains. Irrigation is a straightforward practice which does not necessarily imply farming. Paiute hunter-gatherers were irrigating wild rice in California's Owens Valley less than a century ago.

People in the Ali Kosh area began irrigating their crops some time after 5000 B.C. According to Helbaek, an entire complex of plants marks the change. Barley appeared with six rows of spikelets instead of the two of wild varieties. The new grain required extra water. Flax or linseed grown under rainfall conditions only produces seeds with a maximum length of 0.132 to 0.161 inch, but the largest seeds of irrigated plants consistently range from 0.178 to 0.248 inch. A single large flax seed is considered solid evidence of irrigation.

Silt tends to accumulate along small streams overflowing during the rainy season, raising streambed levels above the surrounding plains and forming elevated banks. The early practice of breaching these natural levees and guiding the water to fields certainly increased crop yields, but not to a spectacular degree. The odds are that people were regarding irrigation as they had once regarded agriculture itself, as a supplement to rainfall farming, something to be done for the time being only. It was the old effort to preserve things as they were, the old illusion that this effort could succeed.

A mound in Iraq more than 130 miles to the northwest of Ali Kosh on the other side of the Zagros Mountains and known as

Choga Mami produced not only six-row barley and other domesticated plants, but the earliest known canals. Joan Oates of Cambridge University uncovered a series of clay deposits at several levels, extending for some distance along the side of the mound. The clay shows that the deposits represent waterways, almost certainly artificial waterways, since they had a characteristically regular U-shaped cross section, and since the later ones ran above the level of the plain.

The most recent of the excavated canals was relatively modern; the oldest dates back to about 5500 B.C. The entire countryside is ideal for irrigation. A number of low eroded mounds are probably remnants of heaped-up dirt from the digging of an ancient canal. A canal in operation today brings water from a nearby river to the modern palm-groved town of Mandali about a mile away. Prehistoric irrigation supported a sizable community, covering more than thirteen acres. Houses were built directly on top of, and sometimes inside the walls of, underlying houses, perhaps evidence of "continuing property rights."

Choga Mami represents a crucial turn of events. Although less than a fiftieth of the site has been excavated, that is enough to suggest developments which were forcing settlers out into the plains. There was nothing casual or makeshift about water control here. It must have been planned and, as Oates emphasizes, the people who did the planning were "among the first deliberately to employ the techniques of irrigation without which their climatically marginal area could not have been effectively settled, and which were fundamental to widespread cultivation of desert lands."

In the unfolding process from 15,000 B.C. to 5000 B.C., hunter-gatherers shifted to rainfall agriculture, which was originally introduced to save the hunting-gathering way of life, and then to irrigation, introduced to save rainfall agriculture. The landscape changed from wildernesses with a wide variety of wild foods to less fruitful regions where a few domesticated species were used upon occasion as dietary supplements, to semiarid country and a swiftly increasing dependence on agriculture.

Many observations focus on subsistence pressure, on slowly increasing populations making do with less land because of melting glaciers and rising seas, as a central factor in Near Eastern developments. Rising seas that covered more than half of the coastal plains of Israel and Lebanon may explain why some people migrated to less abundant areas further inland. The use of a wider variety of wild species in such areas created new possibilities of all-year-round living in a single location. Finally, settling down seems to have been followed by sharp population increases and a need for more food, which could be met only by domestication and more migrations.

It is a strange story, full of paradoxes. People were on the move in a new way, not natural nomads like hunter-gatherers, following great herds or exploiting territories at different times of year. Now settled people were moving, pulling up their roots and looking for new places to settle. Their numbers were on the rise in large part as a result of settling down in the first place, a change resulting in better nutrition, higher fat levels, and increased fertility (see Chapter 3). They spread from abundant lands into less and less abundant lands, and then by irrigation and other forms of hard work, proceeded to make second- and third- and fourth-best areas more abundant by far than the best hunting-gathering lands.

This is one theory about the course of events in the Near East. It will certainly be modified, and perhaps radically altered, by studies already under way or planned. Smith and his fellow Canadian Cuyler Young of the Royal Ontario Museum point to some important directions for further research. They launch their analysis of prehistoric agricultural trends with a reference to the work of Ester Boserup, a Danish economist concerned primarily with agriculture in our own times, and with the relationship between land, work and productivity.

Boserup is interested in what happens when population increases. In the beginning there is land to spare, enough for everyone. People are free to move from one plot to another and eventually to come back to the original plot, all within their home territory. They clear a section of forest by burning off vegetation, cultivate it from one to as much as eight years when crop yields decline and then let it lie fallow for six to more than twenty years. During that period nature has a chance to replenish itself. The cleared land returns to its former state by gradual stages. Dense, tough grasses move in, then bushes and small trees, and finally large trees. The land becomes a full forest again.

This so-called slash-and-burn agriculture or something like it persisted in Sweden until after World War I. It exists in parts of Finland today, and still supports some 200,000,000 people in Africa, Latin America and Asia. It declines when local populations soar, and people cannot afford to let land lie unused. Fallow periods become shorter and shorter, until in extreme cases there is no fallow at all and land yields one or more crops a year. Agriculture becomes more labor-intensive, people working harder, as land becomes scarcer. These changes may call for changes in technology. A digging stick to disturb the soil a bit is sufficient equipment for long-fallow farming. Short-fallow conditions usually require hoes and other implements to break up sods matted and thick with grass roots. Plows to turn over the soil came later in the Old World and, still later, an assortment of farm machinery and fertilizers and weed and insect killers.

Can we detect changes corresponding to the early stages of the land-use process in prehistoric times? Smith and Young believe that research directed to answering this question would put the subsistence pressure theory to the test and lead to better explanations of agricultural developments. As hints of what might be found, they point to the presence of hoes at Jarmo, possibly for breaking up heavy short-fallow soils, and "polished celts" in the Ali Kosh area, which may have been used for the same purpose or to dig canals, since the tools first appear with irrigation.

Further evidence may be expected from more sophisticated investigations of plants and animals, such as gerbils associated with ancient canals (see Chapter 5). Certain species of freshwater mussels live in relatively swift canal waters; others prefer slower waters; the common land snail is adapted to small canals with vegetation growing on the banks. The soil itself may provide clues; concentrations of phosphates and other substances suggest how the land was exploited. All theories, however grand, rest ultimately on detailed observations, multiplied many times and subjected to intensive analysis.

The effort to get more out of the land continues with the benefit of new techniques, but for the same old reasons. Investigators in the Near East and elsewhere, building on the knowledge of times past, are developing increasingly sophisticated methods of irrigation. They are preparing for the twenty-first century, for a world which will contain at least twice as many people as today's world, and 800 times as many people as the vanished hunter-gatherer world of 10,000 B.C.

7

The Coming of Cities and Kings

The road to Uruk/ A survey in the desert/
The evolution of one of the world's first cities/
A labyrinthine temple/ Hierarchies of people
and places/ Early urban planning/ The Death Pit at Ur/
New excavations at an old center in Syria/
The dangers of kingship

THE way to the ruins of Uruk lies south of Baghdad in Iraq, on the dead-flat floodplain between the Tigris and Euphrates rivers, once the most flourishing part of ancient Mesopotamia. I took the trip not long ago, more than a hundred miles along a main highway and seventy more miles on dirt roads. The landscape became emptier and emptier the further I drove.

At first I passed towns and villages and then, on a narrow road raised above the plain like a railroad embankment, only dusty-drab adobe huts in clusters, herds of sheep and goats, occasional camels, women in black and their children, dun-colored tents. The last fifteen miles or so were the loneliest. I found myself moving along on a desert floor without anything to steer by, except for a

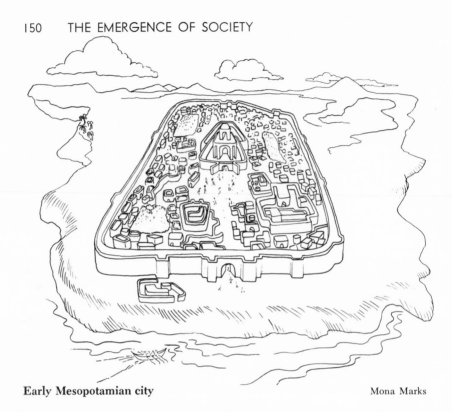

Early Mesopotamian city   Mona Marks

pair of faint wheel tracks which extended ahead of me on the
sand and sometimes vanished entirely.

Then all of a sudden I had a landmark. The ruins appeared low
on the horizon to my right, a series of dark mounds like a range
of mountains far off. Soon I was there on top of the highest
mound, overlooking a sight that made the desert seem emptier
and lonelier than ever—bone-dry acres of walls in shambles,
fallen bricks and columns, and a great pile of earth where a
stepped pyramid or ziggurat once stood. "Of all the desolate pictures which I have ever beheld," wrote one nineteenth-century
traveler, "that of Uruk incomparably surpasses all."

Five thousand years ago the desert here was blooming. The
Euphrates, now shifted ten miles to the southwest, flowed past the
city, and the delta-marshland region where it entered the Persian
Gulf was not far away. Green lands extended for miles in all

Ruins of Uruk temple area, Iraq

The flowering of elites: the world's earliest cities, appearing some 5,000 to 6,000 years ago in Sumer, the southernmost part of Mesopotamia, scene also of the first population explosion

George Buctel

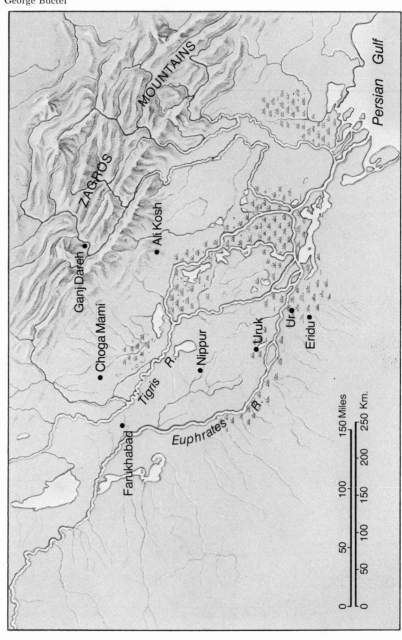

directions, fields of grain and gardens with date palms and flowers, marshes with wild boars and tall reeds, poplars and tamarisk trees. There were artificial lakes, reservoirs, and a system of canals bringing water from the river.

A wall of sun-baked brick six miles long and twenty feet high, with hundreds of watchtowers and gates to the north and south, enclosed homes, fields, gardens, and grazing areas. All roads inside led to the ceremonial district at the center, a complex of platforms and huge columns decorated with red, black, and white ceramic cones arranged in mosaic patterns. There was a holy courtyard or inner sanctum closed to the public and a main temple which loomed high and massive some six stories above street level. According to one estimate, the city contained more than 20,000 persons living in an area of about two square miles.

Uruk was the largest of half a dozen major centers which appeared about 5,500 years ago within a limited period and within a limited region of Iraq—the ancient land of Sumer, southernmost Mesopotamia, located between the Tigris and Euphrates rivers. Most of the centers are desert places today, left high and dry like wrecked ships when the tide is out. We must deduce what we can from ruins, because the waters have gone. The Euphrates has shifted many times, and, according to recent evidence, the Gulf itself may have retreated more than 150 miles to the southeast.

Sumer was something new under the sun. It represents a break with the past, a reversal of the old tendency to stay small and dispersed. Never before had so much come together in one area, so many people, so much knowledge and skill, and so much power. This massing of people into denser and denser communities or population nuclei marks the rise of the city as a localized phenomenon with temples and workshops and close-packed homes.

A pioneer in research on the evolution of urban society, Robert McC. Adams of the University of Chicago calls for regional surveys and studies of aerial photographs in addition to excavations. Alone and with colleagues, he has walked and driven thousands of miles through deserts that were Mesopotamia. His most recently published survey, conducted with Hans Nissen of the Free University of Berlin, involves Uruk and the Uruk countryside, a 1,000-square-mile area of Sumer.

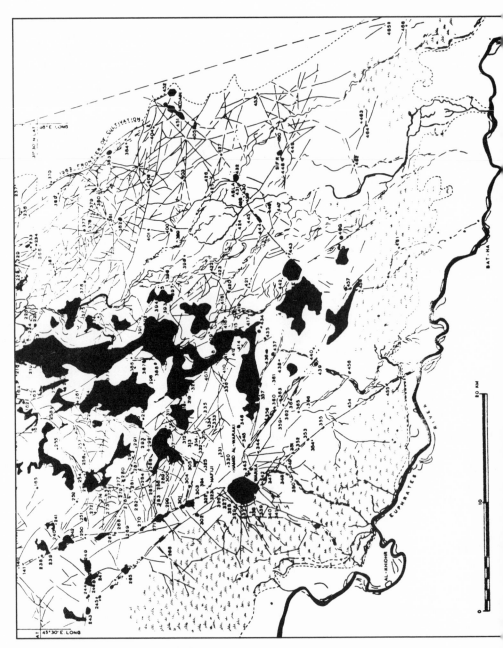

466 sites, countryside of Uruk, Iraq: part of Adams' survey map showing discovery and mapping of sites in archeological survey

The desert in that part of the world is littered with traces of the past. Scattered about the landscape are coins and bits of metal green with age, fragments of stone vessels and bricks, stone weights for fishing nets, sickle blades, and countless pieces of broken pottery. The most littered places, often but not always on or near mounds, where the ground is thick with sherds, are sites. Adams and Nissen estimated site sizes by noting the areas covered with extra-heavy concentration of sherds.

The investigators developed a fine eye for special sherds. At distances of up to fifteen feet or so, and out of a jumble of hundreds of undistinguished sherds, they could spot the rare diagnostic piece, which is unique for a particular period and can thus serve as a reliable time marker—for example, a highly fired, china-like rim fragment representing a large open dish probably made between 5500 B.C. and 4500 B.C., or a coarse, yellowish bit of a narrow bottle dating to about 3500 B.C. plus or minus a century. Since debris found at the surface of a site provides clues to what lies underneath, sherds picked up from the ground may come from deep-buried occupation levels. Prehistoric people kept digging into earlier deposits for building materials and, in the process, brought some earlier remains to the surface. Sherds thus tend to "climb," so that surface collections often include samples from even the lowest or oldest levels.

During four and a half months in 1967, Adams and Nissen mapped 466 sites ranging in size from a fraction of an acre to nearly 600 acres and representing at least 1,500 separate occupation levels. It took more than five years to analyze the material and prepare it for publication. The result is a picture, incomplete and blurred in many places, but one of the first of its kind and definitely something to build on, a picture of some of the elements that went into the shaping of one important prehistoric city.

It is a record of increase, slow at first and then accelerating. One of the region's earliest known sites, a village identified as No. 298 in the survey catalog and consisting of fifty persons or so, appeared some time after 5000 B.C. A number of generations later another village appeared eight miles to the northeast, perhaps founded by descendants of the original settlers, and still another roughly the same distance to the southwest—the three sites forming a compact equilateral-triangle cluster. The survey reveals a second northern cluster some four or five centuries later, and a total of about a dozen sites and 4,000 to 5,000 persons by 4000 B.C.

The region saw a definite rise in population, a common aftermath of settling down. Something else was in the wind, something a great deal more complicated than mounting populations. More people were at large, to be sure. But theoretically, at least, that could have resulted in a relatively even distribution of sites all within the same size range, a straightforward multiplication of villages. Ample room existed for many such settlements.

What actually occurred was something quite different—the massing or centralizing effect, the gathering of people into denser and denser nuclei. Why these centers arose where they did is an unsolved problem. Advantages are never distributed perfectly evenly. The settlements in a cluster are never of exactly the same size or located in exactly equivalent areas. Depending on local conditions, some settlements will become important and one will acquire an edge over the others.

Uruk, the southernmost site in the original triangular cluster, had such an edge. It may have been located in a particularly attractive spot near abundant marshlands, and thus became a natural place for early versions of market days and local fairs, religious ceremonies and other special events which brought visitors from neighboring villages, some of whom might eventually decide to stay on with friends and relatives. It included within an estimated twenty-five acres about a fifth of all the people in the region and was one of two extra-large sites.

Uruk seems to have had a peculiar "double" quality from an early date. A single settlement of no more than an acre or two in the beginning, it gave rise to a second settlement about a quarter of a mile away, probably on the opposite bank of the Euphrates. This pattern was not rare and is found today among Arabs living in marsh areas. One group of villagers moves seasonally, from the west bank of a canal in the winter to summer quarters on the east bank which is only slightly higher, but high enough to provide cooler evenings and fewer insects. The pair of prehistoric settlements at Uruk may have arisen in a similar manner, or as a result of a rivalry between two families or lineages. Later the twin-river straddling sites may have had a practical purpose. They might have served a "toll booth" function, controlling the flow of traffic and exacting tribute from boats moving along the river.

During the next millennium or so, 4000 B.C. to 3000 B.C., the population continued to rise and to centralize. Settlements expanded from a dozen to about a hundred, population from 5,000 to 20,000 or so, and large, densely settled sites from two to five. Uruk, the largest of the lot, still retained its double, twin-site quality, but now it had two prominent ceremonial districts, one dedicated to the sky god Anu and the other to Eanna, the goddess of love. During this period its area increased from about 25 to more than 175 acres, passing the arbitrary 125-or-more-acre level which may be taken as one rough index of an urban center.

Members of the German Archaeological Institute in Baghdad and a small army of local workers have been excavating here ever since 1913. (According to one investigator, completing the job would take another hundred years.) Allowing time out for world wars, that makes a grand total of more than thirty seasons, some sort of record for sustained digging in the region. The most impressive of recent discoveries is a massive temple located under the oldest known terraced pyramid, or ziggurat, in the Anu district and built around 3500 B.C. Unearthed just two weeks before my visit, it ranks as one of the most complicated structures in a site noted for complicated structures. For one thing, it is the only building at Uruk made mainly of stone, limestone carried in from a quarry about thirty-five miles away, the predominant material in all other buildings being the traditional mud bricks.

It has an unusual nested or box-within-a-box design, with three thick-walled chambers, one inside the other, giving the structure a labyrinthine appearance. Inside the innermost chamber, reached by passing through a number of doorways, is a ceremonial pit, possibly where a fire-altar once stood. The inside wall of this chamber is roughly plastered, in marked contrast to the smooth-plastered outer walls, and may have been covered with drapes. Jürgen Schmidt, director of the Uruk excavations, believes that the subterranean temple symbolizes death and the world of the dead. The nested structure and doorways leading to a central pit may represent the devious way into the underworld, as described in a myth recorded from a later period. Whatever its purpose, the temple had a strange history. Within a year and quite possibly within a few months of its completion, it was mysteriously covered with earth, only to be uncovered at some later date—and then promptly buried again, once and for all.

Uruk box-within-box temple, Iraq: entrance to the underworld?

The food quest was drawing people to more and more restricted areas of the region. Early settlers probably lived in the
main by hunting and gathering, as modern Arabs still live in
certain marshland villages of the Tigris-Euphrates delta to the
southeast. They did some cultivating but relied on fish and game,
wild fowl and wild plants. As population increased, they turned
more and more to agriculture based on irrigation.

Survey maps show a change in settlement pattern from early
to later times, a shift from irregularly spaced sites to sites lined
up in rows, indicating a corresponding shift from naturally meandering waterways to artificially straightened canals. One result
was increasing concentration of populations. Estimates are not
available for Mesopotamia, but in neighboring Iran perhaps as
much as two-thirds of the land represented good hunting-gathering territory, mostly grassy plains and mountain valleys.

Good farming territory made up a considerably smaller proportion of the country. When people found it necessary to turn to agriculture, they had a far narrower range of choices. Flannery estimates that about a tenth of the land in Iran, land with a high water
table, and marshy areas, offered the best prospects to early farmers—and only about a tenth of that tenth was suitable for irriga-

tion. In the Uruk region as well as in Iran greater quantities of food were produced and greater numbers of people were living on less and less land.

Survey maps may contain further information about centralizing forces, reinforcing the notion of cities as parts of systems, major centers in hierarchies of lesser places whose emergence may be closely connected with the emergence of states. Wright's concept of the state as a system of three or more administrative levels may be reflected in settlement patterns, as indicated in studies by Gregory Johnson of Hunter College. Focusing on the situation in the Uruk countryside between 3300 B.C. and 3100 B.C., he first prepared a simple chart showing the areas of ninety-five sites which turned out to be distributed into four general size levels: fifty-four villages (one-fourth to six acres), twenty-eight large villages (six to fifteen acres), eight small centers (fifteen to twenty-five acres), and five large centers including Uruk (twenty-five acres and up). A hierarchy of increasingly larger settlements emerged, strongly suggesting a corresponding hierarchy of people, status and authority.

The hierarchy also suggests an evolutionary process. Presumably the first villages in the region were at about the same stage in size and status, with people producing what they needed and no surpluses. Later a few villages began providing ceremonial and other services to the other villages and became larger, still later, villages and larger villages and small centers appeared, and finally the four-level pattern. Such changes represent a trend in human affairs, a notable increase in social complexity involving workers and overseers and people ranking above the overseer and elites above them—involving the emergence of a state.

Johnson proceeded to a further analysis dealing with the spacing of the settlements. For each size level he measured the distance between each mapped site and its nearest neighbor. Larger sites were farther from one another than smaller sites. The five large centers are an average of 11.25 miles apart; corresponding distances for small centers, large villages, and villages are 7.14, 2.84 and 1.75 miles, respectively. A special relationship exists between large centers and certain relatively small sites, which may have served as distribution or control stations, judging by the fact that they yielded ceramic cones, the mosaic elements used in

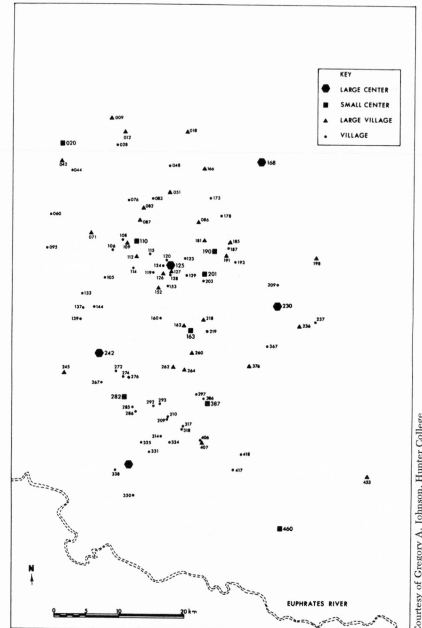

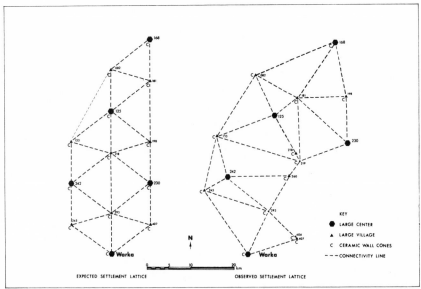

Uruk countryside, central place theory: survey map (left) and abstraction of map showing network analysis (above)

decorating temples and other public buildings. Each large center is associated with two cone sites, an average of six miles away.

The distances are in effect rules which describe a pattern of locations, an "expected settlement lattice," with a clear-cut hexagonal structure. The pattern is idealized, simplified, since it is based on averaged or "smoothed out" distances and takes no account of the presence of rivers, canals, marshes, and other features influencing the locations of sites. But allowing for such differences, it resembles the actual pattern of large centers and cone sites as they appear on a map of the Uruk region, which also shows a hexagonal structure.

This is a familiar geometry. Hexagons turn up in Christaller's central place theory, which deals with distributions and hierarchies of settlements (see Chapter 5). They tend to turn up under specific conditions—in densely settled parts of the world today, and in regions where villages, towns and cities are built into the structure of market networks providing a variety of goods and services. The appearance of hexagons in the study of Uruk implies that a similar system also existed there, on a much smaller scale of course, but involving similar functions.

Courtesy of German Archeological Institute, Baghdad

Ceramic cones in wall at Uruk, marking public buildings

Does archeology support what central place theory suggests? To some extent. Johnson figured that if small sites with ceramic cones were indeed distribution points, places along local trade routes connecting major centers and other settlements throughout the region, they should yield more rare or unusual artifacts than small sites located in less strategic positions. To check this argument, he prepared inventories of clay spindle whorls or flywheels used in weaving to help keep the spindle spinning, mace heads, fishing net weights, stone vessels, hoes and metal objects for fifty-two small sites. He found that about fifty percent more such items were collected at cone sites than at sites without cones, indicating a significantly greater variety of rare objects.

So geometry hints, but only hints, at a link between past and present, at the possibility that forces at work in the twentieth century also affected the behavior of people making decisions in early Sumer. It will certainly take further research to prove the existence of a highly organized trade network within the Uruk region, and to determine whether or not the system operated under the control of a highly organized political system. Enough has been done to indicate the potential of mapping, measuring and analyzing excavated materials.

The city changed dramatically during the century or two following 3100 B.C. At first the number of settlements and the size of Uruk continued to increase together, from about 100 to 150 sites and from perhaps 175 to 250 acres, respectively. But then things tightened up, in all likelihood within a few generations. An extraordinary "implosion" or bursting inward marks the last stage in the rise of Uruk. The center continued to expand, at a faster rate than ever. But now it was growing at the expense of the countryside. About half the settlements in outlying areas were abandoned, and Adams points out that in areas close to the city "the towns as well as the villages virtually disappear . . . all the former inhabitants almost certainly taking up residence within the Uruk city wall." The city grew to about 1,000 acres. Its population may have doubled from 10,000 to 20,000, probably some two-thirds of all the people living in the region.

A city was born in a world that had been without cities, or rather a city-state. By this time the Uruk region probably had five levels of settlement size, with Uruk itself now at its 1,000-

acre peak, at the top. A class of administrators concerned mainly with administering the affairs of lesser administrators probably lived there. On the principle that explanations should be simple unless and until solid evidence dictates otherwise, we assume that it grew largely as a result of local forces, the activities of hunter-gatherers native to the region and their descendants, and perhaps it did happen that way. But the Uruk countryside, like Uruk itself, was never isolated from the impact of outside events.

Immigrants may have played a role from the very beginning. Perhaps they included the earliest known settlers at site No. 298, some of whose pottery resembles in shape and decorations some of the pottery Oates found at her early irrigation site, Choga Mami, about two hundred miles to the north. More than a millennium later immigrants may have come from Saudi Arabia and Qatar, where settlements apparently vanished abruptly some time after 4000 B.C. McGuire Gibson of the University of Chicago believes that still later when the city was approaching its height, more people may have streamed in from the northwest, refugees displaced by a possible shift of the meandering Euphrates.

There were other major centers in Sumer, and one of them was the result of an early venture in urban planning. A new cluster of settlements took shape abruptly around 3000 B.C. some twenty-five miles northwest of Uruk. A canal about ten miles long was constructed in an area previously occupied sparsely if at all, and the sites strung out along its banks were not budding villages but full-fledged, "made to order" towns, presumably built to house overflow populations from elsewhere. Later the towns were abandoned en masse, and a new city appeared in the area.

Another city-state, Nippur, was established some fifty miles to the northwest of Uruk. This center, where Gibson is the latest of a long line of excavators, experienced a population implosion like that at Uruk. It featured a "holy spot," a plot originally sanctified for reasons unknown and serving, century after century, as the site of temples built one after the other on the ruins of earlier temples. At one point, perhaps around 3500 B.C., only a village existed where Nippur was to rise, a small cluster of houses in no way distinguished from others in the region.

Some time later one of the houses, or perhaps an open space where no one was living, became hallowed ground, the site of a small temple some forty feet long and twenty feet wide with an inner sanctum in the center, a nine-by-nine cubicle presumably reserved for special worshipping. From then on, for 500 years, people built ten successively larger and grander temples there, the largest and last covering more than half an acre or about eighty times the area of the original temple. And always, throughout the process, each temple had an inner sanctum of about the same size as the first inner sanctum and located in about the same place.

Every early center in Sumer and elsewhere probably had a holy spot. The subterranean temple at Uruk probably marked such sacred terrain, and so did a structure in a rising town to the south. In a few centuries it would become the city of Ur, which had palaces and objects of gold and royal tombs, including a Death Pit housing sixty-four sacrificed "ladies of the court" arranged in neat rows with golden ribbons in their hair—but which even at its height did not approach the size of Uruk. Another early Sumer center, Eridu, included an eighteen-layer system of temples built upon temples with a tiny holy-spot shrine at the bottom, like a seed from which all the rest grew.

The growth of these centers influenced the shaping of Uruk, in particular its period of implosion, starting about 3100 B.C. The pace of this packing or nucleation argues for a corresponding leap in the concentration of power, a leap occasioned by new dangers from the outside. Even allowing for the lure of big-city crowds and big-city action, people normally come to visit, not to stay; they do not leave their homes suddenly and in droves.

All of which suggests that they had to leave, under double pressure. They were probably pulled into Uruk by a local militia or its equivalent, drafted to provide taxes and manpower for a growing army and the building of a new six-mile wall—and at the same time "pushed" into the city, seeking protection from the armies and raiders of competing centers. There is another sign of consolidation, also perhaps under duress, a new relationship between the people and their gods. The Anu and Eanna districts finally merged into a single religious complex, indicating an institutionalized ending, possibly the ending of an old conflict which the city could no longer afford.

Adams is working toward a wider synthesis based on some of

Ziggurat at Ur, Iraq, excavated (above) and restored (below), where the Death Pit was found

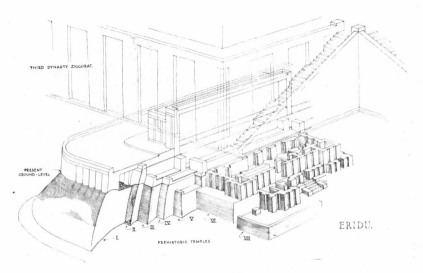

Courtesy of Directorate General of Antiquities, Baghdad, Iraq
Temple levels at Eridu, Iraq: a millennium of superimposed buildings

his earlier and more recent surveys, a synthesis of settlement patterns in a region extending to the northwest as far as Baghdad and beyond. Uruk and the Uruk countryside make up less than a quarter of that region, which presents some interesting problems. Large stretches of the plains yield no traces of settlement and were apparently never used. They may have been barren desert or swamps or perhaps extensive pastures. In any case, population densities in the areas that were settled may have been considerably higher than previously suspected.

There are wider regions to explore, not only in Saudi Arabia and lands to the south, but also west into Syria. In fact, German investigators are excavating a city as large and as old as Uruk on the upper Euphrates about 60 miles from the modern city of Aleppo, a drive of four to five hours over rough roads. They are working extra-long hours, because a dam is being built in the area and the site is scheduled to be flooded within five years. Known as Habuba, it includes a great wall with bastions, a system of canals and paved streets, and a central complex of buildings resembling Uruk's first temples.

The relationship of this center to centers in Sumer and elsewhere remains to be worked out. But a general picture is emerging. People were being built into expanding social networks, state systems of levels within levels. Always at the lowest, basic subsistence level there were farmers and their families, working long hours to produce more food than they needed. They carried the surplus to intermediate centers where a variety of petty officials saw to it that a proper proportion of the food went to the largest centers, including an extra-large share of the best food for people in authority. Things flowed down as well as up the hierarchy. People at lower levels may have received mass-produced pottery, textiles and other goods, along with such specialized services as protection from enemies and elaborate religious ceremonies.

Early cities and city life were signs of new control principles in human affairs, major developments in the technology of organizing people for the common good. Many things were happening all at once, changes that introduced new and prodigious complications, and yet at the same time had constructive effects, acting against strong counterforces to unify diverse groups. Apparently nothing, or at least nothing of any importance, had simple consequences. Status, the coming of haves and have-nots, and hereditary rights and administrative levels drew people apart and gave rise to new conflicts and corruptions and tyrannies. But it also brought people closer together, since they were meeting more often than ever before as fellow specialists, fellow potters and scribes and warriors, and not only as blood relatives.

Considering that most human violence in all societies, from hunter-gatherer bands to cities of the twentieth century, takes place among blood relatives, this trend must have had some beneficial results. A policy of promoting loyalties beyond the traditional loyalties to kinsmen has helped found a number of dynasties in the Near East and elsewhere, some of them during historical times. Henry Rosenfeld of the Hebrew University of Jerusalem describes the tactics of Ibn Rashid, a sheik of nineteenth-century Arabia, who built a kingdom out of rival tribes by deliberately creating a specialist class of mercenary soldiers, slaves and unrelated tribesmen owing allegiance to no one but himself—and by deliberately keeping his own kinsmen out of positions of power.

Another sheik, with the help of the British and other concerned parties, revived an Islamic sect whose members were warriors dedicated to the national interest. Apparently the combination of zealous crusading and fighting prowess proved explosive as the devotees got out of hand. Rosenfeld concludes his account of the episode with a terse footnote: "These military-religious fanatics . . . began to operate independently and their organization had to be liquidated."

Similar aberrations may have occurred from time to time in the remote past. But, more often than not, the higher and more inclusive loyalties served chiefly to reduce rather than aggravate conflict. Ritual came to involve artifacts more elaborate and impressive than village shrines and little clay figurines kept near home firesides, and functionaries more exalted than those who tended the shrines. Frequent ceremonies conducted on the grand scale in wide plazas surrounded by massive buildings brought people together shoulder to shoulder, reminding them that they shared the same beliefs and the same fears.

For all the reassurance of pomp and circumstance, life in the first cities had a fragile quality. Sumer happens to have been in some respects a very bad place for agriculture. Ideally, considerable water in October is needed to give newly planted seeds a good start, then a fairly steady supply from October to March, and a tapering off to give crops a chance to grow firm and free of rot. Unfortunately, the Euphrates, fed by rains in the mountains of Turkey hundreds of miles away, provides scarcity and abundance, and both at precisely the wrong time. It is usually lowest in October, rising very slowly until about February, with chances of floods in May when water is needed least. According to Gibson, farmers "faced a yearly prospect of previously water-deprived plants being washed away by uncontrollable flooding."

If they had been offered any options, lands requiring appreciably less effort to work, they would long ago have moved elsewhere. They stayed because they had to stay and, in effect, made a go of it by working against nature. There was certainly nothing natural about their systems of canals, reservoirs, dams and other water-control devices. They achieved a degree of security, but never anything approaching complete security, only by agreeing to pool resources and spread the risks. That meant sharing hardships as well as available food supplies when trouble came and, more difficult, sharing with strangers from communities two or three walking days away—and, perhaps most difficult and most "unnatural" of all, sharing with leaders who, because they were more important than their fellowmen, expected and usually received most of the best of everything.

Survival in those days presumably demanded an end to equality. A universe, a superartifact, emerged, in which everything that had to be done seemed right and necessary. Planning and trial-and-error development of hierarchies were part of the process. So was religion, not planned in the conventional sense, but a mythology and an associated ethics, which explained and justified the daily round.

In the Sumerian cosmos, man, afloat on a platform of rushes in an ocean encircled by mountains, existed to serve gods. Kings existed to oversee the carrying out of divine commands, which involved labor and sacrifices, animal and human. Sometimes the commands must have seemed unreasonable and arbitrary, in particular during periods of stress when life became more complicated, when the number of administrative levels and the distance between people and their leaders increased.

The status of royalty rose accordingly, and with it the force of royal edicts. Authority evolved from king as hero, an extraordinary individual but still human, to king as something more than human, a glorified intermediary between gods and the rest of mankind. The ultimate promotion is documented on cuneiform tablets where the king's name appears with the divinity symbol before it, a mark originally asterisk-shaped and signifying that he had become a full-fledged god.

Courtesy of A. Leo Oppenheim, University of Chicago

The divinity sign, ancient Sumer, Iraq: evolving symbols placed before names of kings to show divine status

8

Merchants and Middlemen Across the Iranian Plateau

FRONTIERS assumed a new significance with the coming of kings and kingdoms. They were upriver and mountain-pass places rarely visited, glamorous and threatening. They challenged the young, as outer space does today and as Everests and polar regions and Amazonias once did. There was adventure past the horizon, over passes into the next valley and into valleys beyond, and homecomings with tales, tall and otherwise. Frontiers represented danger, too. People seen from afar, coming downstream or down mountain slopes, were not always the returning young. Sometimes they were strangers, and distrust of strangers ran deep. It was a heritage from the remotest hunter-gatherer times when the world was emptier and meetings were rarer and more of a shock.

Now meetings were becoming part of the new order of things. People were crossing frontiers, their own and others', not for novelty and surprise, but to reduce and if possible eliminate surprise—to know and become known, to assess new lands and new possibilities. The crossing of frontiers was part of a search for security. As populations expanded at home and problems of supply and control multiplied, what lay beyond the frontiers became of intense practical importance. Strangers needed the goods and the goodwill of other strangers. They brought gifts, messages from other kings, invitations to trade, and perhaps an unspoken hope of support in the event of hard times.

Sumer seen close up was a major center of growing cities and states. Seen from a continental perspective, it was a speck, a tiny patch of terrain on the edge of the Iranian Plateau—a million square miles of highland that extends halfway across Asia, from the Tigris to the Indus River. With the passing of time its people, lacking more and more things they needed and wanted, reached further and further out into this vast landmass.

About 135 miles northwest of Uruk in an inhospitable part of Iran is a high mound known as Farukhabad, which Wright has excavated and described, not without a measure of affection: "The site at sunset, except for the call of the jackal and the laughter of hyenas, is impressive in its desolation." The site lay along a trade route leading further afield. There was a spring nearby, not of bubbling water but of the first commercially important product of Middle Eastern oil fields, bitumen or natural asphalt, seeping up at a rate of about ten quarts an hour from underground reservoirs. For 8,000 or more years it had been widely used for fastening flint blades to handles and waterproofing baskets, roofs and drains, among other things. Jericho's remarkable growth as an early town may have been partly as a result of its location near Dead Sea bitumen springs.

To obtain a rough index of how much bitumen was brought into Farukhabad town and processed for export, Wright sifted through masses of earth and saved each scrap of the tarry material. From deposits dating to around 3150 B.C. he extracted about a pound of bitumen from every ton of sifted earth. From deposits of a century or so later that figure had increased eightfold, and it is reasonable to infer that one of the chief reasons was the population implosion and general boom period under way in Uruk. Although people presumably were hafting more blades and water-proofing more roofs and baskets, that could account for only part of the increase. An appreciable proportion of the bitumen undoubtedly went elsewhere, to build boats and to seal up seams in the hulls.

River and sea traffic have ancient roots in the Near East. Trade in obsidian came at least as early as trade in bitumen. Obsidian is a hard natural glass which forms when molten lava cools rapidly and can be worked into razor-sharp knives and other tools. Obsidian flakes have been found in Ali Kosh occupation levels of about 7000 B.C. The research of Colin Renfrew of England's University of Southampton and his associates has provided evidence for the source of the flakes.

Obsidian from different sources differs in composition. If a sample is heated to incandescence, each chemical element emits a characteristic wavelength or color. Two elements most useful in identifying sources, zirconium and barium, emit ultraviolet and

Adventure, expansion, trade networks on the Iranian Plateau: where traders ready to fight in case trading failed brought practical and luxury products. (Example of their enterprise: lapis lazuli, "the diamond of the Sumerians," passed from the Hindu Kush Mountains in the east along a southern "low road" through Shahr-i Sokhta and perhaps Malyan and on to Sumer—and along a northern "high road" through centers in the Altin region and Godin)

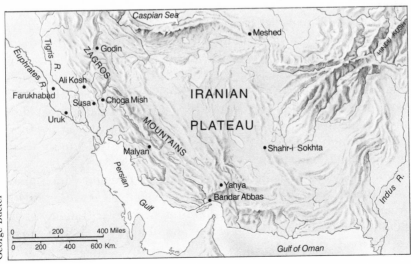

blue radiations, respectively, which can be measured with a light-analyzing instrument known as a spectrograph. The Ali Kosh flakes were made of 1,000–1 obsidian, that is, obsidian containing 1,000 parts per million of zirconium and one part or less of barium.

The 1,000–1 variety comes from quarries 600 miles away near mile-high Lake Van in the mountains of eastern Turkey. It was probably transported most of the way along the Tigris, whose headwaters are not far from the lake. (The river passed within forty miles of Ali Kosh.) Long-established river routes later brought not only obsidian but copper, silver, and other metals which were also found near the headwaters of the Tigris.

Trade was on the rise. Theodore Wertime of the Smithsonian Institution notes progress in metallurgy based on practical knowledge about the uses of heat, knowledge acquired in pottery-making when "in effect, one turns clay back to stone by dehydrating it and heating it to a high enough temperature." For example, the earliest copper artifacts, pendants and other objects, may date back ten thousand years. Improved techniques evolved rapidly during the period from about 5000 B.C. to 3000 B.C. with the development of smelting furnaces and experiments in adding other elements to copper to produce harder and more durable bronzes—arsenic at first, first encountered as a natural impurity and then added deliberately, and later tin.

Booming trade required boats and wood, most of it river-borne. More wood meant clearing forests, a turning away from stone as the traditional material for axes, and an increasing demand for efficient metal axes. Metallurgical advances, in turn, called for additional supplies of wood to feed the hot fires of smelting furnaces. Wertime points out that for all the emphasis on metals and ceramics, wood was "the unsung hero" of the times, the basic raw material for fuel and for building. Timber and a great deal more came from a region about 175 miles to the east near the foot-hills and high valleys of the Zagros Mountains, the 1,100-square-mile Susiana Plain in Iran. For about ten years Wright has been devoting special attention to this semidesert region which grew with the growth of Sumer. He has conducted surveys there with Adams, his former teacher, and Johnson, his former student. Their findings, together with those of Perrot and his French Archeological Mission colleagues, Helene Kantor of the University of Chicago and Pinhas Delougaz of the University of California, Los Angeles, supplement findings in the Uruk countryside.

While the first sites on the Susiana Plain were probably established more than 8,000 years ago, the rise of complex societies came primarily during the millennium or so following 4000 B.C. Settlement patterns changed as they did in the Uruk region. Early in this period people were living in a relatively simple and fragmented world, a two-level world of eighteen villages and averaging some three acres with two small centers of fifteen acres each. The sites were strung out in a line as if located along artificial or natural waterways. Grouped into three or four separate clusters, they seemed to be independent communities or subregions.

Survey maps show a notable difference by 3500 B.C. Now there were 20,000 persons, fifty sites and three levels of settlement size— forty-six villages, three small centers, and a single thirty-acre large center on a river bend in the middle of the plain, the city-to-be of Susa where the French have been digging even longer than the Germans have been digging at Uruk. At this stage the first signs of the familiar hexagonal structure emerged. A fourth level emerged two centuries later, with around 25,000 persons, fifty-four settlements, and four small and three large centers. Susa was the largest center at more than sixty acres. There were two village levels instead of one, thirty-four small villages and thirteen large ones, averaging 2.3 and 5.7 acres.

Central place theory reveals a somewhat more detailed picture of the process observed in the Uruk region. A hierarchy of settlement sizes had evolved and again, as in the Uruk study, archeology and architecture support what settlement patterns imply— another state in the process of taking shape. A number of small sites with ceramic mosaic cones, presumed distribution points for local exchange systems, arose at strategic places in the settlement network. A large settlement appeared to the east of Susa during the four-level stage, at a place where no previous site had existed. This thirty-acre site, known as Choga Mish, is probably another example of prehistoric planning. It seems to have been built in a relatively short time as a major administrative center to coordinate exchange and other activities in the eastern part of the Susiana Plain.

Insights into such matters come from studies of a special kind of pottery. Open bowls with sloping or beveled rims began to appear with the rise of the three-level stage; many millions of sherds have been excavated at Choga Mish alone. Since the bowls are often found in or near large buildings believed to be temples, they were once regarded as ceremonial items designed to contain offerings for the gods, but recent research points to more secular purposes. Nissen, noting among other things that beveled-rim bowls are made of coarse, low-cost materials, suggested that they were used to dole out food to workers. Wright experimented with production methods to see how fast they could be made. He tempered his own clay and learned to form a bowl in an earthen mold, a properly shaped hole dug in his backyard, in about a minute or so.

Johnson took on the formidable task of measuring base angles, rim diameters, side heights, side thicknesses and half a dozen other features of 278 reconstructed bowls. He estimated the volumes of the bowls and found that they tended to come in three sizes, roughly a quart, two-thirds of a quart, and half a quart. The quart size holds enough barley grain to make about 1,960 calories of bread, almost exactly what the average adult villager in the region consumes daily today. Such observations may be taken as indirect evidence for some sort of corvée labor system, with rations for workers drafted and supported by people in authority.

There must have been military rationing as well. Local conflict broke out during the period from 3300 B.C. to 3100 B.C. with Susa on the losing end—it decreased from sixty to about twenty-two acres, while Choga Mish, originally intended as a secondary center, grew from twenty-five to forty-five acres. A previously occupied zone more than eight miles wide between the two centers became a no-man's-land of ghost towns and villages. About a third of the inhabitants abandoned their homes, most of them perhaps heading for more stable places to the west where Uruk was on the rise. This was Uruk's take-off period, when it increased to 250 acres and later to 1,000.

Relations between the two regions, the two trade and administrative systems, had become very close, a development reflected in their pottery. A few centuries before, there were marked differences, mainly differences in shape. Now the shapes were practically identical so that, according to Johnson, "You could throw

Susa sherds into a collection of Uruk sherds and never tell them apart." Much of what the people of Sumer wanted came across the Susiana Plain from points to the south and east. Timber and stone and other common bulk materials, and rare and exotic items, arrived, the rarest and most exotic tending to come from the greatest distances. Shahr-i Sokhta, an important site at the eastern edge of Iran some 800 miles away, yields information about this sort of trade.

Like most of its ancient contemporaries, the site is desert now, a heavy concentration of sherds in the sand. But between 3000 B.C. and 2500 B.C., it became a city of more than 175 acres, dominating a river delta with a most unusual pattern of settlements. On the Susiana Plain, as in the Uruk countryside and other regions, there was a ranked structure of at least four levels—three large centers, four small centers, thirteen large villages and thirty-four small villages. Shahr-i Sokhta, on the other hand, was the only big center. All of the secondary settlements, more than thirty of them, were small villages, none larger than five acres.

The same sort of two-level pattern has been noted in twentieth-century settings. It exists today in western Guatemala, for example. According to Carol Smith of Duke University, a single large center dominating many very small settlements occurs under particular economic conditions—typically, export of a single primary product or a few primary products, and elite control of the exchange system. In Guatemala the exports are cotton and coffee and sugar, grown on lowland plantations by workers who do not own the means of production and do not play a prominent role in marketing the products. Many workers are highland Maya Indians who work on the plantations seasonally. The plantation owners and market middlemen at all levels are Ladinos, non-Indians claiming Spanish ancestry. They make up a minority in the region and are politically dominant. (Elsewhere in Guatemala, under other economic conditions, different types of settlement systems occur, some of them quite regular.)

The people of Shahr-i Sokhta also exported their products over long distances. They also concentrated on a few products, chiefly on lapis lazuli, "the diamond of the Sumerians," brought in over high passes and down rivers from mines in the Hindu Kush Mountains, a westward extension of the Himalayas. As recently as a generation ago, the same mines were providing ninety percent of the world's supply of the deep blue mineral crystals. The nature of labor relations in Iran three to four millenniums ago, however, remains to be clarified.

Maurizio Tosi of the Italian Institute of the Middle and Far East in Rome has uncovered a large lapis workshop at Shahr-i Sokhta. Among the sands and sherds and stones he found lapis wastes, lapis beads and bead fragments, and some remarkable miniature artifacts that might have been missed entirely if it had not been for a special "flotation" technique. Investigators poured samples of excavated earth through a fine screen into a basin of water, scooping off the light material that floated on the surface for future examination (for fragments of bone and plants). Among the particles that remained on the screen they found hundreds of tiny slivers and chips of flint, many about half the size of a little fingernail. Microscopic examination showed that these were microliths, tiny drills with carefully worked edges and tips, used to bore holes in lapis beads. Patches of pulverized lapis were still sticking to the tools.

Most of the valuable mineral was not worked locally but came from the mines imbedded in chunks of limestone. The limestone had to be chipped away carefully, leaving relatively clean crystals, which went to craftsmen in other centers for final working into jewelry and special inlays. Camels probably did the carrying. Camel dung and bones, and fragments of camel hair interwoven with flax have been found at the site. There seems to have been a "low road" or southern overland route extending west from Shahr-i Sokhta and then north between the Zagros Mountains and the Persian Gulf, or along Gulf sea lanes, to Susa and Sumer. A high road, a northern route leading to the same destinations, passed from the Hindu Kush mines through an early urban region in Central Asia and on to a center with a lapis workshop some fifty miles southeast of the Caspian Sea.

Many other luxury items moved toward Mesopotamia along these and other routes. One of the most valuable was produced in a settlement along the southern route about 300 miles from Shahr-i Sokhta and 75 miles inland from the modern Persian Gulf city of Bandar Abbas, discovered late in the summer of 1967 near the end of what promised to be a highly frustrating season. After eleven weeks and 8,000 miles of exploring, an American expedition had found no site old enough, large enough and well enough preserved to provide evidence of early trade across the Iranian Plateau. The successful search, the latest of a long series of leads based on the report of a local mining engineer, started at four o'clock one August morning. It lasted thirteen hours, the first seven hours or so on foot, to the top of a Zagros Mountain pass and down into a valley, and the rest of the way by Land Rover. The journey led to an intact sixty-five-foot mound called Yahya. Carl Lamberg-Karlovsky of Harvard University, leader of the expedition, was "overwhelmed" by the find: "Sherds picked up on the mound and on the surrounding plain as much as a mile away, and a preliminary test trench showed that it was an early and very important site. I thought that three or four seasons of excavating might be required to do it justice."

Doing Yahya justice required eight seasons of digging, concluding in 1975. It has revealed unexpected traces of what Lamberg-Karlovsky calls "an early form of economic imperialism." People first settled in the valley around 4500 B.C., established a small farming village, and put the local stone to good use, particularly a soft, dark green stone known as chlorite. The site's earliest occupation level included a steatite female figurine about a foot high; later levels included stone beads, bowls and other items.

Yahya mound, Iran, 65 feet high, during excavations

Courtesy of C. C. Lamberg-Karlovsky, Harvard University, and Harvard News Office

Some time after 3000 B.C., someone, probably an outsider, intervened and reorganized the village, or a good part of it. Making stone objects became the predominant activity, with a major emphasis on bowls. In one workshop area more than 1,200 pieces of vessels were found in different stages of completion, and they came in a variety of shapes and sizes, usually small, perhaps three or four inches high and weighing a pound or two. The most impressive of the lot demanded considerable time and effort and are clearly the work of superb craftsmen.

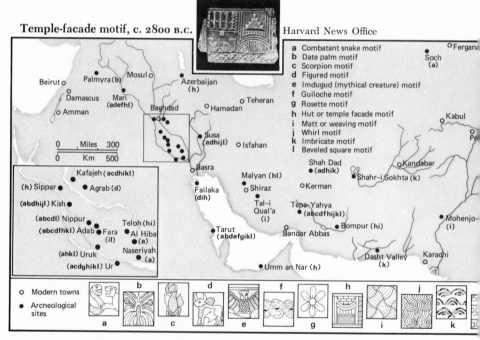

Temple-facade motif, c. 2800 B.C.   Harvard News Office

a Combatant snake motif
b Date palm motif
c Scorpion motif
d Figured motif
e Imdugud (mythical creature) motif
f Guiloche motif
g Rosette motif
h Hut or temple facade motif
i Matt or weaving motif
j Whirl motif
k Imbricate motif
l Beveled square motif

o Modern towns
● Archeological sites

Vantage Art, Inc.

Based on Philip L. Kohl, Wellesley College, "Carved Chlorite Vessels," *Expedition*, Fall 1975

International stylistic "code:" map showing the distribution of some of a dozen principal design motifs on stone bowls, made at Yahya and other centers and excavated at sites from the eastern Mediterranean to the Indus Valley, with carved designs representing a "vocabulary," symbols of elitism

Philip Kohl, of Wellesley College, who worked at Yahya as a graduate student, found that similar bowls were being made for visiting pilgrims some 600 miles away in a modern shop in the bazaar at Meshed, the holy Muslim city in northern Iran. Local workers explained their own methods, which in some ways resembled the methods of times past. The hollowing out of prepared blanks, for example, is still done with metal tools, although smoothing involves a crude hand-operated lathe instead of the ancient rubbing implement, which could have been a wet river pebble.

Production has speeded up, however. Three Meshed workers can turn out at least a hundred bowls a day; while, as a rough estimate, Kohl suggests that three Yahya workers might have produced only half a dozen, although they spent hours carving delicate standardized designs on the outside of their bowls. In their "vocabulary," their repertoire of basic patterns, were twelve major and fourteen minor motifs or themes. Seven of the major themes represent living things: date palm, scorpion, flower-rosette, a pair of fighting snakes, a single fighting snake, a horned animal, a mythical winged creature. The rest are more abstract and stylized: perhaps a hut or temple facade, mat or weaving, whirls, beveled squares (a wall?), overlapping rounded forms (decorative tiles?).

This is communication, a code, and deciphering it would tell us more about the people of the times, particularly the elite. No one knows what, if anything, the bowls contained; incense and rare oils and perfumes have been suggested. But whatever the contents, they were insignificant compared to the carvings on the outside. The motifs convey information as definite as that conveyed by today's Rolls-Royce emblems, Tiffany labels, papal and Maltese crosses, yachtsmen's flags, the stars of generals and the stripes of admirals. They signify brotherhoods of a sort, memberships in exclusive circles.

On the basis of X-ray diffraction tests which "fingerprint" samples of stone by their crystal structure, Kohl postulates that at least four workshops besides the one at Yahya specialized in producing similarly carved vessels, an "intercultural carved-bowl style." These bowls are found primarily in buildings identified as palaces and temples, and in the graves of highly placed individuals. They seem to have been widely owned. Made-in-Yahya bowls have been recovered from sites as far west as Syria, and bowls with the same basic symbols are reported as far east as the Indus Valley, a total span of more than 1,500 miles. Cracking the bowl-motif code might also tell us something about international relations and the existence of an international clique or "set."

Events in Yahya provide only a glimpse, a faint indication, of what must have been going on east of Sumer. A small center of about ten acres, it was probably not the only place specializing in the manufacture of stone bowls for elites. But it has broad implications for the nature of early domination. Lamberg-Karlovsky stresses a crucial piece of missing information, the significance of something that has not been found at the site after eight digging seasons—no elite district has been found, no area with large and elaborate residences. Apparently no local person was getting rich from Yahya's high-value, high-status products. The profits seem to have been going to absentee middlemen. Still, local people must have received something for their efforts, since there is no indication that tribute was being exacted, no signs of military outposts or forts. No evidence exists of what Sumer gave for the bowls it imported, or for all the gold and silver and gems and other valuables that came from other workshops. Presumably its exports consisted almost entirely of perishable goods like grain, dried fish and textiles.

Long-distance luxury trade emerges as a significant development in the evolving technology, the evolving art, of controlling people for the common good. A rare exotic object has an almost hypnotic crystal-ball effect. Viewed in a public ceremony or on the person of a leader, it is above all a symbol of power that attracts and holds attention, preparing the viewer to be impressed and indoctrinated. Such objects are as important in organizing society and keeping society organized as a temple, a monument, an army and music to march by, a police force.

Research on early trade routes and trade networks in the Iranian Plateau, on early lines of communication, demands cooperative studies. Tosi and Lamberg-Karlovsky have visited and dug at each other's sites and have written articles together. Both investigators are in close touch with excavations in Central Asia under the direction of Vladimir Masson of the Soviet Institute of Archeology in Leningrad. Imminent discoveries could easily require profound changes in current theories. New insights are sure to come from work at Malyan, a city on the southern trade route about halfway between Yahya and Susa. William Sumner of Ohio State University discovered it in 1968 during a river-valley survey, three months of "driving down every track as far as possible, and walking to every mound sighted." A low, flat-topped mound more than a mile long, Malyan is the largest of some 350 early sites in the valley and, incidentally, one of the largest in the Near East, with an area of at least 150 acres in 3000 B.C.

Sumner has already worked there for four seasons, but considers this to be little more than a reconnaissance effort. He expects to put in another three seasons to complete the first stages of a preliminary study: "After that, we'll know enough to start real excavations." In other words, Malyan, like Susa and Uruk, will probably become a long-term project, demanding one or more lifetimes of intensive digging. Located in a rich, well-watered plain, it had a number of large buildings during the period from 3200 B.C. to 2800 B.C., and some almost certainly housed administrators concerned with trade records.

New research hints at similar activities during the same period along the northern route. The studies of Harvey Weiss of Yale and Cuyler Young suggest a Susa presence at the site of Godin some 275 miles away, a possible foreign quarter of Susa merchants living on the summit of Godin's central mound or "acropolis." Such findings point to a well-controlled trade network, which was also a political network with lines of command and administrative hierarchies characteristic of emerging states.

Increasing trade, local as well as long distance, brought a spectacular increase in the number of transactions requiring more and more middlemen—and a need for new methods of keeping records. Recent studies suggest that some of the marks painted and engraved on pebbles, ivory, bone and cave walls 20,000 or more years ago may represent numbers and systems of counting. Special meanings were almost certainly assigned to the animals and unexplained symbols depicted in early cave art.

Experience with record-keeping and standardized signs had been accumulating for a long while by the time the first steps toward writing can be traced in the Near East. The beginnings of the process some 7,000 or more years ago can be seen in standardized design motifs on early pottery. There were also tiny pictures cut into button-shaped and hemispherical stones, stamp seals used to impress patterns on jars and other vessels, to identify who was sending them and for whom they were intended. The pictures on the seals are not writing, which came several millenniums later. But they reflect in miniature widespread social changes which would create the need for writing.

Some of the early seals found at sites on the Susiana Plain, for example, date back to simple two-level times, when the region included only a few clusters of villages and two small centers. Wright and Johnson point out that pictures on seals from Susa are also simple, including crosses, stylized human and animal figures, and mostly parallel lines, triangles and other geometric forms. The inference is that no need existed for greater variety since supplies were coming in directly from a small number of hinterland villages, and there were relatively few buyers and sellers, and probably no middlemen to identify.

More complicated pictures appeared during later periods, as Susiana Plain populations quadrupled and the number of settlement-size categories increased from two to four. In addition to stamp seals with simple patterns there were elaborate scenes of herds and people in workshops and boats. Cylinder seals appeared in quantity. They were designed to be rolled over clay surfaces and leave repeating scenes and patterns—including, during Choga Mish–Susa conflicts times, the first representations of armed men, battlefields and captives.

These developments make sense considering that these were middleman times. Goods were passing through more and more hands, and more and more individuals and institutions had to be identified. They make sense for another reason as well, since the very existence of records encourages tampering with records. The temptation to forge seals undoubtedly increased with increasing opportunities for graft of all sorts. The more complicated a seal the more difficult it is to copy faithfully.

Cheating could be further discouraged by the so-called bulla, from the Latin word for "bubble." ("Bull," as in "papal bull," comes from the same root.) The bulla was a hollow clay sphere about the size of a golf ball, with enough space inside to hold a number of tiny cubes, cones, spheres and other geometric clay objects. Bullae probably served as invoices, evidence of orders filled and delivered in good condition. A storehouse clerk would count the containers of barley in a shipment or the sheep in a herd, break open the accompanying bulla, and check the total with the counters inside. If the numbers matched, the fact was duly recorded; if not, there might be trouble.

These are some of the precursors of writing, of deeds and contracts and leases, and ultimately of legal systems. The earliest

Susa-type cylinder seals from tablets at Godin, central western Iran: rearward glancing lions with curled tails

Courtesy of T. Cuyler Young, Royal Ontario Museum, Toronto, Canada

known writing appears on clay tablets unearthed in the Uruk region, specifically in the Eanna district of the city itself. The tablets date to around 3500 B.C., but by that time the script already consisted of about 2,000 different signs, including pictograms like the following which bear some resemblance to, and thus help to remind one of, the objects they refer to:

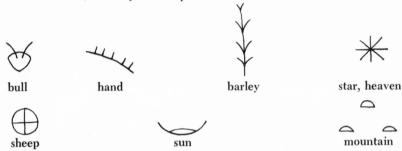

| bull | hand | barley | star, heaven |
| sheep | sun | | mountain |

There were also abstract signs which have no such obvious associations, at least not to us:

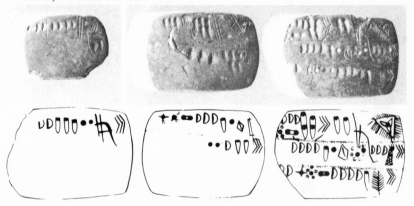

Some of the earliest writing, Susa-type tablets, Yahya, Iran: inscribed tablets and drawings of each, showing detail
Courtesy of C. C. Lamberg-Karlovsky and Harvard News Office

It took some time to standardize the signs. Individuals who knew how to use the new writing system, probably no more than a dozen or two out of a population of 10,000, had represented the same objects in various ways. They used thirty-one versions of the sheep sign. But within four centuries or so the number dropped to two, and the total of all signs decreased from 2,000 to 800.

The people of Susa developed a system of writing based on pictographs at about the same time as the people of Uruk. Their tablets appear along the northern and southern trade routes, including finds at Malyan, Godin, Shahr-i Sokhta, and Yahya. Yahya yielded an "office," a room in a large building constructed between 3400 B.C. and 3000 B.C. Near one corner of the room were ninety clay tablets, each about the size of a book of matches, six with Susa-type writing on them and eighty-four blanks. According to a preliminary study, a triangular mark stands for a corporation or administrative authority which was responsible for distributing some sort of seed, probably barley, during the planting season.

The invention of writing in the Near East was apparently the work of people deeply involved in scheduling supplies of food and other resources from outlying areas. We assume, although it remains to be demonstrated, that at some critical stage the number and pace of transactions became too much to handle solely with the aid of seals, bullae and other recording devices. Perhaps the first schools were places established to teach the use of such artifacts. Perhaps some of the teachers and their brightest students, impressed with the need for greater efficiency in the face of soaring work loads, came up with a set of signs as a kind of time-saving shorthand. The implication is that there was a breaking point in efforts to cope with administrative complexities, a point at which record-keeping would have collapsed if writing had not been invented. In our times the invention of high-speed computers with voluminous memories has a similar significance.

Writing was part of the same process that led to long-distance luxury trade, settlement hierarchies, ceremonial architecture and the rise of the city itself. In considering these and other developments, investigators tend to stress the contributions of settled people, city dwellers and farmers. Less attention has been paid to people who did not settle down. The Near East some five millenniums ago included perhaps one to two million persons out of an estimated world population of about 100,000,000 and perhaps more than a third of them were nomads, people in tents on the move in the no-man's-lands between urban regions.

According to motion pictures and many history books, nomads had nothing to do with the serious business of creating a workable way of life. They are supposed to have functioned as villains in the melodrama, threats to progress of any sort. Popular tales often present nomads as perennial wild men, as barbarians who feared neither kings nor gods, and who periodically descended in hordes from rugged mountain fastnesses to loot towns and cities, and from time to time to topple civilizations.

Raiding, frequently on a large scale, has long been part of the nomads' way of life—and, as voiced not long ago by an angry Turkman nomad in present-day Iran, they may be as ready as settlers to take the law into their own hands when sufficiently aggravated: "I do not have a mill with willow trees. I have a horse and a whip. I will kill you, and go." There is also something to the notion that nomads and settled people had close ties and depended upon one another, and that the supposed gap between them is basically a myth. Nomads, like workers living in the city or like some of the city's leaders themselves, may well have tried to beat the system on occasion and clashed violently with the Establishment, and yet remained part of the system. Real "outsiders" are rare.

Getting at the truth is difficult, particularly when it comes to understanding the role of nomads in the evolution of complex societies. For one thing, educated city folk have written all the books, including records inscribed on tablets and ancient texts. One could hardly expect scribes serving the elite and top-ranking administrators to look kindly on highly mobile people who were hard to control and, above all, hard to tax. Also, the nomads of times past tend to be invisible archeologically speaking, at least their sites are far more elusive than the sites of those who lived in permanent houses.

The first, and to date the only, nomad site to be identified unequivocally in the lowlands of the Near East is known as Tula'i and was discovered on the Susiana Plain in 1973. Frank Hole excavated it in the spring, definitely not the season for archeology in that part of Iran, since temperatures hover around 115 to 120 or more degrees Fahrenheit and the ground is so dry that you raise clouds of dust with every step. But he had no choice. Bulldozers leveling ground for an irrigated wheat field had just exposed the site, and it would soon be destroyed by plowing and other activities. Under such conditions, the time to dig is always now.

The project had a special meaning for the fifteen Iranians Hole hired to do the digging. Ex-nomads themselves, they knew the land well. Twenty years ago they and their families came regularly with their herds to the same area, for the same reasons that brought their remote ancestors. This was familiar grazing territory and their winter tents, very probably like the winter tents of times past, had tops of woven goat hair and faced south away from the prevailing wind. Without land of their own now and without jobs, living in squatter villages, they came to spend ten days in a salvage operation to record part of their tribe's prehistory.

The men helped to interpret some of the things they unearthed. They recognized the feature which more than any other single one identified the site as a nomad site—rectangular stone platforms to keep bedding off damp ground. In fact, they had built similar structures many times before. At one partly excavated location digging had already revealed such a platform. Hole asked

Nomad site, Tula'i, Iran: with rectangular stone platform, support for bedding

Courtesy of Frank Hole, Rice University

one of the workers where the fireplace would be found. The worker promptly paced off two steps to the south, started shoveling, and soon uncovered the ashes.

Other evidence of the nomadic life included rows of stones outlining tent edges, and bones of domesticated sheep and goats. The absence of certain things also served as evidence, no sickle blades or grinding stones which are abundant at farming sites, and no walls or any signs of houses. "It was a camping place," Hole reports. "People first pitched a row of tents there around 6000 B.C., perhaps half a dozen families including thirty or forty individuals and twice as many animals. Like modern nomads, they probably came back to the same area season after season, for two hundred years or so."

It was one of the first known sites on the Susiana Plain and may have been used by people belonging to a permanent village located near summertime pastures in foothills and mountains to the west. It may also have been part of a pattern, determined by the fact that winter pastures were dwindling close to home. If the dwindling were a widespread phenomenon, an appreciable number of similar camping areas must have appeared at about the same time.

Things certainly changed with the coming of irrigation and more and larger permanent settlements on the plain. Perhaps the nomads joined the settlers and became farmers, workers and administrators. If so, new tensions were probably on the rise, as suggested by Lees and her Hunter College colleague Daniel Bates, who has spent considerable time living with nomads in southeastern Turkey. They believe that irrigation had a great deal to do with transforming herding operations from a part-time to a full-time occupation.

Before irrigation became extensive most workers were not specialists. Depending on current needs, they spent time on herding, building and maintaining canals, farming, and so on. But as irrigation spread and canals became longer, settlements were established further out into the plains, further from the mountains. As a result, more time and energy were required to bring herds to and from summer pastures, and some workers adapted by becoming full-time herders. (With the increase in irrigation another specialization, that of the full-time canal worker, presumably appeared during the same period.)

To check the Lees-Bates and other theories, investigators are on the lookout for nomad sites. Hole's site lay buried under several feet of river-borne deposits, and would have remained buried if it had not been for the bulldozers. So the search continues wherever construction is going on, wherever stones in rows and stone platforms and hearths may be uncovered. They may be found in highland or lowland regions, and in caves where layers of sheep dung indicate nomad camping places. According to preliminary surveys, more people were living in caves during the period around 3500 B.C. at a time when administrative complexity and the size of settlements were increasing on the plain.

Nomads were not only a product of changing times, they helped change the times. They almost certainly organized themselves on a larger and larger scale, groups of hundreds of persons on the move and related to other groups by kinship and tribal ties—and in the process had a powerful impact on the place of organization in settled communities. In fact, Wright believes that they may have had a significant role in urban evolution.

Nomads created a demand for new and more flexible organization, and found a special place in expanding trade networks. They raided on occasion, but at this stage large centers probably had more to fear from other large centers. More often than not, nomads came to trade, offering meat, wool, carpets and blankets in return for grain and goods like pottery and metal implements. Because nomads came in large numbers, often unpredictably, planning was called for to stockpile supplies; large workshops were needed to satisfy the demand. Bates points out that prehistoric nomads may have provided an even more important service, carrying crops and other goods to distant markets as their modern descendants still did in Turkey before World War II.

A nomad did not have to remain a nomad, or a farmer a farmer. Roles could change. Owen Lattimore of Johns Hopkins University pointed out that this happened in China during historic times, particularly at remote frontiers of empire where "the poor farmer could become a prosperous nomad by abandoning his underprivileged share of civilization and taking to the steppes," a course followed most easily when central authority was on the decline: "Chinese dynasties did not normally weaken along the frontier until they had first decayed at the core." As the authorities reestablished themselves, of course, many Chinese nomads returned to farming, often against their wills. Adams, citing Lattimore, believes that similar changes may have taken place in the Near East with the rise and fall of competing city-states.

So nomads enter as one more basic element that must be considered in accounting for evolving social systems. Reports multiply and analysis becomes more and more formidable. It is like working on a difficult jigsaw puzzle representing a region, the individual pieces representing sites. You are completely absorbed in the task and have just succeeded in fitting a number of the pieces together, only to discover that many other people are concentrating just as hard on other jigsaw puzzles and that all the puzzles are merely parts of a single superpuzzle. The problem is to understand the large patterns among regions as well as the smaller patterns of settlements within regions. Necessity was creating not unity, because people unskilled at peace were fighting a good deal of the time, but far-ranging communication networks and the still undiminished hope for unity.

9

Planned Cities, the View from India

*Domesticating man/Continents in collision/
Western and eastern tool kits/The rise of cities
in the Indus Valley/The pollen record/
A hoard in Central Asia/The spread of trade
networks/The pictures on stone seals/"Miles of
monotony"/The persistence of tradition*

VOLUTION in India had a direction, a rhythm of its own.
From one standpoint, things happened there more slowly than in
the Near East. Agriculture did not become established until
about 4000 B.C. to 3500 B.C., when Uruk was already a budding
urban center. Once the settled life took hold, however, India's
rate of change picked up. The transition from villages to cities
required about a millennium; it had taken twice as long in Sumer.

India's first cities are striking examples of the imposition of
planning on landscapes and people. They were patterned, sharp-
cornered, gridded places with straight streets and avenues intersecting at right angles, the geometry of control and certainty, the
geometry of rigidity. Human society had departed from the

193

casualness of hunting-gathering and early gardening days. Planning had taken command. People trying to survive had sacrificed some of their individuality. They were domesticating, taming themselves together with their domesticated plants and animals. They were building systems, and building themselves into systems.

From the very beginning, in early hunter-gatherer times and even earlier, India has had a special quality which seems to be particularly elusive when viewed through Western eyes. Walter Fairservis of Vassar College, an archeologist who has been wrestling with the problem for more than a generation, puts it this way: "Countless as the crystals of Himalayan snowfall . . . are the fundamental pieces . . . the essentials of the Indian environment. Indeed so far removed is this environment from the American's comprehension that most of us have been mere tourists in its presence, seeing without understanding."

The record starts about 200,000,000 years ago with some extraordinary geological events. No continents existed then, only a single supercontinent called Pangea in a single ocean, a vast island already starting to split apart in a series of earthquakes and volcanic eruptions. What is now India was one of the pieces. A slab of land forty miles thick, it had just broken loose from Antarctica and was now drifting north like an enormous lily pad of softened rock—on a collision course with Asia.

The collision occurred 50,000,000 years ago and is still going on. India has not yet lost all its momentum, and continues to grind into Asia. More than a hundred peaks in the Himalayas and associated ranges mark the lines of contact, places where the land is buckling up, creating a natural barrier which sets India off as a subcontinent from the rest of Asia. One of the world's great rivers, the Indus, carries the run-off waters of melting snow and monsoon rains a thousand miles from the mountains to the Arabian Sea. The first Indian cities arose in its valley.

An unusually diverse inventory of species came together here long before man appeared on earth. There were wild barley and other cereal grasses, lions, gazelles, and many kinds of birds characteristic of semidesert and savanna lands to the west in the Near East and North Africa. There were also native species characteristic of Southeast Asia's humid tropical forests: wild rice, Indian

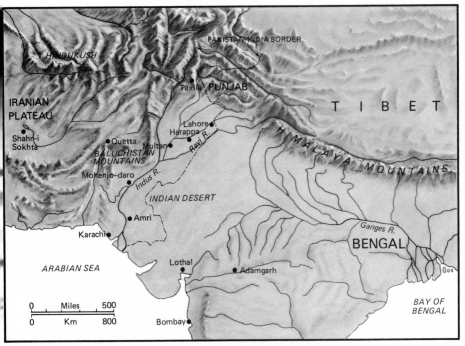

Indus Valley, urbanism and high status move east: sites of the earliest known cities outside of the Sumer-Susiana Plain region, about 4,500 years ago— early centers with city blocks, rectangular grids of long intersecting main streets running between high walls

elephants, tigers, cobras, mongooses, rhinoceroses, crocodilian reptiles. Two worlds overlapped in the Indus Valley to form a transitional zone, a meeting of east and west.

East and west met in another way much later, and the phenomenon remains an archeological mystery. The earliest traces of man in the Indian subcontinent are more than 300,000 years old and include two distinct tool kits, both of which originated in Africa during still earlier times and had largely disappeared by 50,000 years ago. One kit is found in African, Near Eastern, and European sites. It consists mainly of wedge-shaped cleavers and so-called hand axes, oval or teardrop-shaped implements pointed at one end and with cutting edges along the sides. The other kit, typical of sites in Burma and China and Southeast Asia, features chopping tools with rough bashing or cutting edges formed by knocking flakes off the sides of pebbles.

The mystery is what these kits mean. Are they signs of two widespread traditions or cultures? Do they have anything to do with the fact that there were more open spaces in the west, grasslands and savannas with huge herds of big game, while tropical forests predominated in the east, remnants of the worldwide forests of earlier times where animals moved alone or in small groups? To answer these and other questions we must know more than we do about how the tools were used. In any case, the kits reflect separate life-styles existing side by side in northwest India and the Indus Valley region.

Another difference between east and west involves choices of places to live. In Europe and the Near East hunter-gatherers camped regularly in caves and rock shelters. The Combe Grenal cave in southwestern France had some sixty layers of geological and archeological deposits, representing on-and-off occupations over a span of more than 80,000 years. Such continuous records are lacking in India, where people presumably enjoyed milder weather and preferred to camp at open-air sites on river banks. Hunting-gathering has persisted on the subcontinent, although in a modified form. Many hunter-gatherers are still living in Indian forests, not in the self-sufficient style of their prehistoric ancestors or of some present-day aborigines, but by exchanging deer and monkey meat, honey, twine, baskets and other forest products for items such as rice and iron tools which can be obtained in nearby villages.

Hints of forces working to change traditional hunting-gathering patterns, and possible steps toward agriculture, appear in sediments recovered from three Indian Desert lakes east of the Indus Valley. Gurdip Singh of the Australian National University in Canberra used special apparatus to drive pipes into the lake bottoms to haul the pipes to the surface and to remove "cores" or cylindrical columns of tight-packed mud and clay deposited during the past 10,000 or more years. The cores contain the remains of ancient plants, fossil pollen grains with outer coatings so tough they they have retained their shapes and can be identified, permitting a reconstruction of past climates and plant types.

A number of changes took place at about 7500 B.C., no one of them particularly convincing by itself, but taken together adding up to a good case for agriculture. Rainfall decreased slightly as indicated by a slight decrease in pollens of sedges, cattails and other swampland species. At the same time there was a rise in the "cheno-ams," pollens of chenopods (members of the goose-foot family) and amaranths, plants that flourish in disturbed soil such as that found around camping places, plants with nourishing seeds and leaves, likely candidates for early experiments in culti-vation. The pollen record also shows a rise in cereal grasses.

Of course, all the plants might have been growing wild. How-ever, the 7500 B.C. sediments contain charcoal particles, mostly fragments of burned wood, about fifteen times more charcoal than earlier sediments. The sharp increase occurs in all three lake areas and continues throughout the mud-clay cores for sediment levels representing some 5,000 years. Singh interprets his combined pol-len and charcoal findings as signs of deliberate burning to clear away low trees, bushes and shrubs to make room for crops, although hunter-gatherers may also burn off their lands. In any case, confirming the theory will require a search for sites yielding such items as grinding stones, sickle blades and the remains of domesticated plants.

The hunter-gatherers of India, like their brethren in other lands, had undoubtedly accumulated considerable knowledge about plants, and used their knowledge to do some cultivating long before proof positive of domestication appears in the archeo-logical records. They do not seem to have been under any particu-lar pressure to settle down, at least not until relatively late times. Like certain groups of twentieth-century nomads in Iran, Moroc-co and elsewhere, they may have sown seeds in early fall, gone off with their herds to remote pastures, and returned a year later to harvest their crops.

The earliest unquestioned evidence for domestication is of ani-mals rather than plants and dates to about 5500 B.C. That is the carbon-14 figure obtained for deposits at the Adamgarh rock shelter on a low isolated hill in Central India, more than 400 miles northeast of Bombay. The deposits contain abundant re-mains of dogs, sheep, goats, humped cattle and pigs, all appar-ently domesticated. But the people were still hunting; the remains of deer and other wild species are equally abundant. Further-more, Adamgarh and other similar sites have domestication without any traces of permanent settlements, or houses, or walls, an interesting contrast with the Near East where at places like Mallaha near the Sea of Galilee there were permanent settlements without domestication.

The first agricultural settlements appeared in a borderland region which, strictly speaking, lies outside, but just outside, the Indian subcontinent, the eastern edge of the Iranian Plateau. Fairservis has surveyed part of the region, the mountain valley that includes the modern city of Quetta in what is now West Pakistan. He mapped approximately three dozen sites within a radius of 100 miles from the city and excavated one of the earliest, a small mound strategically located near the head of one of the major passes leading down into the broad floodplain of the Indus River.

The mound, known as Kile Gul Mohammad or KGM for short, contained at the deepest levels evidence typical of many early farming villages—walls made of mud bricks or clay rammed between molds, goat and sheep and cattle bones, stones used for grinding, simple pottery, a sickle blade or two. The site's precise age is not known. Fairservis dug an impressive hole, stopping at a depth of more than thirty-six feet because of limited time and the risk of cave-ins. Charcoal from a hearth in one of the deepest levels gave a carbon-14 date of 3600 B.C., but the first settlers probably came at least four or five centuries earlier.

KGM was one of a cluster of five early sites, all within a few miles of one another. During the next fifteen centuries or so population climbed steadily, presumably as a result of settling down, not only in the Quetta Valley where the number of sites expanded from five to more than twenty, but also in other mountain areas to the east, north and south. More and more people began "spilling over the rim." They came down into the lowlands as other people in other mountains had come down some 1,200 miles away and four or five millenniums earlier from the other edge, the western or Mesopotamian edge, of the Iranian Plateau.

Pioneers from the eastern edge left their marks, mainly in the form of pottery, at a number of sites. At Amri, on the right bank of the Indus River about a hundred miles northeast of Karachi, some vessels were painted in the same red-and-black style as that used in the Quetta area and neighboring highlands to the east. Furthermore, highland and lowland sherds share many of the same basic patterns done in strikingly similar manner—checkerboards, chevrons, zigzag, crosslike, and many others.

Change came swiftly from this point on. In one of the most recent studies of the process, Rafique Mughul of the Pakistani government's Department of Archeology in Karachi concentrates on its earliest and least investigated phases. According to his unpublished report, Amri and other villages were established at about 3200 B.C.; and the Indus state, dominated by the cities of Mohenjo-daro and Harappa, among others, took shape within a thousand years after that.

Mohenjo-daro is by far the most impressive of the two today, although the odds are that once there was little to choose between them. Located 100 miles upstream from Amri, its ruins cover a total area of about 240 acres. The site may have been flooded from time to time. Fairservis says that because of Indus meanderings and periodical changes of monsoon rains in the mountains to the north, people were flooded out of their settlements in the valley every two or three centuries and moved to nearby areas. You can see ruins underwater, walls and fired bricks, in lagoons not far from Mohenjo-daro.

Estimates for the population of the ancient city range from 15,000 to 40,000, although 30,000 seems to be regarded as a reasonable compromise. First excavated during the early 1920s by the British archeologist, John Marshall, it has been explored by a number of investigators since then, two of the most recent being Mortimer Wheeler and George Dales of the University of California at Berkeley.

As at Uruk, Susa, and many of the Old World's earliest cities, the river has gone. The Indus has shifted so that its nearest branch flows three miles to the east. The countryside is flat and open. Most other ancient cities have crumbled. They are now sand and shapeless mounds and the stubs of wall. Mohenjo-daro was built of more enduring stuff, of fired, not sun-baked bricks.

You are in the presence of a city. You can walk through it. The main streets extend straight and wide (thirty feet across, the equivalent of two and a half modern superhighway lanes), east-west and north-south, forming blocks and rectangular grids. Running straight and parallel to the streets are long drains on both sides and high standing walls. According to Wheeler, easily the

Courtesy of Gregory L. Possehl, University of Pennsylvania

Mohenjo-daro, Indus Valley: early city, with city blocks, streets, alleys, and stone buildings with garbage chutes to street (see holes in walls, right below)

most articulate of Mohenjo-daro's excavators, all this creates a "regimented" atmosphere: "The miles of brickwork which alone have descended to us, however impressive quantitatively and significant sociologically, are esthetically miles of monotony."

But within the monotony is an element of confusion, almost of chaos. The high walls are "blind," blank surfaces with no doors and few windows. To enter the places where people lived and worked you must turn off the main streets, down dog-leg alleys with side branches where "the prisonlike houses opened their furtive doors." There are alcoves and corners inside the houses, stairs to climb, dead ends and courtyards with rooms opening onto them. One could get lost in such areas; everything has a mazelike quality.

The most prominent part of Mohenjo-daro is a roughly rectangular man-made hill which can be seen for miles and whose long axis points in a north-south direction. Investigators have done most of their digging here. They have uncovered a great deal of monumental architecture, much of it in a fine state of preservation, towers up to thirty feet high, massive walls six to seven feet thick, pillars, verandas, hallways. Unfortunately, the remains are more solid than many of the theories about what they represent.

Wheeler refers to this entire section of the city as "the citadel," but the evidence for a heavily fortified stronghold dominating the area is far from compelling. One archeologist, who describes himself as "disgruntled" and prefers to remain anonymous, considers the citadel notion to be largely a product of the British tendency to see things in terms of conquest and empire—and, more specifically, a product of Wheeler's eloquence and imagination.

One building has been definitely established as a bath. About the size of a large swimming pool, it has bitumen-sealed watertight walls and an arched drain big enough to stand in, and may have been a place of ablution or ritual cleansing. Near the bath is a complex structure consisting of a brick platform covering a

Mohenjo-daro: plan of citadel (heights in feet above sea level)

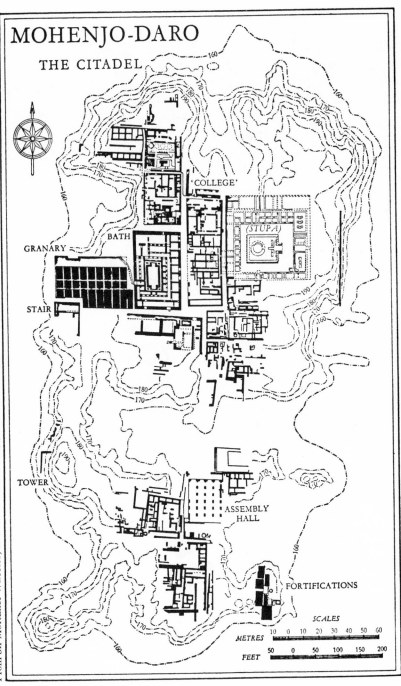

MOHENJO-DARO
THE CITADEL

'COLLEGE'

(STUPA)

BATH

GRANARY

STAIR

TOWER

ASSEMBLY
HALL

FORTIFICATIONS

SCALES

METRES   10 0 10 20 30 40 50 60

FEET   50 0 50 100 150 200

From Sir Mortimer Wheeler, *The Indus Civilization*, 3rd. Ed., Cambridge University Press, 1968

quarter of an acre and a system of brick blocks with crisscross passages between them. There are hints that a large wooden building once existed on top of the platform, perhaps for storing large quantities of grain, possibly received as tribute and meted out to slaves. If so, the passages might have served as a ventilating system to help keep the building dry and prevent the grain upstairs from going bad. This interpretation remains to be supported, however, by the finding of cereal remains or grinding equipment or mass-produced bowls used for rationing, or some other sort of evidence. The only signs of measuring are rectangular and cubical stone weights in graded sizes. The smallest must have been used to weigh such items as gems, precious metals and spices; the longest, which are too heavy to lift, probably measured loads of grain, hay or bricks.

The site's deepest layers have never been probed. The water table has risen since ancient times, and the earliest settlements are submerged too deep for digging. Wheeler once tried, though. With the aid of heavy-duty pumps he managed late one afternoon to expose deposits at the bottom of a twenty-six-foot pit, but the deposits were submerged again next morning. During a later season Dales used drilling equipment to recover mud and clay samples, and found that occupation levels extend to a depth of thirty-nine feet, which effectively puts the beginnings of Mohenjo-daro out of reach.

Harappa, the other large excavated city, was located on the Ravi River, a tributary of the Indus. It is a place doubly ruined, a victim of plundering as well as time. Nineteenth-century engineers managed to do more damage there in a decade than wear and tear had done in more than three millenniums, pirating millions of bricks to build embankments for the Lahore-Multan section of the Western Railway. Apparently Harappa was built very much along the general lines of Mohenjo-daro, with a "citadel" consisting of a huge platform surrounded by high tapering walls forty-five feet thick at the base, and oriented in a north-south direction. All that remained in this zone after the plundering were forty large urns in a row, a well, a long covered drain, and the fragmentary walls of buildings too shattered for reconstruction.

Excavators found structures outside the walls in somewhat

better condition. The remains of a dozen granaries or warehouses, with a total storage capacity about equal to that of Mohenjo-daro's single granary, lie on the banks of the dried-out riverbed, once the chief route for the distribution of food supplies. Sixteen pear-shaped furnaces represent the site's only known workshop, probably a bronze foundry. Cattle dung and charcoal were used as fuels to produce temperatures of more than 2,000 degrees Fahrenheit, judging by the fact that bricks lining the furnaces had melted.

It was once thought that Harappa and Mohenjo-daro, about 350 miles apart in the Indus heartland, were twin capitals exerting joint control over the Indian subcontinent's first state—a situation which seems to have existed in Egypt (see Chapter 11). But new findings argue against this notion as far as the Indus Valley is concerned. According to Dale, aerial photographs reveal the existence of at least two other cities as big as Harappa and Mohenjo-daro, and perhaps bigger. One lies in the foothills of the Baluchistan Mountains, about 150 miles southwest of Harappa; the other lies to the south in the desert near the India-Pakistan border. All of which implies a more complex control network than pictured in the twin-capital theory.

The settlement pattern is not known in anything like the detail available for the Uruk countryside or the Susiana Plain, but there are hints of an evolving hierarchy culminating in a system of four or more levels. By the time the state reached its height around 2000 B.C., it was made up of four to half a dozen major centers, each several times larger than the next largest settlements, about twenty smaller centers, and 200 large and small villages. It extended over more than 400,000 square miles, several times larger than the largest Mesopotamian states, and included a much smaller population of perhaps 200,000 to 250,000 persons.

Again, as in the case of Mesopotamia, long-distance trade in luxury items suggests that higher levels may have existed, relationships among as well as within regions and among the elites of different regions. Caravan routes extended to the west, joining other routes and other networks. More than a decade ago Soviet investigators excavating at Altin, a Central Asian site, found a hoard of ivory subjects made in the Indus Valley some 700 miles away. The hoard included square and oval pieces tentatively identified as gaming counters, and small four-sided sticks with decorations resembling those described in ancient Indian texts and used in fortune-telling. Similar objects have been unearthed in Mohenjo-daro.

Goods from the west are found at Indus sites—turquoise and perhaps copper from mountain areas in Iran not far from Yahya, fifteen to twenty stone bowls with carved Yahya-type motifs, lapis beads possibly made in Shar-i Sokhta, jade from sources in Central Asia. There was even trade, through middlemen and their outposts, with places as far west as Sumer. Some sort of cargo made in India apparently arrived at a city less than thirty miles from Uruk. It must have been perishable, for it has vanished without a trace, but a record endures in the form of a piece of clay stamped with an Indus seal.

The trade between the two regions, however, seems to have been largely a one-way affair. Investigators have never found clay sealings or any other generally accepted remains of Sumer-made goods in Indus territory. If the two regions had been neighbors instead of more than 1,200 miles apart, it might be interpreted as a case of tribute exacted by force from India, with Sumer taking but not giving. However, no signs exist to show that the politics of the times permitted dominion over such distances. The mystery of this strange trade imbalance will remain until fresh evidence appears or until there are fresh insights into evidence already accumulated.

Traders looked east as well as west, to other parts of the subcontinent and beyond. They had a major seaport known as Lothal in a bay of the Arabian Sea, a voyage of about 350 miles from the mouth of the Indus, near the present-day city of Cambay. Judging by the findings of S. R. Rao of the Archeological Survey of India, who completed seven seasons of excavations there about fifteen years ago, the center packed a great deal of activity into an area of fewer than twenty acres.

The town had many features widely recognized as characteristic of Indus centers—the Indus touch, although on a smaller

Lothal, Indus Valley: "dock" and wharf; reconstructed site plan showing warehouse

Photo by Gregory L. Possehl, excavation by S. R. Rao, Archeological Survey of India

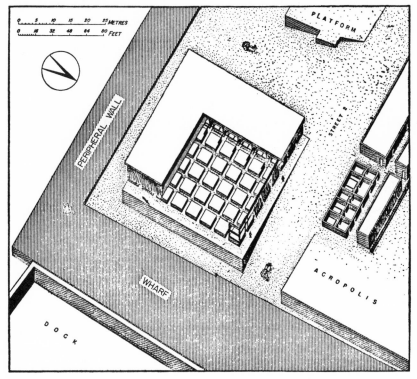

From S. R. Rao, *Lothal and the Indus Civilization*, Asia Publishing House, New York, 1971

scale. There were streets running north-south and east-west to form a grid, elaborate drains and baths, granaries or warehouses, and a raised platform reminiscent of platforms in the "citadels" of Mohenjo-daro and Harappa. There was also a structure like nothing yet reported from any Indus settlement—a pool wide as a football field, more than two football fields long, surrounded by a brick wall fifteen feet high, with a spillway and a sluice gate at one end. Textbooks refer to it as a dock and although few experts accept that interpretation, no one has come up with a better idea.

The site provides evidence for what may have been a far-reaching agricultural experiment. The Indus state had extended itself just about as far as growing conditions for wheat and barley would permit, to the limits of the subcontinent's temperate zones. Further expansion into tropical zones depended on the development of new crops, and farmers, perhaps working in an emergency atmosphere of threatening food shortages, seem to have taken steps in that direction. Imbedded in mud-plaster fragments of a granary-like structure at Lothal are husks of rice, and husk imprints have been found elsewhere on pottery and bricks. Since rice never became an important item in early Indus diets, the suggestion is that the husks represent an effort that did not succeed, at least not for those people in those times. But it may have paid off for later generations who learned from such experiences, who developed rice as a staple, and who established cities and states in other parts of India, especially in the Ganges River plains.

Lothal served as one of the main outposts of the state, a major shipping, manufacturing and trading center. Its most prominent industry was bead-making. A bead factory, several small rooms around a central courtyard, included a furnace for heating carnelian (which intensifies the mineral's natural red color), drills and chisels, and hundreds of finished and unfinished beads of agate, jasper, opal and other semiprecious stones as well as carnelian. Findings in other workshop areas include anvils, bronze drills, crucibles, pieces of conch shell, copper ingots, and whole and partly sawed elephant tusks.

Gregory Possehl of the University of Pennsylvania pictures Lothal as a "gateway," a settlement on the frontier between the Indus state and hinterland territories to the north, south and east, perhaps through the Persian Gulf to Sumer, "sitting at the hub of what must have been a complex and continuous exchange network." It dealt with people in the back country, hunter-gatherers known by several hundred sites in the area. Like their remote descendants, today's hunter-gatherers, they lived by trading forest products for the products of settled communities. In exchange for such goods as grain and bronze tools they provided the copper, agate, ivory and other raw materials required by people in towns and cities.

Other gateways opened on other regions, gateways through which many kinds of people with a diversity of goods and ideas passed in and out of the Indus Valley. The state was exposed to an unusually wide variety of influences and, as a result, it has been regarded as something derivative, a kind of second-rate system which had little of its own to give and took a great deal from others, notably from Sumer.

The extreme version of this viewpoint was more popular a generation or two ago than it is today, a point emphasized in Chapter 1. It represented Sumer as the source of all good things, a place inhabited by a breed of especially gifted and resourceful people. Once they had brought civilization into being, it spread to other areas where enlightened natives proceeded to develop civilizations of their own. The assumption is that civilization offered so much of such overwhelming value that those capable of adopting it did so as expeditiously as possible, and that civilization can be adopted by decision.

Few investigators subscribe to these notions today. Even without Sumer's shining example, states would have emerged in the Indus Valley and in other regions as well. Change was under way in several parts of the Iranian Plateau, for example, in Central Asia to the east of the Caspian Sea and about equally distant from Uruk and Mohenjo-daro. Masson describes Altin, the site which yielded a hoard of ivory objects, as an "incipient urban community." It covered more than a hundred acres and had a six-acre pottery-making area, a large central square and a ziggurat. Furthermore, the 200-acre site of Namazga lay only fifty miles away, suggesting that a new city-state complex was in the making.

Conditions favoring such systems seem to have been widespread around 2000 B.C. What happened in Sumer nevertheless might have accelerated the pace of change. When people are struggling with problems new to them, it helps to have other people around who have been dealing with similar problems for some time and who have learned a thing or two from past mistakes. The elites responsible for organizing the Indus state may have met and exchanged ideas with fellow elites and their representatives from the western end of the Iranian Plateau, and profited from the encounters. Nevertheless they evolved their own traditions and institutions.

Stone seals, usually square or rectangular and about the size of postage stamps, depict various aspects of Indian life. Carvings represent animals first domesticated in India from approximately 2700 B.C. to 2000 B.C.: humped cattle related to the gaur or wild ox of Southeast Asia and Malaya, water buffalos, and elephants. (The chicken or a chicken-like bird, another original Indian domesticate, is not shown on seals; its traces consist mainly of bones found at Mohenjo-daro.) There are men on the hunt, going after deer and other wild animals with spears and bows and arrows; two small animals leaping at birds and women at work nearby; a high-prowed river boat with a central cabin and double steering oar.

A menagerie of imaginary animals appears on the seals—unicorned beasts and creatures half man and half tiger, three-headed antelopes and a bull with an elephant's tusk. An Indian Hercules with feet planted firmly on the ground is strangling two tigers, one in each hand. There are people in processions carrying banners, a man with a horned headdress, and a woman seated before an armed man and apparently about to be sacrificed. These are themes of myth and ceremony.

Vignettes in stone, these scenes reveal disconnected glimpses into an alien and remote way of life. They raise many questions and, for all we know, some of the answers may be inscribed on the seals themselves, because most have "captions," writing in the official script of the Indus state. Although the writing cannot yet be translated, a good start has been made by four Finnish investigators associated with the Scandinavian Institute of Asian Affairs, Asko Parpola, his brother Simo, Seppo Koskenniemi, and Penti Aalto—specialists, respectively, in Hindu sacred writings, Assyrian history, computer science and linguistics. They analyzed the in-

From Walter A. Fairservis, Jr. Vassar College and the American Museum of Natural History, *The Roots of Ancient India*, Macmillan, copyright © 1971 by Walter A. Fairservis, Jr.

Stone seals and potters' marks, Indus Valley: seals with scenes of adoration or sacrifice with predecessor of Hindu deity; early "signatures" of craftsmen

scriptions on nearly 2,000 seals, a total of more than 9,000 occurrences of about 300 different signs, a few of which were borrowed from potters' marks, simple "signatures" identifying the works of individual craftsmen. These raw facts were fed into a computer and in a matter of hours a mass of detailed and highly organized information emerged.

The computer compiled the number of times each sign appeared, the number of times it appeared at the beginning and end of inscriptions, the frequencies of sign-pairs from the commonest to the rarest, and a table listing the complete texts of all inscriptions in which a given sign appears. Deductions from the data included the identification of the genitive or possessive sign ⅂ʃ which, if it occurs at the end of an inscription, is probably associated with the name and description of the individual owning the seal and the goods stamped with the seal.

The Finnish investigators then made the crucial assumption that early Indians spoke a version of the so-called Dravidian languages used today in southern India, northern Ceylon and a small mountain region not far to the west of the Indus Valley. They also concluded that each sign stands for a word rather than a syllable. On that basis they made further deductions; for example, a frequent fish sign probably refers to astral deities since the word "min" in Dravidian means both fish and star. Other tentative translations:

woman   man   merchant   priest

The symbol for woman, by the way, may represent a comb.

The British linguist, John Chadwick, of the University of Cambridge, has criticized this work, yet he ends on a very positive note: "What we still need is . . . the clearest possible demonstration that these meanings, and only these meanings, are correct. . . . We must not be led into admiring a house of cards which, elegant as it seems, will collapse if one prop is withdrawn. . . . But the case itself looks extremely promising." Advances in the continuing study may well enrich the meanings of the figures and scenes on the seals.

Another mark of the Indus state is the "miles of monotony" that so appalled Wheeler. As already suggested, that monotony applies chiefly to the main streets, and things were not so neatly laid out in living areas off the main streets. Yet there does seem to have been a basic sameness among Indus centers which implies the existence of a master plan or blueprint, a single agreed-upon way of doing things, conceived and carried out by skilled architects and builders. As Fairservis emphasizes, it implies a good deal more:

> One cannot but be impressed with the urban order, the modular planning, the uniformity of the great . . . sites. There is little indication of the twisted and chaotic lanes of the traditional Eastern city with its confusion of byways and thoroughfares. Rather it is as if each segment of the population knew precisely that there was only one way to live together—by conformity to a time-honored plan given its validity by one's forefathers.

A further implication is the suggestion that one of the institutions unique to twentieth-century India had its origin in the appearance of the subcontinent's first state. Early efforts to create and maintain order among many different kinds of people in a transition region between east and west may have produced a caste system which later generations refined and elaborated. The system still flourishes.

Some of the beliefs behind the institution have also endured. One of the 1,200 seals recovered at Mohenjo-daro shows a figure adorned with bangles, bracelets and a large buffalo-horn head-dress. He is sitting with his legs crossed under him, feet heel to heel, toes pointing down, arms outstretched and hands turned thumbs outward—a typical Yoga position. He looks very much like contemporary gods, a prototype or forerunner of Shiva the Destroyer, one of the three chief deities worshipped by Hindus today (the other two being Vishnu the Preserver and Brahma the Creator), perhaps the most remarkable example of the persistence of Indus tradition.

10

Ritual and Control in the Far East

*The evolutionary "hot spot" in China/
The oldest known pottery/The writing on
oracle bones/The good earth and the worship
of male ancestors/Mass human sacrifices/
The gardens of Southeast Asia/The evidence for
rice-growing/The earliest bronzes/The city in
Vietnam's Mekong Delta/Effigy mounds/
The most elaborate pyramid*

INVESTIGATORS are having a difficult time excavating a mound in northern Thailand. A bustling modern village of more than a thousand persons is located on that mound; houses cover most of the places believed to contain ancient graves or public buildings. Work must proceed at second-best or third-best places between houses or in backyards, if permission can be obtained. While such problems may turn up anywhere in the world, they seem to turn up more frequently in the Far East, and that was apparently the case long before current population explosions. Archeologically speaking, a "permanent" village is usually one that has been occupied for a few generations or a few centuries. Many Far Eastern sites, the mound in Thailand among them, have been occupied continuously for 5,000 or more years.

215

The Far East, a 10,000,000-square-mile search area: region of some of the richest and most promising archeological finds, where recent studies have provided insights into evolutionary processes in North China and Southeast Asia

North China nuclear area, an evolutionary "hot spot:" the great bend in the Yellow River, China's nuclear area, where human beings have lived for 750,000 or more years, region also of the earliest known farming villages and cities of the Far East, and a flourishing industrial center today

There is a mystery, a challenge, here. This part of the world has not been exceptionally peaceful. It has had its share of turmoil, of raiding and plunder and all-out warfare; its towns and cities have been destroyed and rebuilt and destroyed again. But through it all, in some areas, people have achieved a striking persistence of location, a sustained balance with the land. The story of beginnings is as elusive in the Far East as elsewhere, and perhaps a bit more so. A staggering amount of research remains to be done in the vast region of roughly ten million square miles. But the general outlines of at least two quite different processes are already evident, one under way in northern China and the other in Southeast Asia including southern China, Burma, Thailand, Cambodia, Vietnam, Malaysia and the Philippines.

One area of intensive Chinese development was a remarkable strip or corridor of land, a so-called nuclear area, hemmed in by mountains and high plateaus to the north, south and west, and opening on a wide prospect of flat plains to the east. The Wei River rushes into the corridor through a narrow channel, almost a gorge, 180 miles west of the modern city of Sian and flows due east to join the Yellow River at its great bend on the way to the Yellow Sea.

This area was, and still is, an evolutionary hot spot. Fossil traces show that the first human beings in the Far East, pre-*Homo*

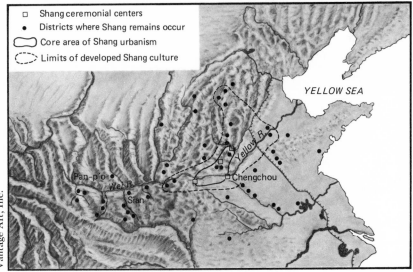

sapiens hunter-gatherers, roamed the hills, forests and plains around Sian more than 750,000 years ago—and their descendants, farmers and artisans and aristrocrats and industrialists, have been active there on and off ever since. China's first emperor, Ch'in Shih Huang Ti who ruled from 221 B.C. to 210 B.C. and built the Great Wall, had his capital not far from the city. Archeologists digging in another part of the region recently unearthed relics of a dynasty that flourished some thousand years later, a hoard of gold and silver vessels, jade objects and precious stones. Today in the same countryside life proceeds more intensively than ever. It is now a major industrial center, and includes one of the nation's largest nuclear power plants.

There can be no easy answer to the question of why so much has been happening in and around this valley for so long. In the beginning it was partly a combination of convenient living sites and abundant waters which nourished plants and attracted man and his prey. Later it was the fish in the waters, providing an additional source of food and permitting people to live in one place year-round. Still later, with the rise of agriculture, it was the good earth.

Ping-ti Ho of the University of Chicago emphasizes the enduring, self-sustaining quality of the pale yellow, wind-deposited soil which could hardly have been improved upon if it had been designed specially for farming. Known as loess, it is rich in organic material, the residue of generations of grass stems and roots. Furthermore, when the stems and roots decay they leave "holes," tubular channels through which mineral salts are drawn toward the surface by capillary action after it rains. The soil also happens to be loose, readily broken up for cultivation, and constantly replenished by fresh dust blown in from the west.

This land supported the people of Pan-p'o, a large prehistoric village located near Sian on the bank of a tributary of the Wei River. A twelve-acre oval with the long axis pointing north-south, it included a cemetery, a concentration of half a dozen pottery kilns, a residential district surrounded by a ditch nearly twenty feet deep and about as wide, and more than 500 persons. The plant and animal remains found there are domesticated millet, leaf-mustard or Chinese cabbage, and an abundance of pig and dog bones, all with a special significance in light of a series of carbon-

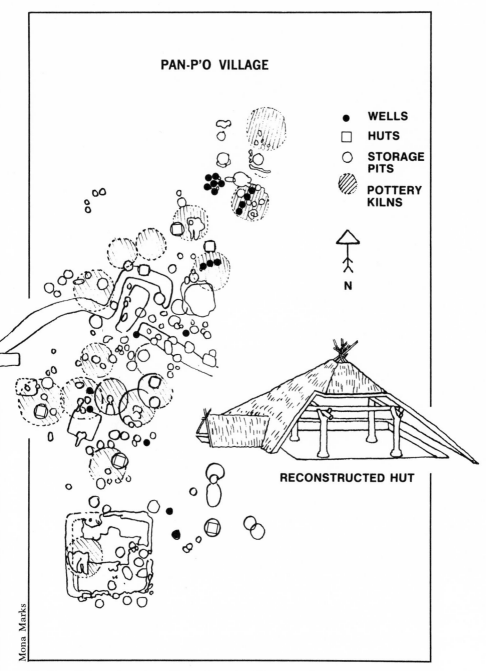

PAN-P'O VILLAGE

- ● WELLS
- □ HUTS
- ○ STORAGE PITS
- ▨ POTTERY KILNS

N

RECONSTRUCTED HUT

Mona Marks

Earliest Chinese farming village: Pan-p'o village, northern Hunan, China

14 dates recently reported by the Institute of Archeology in Peking. The community was flourishing more than 6,000 years ago, making it the oldest extensively excavated agricultural village in the entire Far East.

Pan-p'o, which means "halfway up the slope," was one of some 400 sites occurring in clusters above the Wei River Valley, in narrow side valleys along Wei tributaries. The sites often come in pairs half a mile to a mile apart, facing each other from opposite riverbanks, a pattern which existed at about the same time in the Uruk countryside some 3,500 miles to the west. And the odds are that hierarchies were developing in China as well as Sumer. Pan-p'o, the largest site in its cluster, was near the floor of the Wei Valley, and may have served as a center in a local exchange system which used the river below as a main thoroughfare.

These were early settlements, but not the earliest. Farmers worked in the area and elsewhere long before 4100 B.C., the oldest carbon-14 date from Pan-p'o. The village's pattern of residential district, cemetery and pottery-kiln center is repeated in other villages, a sort of traditional planning. Furthermore, although people still gathered wild grains and vegetables and hunted deer and other game, everything points to a heavy dependence on domesticated species, a dependence which must have been based on previous experience accumulated over a long period.

Research in Taiwan by Kwang-chih Chang of Yale University and his associates suggests the possibility of more ancient origins. They are working in a beautiful river valley not far from the Sun-Moon Lake at the island's center where hills, trees and gorges resemble the "stylized" scenes in Chinese prints. The lake itself has provided evidence of possible early beginnings in the form of a pollen core resembling those obtained by Singh in the Indian Desert and hinting at similar conditions. The record shows warmer climates starting more than 10,000 years ago, a dwindling of the primeval pine-hemlock forests, a gradual increase in cereal pollens, and a sudden increase in fragments of charred wood which may be traces of fires set by slash-and-burn agriculturalists to clear land for cultivation.

Further hints come from a type of decoration on pottery found recently near Sun-Moon Lake as well as at many other sites in

Sun-Moon Lake, central Taiwan: source of pollen samples showing changes in climate and land use

Taiwan and elsewhere during the past few decades. The decoration consists of patterns pressed into soft clay, parallel lines and cross-hatching and diamond-shaped meshes, but the patterns are not nearly as interesting as the material used to make them. The material was cord, probably made from bark or hemp, and in many cases you can see in detail how skillfully it was prepared. The clay contains fine lines showing different ways of twisting many strands together into a strong, tightly interwoven finished product.

The cord was not made simply to decorate pottery. It found extensive use in fishing lines and nets, and Chang speculates that fishing was one sign of a settling-down process like that in the Near East. People in the east as in the west may have multiplied to a point where no more uninhabited valleys were available. If so, they turned increasingly to new food resources close at hand and once of secondary importance only, particularly to abundant and protein-rich aquatic resources. Carl Sauer of the University of California in Berkeley developed this theory more than fifty years ago. He also suggested that the first domesticated plants may not have been food plants, but hemp and other species useful in the manufacture of fishing equipment.

Cord-marked pottery was made not only in Taiwan and the China mainland, but throughout the Far East from Siberia to Indonesia (and is still being made in many places). If future excavations confirm the notion that it is an indirect sign of a settled way of life, of villages and homesteads and fishing on a large scale, then agriculture in this part of the world may have had very early beginnings indeed. The oldest pottery known has been found in two caves, one in western Japan and the other in the central Yangtze River Valley of China, in occupation levels that are more than 10,000 years old, and it is cord-marked.

A long and barely discernible past preceded the clustering of villages along Wei River tributaries. And some time later, perhaps around 3000 B.C., a splitting or budding-off process began. Groups of farmers left friends and relatives and walked down ancestral side-valley slopes for the last time, past the bend in the Yellow River and out onto unfamiliar, sparsely settled lowlands. Apparently it was another "spilling over the edge" of overflow populations, the same sort of phenomenon that occurred in Mesopotamia and India. Chang calls it "a rapid, almost explosive, expansion."

A main thrust of the migration was due east and south into wide plains extending from the loess lands to the seacoast. It takes some kind of pressure, population pressure usually, to bring about such moves. Given a choice, people in China and elsewhere apparently prefer homesteads facing open spaces but with something at their backs, a hillside or cliff or forest, to an exposed life smack in the center of things. Settlements tended to be larger than before on the flat grasslands with a number of new features, among them polished sickle-shaped knives, double-pronged digging sticks, domesticated chickens in addition to pigs and dogs, and distinctive pottery including cord-marked varieties.

The earliest traces of cultivated rice in China, imprints of grains on a sherd, also date to about 4000 B.C. to 3000 B.C. Farmers had entered natural rice country in the course of their move from highlands to lowlands, to rainier terrain with swampy areas along slow meandering rivers. As indicated in Chapter 3, this is the same sort of terrain where the ancestors of all rices, wild and domestic, originated. Stebbins suggests that rice, and other grasses adapted to wet soils, evolved tens of millions of years ago from seeds blown down from mountain slopes in Central Asia.

Increasingly intensive clustering occurred on the northern plains, and the first Chinese cities began taking shape around 2000 B.C. What has endured aboveground is not spectacular. The people built with earth and wood and perhaps, for special structures, with the most versatile and ungrasslike of all grasses, bamboo. Therefore no mounds or citadels or towers mark their passing. The most impressive features are hidden, structures of earth buried in the earth. The wall enclosing one of the oldest known cities, Chengchou, dated roughly to 1600 B.C. and located at the conflux of the Yellow River and two of its important tributaries, was constructed of layers of earth packed tight by pounding to a maximum height of more than 30 feet and a maximum width at the base of about 120 feet.

There are less massive symbols of power, and danger. Outside the city wall at distances of a few hundred yards to a few miles were satellite workshops and settlements catering to elite insiders. The complex included two bronze foundries, among the earliest yet discovered in China, with special molds for the casting of arrowheads, socketed ax heads, and decorated vessels; a workshop for making arrowheads and hairpins out of bones, about half of them animal (pig, cattle, deer) and half human; several pottery-making locations; and a concentration of large jars perhaps from an ancient winery.

As far as the seat of power and the people who lived inside the walls are concerned, Chengchou has little to tell us. Practically all of its walled area lies beneath a bustling modern city of the same name. Another city, about 100 miles to the northwest on top of the Huan River and founded perhaps two centuries later, helps fill the gap. There was nothing overtly urban about the ancient center of Anyang. It was surrounded by forests. In the clearings between the forests and the river banks were wooden buildings with thatched roofs, long houses and rectangular compounds enclosing plazas, fields and clusters of little conical huts. It might easily be mistaken at first for an African village, but that notion changes as one observes the scale of things. The "village" occupied both sides of the river, extended for more than three miles, and like Chengchou was surrounded by a system of satellite communities.

Continuing excavations, begun in 1928 and interrupted for more than a decade by Japanese invasions during World War II, indicate that Anyang was the last capital of China's first archeologically substantiated dynasty, the Shang dynasty. It includes an elite residential section, fifteen houses built on pounded-earth platforms, one of them—presumably a royal palace and appropriately decorated—about 200 feet long and more than twice as large as the next largest. Servants, laborers and other lesser persons had their places ten feet below ground, in circular pit houses about fifteen feet across. Many still smaller pits served as workshops and storage bins.

The site has yielded the earliest known samples of a developed Chinese script inscribed on the shoulder blades of animals, chiefly oxen, and tortoise shells. The beginnings of writing, in China as elsewhere, date back long before writing appears in an advanced form. Some 6,000 years ago Pan-p'o potters scratched twenty-two different marks on the outer rims of certain widely

EARLY CHINESE NUMERALS

	ABOUT 4000 B.C.	AFTER 1300 B.C.	1300- 1028 B.C.	MODERN
	A	B	C	D
1				
2				
3				
4				
5				

Early Chinese numerals: (a) Pan-p'o sherds; (b) Anyang pottery; (c) Anyang oracle-bone inscriptions; (d) modern version

Mona Marks

used bowls and, according to Ho, five of the marks represent numerals (1, 2, 5, 7, and 8), three may identify the family or individual owning the vessel, and the rest remain undeciphered.

Later techniques are known only from references in historical texts. Scribes wrote with pens and brushes, first used in decorating pottery, on slivers of wood or bamboo or strips of silk, and bound the "pages" together like books. They wrote about important state events, but their archives have long since crumbled to dust. Also missing if they ever existed (and they must have) are detailed records of the flow of food and other goods, the sort of orders and bills and receipts preserved on clay tablets from Sumer where writing seems to have arisen primarily to handle such dealings. No traces of the corresponding Shang records survive.

What has endured, what was considered important enough to register on enduring materials, involves status and ritual and religious beliefs. The inscribed objects unearthed at Anyang, some

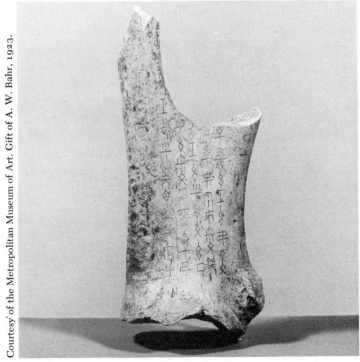

Courtesy of the Metropolitan Museum of Art. Gift of A. W. Bahr, 1923.

Fortunetelling: oracle-bone with inscriptions, Shang dynasty, 13th-11th century, B.C.

30,000 of them, were regarded as communications with another world, the dwelling place of venerated ancestors. Known as "oracle bones," they were part of an elaborate ritual for consulting the spirits of the dead, a ritual still practiced today in some villages.

The middlemen in this procedure, diviners or mediums of a sort, worked on selected fragments of bone and shell. They made carefully placed pits and grooves and then applied intense heat at just the right spot, perhaps using a burning grease-soaked wick or a red-hot bronze point. The heat brought the dead bone to life. Fine cracks appeared on the surface, indicating that a gate had been opened to the spirit world. The job of the diviner was to read in the pattern of cracks ancestors' answers to the questions of the living.

Investigators can translate only about a third of the 3,000 different characters in the inscriptions, but that is enough to provide some insights into the homely concerns of Anyang elites, chiefly kings. They wanted their fortunes told. Is my dream a bad or a good omen? Will I be successful in battle? In the hunt? Will the weather be favorable? My child, will it be a boy or a girl? And, most important, will the gods help me? Sometimes they did not ask questions, but simply informed their ancestors of recent family events.

Consulting oracle bones was not a casual, occasional thing. It was a daily routine and, along with sacrifices and other practices, one of the most important ways of keeping in touch, maintaining intimate and continuing ties, with beings no longer visible but very much present. "The core of ancient Chinese religion is ancestor worship," Ho writes, "and ancestor worship has contributed significantly to the extraordinary enduring quality of Chinese civilization."

Ancestor worship had deep roots. It was related to rural days and the place where one was born and, above all, to the rich self-sustaining yellow earth in which things grew so abundantly for so long. It had the intensity of generation after generation, century after century, of living in one locality where each feature, each hill and stream and grove of trees, was as familiar as family itself. It helps account for the continuous occupation of many Chinese sites, some for 6,000 or more years. The world of the

Shang had five cardinal directions: north, south, east, west, and the place where the king and his ancestors lived. Buildings and tombs at Anyang were aligned in a north-south direction.

All this is part of what made the earliest known religion of China uniquely Chinese. One thing, however, was not unique, the role religion eventually came to play in the Shang and later dynasties. A view of life and afterlife with many distinctive local aspects was adapted to problems which confronted all people, in Sumer and the Indus Valley and elsewhere as well as in China. Belief became part of the apparatus of power. In the beginning, in hamlet and small-village times, ancestor worship was presumably a direct personal experience, an intimate matter between a family and a beloved and recently deceased and still missed parent or grandparent. The event was commemorated by the sacrifice of a sheep or pig buried in a small pit on the home site, perhaps to provide nourishment for the spirit of the departed.

The scale of the ritual had changed by Shang times. People living close to one another in and around cities had to be managed and, according to the Li-chi or Record of Rituals, a second-century text, "rites obviate disorder as dikes prevent inundation." That means a whole new set of elaborate and formal relationships between the living and the dead, as leaders called publicly and grandly on their ancestors for guidance and validation. They called on ancestors less recent, less fresh in memory (belonging to lineages dating back as much as half a millennium), more powerful and dangerous, and rather voracious. Burials, building temples and palaces, holidays and other occasions demanded more frequent sacrifices with larger pits and larger numbers of animals, up to several hundred at a time.

The nature of the sacrifices changed. Among the animals were increasing numbers of human victims, perhaps the most dramatic sign of utter control over people's lives. The royal cemetery of Anyang featured a cross-shaped superpit more than thirty feet deep, the famous tomb No. 1001, complete with artifacts of bronze and jade, including a pair of bronze chopsticks and at least 164 dismembered men. More than 600 individuals were killed in the hallowing of a single temple.

Warfare and sacrifice played a prominent role in ancestor worship, Shang style. It was all part of the current technology of

Photo by K. C. Chang, Yale University

Deep-pit tomb at Anyang, Shang dynastic capital about 1350 B.C., northern Hunan, China

control. Shang armies fought not for conquest or land, but for people. Using the latest military equipment, notably western-style horse-drawn chariots, they developed swift roundup and bring-them-back-alive tactics against their enemies. They marched captives by thousands through the main streets of Anyang to provide vivid reminders for all to see and wonder at of the king's absolute power, to serve as slave labor, and, their ultimate function, to be ceremoniously decapitated as offerings to royal ancestors. Incidentally, the word used to describe most captives is "Ch'iang," a combination of the pictographic symbols for sheep and men, which refers to people living in the northwest and suggests that they were nomadic herders.

Writing provides a clue to another characteristic of the Shang world view. According to Ho, in oracle-bone inscriptions concerned with forecasting the sex of royal babies the word "good" refers to boys and "not good" to girls, one of many indications that women enjoyed secondary status at best. The only ancestors who really counted were male ancestors, and ancestor worship was primarily the worship of males and maleness. The character for ancestor was a phallic symbol.

On the plains of northern China, people confronted with law-and-order problems similar to those that arose in western lands evolved some institutions and traditions that were distinctly their own, their own brand of ancestor worship, attachment to the land, oracle-bone divination and inscriptions, and so on. There were universal responses as well—ceremony on the grand scale, art mobilized for the production of luxury and prestige objects, warfare and human sacrifices, and a strong element of male chauvinism—all part of the bizarre process sometimes loosely referred to as civilization.

Southeast Asia, on the other hand, has until recently been regarded as a prehistoric backwater stuck fast in the stone age. Investigators, predominantly westerners, somehow never expected interesting or important things to happen in a tropical setting. Reflecting old colonial attitudes, they regarded Southeast Asia as white-man's burden, Kipling territory which had borrowed heavily from the rest of the world and given mighty little in return. As the pace of research quickens, however, it is becoming quite clear that change came as early here as elsewhere.

People acting in response to the same forces at work in Sumer and the Indus Valley and northern China evolved different subsistence patterns. Between 10,000 and 15,000 years ago they were exploiting their lands intensively, sometimes concentrating on relatively few food species and sometimes on a wide variety. Rising population densities and rising seas provided the pressure. Waters flowing back into the oceans from melting glaciers covered gently sloping continental shelves and effectively deprived people of large stretches of valuable territory. Although the waters rose all over the world, the flooding was much more extensive in Southeast Asia, where it submerged about half the total land area.

This region featured a life-style unlike anything in the west, a life-style marked by gardening and diversity. People developed their own form of slash-and-burn or "swidden" agriculture. They cleared areas of forest by cutting and burning, cultivated many plants for a few years and then, as fertility began to decline, moved to another part of the forest, usually not far away.

There were probably little gardens everywhere, not unlike the one I saw in the Amazon Basin (see Chapter 3), sources of food and "agricultural experiment stations" where people learned about new plants and ways of growing them. The gardening system has been called "a canny imitation of nature." It may look messy and haphazard, but so does nature. Its strength lies in preserving much of the diversity of things. Harold Conklin of Yale University describes a highly evolved version of the system as practiced late in the rice-growing season by present-day farmers in the Philippines:

At the sides and against the swidden fences there is found an association dominated by low, climbing or sprawling legumes (asparagus beans, sieve beans, hyacinth beans, string beans and cowpeas). As one goes out into the center of the swidden, one passes through an association dominated by ripening grain crops but also including numerous maturing root crops, shrub legumes and tree crops. Pole-climbing yam vines, heart-shaped taro leaves, ground-hugging sweet potato vines and shrublike manioc stems are the only visible signs of the large store of starch staples which are building up underground, while the grain crops fruit a meter or so above the swidden floor before giving way to the more widely spaced and less rapidly maturing tree crops.

A highland cave nearly half a mile up the face of a steep limestone cliff in northern Thailand, near the Burma border, has yielded evidence of simpler prehistoric gardens. It includes a hearth, charred pieces of bamboo two to three inches in diameter, bone fragments, shells and fish vertebrae, and abundant remains of bottle gourd as well as water chestnut, a cucumber, pepper, almond, and a beanlike seed. Chester Gorman of the University of Pennsylvania, who found and excavated the so-called Spirit Cave site, describes a meal eaten there at least 9,000 years ago. The cave dwellers built fires, chopped pork, venison and other meats into small pieces, added selected vegetables and seasonings, boiled the ingredients in bamboo "pots" as peasants do today in the same area, and prepared tasty soups and stews.

Gorman believes that this sort of living may represent one form of a pattern that evolved thousands of years earlier, perhaps in low-lying country. The gardeners were not farmers. They were hunter-gatherers supplementing their diets by bringing local plants to plots near their huts. They grew varieties of taro and yams with tubers weighing from five to ten pounds on the average, and sometimes swelling to ten times that bulk. Rice may also have been present, but on the outside looking in, as it were.

According to one theory, rice—the grass which now serves as a food staple for more than half the world's population and permits rural densities of as many as 5,000 persons per square mile—may once have been a perennial and persisting weed on the edges of taro gardens. Later it was brought in and accepted as a member of the garden club, but only as a second-class member. There is some disagreement on when it became an important crop. Gorman favors an early date on the basis of evidence which appears on a Spirit Cave living floor: pottery, adzes which may have been used to break up the soil, and small slate knives like those used today in harvesting.

He is convinced that these artifacts were associated with the large-scale exploitation of rice, and domesticated rice at that, by lowlanders—and that highlanders at Spirit Cave and elsewhere borrowed the practice. This implies rice agriculture earlier than 6800 B.C., the date of the Spirit Cave living floor, rather too early for most investigators. The general opinion is that rice became a major crop probably after overflow populations began moving from highlands to lowlands as they seem to have done between 5000 B.C. and 4000 B.C. in Southeast Asia (as compared to about 7500 B.C. in the Near East and 3000 B.C. in northern China).

Direct evidence of rice comes from a site in the foothills of a "ring mountain," a craterlike formation fifteen miles across and located nearly 300 miles southeast of Spirit Cave. Non Nok Tha, a low mound set like an island in a sea of rice paddies, has been excavated by Donn Bayard and Hamilton Parker of the University of Otago in Dunedin, New Zealand. They report grain imprints on sherds and rice chaff as a tempering material in pottery clays from levels dating to at least 3000 B.C., although those traces cannot be positively identified as signs of domesticated rather than wild rice.

Although the site is small, little more than one acre, it was by no means a simple village. "I was walking toward the site across the rice fields," Parker recalls, "when I saw Donn jumping up and down and waving to me. He had found something we never ex-

Courtesy of Northeast Thailand Archaeological Projects,
University Museum, University of Pennsylvania

Ban Chiang, northeast Thailand: village with houses on stilts on ancient
burial and habitation mound; early bronze spear head and pottery,
circa 3600 B.C.

pected to find in an early occupation level, something at least a millennium 'premature'—a pair of sandstone molds for the casting of socketed bronze ax heads. After that, nothing surprised us." The molds indicate that advanced bronze-working may have appeared in the region around 3000 B.C., or at least a millennium before it appeared in China.

Even earlier dates may come from Ban Chiang, a village which lies more than 100 miles to the northeast and, along with other villages in the surrounding countryside, has become a center for illegitimate as well as legitimate digging. Ban Chiang is a community of houses on stilts built on an ancient burial mound about a mile square. It was excavated during the 1960s by an archeologist of the National Museum in Bangkok and later by a number of amateurs who unearthed a variety of items featuring beautiful pots painted in red and white.

News of these finds, and rumors of associated bronze tools, produced feverish activity in the village. One reporter on the scene included the following account in a cable to his New York office: "With this extraordinary dating, two thousand years earlier than expected, the rush was on, and collectors with truckloads of pots, bronze and other artifacts were soon hauling out tens of thousands of pieces. For forty or fifty dollars a pot, villagers literally destroyed their houses (fifty dollars a pot being half the annual income in this, the most impoverished part of Thailand), while collectors would sell the pots for thousands."

Allowing for some exaggeration, this is a reasonably sound version of what happened. The site was too big and too deep to be destroyed completely, however. Digging more than twenty feet deep, Gorman and Pisit Charoenwongsa of the National Museum of Bangkok found undisturbed graves with pots and bronze tools and jewelry which may have been made as early as 3600 B.C. Such investigations suggest the existence of trade networks involving, among other things, supplies of copper and tin for the making of bronze, and perhaps people in charge of the mining and trade.

Analysis of the grave goods associated with more than 100 Non Nok Tha burials indicates power beginning to emerge, and a widening of the gap among classes during the time that bronze first came into use. The proportion of elaborate burials, measured by the quantity and variety of pottery, beads, ax heads and large bronze bracelets, increases between about 3000 B.C. and 2000 B.C. Bayard distinguishes three classes by their graves: poor, wealthy, and very wealthy. Almost all of the bronze artifacts are found in wealthy burials, a mark of the alloy's importance as a status symbol.

Perhaps the most significant point about the coming of highly developed agriculture, metal-working, trade networks and hierarchies in Southeast Asia is something negative, something that did not happen. While in Sumer, the Indus Valley and northern China such changes accompanied mass movements into urban centers and the coming of a centralized political authority, in Southeast Asia there may have been a lag of as much as three to four thousand years. According to Wheatley, city-states did not appear until early in the Christian era, although other investigators believe that the region's first urban centers may have appeared nearly a millennium earlier.

Research at Chansen in south central Thailand illustrates the pace of development. This is primarily an "indicator" site, in the sense that its chief importance lies in what it reveals about events in other areas, at sites many of which have not been discovered

Chansen, Thailand, ivory comb from the National Museum, Bangkok: possibly earliest Hindu-Buddhist object (c. A.D., 50–200) found in Southeast Asia, photo (left) and drawings of front and back (above)

and may be lost forever. Bennet Bronson of Chicago's Field Museum of Natural History and Dales report that settlers first came here some time before 500 B.C., and have found in successively higher and more recent archeological levels evidence of major changes under way elsewhere.

The first clear-cut sign of change appears in the record half a millennium later. The pottery contrasts sharply with that found in the earliest levels, with its several distinctive types of decorated bowls. It resembles pottery found at a number of cities in India, implying influence from the west—some thousands of miles away —and a rather pervasive influence at that, since Chansen was off the beaten-track trade routes of the times. Another find points in the same direction, an ivory comb engraved with horses, a plumed goose, and Buddhist emblems characteristic of a city on India's east coast, dated as early as A.D. 50. It may be the earliest Indian artifact yet found in Southeast Asia.

Two or three centuries later the village of Chansen reflected further changes, this time from the east. The markers include many twisted bands and cast rings made of tin, ceramic stamps perhaps used to print designs on fabrics, small bronze bells with spiral decorations, gold jewelry and molds for making the jewelry —all closely resembling artifacts found in the seat of a half-legendary kingdom in a war-ravaged land 450 miles to the southeast.

Paul Wheatley of the University of Chicago describes the countryside: "Behind its broad fringe of glaucous mangrove, it constituted an enormous sponge of coherent muds and vegetable debris —where a mantle of swamp forest masked such diversification as parallel-trending sand ridges. . . . Through this waste of swamp seeped rather than flowed an infinitude of strangulated streams, a labyrinthine network of waters."

This is Vietnam's Mekong Delta region, the mouth of a river that rises more than 2,500 miles away in the mountains of China and Tibet. A group of half a dozen little mounds with scattered bricks was bombed frequently by American planes during the late war because, like many archeological sites, it looks like a military installation from the air. But looters have done more damage than bombs. The mounds are all that remain of Oc-eo, the earliest known city of Southeast Asia, the probable source of the unusual artifacts found at Chansen, and the probable capital of a kingdom first visited by Chinese envoys around A.D. 220.

Wheatley has recently reconstructed the 1,100-acre center and its surroundings. Some fifteen miles inland from the Gulf of Thailand, it spread out from the foot of a three-peaked granite hill which may have served as a sacred place. The hill's spring provided drinking water when local wells failed in dry seasons. Oc-eo was a city on water, a small-scale Venice. Traffic moved along a system of canals. A 60-mile "Grand Canal" connected the city with back-country villages to the northeast and with the sea.

King and court and commoners lived within a wooden defense wall or palisade in wooden houses thatched with bamboo fronds and raised above the water on wooden piles. Only the gods rated stone and brick, and their temples dominated the city's center. Some looted artifacts bought back at a price are on display in the Saigon Museum. They are gem-studded buckles, pins and rings made of gold, crystal ear pendants and beads, small rings with Sanskrit inscriptions, a Roman gold medal dated A.D. 152, and a life- sized statue of a Hindu-style god.

Oc-eo did not evolve in its delta setting. It was planned, built from scratch. It came full-blown out of a culture about which practically nothing is known. For all the world's billions, there are still wide areas to be explored; there are still a few lost worlds. Notes and abstracts in obscure journals mention great earthworks to the north and west toward the Burma border, enclosures extending several miles, long "effigy" mounds built in the shape of chariots, spearheads, and other forms. We do not know what lies buried in the enclosures and mounds. They have never been excavated, although museums and private collectors undoubtedly possess objects which looters found there and smuggled out of the country and sold for high prices.

From Oc-eo on, the story in Southeast Asia is one of increasing concentration of power and people. The great symbols of power, monumental architecture and towers and pyramids, appeared in central Java between A.D. 700 and A.D. 850. There was a complex of 250 shrines, the grandest of which, the Borobudur not far from Jogjakarta, is being restored with the aid of funds from the United Nations. Probably the most elaborate pyramid ever built, it is a system of stone terraces some fifteen stories high on the

World's most elaborate pyramid, with multiple stone terraces: the Borobudur, Buddhist temple completed in 863 A.D., Java

Detail of temple facade

Sacred city, Angkor Wat, Cambodia: tower foundations

slopes of a natural hill, with more than three miles of winding galleries. According the Wheatley, "the progression from ground level to the summit symbolized successive phases in the attainment of spiritual enlightenment."

The blending of city and symbol culminated around A.D. 1200 with a coalition of chiefs under a paramount chief—and with the spectacular center of Angkor in the lowland jungles of Cambodia, about 100 miles north of Phnom Penh. Angkor was surrounded by a massive ten-mile wall and an outer moat more than 100 yards wide, representing the mountain range and ocean believed to encircle the universe. The king's palace floated above the city on huge columns carved with winged, half-man–half-bird figures.

Divine kingship may have resulted from the intervention of India and China. Picture a countryside of rival leaders, men continually making and breaking alliances with their neighbors but never having the resources necessary to dominate on an enduring basis. Into this setting sail traders from distant places, people looking for metals, spices, gems and timber, and bearing a variety of items to give in exchange. The outsiders land near water, on a coast or inland on the bank of a river, and the entire order of things began to change.

The native leaders nearest the coast or river bank immediately have advantages over their back-country counterparts. Depots grow up, collecting and redistributing centers where goods come from the interior and are exchanged for alien goods. The interests of the coastal leaders, who become middlemen by virtue of geographical location, are more and more closely associated with the interests of the outsiders. The outsiders naturally support them and everyone profits, nuclei of power take shape and a self-amplifying process gathers swift momentum. Somewhere along the line the scale of things changes and one man and one area becomes paramount—and that man justifies his preeminence by claiming divinity.

This happened during the nineteenth century as the British moved into Malaya, and probably nearly 2,000 years ago in Vietnam and Cambodia and Thailand with the arrival of trader-entrepreneurs from India and China. The columns of the king's palace in Angkor were made of stone rather than "mortal" wood, a solid sign that he had achieved immortal status. This sort of development is still taking place in some remote areas, for instance among tribes living in the hills between Burma and Bengal.

So centralization breeds centralization, and there are time lags between early and more recent city-states. The objectives are always the same—power and control. Certain elements like ceremony and hierarchy seem always to be present. But the vernaculars, the forms and expressions, the art styles and human relationships, may differ radically. To cite only one example, Southeast Asia borrowed a great deal from India and China, but never their male chauvinism. For reasons yet to be determined, men and women live together more nearly as equals in Southeast Asia than in any other part of the world.

Another important feature of "the rice-growing world of Southeast Asia" is the observed pattern of change in times past. People adapted differently in different areas, often in areas located quite close to one another. A representative situation existed in the Philippines about a millennium ago on the island of Samar. Here Karl Hutterer of the University of Michigan investigated one area where hunter-gatherers, swidden farmers with stone tools, and more advanced iron-using farmers were all living within a six-mile radius of one another.

This is only one example of a widespread "mosaic" pattern, essentially a mosaic life-style. The variety of adaptations itself is in effect an adaptation. In fact, as Hutterer points out, the variety of human cultures reflects the variety of living things in the tropical forests of Southeast Asia. The dwindling lowland forests of the Malay Peninsula may contain more than 200 different species of trees within about five acres, contrasted with only two dozen or so species for the same area in an exceptionally abundant temperate-zone forest. A similar contrast holds for animals.

People exploited whatever foods and raw materials were available within restricted areas, using whatever hunter-gatherer or farming techniques were appropriate—and instead of changing their techniques when populations increased and scarcities threatened, simply made up for what they lacked by exchanging goods with their neighbors. Such solutions were common in Southeast Asia, but they may also represent an extreme version of a more widespread phenomenon. They probably existed in India and

China as well as in Sumer, where people settled in villages and towns and did business with nomadic hunter-gatherers.

All of which serves as a reminder that stages of development are abstractions, artifacts. Obviously the broad trend has been away from hunting-gathering and toward increasingly intensive farming and city life. Viewed in the process of changing, close up, nothing appears quite that neat. Real life is sloppier, more inventive, rather more complicated and much more interesting.

11

African Origins, African Power

*"The city of the hawk," an early Egyptian capital/
A prehistoric site in the desert/Yam cultivation
in West Africa/Trade routes across the
Sahara/West Africa's first cities and first divine
kings/The iron age in southern Africa/Cast
copper currency/The evolution of
a state in Madagascar*

P REHISTORY began in Africa. The first members of the family of man, chimpanzeelike creatures moving out of forests into open savanna lands, appeared there some fifteen million years ago. Traces of the earliest human beings have been discovered in Kenya and Ethiopia, along with their tools and kill sites and camping grounds. In more recent times the most spectacular and one of the first explosions of power occurred in the great oasis of Egypt, a ribbon of fertile land nourished by the Nile River. Power appeared at successively later times south of the Sahara, in the forests of West Africa, in East African savannas, and in South Africa's Transvaal where all people were hunter-gatherers as recently as fifteen hundred years ago.

243

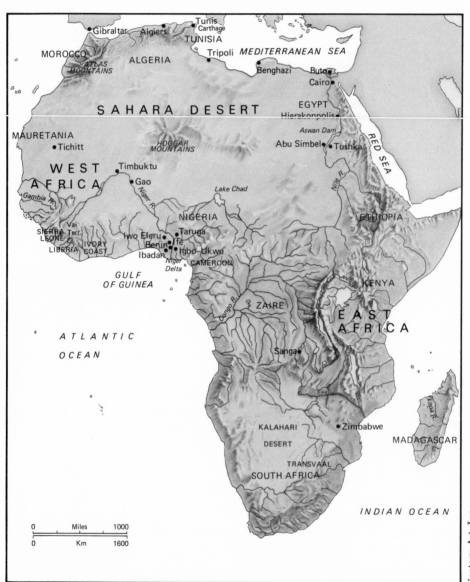

Africa, continent of spreading social change: Egypt, site of early villages and
cities and first appearance of divine kings; further development, south of the
Sahara in West Africa and East Africa; still later in southern Africa; and less
than two centuries ago in Madagascar, perhaps the world's most recent "pristine" or independently evolved state

A spectrum of early-style societies exists in the Kalahari Desert. There are full-time hunter-gatherers, hunter-gatherers doing some farming on the side, hunter-gatherers in the process of settling down, full-time farmers who were hunter-gatherers only a decade or so ago. Africa also includes a state which during the past century or so grew up from simple agricultural beginnings on the island of Madagascar. If archeologists had no other continent to work in, they could dig here and deduce the most important parts of the human story—the passing of equality, the rise of conflict and complexity, the appearance of big men, chiefs, mortal kings, and divine kings.

An important part of the prehistory of Africa lies submerged under 180 feet of water. The flood that reached its height in 1971 was a man-made flood. The Nile, backed up by the Aswan Dam, inundated thousands of square miles of desert rich in remains of times past. "I remember the last day of our work before we had to get out," recalls Fred Wendorf of Southern Methodist University in Dallas, "walking around and seeing sites we had no time to study and being overwhelmed by the vast amount of material left behind."

Before the Aswan flood, Wendorf walked along the west bank of the Nile more than 600 miles south of Cairo, not far from the Abu Simbel cliffs where more than three millenniums ago Rameses II had two temples and four colossal statues of himself carved out of solid rock. He found an earlier and less prepossessing site near the town of Tushka, a patch of desert covered with the debris of old camping grounds, fire-cracked rocks and fossil bones, and thousands of stone tools.

There was also evidence of a change in life-style among hunter-gatherers who had been at large in and around the Nile Valley for several hundred thousand years. Among the traditional-type tools, mainly bladelets and other microliths about three quarters of an inch long or less, were more than a hundred stones heavily worn from grinding, too heavily to have been used solely for making red-ocher powder for paints and cosmetics. The site also included microliths with sickle sheen and signs of having been hafted to a handle and, extracted from the fossil sediments of what had once been a pond, "a few pollen grains of a large wheatlike grass."

This sort of pattern, indicating an increasing dependence on cereal grass seeds, can be interpreted as a mark of subsistence pressure. The unusual thing is that it seems to have happened earlier in Egypt than in the Near East. The Tushka site dates back about 15,000 years, or about a millennium or two older than similar sites in the foothills of Israel and Lebanon. The discovery of further sites to the north suggests that people under pressure were harvesting grasses all along the Nile Valley. There is another sign of stress, perhaps but not necessarily a sign of fighting because of subsistence pressure—a cemetery including six skeletons with sharp stone points imbedded in the bone, the earliest direct evidence of group warfare.

The grasses may or may not have been domesticated. Although no good evidence exists either way, such developments generally represent the early stage of a process that leads to full-scale agriculture. Egypt had a kind of false start. Things ground to a halt, or, more precisely, went into reverse. Instead of becoming farmers, people remained hunter-gatherers and relied less and less on cereal grasses. Fewer grinding tools and sickle blades have been found at later levels. Apparently they solved their problems in other ways, in large part by exploiting fish more intensively.

The pressure was off, but only for the time being. Man's prehistory and history seem to have been a long process of postponing food crises. At this stage in early Egypt it was a long postponement. The problem did not reach major proportions again for more than five thousand years. Full-scale agriculture was established between 5000 B.C. and 4000 B.C. with a complete line of domesticated species: sheep, goats, cattle, pigs, wheat, barley, and associated crops.

Courtesy of Musée de l'Homme, and Guido Majno, University of Massachusetts

Flint arrowhead in a human sternum

From Fred Wendorf, Southern Methodist University, *The Prehistory of Nubia*, vol. 2, Southern Methodist University Press, 1968

Early burial, southern Egypt: markers indicate stone projectile points inbedded in bone

Hunting and herding gazelles on early Egyptian frieze (upper and middle)

A long period of trial and error, dealing with temporary but increasingly urgent subsistence problems one by one as they came up, probably preceded these changes. Saxon has provided hints of what happened. After his studies of prehistoric gazelle herding in Israel, he spent nearly three months conducting a similar survey in North Africa, along some 200 miles of Algerian coastline near the frontier with Tunisia. He investigated about eighty sites, including sites strategically located to exploit herds on the coastal plains. Some of the sites, for example, lie along narrow passes on migration routes leading in and out of basins surrounded by high hills.

The exploitation of a single species was even more intensive in Algeria than in Israel, only here it was the large heavy-horned Barbary sheep rather than the gazelle. This species served as a major dietary staple, accounting for more than ninety percent of the bones excavated at one typical site, more than half the total being juvenile animals. That certainly argues for herd management. Even more significant, it argues for an extra-close form of management. Of all wild game the Barbary sheep is one of the most elusive, swiftest, and best camouflaged—and, in the words of one nineteenth-century observer, "so capable of disappearing into the landscape that it can evade virtually all predators." Furthermore, it is quick to move away from regularly hunted regions.

Saxon emphasizes that the "successful economic exploitation of such animals depends on a strategy which encourages them to remain in the most productive grazing territories." In other words, 15,000 and more years ago people in North Africa were practicing a rather sophisticated form of herd management, until rising seas and disappearing coastal plains and subsistence pressure called for a change of tactics. Less grazing land for herds meant less food for people, and led ultimately to the exploitation of previously unexploited resources.

Judging by later evidence, domestication and predomestication have a long prehistory. Carvings and paintings on the walls of tombs show that the early Egyptians, like many people before and since, were inveterate experimenters. These carvings and paintings show that they tried to tame a whole menagerie of beasts, practically every species in and around the valley from gazelles, ibexes, wild cattle and hyenas to geese, ostriches and cranes. Desmond Clark of the University of California in Berkeley believes that such practices date back to very early times. He emphasizes the remarkable continuity between the remote past and the present. Scenes drawn thousands of years ago show in clear detail traps, lassos, and other devices that are still used by nomads living in the Sahara.

Lands along the Nile were filling up. Recent studies in a 144-square-mile region more than 200 miles north of the Tushka site show that after 4000 B.C. villages were larger and more numerous and closer together. People were living not only along the river but also up to two miles inland, back from the banks, in what is now the western desert and was then territory with barely enough rain, perhaps as little as a couple of inches a year, to support some wildlife and crops.

That distribution of settlements changed dramatically and suddenly, within two or three centuries, starting about 3200 B.C. People began streaming back again into the floodplain, a phenomenon which, according to Michael A. Hoffman of the University of Virginia, poses "one of the most fascinating and vital questions in later Egyptian prehistory—a question whose answer may well serve as the basis for understanding the rise of civilization in the Nile Valley." He points out that the streaming-back process was very much like the population implosion which took place along the Euphrates at about the same time, as Uruk expanded from 250 to 1,000 acres.

A center arose along the Nile, too—Hierakonpolis, "the city of the hawk," a traditional capital of southern Egypt, when the country was unified for the first time. It included a raised area, the Kom el Ahmar or Red Mound (so-called because the earth there had a reddish tinge, probably due to the accumulation of painted sherds), which had been a sacred place for a long time, perhaps a millennium or more. Buried beneath one early temple are the fragmentary remains of another temple of public building. A high water table prevents exploring for structures at still lower levels.

A wall of mud bricks apparently enclosed the Red Mound area. It had a gateway which John Wilson of the University of Chicago believes may have been located at one end of a wide processional avenue. His guess is that some 5,000 to 10,000 persons lived in houses outside the wall, and that the entire city covered some forty acres, plus a large cemetery or necropolis at the western edge in the desert. This pattern, the Egyptian pattern, was reflected later in cities where people lived on fertile floodplains and in nearby cities of the dead with massive tombs on sands where nothing grew.

Writing came around 3000 B.C., or perhaps a few centuries earlier, mainly in the form of titles and epithets commemorating the elite. One of the earliest specimens consisted of four hieroglyphs on a little gold band, probably part of a bracelet found in a tomb more than 200 miles north of Hierakonpolis. It says "the Fighter," that being an epithet for Menes, Egypt's first king. The Egyptians undoubtedly kept records of business transactions but, like the Indians and Chinese, they must have used perishable materials since no records have been discovered. Incidentally, that gold band has an unfortunate history. Before World War I a professional thief stole it from a display case in the Oriental Institute in Chicago, hammered out the hieroglyphs, and sold it to a pawnshop. Caught not long afterward, he was released after paying a fine of twenty dollars, the price of the gold in those days.

So inscriptions, monuments and ceremony on the grand scale appeared in Egypt as they did elsewhere. People in the process of assuming power were learning from fellow elites to the east, making use of Sumerian-type cylinder seals and art motifs and architecture. The gateway at Hierakonpolis included a wall with niches and recessed brick facades exactly like those being built in Uruk. Similar activity was probably under way at the other end of the Nile Valley. Hierakonpolis was the traditional capital of southern Egypt. A northern capital, Buto, existed in the Nile delta, although little is known about its beginnings because the lowest levels, representing everything before 500 B.C. or so, are underwater. The twin centers, established before the pyramids, remained sacred cities for nearly three thousand years.

The rest of Africa may be viewed in panorama from its remote northeastern corner, from the vantage point of its first and most enduring kingdom. New life-styles were evolving outside as well as inside the land of Egypt between 5000 B.C. and 3000 B.C.—for example, due west in the Sahara which one investigator has described as "the southwestern extremity of a belt of more or less arid regions extending diagonally across the ancient world from Mauritania to Mongolia . . . unquestionably the largest and most beautiful desert in the world."

The position of the Sahara is linked in some way, by no means a simple way, with the ice ages. In general, as the glaciers approached their peak, this vast wasteland moved south, while its northern edges were invaded by winds out of the west with their cyclonic rains. During warmer times, as the glaciers retreated, the Sahara moved north toward the Mediterranean and its southern areas and the Sudan apparently became somewhat drier. The relationship was never hard and fast, but it does represent a definite tendency.

During Egypt's early days the Sahara was a rather more hospitable place than it is today. Dunes and extensive bone-dry areas still dominated the landscape. Around 7500 B.C., however, after a long period of drought, rainfall increased in certain regions, particularly around the central mountains. Runoff waters nourished stands of open forest in the highlands, stretches of grassy savanna, green ribbons of trees along rivers draining into inland basins, lakes and swamps and transient pools among the dunes, and herds of elephants, giraffes, giant buffalos and antelopes. Lake Chad covered some 120,000 square miles, more than the five Great Lakes combined, compared to 8,000 square miles today.

And people exploited the countryside. At first they lived chiefly as hunter-gatherers but later, approximately 5000 B. C., when populations were presumably increasing to the point where wild species could not provide enough food for everyone, as harvesters and pastoralists. In some areas surprisingly large settlements appeared, relying heavily on cereal grasses, possibly domesticated. Pastoralists moved from pasture to pasture with sheep, goats and cattle. Upon occasion they may have conserved resources on the hoof by bleeding rather than butchering their animals, obtaining their protein in the form of blood rather than meat. Turkana herdsmen in desert regions of Kenya today obtain 3 to 4 million quarts of blood a year from some half million animals, mainly sheep and goats.

Living in the Sahara became more and more of a problem after 2500 B.C., a change that may have had more to do with man than with glaciers. It has been known for some time that overgrazing ruins even well-watered terrain, with rains on denuded surfaces washing away fertile topsoil by the ton. Recent studies by Jule Charney and Peter Stone of the Massachusetts Institute of Technology suggest an even more basic effect of uncontrolled foraging. Bare ground reflects considerably more of the sun's radiation than ground with plant cover, producing major changes in the atmosphere—a cooling and sinking of large air masses, reduced formation of cumulus clouds, and up to 40 percent less rain. Less rain, of course, means less plant cover, so the process is self-aggravating. It may well have helped bring on increasingly severe prehistoric droughts.

A vivid record of people living under such conditions, and the ability to dig in and adapt when they had to, comes from sites near extinct lakes at the base of a 660-foot cliff in the southwestern Sahara, not far from the town of Tichitt in central Mauritania. The record, as reconstructed by Patrick Munson of Indiana University, starts during abundant times perhaps 4,000 to 5,000 years ago. There were rains, large lakes, the marks of hunter-gatherers, a few small grinding stones and stone projectile points, and engravings of giraffes, wild cattle and antelopes on the walls of local rock shelters.

Extreme drought set in around 2000 B.C., as part of a general drying-up throughout the Sahara. The desert expanded and people moved south away from advancing sands, only to move back some four to five hundred years later when rains came again. They returned with domesticated goats and cattle, indicating that the region may no longer have had enough wild game for everyone, and enjoyed good times until about 1100 B.C. when the desert expanded again and lakes shrank. But this time they did not move away, most likely because savannas to the south were too densely occupied.

The mounting pressure provides a model of what may happen when land begins to go bad and people must stay put. The first stone houses appeared, and the rising population clustered together in two large villages near the lakes, each with 500 to 1,000 persons. Munson reports sharp increases in the number and variety of plant foods. Chaff has been found, and seed impressions on pottery, including a wild millet and another native grass that may have been cultivated, and grinding stones, some weighing up to a 100 pounds with deeply worn hollows or basins.

Rainfall dwindled from perhaps fifteen to six or seven inches a year; population expanded roughly four times. People turned to full-scale farming—all in two centuries or less. Sixty percent of the grain impressions on pottery were domesticated millet, identified by characteristic conical seeds. The crop must have been grown and harvested in a hurry. Most of the year's rain fell within two or three months, forming temporary lakes at the foot of the cliff. As the lakes shrank, farmers probably followed the receding waters and planted seeds in the exposed rich sediments, a practice used by present-day farmers in the Niger River Valley.

This was a time of conflict, a time of fighting for food and land. From the flats near the lakes, people moved on to the top of the cliff, building eight large villages surrounded by thick walls, presumably to protect stores of grain from invaders. But the walls did not protect farmers at work in their fields. That would have required armed defenders. Raids and counterraids may have been common, particularly during harvests.

What apparently emerged was some sort of central authority. Although the record is not clear on the details, by 700 B.C. the population had increased to perhaps 10,000 persons in some twenty villages. There were no longer any walls. A system of law and order had apparently been organized with sufficient power to make walls unnecessary. Possibly a paramount chief had arisen. Only further digging can reveal the extent of the system. Munson's study area included only that twenty-five miles of cliffs near Tichitt, and the total length of the cliffs is more than 300 miles. Reconnaissance flights show many sites on the top and dried-up lake beds below, which suggests a repeating pattern and a series of related chiefdoms. Traders were bringing status markers to the Tichitt area, among them marine shells from the Atlantic Coast and green amazonite minerals from mountains more than 700 miles away in the central Sahara.

Everything collapsed during the next three hundred years. Disintegration and fear are reflected in the archeology. There are no more large sites on the cliff tops, only small clusters of three to twenty houses, a last-resort breaking up into isolated groups of families, in effect, minimum survival units. The clusters, concealed among jumbles of rocks and boulders, are extremely difficult to get at. One is so well concealed that it has never been found on the ground. Munson spotted it from the air, marked it

Sénégal: Megalithic tombs, (right, above), stone circle (center), and burial mounds (below)

on a map, climbed the cliff to look in the specific area, and gave up after several hours of futile searching. The houses may have been built into some crevicelike formation with crawl-in entrances. They remain known but still elusive.

The collapse resulted in part from the coming of even drier times. The bones of desert-adapted rodents and other species indicate a rainfall of fewer than six inches and perhaps as little as four inches, the level in today's badlands. But that was not enough by itself to bring about abandonment. People could probably have coped with changing climates. What they could not cope with or, in the last analysis, hide from, was outsiders on the warpath, Berber raiders from North Africa equipped with horses and metal spears and shields.

More elaborate and enduring systems evolved further south, in the savannas and evergreen tropical forests of West Africa. They came later in the game, around A.D. 500 and later, by which time Egypt's last dynasties were more than a millennium in the past, and Greece and Rome had risen and fallen. The remains are no less impressive—megaliths, stones lined up in rows and circles, and 4,000 burial mounds on the north bank of the Gambia River; walls and earthworks and roads buried beneath roots and vines in the jungle; iron, tin, copper and gold mines; fine bronzes and figurines; trade routes stretching across the Sahara from Gao, Timbuktu and Walata toward Gibraltar, Tripoli, Carthage and Cairo.

The earliest agriculture, here as in Southeast Asia, may have involved tubers rather than seeds, notably yams, the starchy roots of certain climbing vines. The vines wither in the dry season and the roots swell into bulbous potatolike storage organs, which still serve as a major food in the yam belt, a forest zone extending some 1,200 miles from the Ivory Coast to Cameroon. Hunter-gatherers probably started using the wild yam as soon as they moved into the forests 60,000 years ago. They used special tools such as sharp-pointed picks, possibly for digging up buried roots. Yams grew close at hand in disturbed soil, ready to be exploited; they spread naturally around camping grounds, since whole plants may develop from discarded pieces that take root and sprout on the spot.

It may not have been long before man began tinkering with

evolution, modifying tubers as he modified cereal grasses, without realizing what he was doing. Until recent times the New Yam Festival was the big event of the year in villages throughout the yam belt. It came just before the harvest, heralding a season of plenty and the beginning of the New Year. Digging up yams before the appointed time was punishable by banishment or death. In some communities if you even looked at an offender you were contaminated, an object to be shamed.

According to Pat Coursey of the Tropical Products Institute in London, the festivals probably developed from rituals originating 10,000 and possibly as long as 30,000 years ago. The act of creating taboos represented a kind of unconscious domestication. Yams over the ages have evolved various characteristics that discourage foragers, nonhuman as well as human. The tubers may lie several feet underground and contain bitter poisons; the vines may have sharp spines and spikes. Protecting the plants by rituals, or simply letting them grow near camp sites where animals fear to tread, would have made natural defenses unnecessary and permitted the selection of forms with more accessible, more palatable tubers. Full-scale yam cultivation may have come much later, between 3000 B.C. and 2000 B.C. when droughts forced people out of the Sahara into moister regions.

It has not been possible to check these and other speculations archeologically. Since root crops do not leave visible remains and West African sites have not yet produced yam-processing tools, new techniques such as soil studies may be necessary to identify chemical traces of wild and domesticated tubers. Signs of the early use of seeds do exist, artifacts that hint at basic changes wherever they are found, and they are found almost everywhere.

About a decade ago, months of searching and a seven-mile tramp through the overgrown rain forests of western Nigeria, Thurstan Shaw of the University of Ibadan found a huge rock shelter known to local people of the Yoruba tribe as Iwo Eleru, "the rock of ashes." It contained artifacts similar to those recovered from sites in India, Egypt, China, the Near East—tiny blades with sickle sheen such as may be produced by cutting wild or cultivated grasses.

The microliths first appear at the site in levels dating back to about 9000 B.C., the earliest date for such tools in West Africa. By

3000 B.C., they are accompanied by the region's oldest known pottery—and by stone axes used to shape timber and clear forests perhaps for gardens, and believed by the Yoruba to be "thunderbolts," meteorlike objects fallen from the skies during lightning flashes. This superstition, incidentally, bears some investigating because the natives of nineteenth-century Europe believed precisely the same thing about so-called hand axes and other prehistoric tools.

Further changes are reflected in changing artifacts. After the microliths, at other sites and in more recent levels, other familiar items appear, including grinding stones, charred seeds and bones of domesticated species, walls and storage pits and ovens. The general trend is clear. West Africa also saw a shift from hunting-gathering to agriculture, from bands seasonally on the move to settlers in villages, and later in towns and cities. Enormous gaps exist in the record, partly because so much was built of mud and wood and has been lost in the rain forests, and partly because there are too few archeologists to find and study what remains.

Many sites, probably the vast majority of sites, are so deeply buried that you can see nothing at all on the surface. Evidence which would otherwise have remained undiscovered is turning up regularly in plateau regions of north central Nigeria, in an area of more than 10,000 square miles where between 20,000,000 and 30,000,000 tons of earth are being excavated annually in a continuing search, not for traces of times past, but for tin and other metals needed to keep the wheels of twentieth-century societies turning.

For more than three decades prospectors and miners have been picking up artifacts among the ores, clays, gravels and churned-up earth—notably superbly shaped terra-cotta figurines which show people with headdresses, clothing and ornaments, and suggest possible differences in status. At Taruga, a site in the region isolated among low hills in savanna woodlands, Bernard Fagg of Oxford University has found similar figurines, as well as decorated graters made of clay and perhaps used to process tubers, and quantities of iron slag. With the aid of a magnetometer, an electronic instrument designed to detect distortions of the earth's magnetic field produced by buried materials, he located ten iron-smelting furnaces.

But the record is still fragmentary. Taruga has yielded no residences of any sort, no elaborate burials of special people, no signs of its relationships with other sites in the region and beyond. It tells us only that increasing time and energy were being put into art and technology, and it offers only the faintest hint of something more—pieces of a statue nearly three feet tall representing a standing figure which holds an unidentifiable object firmly clenched in her or his right hand. The statue provides no answers. But it does raise some interesting questions. For whom was it created, and for what purpose? Was it intended for local use or export? To be placed in a shrine or temple, or in the home of a head man or chief?

These developments occurred some time after 500 B.C. Dated within a millennium or so after that are other artifacts which indicate a widening of contacts among widely separated peoples. Several hundred paintings and engravings of horse-drawn chari-

Trade routes in the Sahara Desert: two of the routes of early traders bringing precious metals, ivory, timber, and other goods across the desert for the cities of Europe and Asia, routes indicated by rock-art paintings and engravings of chariots, one running west of Timbuktu and northeast through Mauritania and the Atlas Mountains toward Algiers and Gibraltar; another, past the Hoggar Mountains in Algeria with branches toward Tunis, Tripoli and Benghazi

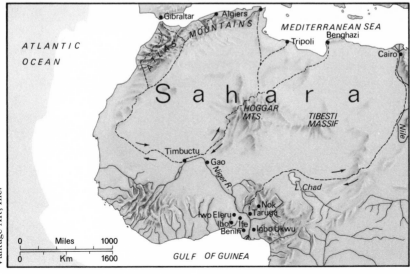

Vantage Art, Inc.

ots, discovered on the walls of caves and rock shelters in the Sahara, serve as "road signs" of a sort. Their locations, plotted on a map, mark possible travel routes and suggest the beginnings of a trade network that was to become more and more extensive in succeeding centuries.

One route ran west of Timbuktu, and looped northeast through Mauritania and the Atlas Mountains of Morocco toward Gibraltar and Algiers. Another route, also starting in the Timbuktu area, passed through the Hoggar Mountains in Algeria and has branches leading toward the present-day cities of Tunis, Tripoli, and Benghazi. Still another route, which is not marked by pictures, may have extended from the Taruga area northeast past Lake Chad and on to the Valley of the Nile. All routes connected with sea lanes in the Mediterranean and markets in Europe, the Near East and Asia.

West Africa's first cities arose 1,000 to 1,500 years ago, and many of them were forest cities. In certain ways they resembled early Chinese cities like Anyang, spread-out settlements in cleared areas with mud-and-wood structures. They differed little from forest cities of historical times which seemed rather second-rate to some European travelers interested primarily in converting heathens and trading in ivory, gold and slaves. In the words of one British missionary of the nineteenth century: "African towns have no public buildings except shabby little temples and . . . houses so rude in appearance as to attract no attention. Architecture, monuments . . . are unknown. The house of the kings differs from the others only in size and in high sharp gables . . . weatherboarded with grass thatch."

So power appears in diverse forms, and people with different backgrounds are impressed by different things. The early Yoruba site of Ife, at the edge of the Nigerian rain forest about forty miles east of Ibadan, was almost certainly built in line with West African traditions as known from later times, and in line with traditions in other parts of the world. It had an inner precinct for king and temple and nobles, and about half a dozen roads radiating out into a region of supporting villages and hamlets. The long arm of tradition may be seen in terra-cotta figurines and bronzes found at the site. They are done in a style that originated at least a thousand years previously, the same style as the figurines of Taruga and the plateau mining area, which does not necessarily mean a definite connection but, according to some investigators, points in that direction.

Ife and other early Yoruba centers had certain features which do not jibe with western notions about cities. For one thing, there were no public projects on a massive scale commemorating the glory of kings, no monuments, citadels or royal tombs, requiring large numbers of workers and rationing systems and overseers. Farming seems to have been by far the predominant occupation. Even as recently as 1952 about two-thirds of the adult males in Ibadan, West Africa's largest city with a population of 318,000, were full-time farmers—prompting Michael Horowitz of the State University of New York in Binghamton to ask: "Are the Yoruba somehow exceptional, effectively combining farm and city, despite assertions supposing the two to be incompatible?"

Another question concerns the crucial relationship between kin and king. Controlling people, holding them together, becomes increasingly difficult with increasing populations, and one critical-mass stage may be reached at levels above 10,000 to 15,000 persons. As a group begins to grow beyond that level, its leader must broaden his base of support, relying less and less on the loyalties of his family and ancestral lineage and more and more on loyalties that cut across family ties.

In the sense that such ties appear to have been dominant, early Yoruba city systems were folk systems. They were competing with one another, making and breaking alliances, and perhaps evolving toward wider unities. The social setting was such that more centralized political institutions came with the coming of Europeans during and after the sixteenth century. It was a dramatic example of the same "take me to your leader" effect noted in connection with urban evolution in Southeast Asia. Newcomers in search of a leader may create one.

European captains sailing down the African coast during the fifteenth century anchored off little coastal villages to do business, or to raid and loot, and soon learned that these innocent—and vulnerable—appearing places were not what they seemed to be, that they were outposts of powerful centers located deep in the interior. And dealings on the periphery brought about massive changes in the interior, in traditional balances of power. As demands soared for gold, slaves and ivory, those centers with easiest access to the coast had great advantages when it came to

Painting by Caroline Sassoon in consultation with Thurston Shaw; photograph by R. A. Osoba.

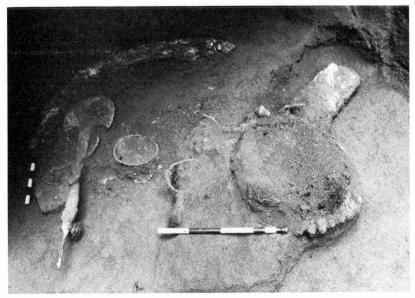

Igbo-Ukwu, near Niger delta: reconstruction of royal burial (left); excavated tomb area with remains of copper-studded king's stool at left, copper fan-holder and ivory tusk at right, center scale = 1 ft. (above); bronze shell, 30.5 centimeters (below)

Photographs, courtesy of Thurston Shaw, Cambridge, England

acting as middlemen or agents, and collecting and redistributing merchandise for markets abroad.

City-states had existed in the interior up to three hundred or more years before Europeans came, and not only among the Yoruba. Their Nigerian neighbors to the southeast established a state with its capital at Benin about fifty miles from the coast, where excavations by Graham Connah, one of Shaw's colleagues at the University of Ibadan, have revealed defenses consisting of an inner district surrounded by high earthen walls as well as outer ramparts. Another site, excavated by Shaw in the town of Igbo-Ukwu near the Niger delta, included bronzes, bead and ivory ornaments—and the wood-lined tomb of a king buried sitting upright on his throne and holding a staff topped by a bronze leopard's skull.

What apparently emerged after the coming of the Europeans was the "Establishment," that is, full-scale centralization with supernatural sanction. Paul Wheatley speaks of "translating the source of authority from consensus to charisma," from leadership because you have won and maintained loyalties to leadership because the gods have chosen you. The Yoruba among others, confronting new complexities in the shape of foreigners and ex-panded trade, developed the divine right of kings, as other people had elsewhere under analogous circumstances.

Cities and states came somewhat later in southern Africa, in the lands of Africa south of the equator—and they appeared following a series of dramatic and rapid changes. Before 500 B.C. or so, the people of these lands lived primarily as hunter-gatherers, with stone tools and without pottery. After A.D. 1000, from the Congo to Cape Town most of their food came from domesticated species, pottery was widespread, and in the vast majority of cases iron tools replaced stone tools. The most extensive and swiftest changes were concentrated within an even shorter period, from about A.D. 100 to A.D. 400.

Newcomers appeared on the scene. Studies of skeletal remains show that increasing numbers of African Negroes were moving into territories hitherto occupied almost exclusively by Bushmen and Hottentots; linguistic and other studies suggest where they came from. Today almost all the Negroes of southern Africa (that is, south of a line running roughly from the Niger delta to the coast of Kenya) speak Zulu, or another of some 300 Bantu lan-guages so closely related in grammar and vocabulary that they probably descended from a single ancestral language. The most closely related tend to cluster in east central Nigeria and part of Cameroon, and it is here that investigators believe that ancestral language arose two to three millenniums ago.

The newcomers may have moved out of West Africa in search of more living space. Over the centuries subsistence pressure had kept mounting in their home country. For a time hunting and gathering and fishing sufficed, supplemented mainly by yams grown close to home. Later they depended more on domesticated yams, and still later on yams and domesticated animals and grasses, plus iron tools to clear and cultivate wide stretches of forest. Finally, for some there was nothing to do but move on. Small groups of pioneers, followed by others, found their way along rivers through dense Congo forests into wide savanna lands to the south.

The process has been compared to what happened when Europeans discovered the Americas, except that in this "New World" there are no traces of wars with the natives. Conflicts undoubtedly occurred. Sites gradually shifted from stone to iron tools, and from wild to domesticated species. Some hunter-gatherers had adopted the agricultural life; other bands probably did business with farming communities as they do today in parts of India; and still others went their separate ways and conducted business as usual.

Excavations document the rise of complex systems south of the equator. One huge ninth-century cemetery known as Sanga lies along the shores of a lake in southeast Zaire in the heartland of Bantu-speaking Africa, where a number of states were flourishing when Europeans arrived during the 1890s. The graves contained a variety of status objects such as fine pottery, ivory bracelets, and ceremonial knives of iron and copper, all testifying to the existence of an established and perhaps hereditary elite. A number of unusual artifacts may have served commercial as well as prestige purposes: 600 small crosses, H-shaped and made of cast copper. In a recent study Michael Bisson of McGill University in Montreal measured these items and reports that they apparently fell into at least three size ranges: 0.28 to 0.6 inch, 0.8 to 1.0 inch, and 1.28 to 2.6 inches. A few pieces are larger, suggesting the possibility of a fourth size category ranging from 3.6 to 5.0 inches.

The fact that the crosses were made of a valuable metal, came

in standard sizes, and in some cases were tied in packets of five suggests they may have been a kind of money. Historical records support this point, similar artifacts being in common use less than a century ago. Among tribes living in northwest Zambia a rifle cost 24 crosses, an ivory tusk 100 crosses and a female slave 150 crosses. Bisson believes the Sanga crosses represent a transition currency, the currency of people in the process of changing from special-purpose money which, like cowrie shells or pigs or strings of beads, can be used to purchase certain items only, to general-purpose money which can be used to purchase practically anything anywhere. This transition in turn implies more basic changes, such as regularly produced surpluses of foods and other goods, markets, and an advanced form of early political organization.

Most of Africa's cities, early as well as later, were in essence supervillages. They were supervillages not only in appearance—great aggregates of simple wood-mud-and-thatch homes—but in spirit. People did not live in individual houses lined up along streets, but in compounds, in clusters of houses which sheltered several generations of kinfolk. The dwelling place of the king or paramount chief himself was the palace, merely a hut slightly larger than the huts of his subjects.

For a time the rulers of the Old Kingdom of the Congo, a state established in the fifteenth century boasting a capital of some 50,000 persons, did live in a special two-story wooden house. They had been talked into the move by the Portuguese. Later kings, thinking better of it, moved back into huts. The ruins of Zimbabwe, built 600 to 1,000 years ago in open woodlands at a cliff edge in eastern Rhodesia, are outstanding for their monumental stonework. In the center were a granite temple and a great curving granite wall thirty-two feet high and seventeen feet thick. But for all its grandeur, the wall enclosed a community of traditional huts.

There is an African style in the evolution of cities and power structures, an African pattern which may still be seen in present-

Burial with copper currency (cross) at Sanga, Zaire

From Robert Netting, University of Arizona, Hill Farmers of Nigeria, University of Washington Press, Seattle 1968

Kofyar hill homestead, Nigeria: a city-state in the making?

day societies, and in the recent as well as the remote past. Because people everywhere confronted with similar conditions tend to adapt in similar ways, the African pattern provides insights into adaptations elsewhere and in other times. Robert Netting of the University of Arizona lived for more than two years with the Kofyar in a pocket of hill-enclosed land in central Nigeria, on the same plateau where miners and archeologists have been finding ancient terra-cotta figurines.

The Kofyar have been getting along as rugged individualists, without strong men or administrative hierarchies, spread out in clusters of three to eighty homesteads. Their system depends on intensive and sophisticated agriculture, and provides enough food to support more than 55,000 persons on some 200 square miles of plains and "tumbled rocky hills." It is a hair-trigger situation, because populations are still on the rise. No one knows what will happen. But more than 5,000 years ago the Egyptians at Hierakonpolis, and the Sumerians in the Uruk countryside, may have faced similar problems—and the result was apparently a mass

movement into concentrated settlements, highly centralized political control, and the first city-states.

One of the world's most recently formed-from-scratch states
emerged in Madagascar. According to one of a number of theories, the island was first settled some time after A.D. 1000 by
people who came from the east (probably Borneo) and were
later joined by people from the African mainland. It seems to have
become a place of chronic warfare among competing chiefs. In
a survey of one central highland region Wright and Susan Kus
of the University of Michigan found some 140 sites, added 130
more from previous surveys, and obtained a preliminary picture
of early developments.

Some of the earliest lowland sites lie in unprotected positions
and tend to occur in pairs, as in Uruk and North China. Later
sites appear on the tops of hills, and still later there are major
centers with "an inner ring of small dependent settlements and
an outer ring of large border settlements." The trend, confirmed
by historical records, was toward greater centralization and increased fighting. During the early eighteenth century practically
every mountaintop in central Madagascar was a fortified center,
where chiefs lived above, in isolation from, and on rice and other
foods produced by villagers in the valleys.

Maurice Bloch of the London School of Economics speaks of
the chiefs and their followers as "gangs of brigands" who obtained
"continual gifts" from the villagers, "especially regular gifts consisting of the rump of any animal killed in the area" as well as
rice grown on terraced slopes. Eventually, instead of depending
solely on the villagers, some chiefs began growing rice on their
own, moving down from the mountains and using hitherto unexploited marshes on valley floors. Although the marshes were
considerably more productive than the hillsides, they required
large dikes and elaborate drainage systems.

Radical changes followed these developments. Most of the
villagers became soldiers instead of farmers, their main job being
to invade their neighbors and come back with slaves to work the
marshlands. There was an increasing demand for more and more
rice, more and more slaves, and larger armies to capture the
slaves, perhaps because of rising populations and the need to
feed an expanding class of elites and their administrators. This

amounted to an expand-or-collapse situation, which actually boiled down to expand and collapse. Sooner or later neighboring chiefs united against a rising chief, who was generally defeated and forced to retreat to his old mountaintop camp while his drainage systems fell into disrepair.

A more stable society, a "take-off state," evolved late in the eighteenth century. One of several competing groups living near the headwaters of the Ikopa River in central Madagascar began winning fights and gaining control over more and more people and territory. The group might also have collapsed eventually, but its rise happened to coincide with the rise of new European trading centers on the island's east coast. Receiving rifles and cannons in exchange for slaves, they achieved military superiority over their neighbors and by 1895 ruled about two-thirds of the island.

These people provide a possible model for one sort of state formation, statehood attained with an assist from the outside. As as result of their own internal evolution, they may have reached a crucial stage where further expansion depended on a new technology, a technology of control involving, among other things, advanced firearms. They were ready to learn from outsiders who had experienced similar problems before, a pattern that seems to have been repeated in other parts of Africa and elsewhere.

12

Europe, the Diminutive Peninsula

*The wave-of-advance model / Agricultural traces
in a cave by the sea / Temples and chiefdoms
on Malta / Europe's first city / The appearance of
megaliths, "tombs for the living" / Sunrises
and Stonehenge / The rise and fall of the Celts*

Oɴᴇ autumn day some 9,000 years ago three or four families left the overcrowded town of Jericho to find a new place to live. They did not travel far, no farther than necessary, no more than about six miles into the surrounding countryside where they could grow crops on unoccupied land. Another group of about the same size left the town the following year, still another group the year after that, and so on year after year.

It all happened on a purely local basis, as the result of decisions made within and among families. People moved always so as to stay as close to friends and relatives as possible, always settling themselves five to ten miles from the nearest community. There was no plan or large-scale migration. But there was a general

Continental shelf

SCOTLAND
DENMARK   BALTIC
NORTH SEA   SEA
IRELAND
Wales
EUROPE
Stonehenge
Cornwall   •Bylany
English
Channel
FRANCE
ATLANTIC   Brittany   •Vix
Bibracte•
OCEAN   Mount Dardon•
BAY OF
BISCAY   YUGOSLAVIA   BULGARIA
ITALY
GREECE   •Troy
Franchthi•
Cave
° Malta   Knossos
AFRICA   Crete
MEDITERRANEAN SEA

| 0 | Miles | 1000 |
| 0 | Km | 1600 |

Vantage Art, In

Elites and power in the west: following the rise of the earliest cities, trade
networks, and elites near the coastlines and among the islands of the Aegean
and Mediterranean Seas, society developed slowly in central and northwestern
Europe

trend, a tendency to avoid going east where the population
centers were and to move in a northwesterly direction. Within a
millennium, forty generations later, farmers had established themselves on a Mediterranean island 900 miles from Jericho. Settlers

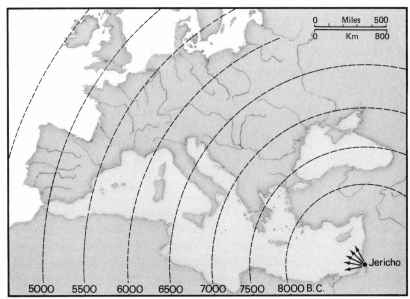

Vantage Art, Inc.
Based on Albert Ammerman and Luigi Cavàlli-Sforza, Stanford University

Wave-of-advance model: the spread of agriculture through Europe, emanating perhaps from centers in the Near East, at an average rate of about two-thirds of a mile per year. Based on findings of a Stanford University study

had reached mainland Greece and Bulgaria 7,500 years ago, Yugoslavia and southern Italy 7,000 years ago, and the northern regions of Europe including Britain and parts of Scandinavia about 5,000 to 6,000 years ago.

This account of the spread of agriculture from the Near East to Europe, "that diminutive peninsula projecting from the western marches of Asia," is part fact and part fiction. Albert Ammerman and Luigi Cavalli-Sforza of Stanford University compiled a list of seventy-three European sites with relatively reliable dates and good evidence for domesticated wheat and barley. They found a regular relationship between the date of a site and its distance from the earliest Near Eastern farming communities, the closest sites being the oldest and the most remote the most recent. They also found that, allowing for local variations, the overall rate of spread was remarkably constant, averaging about two-thirds of a mile per year.

So much for the facts. The hypothesis, the scientific fiction or theory, is a matter of trying to explain the facts. Neither the California investigators nor anyone else believe that prehistory ever proceeded so smoothly. Agriculture did not spread from Jericho, Ali Kosh or any other single center, and it was not always introduced into new areas by outsiders moving short distances. As in the case of the spread of agriculture from West Africa to southern Africa, local bands of hunter-gatherers probably recognized the advantages of farming and often switched over within a few generations.

The so-called wave-of-advance model of Ammerman and Cavalli-Sforza simply provides a working hypothesis of how the spread may have taken place, a guide for further research. It is a step toward a broad theory of diffusion, of how things spread—diseases, rumors and hereditary traits as well as ideas and techniques. (The mathematics of the wave-of-advance model was originally worked out some forty years ago to describe how beneficial genes spread through neighboring populations.) One major factor in the earliest European transition from hunting-gathering to agriculture was a gradual, locally limited movement of small groups of farmers from the Near East.

Evidence for population growth comes from the increase in the number and size of sites. A number of excavations attest to the arrival of newcomers, moving on a wave-of-advance basis over the centuries from the Near East, through Turkey and across the Dardanelles into Greece and Bulgaria. One of their stopping places may have been in southern Greece, at Franchthi Cave overlooking the Gulf of Argolis, a favorite spot not only for prehistoric people but also for modern picnickers, that is, until Thomas Jacobsen of Indiana University started digging there in 1967. It is a large coastal cave, well worth exploring for sheer adventure as well as in the name of science. More than 130 feet wide and 30 feet high at the entrance, it extends at least 500 feet into the side of a limestone cliff—"at least," because no one knows what lies beyond a deep and chilly pool at the end of the galleries, a vast sunken chamber which skin divers have investigated briefly and which the Greeks and Romans apparently used as a secret shrine.

Courtesy of Thomas Jacobsen, University of Indiana

Franchthi Cave, southern Greece: interior looking out toward entrance

The archeological record starts some 20,000 years ago, during ice-age times of extensive glaciers and low ocean levels. A broad plain separated the earliest known occupants of the Franchthi Cave from the sea, and the countryside provided them with a diet including deer, wild goats, wild asses, small fish, snails, and a variety of wild plants. Meanwhile, glaciers began melting and the sea crept closer and closer. By 7500 B.C. to 7000 B.C., waves were breaking nearer the cave, and the local hunter-gatherers had become part-time sailors. They built boats, perhaps the same sort of reed boats Greek lobstermen were using as recently as a generation ago. They returned with tuna and other large deep-sea fish. They also obtained obsidian which, according to chemical analysis, came from quarries on the extinct volcano island of Melos nearly 100 miles to the southeast.

That way of life seems to have ended abruptly a millennium or so later. This was no gradual development. The shift from characteristic microliths, bones of wild animals and flint and bone points, all typical hunter-gatherer remains, to the remains of farming populations—pottery, sickle blades, mortars and pestles, figurines, the bones of domesticated sheep and goats, and so on—came all of a sudden. The simplest explanation is that one group of people moved out and another group moved in. Although there is no evidence of conflict, it would be surprising if local hunter-gatherers had been displaced from their ancestral site without putting up a fight.

Future researchers, perhaps with the aid of skin-diving archeologists, may learn something about their village. Although some of the walls have been uncovered on slopes below the cave, the principal part of the community may lie underwater a short distance offshore. It probably did not differ radically from other early farming villages in Greece or, for that matter, in Bulgaria and the Near East. Judging by other excavations, most of these contemporary settlements had 100 to 300 inhabitants in rectangular one-room houses, sometimes lined up along streets or arranged in a semicircle and equipped with hearths, ovens, and storage pits.

Life had not yet become sufficiently complicated to warrant wide status differences or large-scale ritual. Figurines of clay or stone, usually female, have been found at many sites, among them Franchthi Cave and Near Eastern villages like Ganj Dareh, Ali

Kosh and Jarmo. Resembling similar objects made as much as 20,000 to 30,000 years ago in the houses of hunter-gatherers, they are often cited as evidence for the existence of fertility cults and fertility goddesses. An extra-large, mud-walled building excavated in northern Greece has been interpreted as a shrine, because it occupied a central position in the settlement and included five clay figurines as well as clay animal heads and a pair of finely polished greenstone axes. Some 200 miles to the northwest at a fish-rich site along the Danube, investigators found sculptures suggesting a "fish god," crude sandstone heads with gaping mouths and goggle eyes.

Temples, monumental places of worship and burial and sacrifice, came later—and some of the oldest and most remarkable appeared on Mediterranean islands. Early builders were especially active on Malta. A series of underground chambers, vaults with doorways and columns and curved ceilings all carved out of solid rock, served as tombs for more than 6,000 persons. Not far away are the ruins of a temple, one of sixteen—a high stone wall, large limestone blocks, spiral-motif carvings, friezes of animals, and the shattered six-foot statue of a seated woman. The largest Malta temple, known as the "Tower of the Giants" in medieval times, has several courtyards and a wide terrace supported by a retaining wall that may have been more than fifty feet high. It required an estimated million man-hours to build. Construction was probably well under way by 3000 B.C., when Hierakonpolis and Uruk were on the rise along the Nile and Euphrates.

The distribution of the temples is significant. Plotted on a map, they occur in six clusters of two to four temples, and each cluster is strategically located in a major area of good farmland. Colin Renfrew believes that the six areas, each with its clusters of temples, represent tribal territories controlled by as many prehistoric societies, each numbering from 500 to 2,000 people and led by a chief with sufficient authority to mobilize workers and provide them with food. The intriguing thing is that such impressive projects can be planned and carried through with techniques and under political systems that are not particularly impressive themselves.

Except for the temples and underground vaults, there is nothing special about the archeology of Malta—no elite residences, no avenues or towns with central plazas, no treasure hoards, no writing. Workers shaped and carved great stone blocks and slabs using stone tools. The entire display of power and priestcraft was something like that encountered at Zimbabwe in southern Africa, where a high and massive wall of granite enclosed only humble thatched-roof huts. Given enough rock and enough people taking orders, monumental architecture is always possible. The development of hierarchies and urban centers calls for something more.

In Europe that process first took place east of Malta, on a Greek island some 180 miles offshore from the Franchthi Cave. Emigrants, probably from western Turkey, landed on the shores of Crete in about 6000 B.C., at about the time when the cave site saw its shift from hunting-gathering to agriculture. They came as full-fledged farmers, with boatloads of sheep and goats, pigs, cattle, wheat, barley and lentil seeds, and established a village known as Knossos on a hill overlooking a fertile plain a few miles inland from the northern coast.

According to John Evans of the Institute of Archeology in London, who has investigated early developments at the site, the original settlers numbered 50 to 100 individuals and occupied about half an acre on the hill. During the next three millenniums the community seems to have enjoyed a steady growth, like that experienced at other contemporary sites, expanding to a dozen acres and a population of 2,000. At just this crucial point, the take-off point for spectacular changes to come, there is a tantalizing gap in the record. Prehistoric work crews removed most of the evidence, walls and pottery and other artifacts, in the course of clearing and leveling the land to make way for large-scale construction projects.

But evidence for major changes after 3000 B.C. exists outside Knossos. It reveals the same fundamental phenomenon that occurred in many regions throughout the world, a marked and gradually intensifying concentration of populations, a clustering which cannot be explained simply by the fact that populations were increasing. Another hilltop site on Crete includes a large complex of some two dozen rooms which has been called a mansion but is probably an entire village or most of a village of people living very close together. Clustering also took place on the western coast of Turkey at the fortress site of Troy, an early version of the city of Homeric and Trojan Horse fame, which the Greeks were to destroy thirteen centuries later.

People came together out of a need for tighter organization. Renfrew has analyzed the process for the Aegean region, and believes that wine and olives had a lot to do with it. People were using wild grapes, presumably fermenting them, by 4500 B.C. if not earlier. Characteristic spherical seeds with very short stalks have been found at a site in northern Greece. The earliest known seeds of domesticated grapes, pear-shaped with long stalks, turn up some two thousand years later. Olives, a calorie-rich food as well as a source of cooking oil and oil for lamps, were being cultivated at about the same time.

Growing such crops implies a certain amount of social stability, a variety of property rights involving long-term investments and delayed payoffs, a special confidence that the land will continue to be your and your children's. Orchards and vineyards require more tending than cereal crops, and may take five to twenty years to reach peak yields. New skills and specialties were being created, new high-demand products to be distributed with profit, on a local or regional basis at first and far more widely later.

Where there are profits there will soon be status and status symbols. Opportunities for accumulating wealth called for controlled farm labor and schedules, and for more potent ways of impressing the less wealthy—"impressing" in its double sense of arousing respect and awe, and forcing others to supply labor. Under such conditions metallurgy came into its own in the Aegean region. Known for several thousand years, the art was highly developed elsewhere. Renfrew suggests, however, that the demand soared from this time on in this part of the word: "Suddenly people in power found it advantageous to exploit the possibilities of materials that were at once useful from an immediate, practical standpoint, and also enviable and thus prestigious. Imagine the impact of bronze and silver and gold on people who had seen only wood and pottery, even the most beautiful pottery."

Warwick Bray of the Institute of Archaeology in London disagrees. He believes this explanation "ducks the question of why increased productivity should cause class distinctions," pointing out that small individually owned farm buildings can, and often do, provide abundant supplies of grapes and olives without the

Knossos, Greece: the ruins

Storage area

Courtesy of Greek National Tourist Office

Palace with frescoes of vase-bearers

benefit of bureaucracies and ruling classes—and that something more is needed to account for the rise of elites and elite institutions and all that went with them. This is a penetrating criticism. It draws attention to the fact that we know enough to describe certain aspects of the rise of prehistoric power structures, but not enough to account for them. Part of the answer may involve the need in early times for "an ethics of providing and providence" mentioned in Chapter 4.

Knossos evolved in the thick of such developments. The English archeologist, Arthur Evans of Oxford University (no relation to John Evans), started digging there in 1899 and found above the early farming villages more recent levels containing evidence for what he termed a "Minoan" civilization, named after the mythical King Minos who built a labyrinth to house the half-man, half-bull Minotaur slain by Theseus. The center flourished during the period of peak urban development in the Indus Valley and North China—from about 2000 B.C. to 1700 B.C.

It collapsed suddenly. There are shattered buildings and signs of widespread fires, once believed to be the work of invaders. Now it seems that the end was not man's doing. It came with a bang around 1500 B.C. when a volcano exploded on an island eighty miles away. According to current theory, that explosion produced earthquakes and tidal waves which destroyed Knossos and other Cretan centers. (Volcanic ashes tracing to the explosion have been found in the ruins.)

Knossos has been described as Europe's first city, despite the mild objections of some investigators who suggest that Arthur Evans may have exaggerated the significance of his work, a common tendency in archeology and other professions. But even allowing for overglamorizing, it must have been a reasonably glamorous place. At its height, Knossos controlled 600 square miles of countryside, about a fifth of the island, and an estimated population of 50,000. Perhaps 10,000 persons were concentrated in an area of 60 acres, half of them within a ten-acre, walled-off inner district city. Four palaces at the center, stone-and-brick complexes of stairways, colonnades and air shafts and columned balconies, rose three or more stories high and covered a total of some three acres. One palace included the seat of power, the king's room with an alabaster throne.

The palaces have been described as places "to house the wealthy and minister to the luxury of a human king and a pleasure-loving court." They were certainly that, and more. There were basement warehouses, the largest of which contained hundreds of storage chests and more than 400 tall decorated jars with capacity enough to hold 16,000 gallons of wine or olive oil. These supplies, as well as grain and other products, went not only to palace elites but to craftsmen and workers, overseas markets, and to the clerks and administrators responsible for organizing and keeping track of the flow of goods.

People at Knossos and other Cretan settlements had a developed form of picture or hieroglyphic writing known as Linear A, and believed by some specialists to represent a stage on the way to syllabic writing where the symbols represent sounds rather than ideas or objects. Linear B, definitely a form of syllabic writing, which Michael Ventris, an architect and amateur cryptographer, deciphered a generation ago, was used on the mainland as well as on Crete to write an archaic version of Greek. The scripts have

Courtesy of John Chadwick, Cambridge, England, and the Department of Classics, University of Cincinnati

Samples of early Greek writing: broken tablet showing a tally found at Knossos; symbols at top mean "horses," at bottom, "asses"

provided only a limited amount of information. "It is as if we had salvaged the contents of a few wastebaskets," John Chadwick reports. "They seem to be temporary records, written for immediate use and kept on file only until the end of the current year."

If it had not been for fires which swept through early administrative offices, the evidence would never have survived. Preserved specimens of Cretan-type writing were originally inscribed on disposable "memo sheets," flattened pieces of soft clay baked into solid pottery tablets. Chadwick points out that "by a fine irony" the same accidental fires probably burned to a crisp records intended to be permanent, pen-and-ink entries made on the pages of special palace ledgers.

The linear scripts, like the earliest scripts invented some two thousand years before in Sumer, were used primarily for routine business transactions—goods received as tribute, goods distributed as rations and offerings, inventories. Such details are hardly exciting. Still, they represent the culmination of a system which started out on a regional basis with groups of villages and towns, settlements on the plains and in the hills and mountains, organized to exchange local goods with one another. It was a kind of preliminary to the main event, long-distance trade taking advantage of Crete's position as a large island at the mouth of the Aegean Sea with access to Greece, Turkey, Israel, Egypt, North Africa and its trans-Saharan networks, and other Mediterranean lands.

This is the world of southeast Europe, the world nearest to the Near East, culturally as well as geographically. It gave rise to the nostalgic golden ages of the West, the classical civilizations of

Greece and Rome, featured so prominently in the West's history books. The rest of prehistoric Europe tends to be rather less well publicized, often being recorded as a dark hinterland, a backcountry region inhabited by savages and frequently overrun by hordes out of Asia.

The rest of Europe was indeed a different world, but the above description does not do it justice. It had a golden age of its own long before the coming of agriculture, from about 15,000 B.C. to 10,000 B.C., when artists selected special spots in the deep galleries of caves in France and Spain and covered the walls with paintings and engravings. The times also saw escalating populations, large communal settlements in rock shelters and open-air sites, and probably tribal alliances and great annual get-togethers for feasting and ceremonies.

That way of life passed because, of all things, the climate improved. Good times had depended on ice-age conditions, glaciers nearby and long rigorous winters and treeless tundra lands providing ideal territory for vast herds of migratory reindeer and other big game—and for big-game hunters. Everything dwindled with the warmer weather after the end of the ice age, with the milder winters and gentle rains. Melting glaciers retreated to the north. The herds followed. Dense stands of trees covered what had once been wide open plains; elusive solitary species like wild boars and red deer replaced the herds.

There was less meat on the hoof, and it was much harder to get. Hunter-gatherers dispersed into small groups, manufactured increasing quantities of tiny flint blades, microliths for hafting in harpoons and othedr special-purpose weapons, and turned increasingly to plants and small game. They adapted to new and less abundant forest conditions, but at a price. According to one estimate, the population of Europe may have declined from about 500,000 to 250,000 during the two or three millenniums following the last ice age.

This was the state of affairs confronting the agricultural pioneers of central and northwestern Europe around 5500 B.C. to 4500 B.C. In one of the most thorough investigations of a farming village on record, Bohumil Soudsky of the Czechoslovakian Institute of Archeology and his associates have been excavating a site known as Bylany fifty miles east of Prague. In some twenty seasons they have uncovered about twenty acres and, with the benefit of some ingenious arithmetical reasoning, have figured out a complicated series of successive and overlapping occupation levels.

Of the 500 acres covered by Bylany not all were occupied at one time. The first settlers, about 125 strong, built houses with wattle-and-daub walls (frames of interwoven branches plastered with mud or clay), big enough for up to four families each. The village also included an extra-large "clubhouse" half the length of a football field, with a spacious plaza in front, presumably for meetings and ceremonies.

The settlers had to shift their farms from time to time. They used traditional slash-and-burn methods to clear about sixty acres which produced ample food for three to five years. At that point the soil lost so much nitrogen and other plant-nourishing elements that yields fell sharply, and the land had to be abandoned. So another sixty-acre area nearby was cleared and exploited for another three to five years. When yields fell the settlers switched back to the original land, which had been lying fallow. Having regained much of its fertility, the land was ready for a third three-to-five-year span of cultivation.

That was the end of a cycle. After ten to fifteen years the fertility of the entire region had apparently fallen so low that the forest needed time to regenerate. The residents deserted their villages, built another one on a new site about a quarter of a mile away, and stayed for another cycle of ten to fifteen years.. During the region's prehistory there was a complex of field and site rotations, with several such cycles and returnings to the general area of the first village, and a total occupation of at least 700 years, roughly from 4500 B.C. to 3800 B.C.

The regional population probably increased during this period, but not at Bylany. The village stayed the same size, suggesting a continuing budding-off process along the lines of the wave-of-advance model. As long as farmers could afford to rely on slash-and-burn methods, as long as deep forests were available for clearing beyond the edges of local fields, that was the easiest and most direct way to relieve subsistence pressure. They spread gradually out of central Europe, created new stretches of open land, and established new villages to the north and west.

Megaliths, stone monuments on the Orkneys: side chamber, island of Sanday (above); scattered bones on floor of side chamber (right)

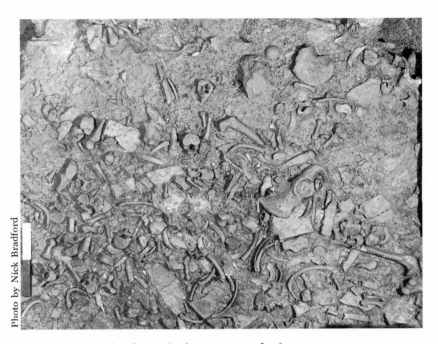

A new archeological feature marked moves into western Europe. People built distinctive rough monuments which have outlasted their homes, artificial caves of a sort, tens of thousands of megalithic tombs in a number of shapes and sizes. According to Andrew Fleming of the University of Sheffield in England, those structures may well be "the earliest ceremonial monuments in the world." Examples of the simplest and earliest type, a straight passage leading to a stone chamber buried in a circular mound, are found in northwestern France, on the Brittany peninsula between the English Channel and the Bay of Biscay. They date to 4500 B.C. or earlier, half a millennium older than the oldest known tombs in the mountains of Iran and more than a millennium before the oldest Egyptian tombs at Hierakonpolis, the precursors of the pyramids.

The stone-chambered structures raise some interesting questions. They required about 5,000 to 10,000 man-hours of labor, seven to fourteen weeks of ten-hour days for ten men, a major effort considering that they were built by small communities, hamlets probably averaging fewer than fifty persons, and that the builders were not full-time specialists, but farmers taking time off from their chores. The reason for all that activity, however, is far from clear. The tombs did not exist primarily to commemorate important individuals. They included large numbers of burials, and generally contained modest grave goods such as flint blades and simple pottery, neither of them high-status symbols.

Recent studies suggest that they served the living as well as the dead. In fact, Fleming calls them "tombs for the living," which in the last analysis means they were not primarily tombs at all, but meeting places with many purposes. A tomb and the area surrounding it may have been something like the "ilo" or commons of Ibo villages in West Africa today. It is a cemetery, among other things, including a sacred hut, the home of ancestral spirits who move about in the underground world and are consulted whenever important decisions must be made. Not far from the hut live future generations, the spirits of children as yet unborn. People gather in the commons to celebrate New Yam Festivals, to hear the beating of drums and feast and drink palm wine and watch wrestling, to have disputes settled by masqueraders impersonating their ancestors.

Stone-chambered tombs very likely played an analogous role in the hamlets and villages of prehistoric Europe. The distribution of the tombs, however, is a puzzle. The vast majority have been found in western Europe, from Gibraltar to the peat bogs of Ireland and islands off the northernmost point of Scotland; many are concentrated in regions along the coasts of the Atlantic Ocean and North Sea. This pattern may have something to do with the last stages of the wave-of-advance process. Renfrew suggests that as people approached the coastlines, the land's end, there was nowhere else to go. Farmers in search of new territory and local hunter-gatherers and fishermen had to live near one another and try to solve by new means problems that they had previously solved, or rather postponed, by moving away. A cemetery where one's ancestors are buried represents a kind of "deed," legal evidence of established property rights, and in time of increasing competition for land, mounds and large stone markers may have helped put such claims on a more solid and conspicuous basis.

Builders designed increasingly conspicuous structures during the last two or three thousand years following the earliest tombs. It was part of the advancing art of mass hypnosis, the theatrical, stage-setting kind of mass hypnosis required to catch, hold, and focus the attention of spectators so that they tend to act automatically and in unison. Similar developments were taking place with varying degrees of sophistication in Sumer and Malta and Egypt and the Far East, in all regions where individuals were in the midst of forming dense population clusters.

In western Europe, as in Africa later and even today in parts of Southeast Asia, architecture and landscaping were used to enhance the impact of megalithic tombs. Long lines of huge upright stone slabs marked avenues of approach, and circles of stones surround the mounds and chambers. Society became organized on a larger and larger scale, as people came together in bigger groups and as chiefs competed for influence. Monuments of all sorts became larger, as well as burial places. It took about 5,000 man-hours to build an early Brittany tomb and as indicated in Chapter 4, more than 30,000,000 man-hours to build Stonehenge. The difference is a good index of power on the rise.

Stonehenge and its setting were well calculated to produce awe. When during midsummer dawns an arc of the sun's disk first moved above the horizon line, directly between two upright stones and split by a marker stone in dead center as if viewed through a giant gunsight, there must have been murmurs and cries among people assembled to watch. It was no natural event, but an act of magic and a demonstration of power. The sun had appeared on schedule precisely where it should have appeared, and the inference was plain—it was obeying the will of the priests and their gods. Eclipses and other events predicted by use of the great observatory-monument implied an even more amazing control of the heavens.

Stonehenge's peak period, 2000 B.C. to 1500 B.C., coincided with the rise of palace centers in distant Crete and on the Greek mainland. It was also a boom time in the rest of Europe, a time of expanding trade in rare raw materials for luxury goods. There was copper and tin and gold in the hills of Ireland, Wales and Cornwall as well as in Brittany and central and eastern Europe. Graves in Greece contained beads made of the fossil resin amber from the shores of Denmark. Treasures found in "princely burials, like the megaliths themselves, attest to the increasing concentration of wealth and power—from Rumania, part of a solid gold dagger

Photos courtesy of Irish Tourist Board

Megaliths in Ireland: Poulnabrone Dolmen, County Clare; Stone circle, Drumbeg, County Cork

weighing three pounds; from southern Russia, a hoard of alabaster maceheads, jade battle axes, and silver spears inlaid with gold."

Trade networks created what has been called an early "European Common Market." Yet for all the mining and quarrying, all the skilled craftsmanship and middlemen and scheduling, life apparently went on without the benefit of high population concentrations in large towns or palace complexes or urban centers. In this respect western Europe resembled Southeast Asia, another forested region where people took part in similarly sophisticated activities primarily at a village level. Many high-status individuals were buried in the Stonehenge area, for example, but no traces of where they lived have been found. Renfrew suggests a hierarchy of people and places in southern England, an evolutionary process starting with a number of independent tribal chiefs each controlling a small territory, comparable to the situation he pictures for the island of Malta, and ending with a group paying tribute to a paramount chief with Stonehenge as his ceremonial center.

Cities, or rather the forerunners of cities, came somewhat later. Population rose beyond the capacities of Bylany-style, slash-and-burn agriculture. Farming became more intensive, farmers' lives harder and more complicated. Forced to allow shorter and shorter fallow periods, they relied increasingly on manuring and plowing to replenish the earth. They moved into less populous areas, into densely forested lowlands, often waterlogged, which in the words of the British archeologist Cyril Fox consisted of "heavy soils unbelievably sticky in winter, caking into ironhard clods in the summer . . . an unending canopy of oak with interlacing undergrowth of hazel, thorn, holly and bramble."

Such heavy soils can be very productive, rather more productive than lighter, readily draining soils which are not as effective in holding water and minerals. But cultivating them is something else again. That demands correspondingly heavier labor and heavier plows. In western Europe during the first millennium B.C. there was a mounting demand for more and tougher implements of all sorts. Iron, originally a luxury material used mainly in ornaments, became the metal of choice for weapons, sickles and hoes and plows. Ralph Rowlett of the University of Missouri notes a marked shift in iron technology around 500 B.C.: "Some hand tools, such as woodworkers' saws, chisels, files and gouges take on the same appearance as they still have in modern hardware stores."

This was the heyday of the Celts, the dominant people of western Europe for more than 500 years. Among them, as among other groups, elaborate burial sites mark the emergence of chiefs and paramount chiefs. One of the most elaborate burials, located near the village of Vix in central France some 120 miles southeast of Paris, and dating to about 500 B.C., contained a young woman of status wearing a diadem of gold with two tiny golden winged horses. To her right was a bronze wine vessel more than a yard in diameter and, to her left, a four-wheeled vehicle, which in modern terms is something like being buried with your favorite sports car.

The Celts were part of a continental trade network (the Vix diadem and wine vessel came from Greece), which, judging by oriental motifs appearing in some of their most striking works of art, included groups to the east in the steppes of Asia. Celtic armies moved early into Greece and Italy, and in 390 B.C. they became the first people to sack Rome, something the Romans never forgot. They built western Europe's first cities, among them Bibracte, the largest site in a region currently being studied by Carole Crumley of the University of Missouri and her associates.

Perched high on a granite mountain in eastern France not far from the Loire River, the city represented a major concentration of people and power. Its sixty-acre inner precinct was surrounded by a wall of stone and iron-nailed timbers and a ditch twenty feet deep. The city had a system of roads, and special quarters including a business district, marketplace, ironworking area, religious section, and a section reserved for elite residences. Its 330 acres housed an estimated 40,000 persons.

The capital of a Celtic state-to-be, Bibracte served as a center for settlements in a region of perhaps 800 to 1,000 square miles, a region which even today, in the midst of Western civilization, commemorates some of the traditions of times past. Springtime country fairs are held here in the same marketplaces where pagan festivals greeting the spring were held some 2,500 years ago. Every June 23 a local village still celebrates Midsummer Eve, when witches were supposed to be on mischief sprees, by burning a wickerwork bundle of sticks crowned with a wooden bird on a pole. "Today, when the pole and the bird fall in a shower of sparks," Crumley notes, "the spectators drive home in Renaults and Citroens."

Crumley is studying the settlement system with Bibracte as the central place, the central fortified city—and a hierarchy of about a dozen fortified towns and an undetermined number of hamlets and villages and special refuges for protection against invaders. In a recent dig she identified Mont Dardon, a site on a 2,000-foot hill some fifteen miles south of Bibracte, as a fortified town by its triple ring of ditch-and-wall defenses.

Bibracte was more than a city. The capital of a powerful Celtic group, it held an important place in the network of centers that was the emerging Gaulish state. Past studies suggest the existence of three administrative levels as in Uruk, Susa, and other early city-states. Certainly there were at least three levels in its social hierarchy; priests and aristocrats at the top, administrators and merchants and craftsmen comprising a broadly based middle class, and farmers and temporary laborers in the lowliest positions.

Given a bit more time, perhaps as little as a century or less, the city might well have evolved a new and distinctive style of art and monumental architecture. It might have become one of the key centers of a far more powerful and widespread state, a state powerful enough not only to beat back invaders but to engage in successful invasions of its own. Western Europe might have left an early legacy as glamorous as that of the southern subcontinent. That prospect never materialized. Roman legions conquered the area in 52–51 B.C.; Caesar made his winter quarters in Bibracte. It was the end of Gaul's war for independence.

13

The Navigators,
Pioneers of the Pacific

*The crossing into Australia/ A subcontinent
without farmers/ The evidence for gardening in
New Guinea/ Exploring Oceania/ Sailing by
the stars and waves/ Underwater lightning/
The chiefdoms of Polynesia/ Island plazas and
pyramids/ The Maori forts of New Zealand/
Divine rulers in Hawaii/ The limits of
primitive society*

I T was not much of a voyage in itself, only fifty miles or so from
a small island somewhere off the coast of Southeast Asia, out
beyond landmarks into open seas, and then toward a long smudge
of shoreline sighted on the horizon. Nevertheless, it demanded a
degree of skill and courage to maneuver the craft, a bark canoe
or perhaps a raft—especially considering the times, 40,000 or
more years ago. The pioneers landed on a huge island where no
man had ever been before, an island continent bigger than the
United States.

There were many trips after that. Some people spread over
their new continent along rivers and coasts, across wide plains
and up mountain passes into valleys ripe for exploiting. Others

295

spread over the waters, sailing hundreds of miles across the seas, out of sight of land, guided by stars and birds in flight and the behavior of the sea itself. Theirs was one of the last frontiers, one of the last habitable regions on earth to be settled. Five centuries before Columbus they had completed their exploration of the vast and dispersed world of Oceania, which includes New Guinea and the 7,000 or so other islands of the open Pacific to the east (and does not include the estimated 15,000 islands to the west, about half of them in the Philippines and half in Indonesia).

At the time of that early voyage and early landing, the island continent was larger than it is now. People arrived during the last ice age, when glaciers had locked up so much water that the

A single land-mass: island continent about 40,000 years ago when the seas were several hundred feet lower, and Australia and New Guinea together made up a continent, reached by people island-hopping in primitive canoes

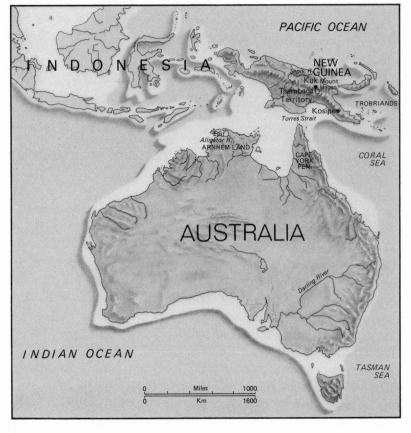

Vantage Art, Inc.

Courtesy of the American Museum of Natural History

Highland landscape, New Guinea

seas were 300 to 400 feet lower than they are today. New Guinea and Australia formed part of the same landmass. Travelers could walk from one to the other across a wide semidesert savanna more than 800 miles wide connecting northern Australia, from Arnhem Land to the Cape York Peninsula, to southern New Guinea. About 20,000 years ago, the glaciers began melting. Waters rose an average rate of three to four feet a century, submerging the plain around 5000 B.C. to 6000 B.C. and creating two regions with quite distinct prehistories.

The record of Australia includes a major puzzle. Of all the Pacific islands inhabited by the time the first European arrived, it was the only one without agriculture of some sort. The original population consisted of hunter-gatherers, and their descendants remained hunter-gatherers for approximately 40,000 years, a state of affairs which puts general theories about agricultural origins to a rather stiff test. Any such theory should be able to explain not only why people turned to farming in some areas, but also why they failed to do so elsewhere.

The Australians of prehistory knew enough to become farmers at least as early as people in other parts of the world. In the tropical Northern Territory they were well equipped to clear the forests effectively if they had wanted to. About a decade ago Carmel Schrire of Rutgers University found stone ax heads, complete with ground edges and grooves for hafting, at a rock-shelter site near the East Alligator River in Arnhem Land. Carbon-14 tests, run on tiny fragments of charcoal painstakingly separated by sieving from half a ton of sand, show that the tools were associated with hearth fires which burned 20,000 to 25,000 years ago.

That date came as a surprise to many investigators. The axes are the oldest yet discovered anywhere, and provide evidence for a higher degree of tool-making proficiency than had been expected of early aborigines. Such axes also appeared early in Japan. They did not appear in the Near East, Europe, or in most other regions until thousands of years later; even though modern hunter-gatherers in Australia used them, they were generally regarded, along with sickle blades and pottery and grinding stones, as artifacts that go with the farming life. In Australia they were probably used to chop off branches for spears, spearthrowers and shelters, and to get at honey-rich bees' nests in tree hollows.

Aborigines living along the Darling River in southeast Australia probably came as close to taking up agriculture as any of their fellow hunter-gatherers. Harry Allen of the University of Auckland says that their problems started with the worldwide warming that ended the last ice age and dried up many local lakes and tributaries. Previously plentiful foods like fish, shellfish, and waterfowl declined severely. There was an increased use of seeds, marked by the appearance of grinding stones some 12,000 years ago.

Forced to work harder for their food, aborigines probably moved seasonally into semidesert back country away from the banks of the river, as their latterday descendants were doing as recently as fifty years ago (and as Egyptians in the Hierakonpolis area did when they moved away from the Nile around 4000 B.C.). The back country offered kangaroos, wallabies, tubers, and abundant stands of wild seed plants, including native millet.

At harvest time in this part of Australia plants were pulled up by the roots while still green and before seeds had ripened to fall off and scatter. The plants were gathered into stacks for sun-drying on the outside, and then burned, leaving the seeds to be collected on the ground. According to one nineteenth-century traveler, the hayricks extended for miles: "The grass was beautifully green beneath the heaps, and full of seeds." People stored seeds in kangaroo-skin bags and containers of mud-coated grass. They also observed that the best seed plants grew on plains flooded during heavy summer rains, and built makeshift stone-and-earth dams across stream channels to distribute water more widely, a technique also used by Paiute Indians in California (see Chapter 6).

In the Torres Strait region, where Australia and New Guinea are only about 100 miles apart, David Harris of University College London recently found a north-to-south spectrum of subsistence styles. Combined gardening and hunting-gathering was the rule in coastal New Guinea and the northern strait islands—and almost 100-percent dependence on wild species in the southern islands and Australia's Cape York Peninsula. The "almost" is significant, because Harris's findings support the notion that the Australian aborigines could have developed agriculture if the pressure had been sufficiently strong.

People living in the southeastern part of the cape, for example, exploited a cycad or palmlike plant which served as a staple, producing large quantities of high-calorie seeds; it is still a major food in certain regions. Harris believes that this plant was probably "managed" in the sense that its productivity was increased by the deliberate use of fire to clear away competing vegetation and make harvesting of the seeds easier. In such cases, it is difficult to draw a sharp line between foraging and gardening. Certainly, plant use involved more than simple gathering. The aborigines even cultivated plants for a while, sometimes to please missionaries and anthropologists eager to be of help.

The aborigines never became farmers, but there were signs of increasing pressure in 1788 when the first Europeans came to stay. Some 200,000 of the continent's 300,000 natives were concentrated in the most abundant regions, such as the tropical coast of Arnhem Land and river and coastal areas in the southeast. The rest lived in less favorable territories with some of the world's harshest deserts to the west. Agriculture might have appeared under such conditions, given another few centuries of uninterrupted evolution.

Nearby New Guinea, only a sunken plain away, presents a dramatically contrasting record. Compared with Australia, which somehow seems to have been out of the action, it was in the thick of things, at least during the past 5,000 to 10,000 years. Many migrations started along its coasts, journeys inland as well as over water toward other coasts. The highland heart of the island was a place of steep gorges between mountains and mountain valleys and high eroded ridges, the highest lost in clouds—and over it all, plunging into the gorges and up the mountainsides, a covering of tropical rain forest, broken only by scars of recent landslides and white stretches of massive limestone cliffs showing through.

People moved early into this wild up-and-down land. They endured rains that fell in torrents "the thickness of a lead pencil," and built slender, vine-suspended footbridges which sway like loosening tightropes over raging streams in the gorges below. Their oldest known site, Kosipe, dates back some 25,000 years. About eighty miles due north of Port Moresby, it is conveniently located on a flat-topped ridge more than a mile above sea level, with water near and a view of the surrounding countryside. In 1960, Catholic missionaries, choosing the same spot for the same reasons, began digging foundations for a new church and came upon stone axes and blades, the remains of their prehistoric predecessors.

Peter White of the University of Sydney, who arrived later to conduct official archeological excavations, points out that Kosipe could not have offered comfortable, long-term camping and foraging. Those were ice-age days, and temperatures at that height averaged ten to fifteen degrees Fahrenheit below present levels. Yet there are no signs of shelters. Tools are scattered over a wide area, suggesting shifting occupations, perhaps only a few weeks at a time over a period of many centuries. White believes that the campers lived in a lower and warmer place, and may have climbed up the ridge for brief, seasonal visits to collect high-protein nuts from pandanus or screw-pine trees growing in a nearby swamp.

The beginnings of agriculture are as difficult to trace in New

Guinea as in West Africa or Southeast Asia, because in a tropical-forest setting slash-and-burn methods have little effect on the primeval balance of things. Forests grow back so fast that abandoned cleared-off areas are soon covered completely. Nevertheless, deducing the nature of early gardens presents no particular problems. They could not have differed much from the gardens growing throughout the highlands only a few decades ago, and those still growing today in remote mountainside villages—some of them so close to one another that they are within shouting distance, and yet separated by many hours of hard walking.

In certain respects these plots serve as commonsense energy savers. They concentrate in one small close-at-hand area species that are generally dispersed over a wide area, and thus reduce the amount of climbing and long-distance collecting. A representative garden produces good yields for three years or so until soil nutrients are depleted; then it must lie fallow for ten to fifteen years. It might contain thirty or more kinds of food plants, tuber staples such as taro and sweet potatoes, bananas, sugar cane, breadfruit (a leafy green which tastes something like spinach and goes well with roasted pig), one or more varieties of bean, and a member of the carrot family, often appearing uninvited as a weed.

The gardeners are usually inveterate and perceptive innovators, always on the lookout for new species or varieties. Each plot probably includes two or three plants being tested as possible supplementary foods. They may climb half a mile or more in search of likely-looking specimens, a herb that might be useful as a pig medicine found growing at 9,000 feet and brought back to a garden at the 5,000-foot level, or a new variety of wild ginger with an extra-strong taste. (Some condiments "tamed" too long in gardens tend to lose much of their flavor.) This deep-rooted tradition of innovation may help account for a phenomenon which contradicts some popular notions. People living much as their forefathers lived many generations ago are often regarded as conservatives who will resist bitterly any suggestions that they give up their old ways. This does not hold for many New Guinea highlanders. They are noted for their readiness to take on new life-styles almost overnight. Swift acceptance of novelty has been the rule rather than the exception.

People lost no time in accepting steel axes, roads, and courts to settle disputes. Richard Sorenson of Stanford University reports on the effect of Australian patrols on one highland tribe: "Fighting ceased almost spontaneously throughout the entire area. Most . . . groups did not wait to be told to cease fighting, but stopped on their own—almost as if they had been waiting for an excuse to give it up." There seems to be a widespread tendency to give up too much too soon. Some villagers abandoned their art quickly and found beauty in tin cans and oil drums. Some abandoned their religion to become Christians, although, in the words of one commentator, "they stayed poor and did not stop dying."

In the prehistoric context early gardening and experimenting with new plants were a matter of convenience to ease the job of food-getting. They became increasingly important as populations grew, in large part because of the settling-down process itself. It always takes energy to save energy. Gardening in New Guinea is an unending battle with weeds and pigs. Weeds, like human beings, continually push for living space. Keeping them out is a major task. Fences keep the pigs out, but they must be in good repair. Pigs are constantly "patrolling" closed-off areas, constantly probing and snuffling about to detect rotting wood or any break in the barriers. Once they get in, they devour everything in short order.

New Guinea's first gardens may have been growing as early as 6000 B.C. to 7000 B.C., about the time of the earliest farming in Egypt and China and the Near East. This guess is based on evidence coming from sites near the frontier town of Mount Hagen in the highland valley of the winding Wahgi River, where Jack Golson of the Australian National University in Canberra and his associates are carrying out one of the most ambitious studies of garden agriculture ever launched.

The project started about ten years ago with the discovery of wooden artifacts in a swamp being drained for growing tea. Buried beneath as much as six feet of soggy peat were well-

Kuk site, highland New Guinea: palimpsest of drainage ditches, black and gray, traces of ancient systems.

Local tribesmen, Korowa and Ul, with wooden spades preserved in swamp, similar to tools still in use

Courtesy of Jack Golson, Australian National University

Photo by J. K. Gollan

Photo by P. J. Hughes

preserved digging sticks, fence posts and paddle-shaped spades; they stirred up memories in one villager, who knew exactly what to do with them. An old man gave an on-the-spot demonstration, using a pointed digging stick to pry out deep roots and a spade to make plot lines, cut turf, and dig small holes. The spade is identical to spades he had used in his valley forty years ago, before Europeans came. Tools exactly like the digging stick, which is about 2,300 years old, are still used today.

Under the peat appeared traces of prehistoric ditches, some of them twelve feet wide and twelve feet deep, running under and across modern ditches and showing up clearly in black-earth profile. This drainage network and a similar network unearthed over the past few seasons at the Kuk Tea Research Station, a 770-acre plantation some six miles away, may be parts of a larger integrated system. The first ditches may have been dug 6,000 years ago, the generally accepted time for the establishment of agriculture in the New Guinea highlands.

Golson argues for a still earlier date. He believes that the first slash-and-burn agriculturalists cleared bushes from the slopes of hills overlooking the Kuk swamps, thereby exposing the ground to the direct impact of heavy rains and increasing erosion. Deposits of gray clay found in the swamps, presumably washed down when the hills were cleared, began forming some 9,000 years ago. Even earlier evidence exists in the form of hollows uncovered under the clay, possibly places where prehistoric pigs wallowed. Some of the hollows have troughs and stake holes, suggesting that the animals were sometimes tied to their wallows to keep them out of gardens. The presence of pigs directly attested by remains at least 6,000 and perhaps as much as 10,000 years old, is one of the surest signs of agriculture in New Guinea, since they are mainland animals and had to be brought in by boat.

Studies of present-day farmlands in a valley more than 300 miles to the west may provide insights into the kind of farming practiced in the Wahgi Valley long ago. There crops are growing on both the slopes and flats with the aid of dams, earth-retaining stone walls and other advanced water-control techniques. If signs of similar techniques are uncovered in early levels at Kuk or elsewhere, it will be proof positive that the highlanders of New Guinea were engaged in advanced communal planning far earlier than has hitherto been suspected.

The evidence also suggests considerable activity along the coasts. New Guinea played a double role in prehistory, looking inward as it were, and looking outward and away. It was a place where people turned their backs on the sea and ventured deep into the interior and learned to live in clearings on the edges of dark forests. It was also a launching platform, a place to leave behind for voyages toward new and distant landfalls, one of the principal setting-out points in early explorations of the Pacific.

Before the long-distance explorations there must have been considerable activity in local waters. Historical records describe regional trade systems which have ancient origins, for example, the famous "kula ring" or circular chain involving the Trobriand Islands and neighboring archipelagoes, off the eastern tip of New Guinea. Once or twice a year people included in the ring launch their canoes and sail across up to 200 or more miles of open seas to other islands in the system. They arrive bearing gifts for established trading partners, the type of gift depending on the direction from which they came. People sailing in a clockwise direction give necklaces of red shell from the Spondylus or thorny oyster, a species collected by skin divers from deep coral reefs; people sailing in a counterclockwise direction give white-shell armbands. These rare and highly valued ornaments serve as goodwill tokens, creating an atmosphere of friendship. Carol and Melvin Ember of Hunter College compare the procedure to "the ceremonial exchange of musk oxen and pandas . . . between the United States and China." In both cases the ritual serves as prelude to hard bargaining and trading. The islanders' canoes include a great deal besides shell gifts. They are crammed with pottery, yams, fish, taro, pigs and other practical items.

In prehistoric times more far-ranging voyages probably followed such local trips. From its position just below the equator New Guinea looks out over the world's largest ocean, where most of the spectacular scenery lies underwater. Within 200 miles of its northeastern coast the ocean floor plunges down from the ninety-foot level of the continental shelf to a trench, a split in the earth, more than five and a half miles deep. In all directions the bottom is dotted with mountains, the vast majority completely submerged, some only fifteen to thirty feet below the surface or barely awash. A small proportion of the mountaintops break the surface, and they are Oceania's 7,000 islands.

People moved from island to island as their landlubbing ancestors on the continents had moved from valley to valley in a process born of adventure, necessity, and, sometimes, desperation. There was always the excitement of taking risks, testing one's nerve and endurance to the limit. Races and "challenge" voyages beyond the horizon, perhaps looking for new islands reported by sailors blown off course and returned to tell the tale, provided an ideal way of doing something that had never been done before. They also provided numerous opportunities to try out newly designed canoes and sailing tactics.

The boldest young competitors acquired considerable "useless" information during leisure and in the spirit of play, and much of it was continually applied to serious endeavors, especially when the pressure was on. It went into the design of canoes up to 100 feet long with outriggers and two or more hulls, for wars and raids and trade and the search for new outposts, all of which called for skilled navigation. So did those voyages of voluntary or semivoluntary exile occasioned by tensions on home shores. In times of threatened famine when disease or hurricanes ruined crops, some of the people had to leave their islands, often with the blessings and encouragement of priests, and some of their voyages may have ended successfully with landfalls on habitable islands.

Most of the seafaring lore accumulated during prehistoric times has been lost. Recent studies, based largely on voyages and interviews with navigators versed in the art of steering without compass or charts, have retrieved part of what remains, and it is impressive. Thomas Gladwin, an ex-anthropologist now living in Oakland, California, describes his sensations while sailing with one such expert from Puluwat, an island in the central Carolines:

Hours go by, miles of water have flowed past. Yet the canoe is still underneath and the stars are still above. Back along the wake, however, the island you left falls farther and farther behind, while the one toward which you are heading is hopefully drawing closer. . . . You know too that there are islands on either side of you, some near, some far, some ahead, some behind. The ones that are ahead will in due course fall behind. Everything passes by the little canoe—everything except the stars by night and the sun in the day.

So it is as if the canoe were standing still, an island in a wide terrestrial river, while the rest of the world drifts past. Familiar places exist in the skies, stars and star patterns to steer by—and in the ocean, seamarks such as coral reefs, built up on mountain-tops, some of them submerged more than thirty feet yet clearly visible in clear tropical waters. They are recognized at a glance in passing, the way travelers by land recognize the contours and features of familiar hills and valleys. During the day reefs can be spotted a mile or two off by telltale whitecaps and a change in water color from blue to green. At night the whitecaps produce a characteristic "uneasiness" or roughness in the motion of the canoe.

This is only one example of the fine art of reading waves. A small boat serves as a sensitive instrument, a kind of natural seismograph, for those "tuned in" on the vibrations it picks up from the water. David Lewis, an investigator at the Australian National University and a first-rate helmsman himself, has learned a great deal about wave messages from veteran native navigators guiding his thirty-nine-foot ketch as well as their own canoes.

In the open ocean, they may steer by the rhythm of a gentle sea swell rolling in from the southeast and moving under and past

Mona Marks

Steering by reflected waves: (1) waves coming head-on, maintain course; (2) waves striking side of canoe, change heading

Settling the world's largest ocean: the great expansion into the Pacific, under way between 3000 B.C. and 1500 B.C.; the Establishment—South Seas version —reached a high point in the Hawaiian Islands

NORTH

AMERICA

OCEAN

DS

LYNESIA

MARQUESAS

TAHITI

SOCIETY IS.

PITCAIRN
IS.

GALAPAGOS

EASTER
ISLAND

the vessel. Even during storms when shifting high winds are blowing up cross waves they can stay on course by detecting that rhythm as a steady signal coming faint but clear through the tumult. Under conditions of low or zero visibility they may use another rhythm to detect a coastline twenty or more miles away. When an ocean swell strikes an island it produces faster and smaller reflected waves which bounce back against the vessel, and indicate the presence and direction of nearby land.

Waves by their steep sharp profile marking strong currents, terns diving for fish twenty to twenty-five miles from their nests on coral islands, clouds that tend to be greenish over lagoons and unusually bright or white over stretches of white sand or surf— these are some of the other signs Lewis learned about during his voyages. One night he was shown flickering streaks and flashes of phosphorescence up to six feet deep, underwater "lightning" which appears in forked patterns far out at sea, moves in the direction of land, and vanishes by the time land is sighted.

His studies show how experienced navigators, by their powers of observation and reasoning and memory, find land in open seas. Given clues accumulated from times past, an expert is almost certain to detect an island if he passes within thirty miles of it, in effect, adding an extra sixty miles to its actual diameter. Each island becomes an "expanded target" and, since the detectable distances of many islands overlap, it has the effect of solid blocks of land. In the 300 Fiji Islands, the overlapping forms an effective superisland of 122,000 square miles, about the area of the state of New Mexico.

Prehistoric sailors, like their few remaining present-day counterparts, had the knowledge to move with confidence across the wide Pacific. Venturing into unknown waters, they steered by stars and waves, noting and mapping islands and reefs in their minds and, because of the distribution of islands, hardly ever having to travel more than 300 to 350 miles without a landfall. In 1976, a new effort was launched to relearn some of the sealore that passed with their passing. A Hawaiian crew captained by Kawika Kapulehua of the Polynesian Voyaging Society successfully sailed a specially built, sixty-foot, double-hulled canoe to Tahiti and back.

By 6000 B.C. there were people, presumably from New Guinea,

on the neighboring islands of New Ireland and perhaps New Britain and the westernmost Solomons. The great expansion into more remote regions came later, starting between 3000 B.C. and 1500 B.C. with pressure that arose nearer the Asian mainland. Waves of families from northeastern Indonesia, the Philippines and Taiwan had to move, probably because of overcrowding, and embarked for points west and south. Some of their descendants landed on the coasts of islands in the New Guinea region; others made landfalls in the New Hebrides and further east. They brought food with them, species originally domesticated in Southeast Asia including taro, yams, bananas, coconuts, breadfruit, pigs, chickens and dogs.

They left traces of their migration. Their tool kit included adzes made from the shells of giant clams and resembling adzes used more than a millennium earlier in the Philippines, bored shark teeth, occasional whale teeth, files made of stone and coral, pig-tusk engraving implements, and sling stones. They made Lapita pottery, named after a site on the west coast of New Caledonia and noted for elaborate maze, crescent, arc, and triangle patterns produced with a stamping tool. Tattooing was practiced as indicated by tattooing chisels and what is probably the decorated buttocks of a pottery figurine. Surfboard riding, a popular Oceanian sport with ancient origins, may have been popular.

Roger Green of the University of Auckland in New Zealand has found a number of sites with such remains. There are sites on coral islands of the Santa Cruz archipelago east of the Solomons, where villagers adapted to "an impoverished environment by importing over great distances." From about 1300 B.C. on they were obtaining obsidian and flintlike stone and other materials, passed along from island group to island group in down-the-line fashion, from sources as far as 600 to 1,200 miles to the west.

Judging by nineteenth-century records, trade also developed within the archipelago itself. Local sailors made frequent voyages of 100 miles or less to exchange canoes, food, women, shell ornaments and fabrics. They often paid for the wares with red feathers from birds on one of the southernmost islands. It was in Santa Cruz waters, by the way, that Lewis first saw displays of underwater phosphorescence.

The spread through Oceania continued. "Lapita" people, people

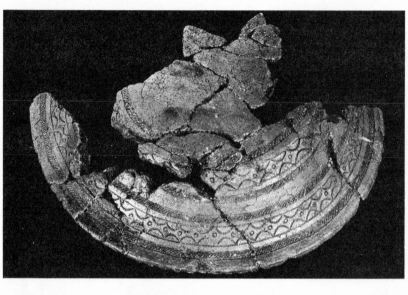

Mona Marks

Lapita pottery designs: dish from Reef Islands; sherds from New Caledonia; motifs from New Caledonia

using the distinctive decorated pottery and associated artifacts, moved into more easterly archipelagoes. Green notes that many of their sites are found on peninsulas or on small islands off large ones, the sort of places seafarers might be expected to choose. By 1200 B.C. at least, they had already reached the Fiji Islands—and, beyond that, the Tonga and Samoa Islands at the western edge of Polynesia, the 10,000,000-square-mile roughly triangular stretch of ocean with Hawaii, New Zealand and Easter Island at the corners.

It took about two millenniums for their descendants and other peoples to explore the rest of Polynesia, often migrating by a kind of leapfrog process to more remote islands first, and, later, working backward to nearer islands. They reached the Marquesas nearly 5,000 miles east of New Guinea around the year 300, bringing pottery tempered with quartz sands that have been traced to the Fijis. Landfalls may have been made at about the same time on Hawaii, a century later on Easter Island (requiring a voyage of some 1,100 miles of open ocean), on New Zealand about 750 or somewhat later. By 1000 or so, when Leif Ericson and his Norsemen were sailing somewhere off the coast of Labrador or New England, almost all the habitable islands of Polynesia were settled.

Despite the fact that people were dispersed over such a wide expanse of the Pacific, they exhibited a remarkable degree of cultural unity. As far as languages are concerned, for example, all Polynesians were practically fellow countrymen. Maori tribesmen in New Zealand can understand Hawaiians, and the region's thirty languages share similar words for sixty to eighty percent of the items on a basic vocabulary list. This is in marked contrast to Melanesia, the region from New Guinea to Fiji, with its more than 1,000 different languages, most of which have only fifteen percent of their words in common.

There are other contrasts between Melanesia and Polynesia. Marshall Sahlins points out that the general rule for Melanesians is "small, separate, and equal." Most of them live in self-governing groups of 70 to 300 persons, with a maximum of several thousand among New Guinea highlanders, and each small village and cluster of hamlets tends to have its own "big man," the head of an independent clan who leads by charisma and personal abilities and as long as he can command the respect of his fellowmen.

In Polynesia, on the other hand, the scale of things is big and unequal. Dispersed communities of 2,000 to 3,000 persons are common, and the largest may number 30,000 or more. Controlling such groups, reducing conflict and resolving conflicts when they arise and organizing the flow of food, demands more formal and institutionalized leadership. Polynesia is a world of hierarchies, ranked clans and chiefs. According to Sahlins, "the qualities of command that had to reside in men in Melanesia, that had to be personally demonstrated . . . to attract loyal followers, were in Polynesia socially assigned to office and rank." These differences had ancient origins. Geography, the lay of the land, was in part responsible. The Melanesian pattern evolved on large islands like New Guinea, especially in gorge-separated highland villages where depths rather than distances kept people apart. In such terrain effective day-to-day communication is difficult enough, even today. It was impossible in prehistoric times, and Melanesians tended to bring their ancient big-man, small-group life-style with them wherever they went.

What became the Polynesian life-style also arose in Melanesia, but the settings were widely different from the New Guinea variety. They consisted mainly of small islands like those of the Santa Cruz archipelago, and the eastern Fijis which have been called the homeland of the proto-Polynesians. Small islands offer little room for hiding. Things tend to be out in the open, land is limited, good farmland rather more limited. Populations may rise rapidly, in part because the islands are healthy places isolated from most of the world's diseases. Long voyages in open boats may tend to kill off weaker migrants.

Survival depended on controlling land use and sharing food. It also depended on taking drastic measures when populations increased beyond the land's capacity to feed them—forced voyages and sometimes massacres usually sanctioned as the will of the gods. Dealing with subsistence pressure was one of the factors involved in the rise of central authority. Peter Bellwood of the Australian National University suggests that a single society of early Polynesians evolved appropriate institutions "somewhere on the western periphery of Polynesia" and that their descendants "adhered to this system with remarkable tenacity."

Among the marks of the system are remains of thousands of

Courtesy of the American Museum of Natural History

Stone heads, Easter Island

open courtyards or plazas, sacred ceremonial places with raised stone platforms and upright stone slabs rather like those in the megaliths of prehistoric Europe. As a refinement of the upright-stone tradition large stone statues appeared on some islands, including Pitcairn of *Mutiny on the Bounty* fame, the Marquesas—and, most widely publicized, on Easter Island which Renfrew compares to Malta as a place where early chiefs mobilized people for the building of impressive monuments.

Ten recently discovered plazas have been excavated on an atoll north of Tahiti, with the aid of funds provided by the atoll's owner, Marlon Brando. One of the most spectacular structures in Polynesia was located on Tahiti itself, a ten-stepped stone platform or pyramid which is about 270 feet long and five stories high and was built in the eighteenth century. (As a reminder that monumental architecture is not confined to Polynesia, Ponape Island in the Carolines some 4,000 miles northwest of Tahiti has a 170-acre district of tombs and platforms built out of prism-shaped chunks of basalt.)

So much has happened so recently in Polynesia that historical records as well as archeology provide important insights into the

Courtesy of Clifford Evans and Betty J. Meggers, Smithsonian Institution

Ponape, Caroline Islands: wall of prism-shaped basalt blocks,
apparently brought on rafts to the island

evolution of complexity. The pace of events tends to blur the picture, however. New Zealand's entire prehistory is packed into a millennium or less, starting between 750 and 1000 when voyagers arrived from tropical islands to the northeast, and ending in 1769 when Captain James Cook of the Royal British Navy put in at the Bay of Islands.

The aboriginal New Zealanders, known as Maoris, came with a knowledge of agriculture and with taro and other domesticated species. Although their first efforts must have gone into adapting these plants to the new, colder environment, they did not ignore wild foods—birds, especially the ostrichlike moa (eventually hunted into extinction), seals, dolphins, eels, waterfowl and more

Maori hill forts, New Zealand
Courtesy of Richard Cassels, University of Auckland; photo by A. R. Buist

than seventy wild plants, notably the thick starchy underground stems of the bracken fern.

By the fourteenth century the natural abundance of the land was seriously depleted. Agriculture became increasingly essential, as Maori populations continued to climb toward 100,000, the estimated total at the time of European contact. The sweet potato, one of many foods, became a staple. People prepared selected fields especially for the crop, spreading sand and gravel and charcoal over the ground to increase fertility, heat retention and drainage. About 5,000 acres of these artificial "Maori soils" have been found in one area along a river south of Auckland.

Warfare increased with increases in population and farming. Signs of ancient tensions can be seen in Auckland itself from the top of Mount Eden, a terraced volcanic cone overlooking the city. Mount Eden once served as a fort and so did many other hills which rise abruptly from the surrounding plain. Most of the estimated 4,000 Maori forts were located on hills along the coast. They included pits for storing sweet potatoes, earthwork defenses, wooden palisades and fighting platforms, and houses inside grouped around a central area, probably used for special meetings and ceremonies.

There were hierarchies of forts and settlements and chiefs. Preliminary research by Bellwood, Richard Cassels of the University of Auckland, Wilfred Shawcross of the Australian National University, and Kathleen Shawcross of New Zealand's Department of Internal Affairs in Wellington suggests that small groups with minor chiefs lived near or in relatively small forts and, during dire emergencies, might retreat to bigger forts maintained by the higher-ranking chiefs of bigger villages. In times of large-scale warfare, or the threat of large-scale warfare, entire tribes of 2,000 to 3,000 persons came together, and on occasion apparently remained together. In at least one case a major fort was surrounded by clusters of houses and about 200 acres of stone-walled fields, forming a permanent concentration of people under a paramount chief.

Apparently the prehistoric Maori never moved very far toward a grand alliance or superhierarchy of all paramount chiefs, a system bringing the entire country under a single leader. The development, the way to statehood, occurred elsewhere, in Tonga and Tahiti, among other places—and in certain respects things proceeded furthest of all about 4,600 miles from New Zealand, at the northernmost corner of the great Polynesian triangle, in the Hawaiian archipelago.

Pioneering families, probably setting out from the Marquesas to the southeast, may have reached the archipelago by about A.D. 300, the earliest date yet recorded. They settled on flat coastal areas and in deep-cut valleys coming down from mountains in the interior. In a recent analysis Ross Cordy of the University of Hawaii points out that they usually chose sites along coastlines exposed to prevailing trade winds from the northeast, rain-laden winds which watered valley slopes and made for easy slash-and-burn agriculture. They raised pigs and fished with characteristic pearl-shell hooks, bonito trolling hooks and special octopus lures.

The story from here in is familiar—simple beginnings and rising complexity, with population increase as one of the driving forces. Archeologically the change involves more and more sites in marginal lands, drier places requiring terracing and large-scale irrigation to produce higher yields of taro, sweet potatoes and other crops. Direct proof for the coming of political centralization on a large scale includes the appearance of large temples and housing complexes. A number of carved whale-tooth pendants indicate high rank as surely as five-star army insignias, since only chiefs were allowed to wear them.

This sort of evidence dates to the early seventeenth century, but advanced authority of some sort must have existed at least a century or two before that, when the islands' population probably reached a peak of about 250,000 persons. By that time the distance between chief and commoner had widened from a mild gap to an enormous gulf. Marion Kelly of the Bishop Museum in Honolulu summarizes what happened: "The high chief once took a leading part in planting, building irrigation ditches and terraces, fishing, and so on. This role gradually passed to lesser chiefs, while high chiefs became increasingly involved in temple worship —and increasingly occupied with worshipping Kukailimoku, god of war, and with military conquest."

At the time of European contact, marked by the arrival of the ubiqitous Captain Cook in 1778, Hawaii's eight main islands were ruled by four paramount chiefs, each having perhaps 200 to 300 attendants and advisors and 25,000 to 100,000 subjects. At the next lowest level were 33 administrative subchiefs responsible for as many districts, which included up to a dozen valleys and which were shaped like pieces of pie, with a wide curved ocean frontage and coming to a point inland in the mountains. Ranking below the administrators were district officers or stewards in charge of the affairs of individual valleys, small pie-cuts—and commoners of course, the workers of the land, made up the bottom-most level of the social pyramid.

The paramount chiefs ruled by divine right. In fact, judging by the behavior demanded of their subjects, their rights were considerably more divine than those of most kings. The amount of awe and humility due to a paramount chief often rose to remarkable proportions in Polynesia and elsewhere, but it seems to have reached an extreme in Hawaii. People prostrated themselves at his passing, faces in the dust. They did this for Captain Cook when he landed, mistaking him for a god (although they rose and followed as soon as his back was turned). Their shadows were not allowed to fall on the chief or any of his possessions. Violations were punishable by stoning, burning or strangling.

The Establishment, South Seas version, may have had the look of stability to some early visitors, but there had been many conflicts in the past and there were many conflicts to come. Robert Hommon of the Bishop Museum cites records of eleven generations of kings on the island of Hawaii, which had 500 communities, six districts and six high chiefs. That 275-year period saw the position of paramount filled twenty-two times, more often than not as a result of warfare. In only eight of the accessions was the entire island unified politically, and in at least three cases by a usurper—that is, by someone not the first son of a first son, the traditional route. The rest of the time one or more chiefs remained aggressively outside the coalition.

Similar situations prevailed on other Hawaiian islands. A chronic instability was built into the system. In a continuing study, Sahlins is concerned with the reasons for such conditions, why the Hawaiians lived always "on the threshold of fission." For one thing, it was a formidable problem to feed and arm warriors away from their home bases. The dietary staple, taro, is very bulky and a man must eat more than five pounds a day, thus putting a severe strain on supply lines supporting sieges by armies of several hundred or several thousand warriors.

High chiefs replaced lower chiefs related to people in individual valleys with their own relatives, a move calculated to centralize control. But it also centralized conflict. It substituted large-scale in-fighting at the top for rivalries at the grass-roots or taro-roots level. As has been noted, there is no fighting more bitter than fighting among close kin, blood relatives. Details of how the system operated exist in missionary records, state archives, land claims and other documents currently being studied by Sahlins and his associates. He points out that the case of Hawaii has broad implications as far as understanding efforts to achieve unity are concerned: "The limits of chieftainship are the limits of primitive society itself. Where kinship is king, the king is in the last analysis only kinsman, and something less than royal. The same bonds that link a chief to the underlying population and give him his authority, in the end tie his hands." Hawaii was finally unified for a time by a chief using European weapons, ships and political strategems. Later all chiefs and tribal institutions passed.

14

The Evolution of Ritual in the New World

P EOPLE first entered the New World during the ice-age days when seas were several hundred feet lower than they are at present. They came over a so-called land bridge, actually a plain more than a thousand miles wide which connected Siberia and Alaska in the Bering Strait region. No one knows when they made the crossing. As usual, in the absence of clinching evidence, there are many estimates, all by qualified investigators and all reasonably plausible, ranging from about 15,000 to 100,000 years ago.

Right now the tendency is to push the event back in time. In recent studies based on analyses of protein in fossil bones, Jeffrey Bada of the Scripps Institution of Oceanography in La Jolla, California, concludes "that man was present in North America at

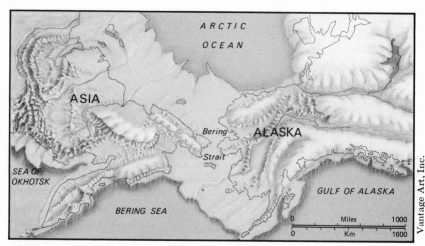

Principal route into the New World: people entering the Americas within the past 20,000 years across the Bering land bridge—and perhaps 30,000 or more years earlier in rafts or canoes, or across seasonally frozen waters

least 50,000 years ago," and 25,000 years ago, once considered a radical estimate, is beginning to look a bit conservative. Crossings could have been made at an early date, over land routes during ice ages, or even by water. The strait is only fifty miles wide with two islands in the middle, and could have been negotiated by raft or canoe, or simply by walking, since the channel often freezes solid.

Pioneers from Siberia and their descendants ultimately broke out of glacier and tundra lands in the far north, and spread through two virgin continents. Within four or five millenniums, according to wave-of-advance models, they had moved down across prairies and semideserts and over the long corridor extending from Mexico to Panama into South America, reaching its southernmost tip by 8000 B.C. And the record they left is remarkable, especially when compared to the course of events in the Old World.

People in the Near East and Mesoamerica, the region including most of the Mexico-to-Guatemala corridor, and in the Andes started domesticating species during roughly the same period. Although further developments may have occurred in a somewhat different order and at a different pace, they involved the same basic pressures and displays of power—rising populations, the

Vantage Art, Inc.

Power in the New World: Mesoamerica, with some of the Valleys of
Tehuacan and Oaxaca where earliest known villages and ceremonial
buildings have been discovered; the Olmec territory along the Gulf Coast,
where early art and religion reached a high point about 3000 to 2500 years
ago, followed soon after by the emergence of the first cities, including
Teotihuacan and Monte Alban and Tikal

clustering of people and settlements, and monumental works erected by elites to their own glory and to the glory of the gods. There were other universals or near-universals, common elements in ways of looking at the universe. The concern with order, with a proper place for everything and everything in its proper place, was as intense in the New World as anywhere else. Here also enormous effort went into studies of the skies, the seasons, divisions of the year and calendars, recurrent astronomical phenomena of all sorts—into the discovery, the creation, of harmony and of ways to restore harmony when things went wrong.

One of the places where people came to stay and changed with changing times is the Tehuacan Valley about 150 miles southeast of Mexico City. A small pocket of land nearly a mile high and enclosed in a wall of mountains, it has been the scene of intensive studies headed by Scotty (Richard) MacNeish, director of the Peabody Foundation for Archeology in Andover, Massachusetts, who cites with some pride as No. 1 on his list of professional honors the winning of a Golden Gloves boxing championship (bantamweight, 1938).

To reconstruct the past scientifically, he and his associates located more than 450 sites in the valley, selecting a dozen for large-scale excavations. These were multilevel sites, with a total of 138 separate living floors, one above the other, representing occupations as they existed at different periods. They yielded many thousands of artifacts, spindle whorls, some thirty types of projectile points, textile and basket fragments, whittled wooden plugs (purpose unknown), burned bones and much more, the position of each one being recorded in field notebooks to be transferred later to file cards and the memory units of a high-speed computer. Among other things, the computer automatically printed charts showing the positions of items found on living floors and providing clues to where people were working and what they did. The raw facts for early developments were collected during five digging seasons, ending in 1965. Analysis is still under way. The findings of MacNeish and his associates already fill five volumes, with a sixth in the works and perhaps two more to follow.

The first families, some twenty-five to thirty hunter-gatherers in all, arrived 12,000 or more years ago. They found a valley of open grasslands already supporting populations of pronghorn antelopes, horses, large jackrabbits and other grazing animals, and geared their movements mainly to the movements of the antelope herds, shifting from ambush point to ambush point. MacNeish estimates that they set up new camps about twenty times a year. In the beginning meat made up perhaps as much as fifty percent of their diet, an ideal state of affairs for hunter-gatherers. But it did not last long. With the end of the last ice age the climate changed in the highlands of Mexico as it did during the same period in other parts of the world, for example, among reindeer-hunting cave painters in southwestern France and Spain. The times were warmer and somewhat dryer. In Tehuacan grasslands gave way to semidesert thorn and cactus forests, and small scattered bands of white-tailed deer replaced the antelope herds.

Domestication was one way of adapting to the new conditions, particularly during the rainy season. Gardens were probably located on the moist, often spring-fed floors of steep ravines and canyons. Families created little local abundances, places they could return to in the spring after foraging throughout the valley and living off wild species, since hunting and gathering continued to provide all but a fraction, say five to ten percent, of their food. The gardens, as usual, were probably messy affairs, in the words of one investigator "the ground completely covered with vegetation, hodgepodges, but strategic hodgepodges."

Maguey, the rugged and versatile century plant which thrives even in the driest part of the dry season and can be grown from cuttings, may have been among the earliest cultivated species. Roasted from one to five days to get rid of the bitter taste, it provided an untempting but reasonably nourishing hard-times food (as well as tough fibers and the still-popular fermented drink, pulque). Thoroughly chewed and spat-out maguey quids were found on Tehuacan living floors. By about 5000 B.C., early gardens included chili peppers, beans, and perhaps squash.

There was a "sleeper" in the garden, a less important cereal which would become the main dietary staple of Mesoamerica and the whole New World. Corn has been called the most highly specialized grass in the world. It furnishes a striking example of artificial selection, evolution guided, not always consciously, by man—a process Darwin described as "a magician's wand" permitting the plant breeder to "summon into life whatever form and mould he pleases." In this case selection was to transform a tiny tasseled ear with less than a dozen kernels into the hybrid giants of the twentieth century with hundreds of kernels, each one of which may provide as much energy as an entire ear of the original plant.

The major part of that transformation was achieved in prehistoric times, representing the American Indians' most notable contribution to the agricultural art. According to a current theory, they started with a grass known as teosinte, which like many grasses is designed to flourish in disturbed soils, including the disturbed soils of human campsites. It exists in massive stands today. This plant had no cob. Indeed, the creation of a cob stands as a spectacular result of domestication. It is a vivid reminder of the fact that of all major cereal grasses, corn is perhaps the most plastic, the most readily shaped into new forms and races, largely because it is the only one with separately developed male and female flowers borne on the same plant, which makes for a high frequency of self-pollination and genetic variability.

The theory suggests that before man began to tinker with teosinte, wild corn, it was a low bushy plant with many stalks and side branches. It had 50 to 100 slender spikes, each about three inches long with eight to ten seeds or kernels. Each kernel was shut up tight in a hard woody cupule or seed case which evolved over millions of years, permitting it to pass through an animal's digestive tract unscathed and ready for sprouting. The seed cases were attached to each other by brittle connections. When the wind blew, the cases broke apart, scattering their enclosed kernels on the ground in a self-sowing action.

That mechanism served nature's purposes admirably, but not man's. Efficient gathering depended above all on tough, non-shattering spikes, on plants whose seed cases would not break off so easily in a high wind, but would tend to remain obligingly in place, ready for harvesting. In fields of wild corn a small proportion of "freaks" or mutants met this precise specification. Selecting such varieties was the first step in the domestication of corn, as in the domestication of wheat and barley in the Near East. And in both regions the results were plants which could not seed themselves and depended on man for their existence.

According to the theory, people began selecting for conveniently harvested strains of corn, 10,000 to 15,000 years ago. They probably did not realize what they were doing, at least not at first. They came back from the fields with an extra-high proportion of tough spikes, simply because those were more readily available—and kernels dropped later by accident or sowed deliberately year after year yielded successively higher proportions of plants with tough spikes. Furthermore, the ears tended to be somewhat shorter and clustered, with closely packed kernels, a trait which may have been favored in the wild because birds found the seeds more difficult to get at.

A new plant was in the making by 7000 B.C. It had shorter spikes, perhaps about two inches long. But the kernels were packed closer and there were more of them, say, twenty or so. Their cases were softer, soft enough to pry open with the fingernails. The packing or compaction process continued in varieties developed during the next two millenniums. The ears MacNeish found at Tehuacan were only about an inch long, but many of them had eight rows totalling twenty-six to seventy-two BB-shot-sized kernels imbedded in a brand new structure, a cob formed out of condensed seed-case tissue that had evolved originally to protect them. Later plants had fewer stalks and side branches supporting fewer and increasingly larger ears.

This is one man's version of how corn was domesticated, a theory outlined by Walton Galinat of the University of Massachusetts' Suburban Experiment Station in Waltham. There are other theories, and arguments about which one comes closest to what actually happened have on occasion aroused intense emotions and hurt feelings. Personal relationships have been strained upon occasion, investigators warned forcibly not to publish controversial results; and graduate studdents with insights and evidence of their own have kept quiet for fear of displeasing their teachers and making the difficult ritual of earning their degrees even more difficult.

All this will come as a surprise only to people who still think that science is pursued without passions, and that scientists are any more willing than the rest of us to change long-cherished opinions in the light of new findings. The debate centers on the century-old question of whether or not teosinte is the mother

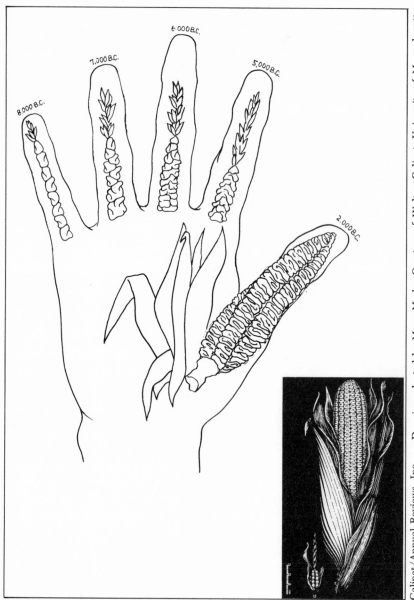

Galinat/Annual Reviews, Inc.   Drawing adapted by Mona Marks. Courtesy of Walton Galinat, University of Massachusetts.

Galinat's schematic rendition of his theory of corn-cob evolution: successive stages of corn domestication, from wild grass (teosinte) to modern-style ear (index finger depicts tiny ears found by Scotty MacNeish at Tehuacan)

Corn now and then: 7,000-year-old pygmy ear from Tehuacan Valley, Mexico, and modern giant plant, the ancestor of today's 200 to 300 races of corn. Galinat, who has been studying corn ever since his high-school days more than three decades ago, believes it is, placing major emphasis on two types of studies—one documenting its close genetic relationship to teosinte, and the other indicating how the teosinte cupule evolved into a cob.

Galinat's work and general ideas are supported by a number of investigators, among them George Beadle of the University of Chicago, who became interested in the problem during the late 1920s and returned to it recently, "after forty years of diversionary academic activities," including a Nobel Prize for basic research in genetics. Chief proponent of the opposing view, that corn arose from an extinct wild ancestor rather than teosinte, is Paul Mangelsdorf of the University of North Carolina. He has been studying corn longer than anyone else, for more than half a century, so his views carry considerable weight. Right now the teosinte theory looks promising. Galinat's research implies that the cobs and other material found at Tehuacan represent not the original wild corn as Mangelsdorf and others believe, but domesticated forms developed from still earlier wild ancestors. Discovery of such forms would certainly reinforce his views.

In their combined corn-bean diets early Mesoamericans achieved what twentieth-century research has revealed as a most effective nutritional balance. Corn is high in calories but low in total protein and lacking in two so-called amino acids, protein units or building blocks necessary to life. Beans are not only protein-rich, but they also happen to contain high proportions of the two amino acids missing in corn. Corn and beans also help one another to grow. In present-day gardens firm corn stalks provide natural "poles" for the climbing vines of bean plants, a mutually convenient arrangement which undoubtedly existed in prehistoric gardens.

The Tehuacanos continued to live predominantly on wild plants and small game. During most of the year theirs was a family way of life. A man, a woman, their children and perhaps a grandparent or two spent most of their time on the go, moving from one area to another within their territory and coming together mainly in the summer when food was abundant. Population increased slowly. MacNeish estimates that it reached 400 by 3500

B.C., which he feels is just about the maximum that could be supported in that valley by nomadic hunter-gatherers supplementing their diets with a small amount of garden produce. The population increased to about 800 persons during the next millennium or so, and farming villages appeared some time thereafter.

This was the typical Mesoamerican pattern, and apparently differs somewhat from the pattern observed in some other parts of the world. For one thing, it took a long time. In the Near East large herds favored collective hunting, the coming together of a number of families to form permanent groups, and a sharp increase in population. As one result, farming villages appeared about 7500 B.C., only 1,500 years or less after the earliest cultivation of wheat and barley. There were no such herds in Mesoamerica after the climate changed and, until the development of increasingly productive varieties of corn, no resource base for settled communal living. Families continued to move from area to area; populations increased slowly. Furthermore, when settlements finally appeared, about 5,000 years after the earliest cultivated corn, each family ran its own garden and kept its own storage pit full.

Different life-styles may be reflected architecturally. As Kent Flannery suggests in Chapter 6, early villages in the Near East often included small circular huts which may indicate segregation of the sexes. They may have housed the wives and children of men living together in a single large communal house, and organized for hunting. Rectangular houses with enough space for entire families came later, with increasing reliance on farms and domesticated species. Mesoamerican villages, on the other hand, had no herds and no big-time hunters. The family had long worked together as a unit, and large houses were built from the very start.

With the rise of villages in the New World, although traditions of equality endured, and indeed were to become even more widely and loudly proclaimed, people were no longer equal. If the hunter-gatherers of early Mesoamerica, like the Kalahari Bushmen and other present-day hunter-gatherers, discouraged the accumulation of wealth and status, and made a special point of putting down the would-be big man, that policy crumbled soon after they settled down.

Among nomadic bands foraging for a living in the wilderness, individuals who were restless or unhappy or angry could move away from it all and join other bands, other kinfolk. But escape, a change of scenery, was rather more difficult for men and women committed to the settled life. The tensions of people living close to other people had to be faced and controlled on the spot, and apparently equality did not work under such conditions. Adapting to the times and the setting demanded new habits, new attitudes, new rituals—and, most important, a stepping up of the scale of things all along the line.

Evidence of what was to come has been uncovered in the Valley of Oaxaca, the current archeological beat of Flannery and his colleagues. Two kinds of public space appeared, two kinds of courtyard, one for the shared activities of family groups within the community, and one for the entire community. Even at the early hamlet and small-village level houses tended to cluster in groups of three or four set around a central courtyard where members of closely related families prepared food for cooking, made pottery, and so on.

Excavations have revealed other spaces apparently cleared for the uses of the entire community. A large fig tree grows today in the village of San José Mogote where around 1600 B.C. local Zapotec Indians, perhaps half a dozen families, built wattle-and-daub houses on a low ridge overlooking the Atoyac River. They also cleared off an area more than twenty feet wide and separated from the rest of the settlement by a double row of posts.

Areas removed from places where people lived were not new. In about 4000 B.C., hunter-gatherers at a summer camp in the same valley had built a similar enclosure, clearing an open space of about the same width and marking it off with two rows of boulders. The enclosure was unusual in that its long axis was aligned slightly west of true north. It is the earliest record of a New World pattern that was to be repeated in later times. (As indicated in Chapter 9, by 2000 B.C. or earlier the so-called citadel areas of the Indus Valley cities, Harappa and Mohenjo-daro, were also oriented roughly in a north-south direction.)

This sort of public space marked the beginning of an evolutionary process that has been traced in Oaxaca and probably took place elsewhere as well. It was followed by general-purpose public

buildings, places where people did many kinds of things together, for meetings, announcements, feasting rituals. Later each
activity tended to have its own separate space. Special-purpose
buildings appeared, temples and palaces and workshops representing new divisions of labor and new social complexities.

The first Zapotec public buildings date to about 1350 B.C. The
people of San José Mogote, by that time a two-acre hamlet of
fifteen or more families, set pine posts into bedrock, raised a
platform of clay, lime, sand and crushed volcanic rock, and built
a rectangular structure about eighteen feet long and fifteen feet
wide. They centered a low adobe altar against the south wall
and a storage pit directly north of the altar. The building was
repaired and renovated from time to time, and probably lasted
three to four decades. Then a new building was built on top of
the old foundations and, later, a third building.

The first temple appeared still later. It can be identified archeologically by a large upper area which includes the remains of little
plaster basins and signs of burning on the floor, and a short flight
of stairs leading down to a lower area. We have a fairly good
idea of what was going on in such places. Descriptions of Zapotec
temples with exactly the same basic ground plans are found in
historical Spanish documents. Priests lived in the upper parts of
the temples, and the basins and burning represent a variety of
sacrifices, everything from dogs and turkeys to human infants and
captives.

The temple was probably built on hallowed ground as were the
earliest temples at Eridu, Nippur, and Uruk in the Near East. The
holy-spot tradition may date back 25,000 or more years ago to
special ritual galleries and grottoes in caves, and has lasted into
our own times. Eva Hunt of Boston University points out that
practically every village in Mexico still has a holy spot. Often a
water hole or a small mound where a pyramid stood in the prehistoric past, it marks the center or "navel" of the world, the
point where all axes intersect and from which the locations of
everything else can be measured.

Another theme, another tradition which can be traced to early
hunter-gatherer times, comes through strongly with the first
temples—the appearance of thousands of clay figurines. Like
figurines found in Greece's Franchthi Cave, the great majority are

found in household debris. According to Flannery and others, they may represent ancestors, since the Zapotec believe that the spirits of deceased ancestors continue to take part in village life, as intermediaries between the living and natural forces. A group of figurines found under the floor of a shed attached to one San José Magote house consists of three adults, arms folded in burial position, with a fourth and smaller adult seated Yoga-style in front of them.

Many of the figurines seem to be masked, which suggests dance rituals and fits into the picture of evolving ceremony and the central importance of rhythm and the dance. Flannery compares the boulder-lined clearing in his valley with Shoshoni Indian "dance grounds" in the western United States, where fandango festivals celebrated the springtime flowering of the desert and piñon-nut harvesting in the fall. Dances with roots in prehistory are still performed in Oaxaca City, mainly in summer and for the entertainment of tourists.

Grouped figurines found under San José Mogote shed, Valley of Oaxaca, Mexico

Courtesy of Kent Flannery and Joyce Marcus, University of Michigan

Ceremony provided times and places for sharing plans and hopes and affections as well as food and other material goods. It was part of an intensifying struggle to unify, for survival's sake, individuals who find getting along with one another difficult over extended periods. Rituals repeated at regular intervals—word for word, gesture for gesture, note for note—had an "imprinting" effect, extending the notion and feeling of family to a number of related families or clans, and ultimately to an entire tribe or state. The process tended to create its own tensions. Rituals tended to build up as people clustered into larger and larger groups, and to separate in the very act of bringing together. There was a demand for more and more complex symbols, bigger and more elaborate temples, for special men and women exalted higher and higher above common folk.

The build-up occurred in the Valley of Oaxaca in due course. It reached an early high point in tropical lowlands to the north, along the coast of the Gulf of Mexico. Here so-called Olmec people flowered in a hothouse atmosphere. Of all places in the world where archeological digging is done, the lowlands are among the least attractive. Digging must go on in moist sticky summertime heat, in swampy terrain; mosquitoes, ticks, giant wasps and poisonous snakes such as the fer-de-lance add to the general discomfort.

The region, however, offers abundant game, fish and waterfowl as well as fertile flood-deposited soils that are annually renewed, requiring no fallow period, and yield nearly twice as much corn as do fields in higher, less humid country. These and other resources supported some remarkable settlements in times past. Michael Coe of Yale University directed excavations at one of the most remarkable of the lot, the site of San Lorenzo located on top of the 150-foot mesa overlooking the jungles and wet grasslands of eastern Veracruz, about thirty-five miles from the Gulf Coast.

There are no grand ruins on this mesa. Clearing the land exposed some 200 "undistinguished little bumps," low mounds on which wattle-and-daub houses once stood, two or three often sharing a family courtyard. The houses themselves vanished long ago. Only the garbage survives, ashes of old hearths and metates for grinding corn, and charred and shattered bones indicating three meat items in the Olmec diet: dogs, a basslike fish known as the snook or robalo, and human beings. Ritual cannibalism was a common practice.

The 600 to 700 inhabitants of San Lorenzo used their most enduring building material, basalt, not for homes and temples but for a number of outstanding monuments, many of them with graven images. One of Coe's first and most exciting finds started with the most routine sort of problem, simply how to get at the side of a large upright basalt slab or stela in the process of being excavated. That called for digging in a new place about a yard or two to the north, moving to a new square of the site's grid system; Coe calls it "the luckiest thing I have ever done." Workers soon uncovered a headless and armless, larger-than-life statue of a kneeling figure. Judging by the insignia and protective belt, it probably represents an athlete equipped for an early version of a notoriously rough ceremonial game involving a large rubber ball, up to eleven men on a side, and perhaps postgame decapitations.

On the off-chance that more monuments might lie further on in a north-south line, Coe kept digging, and his hunch paid off. Along the line he unearthed a headless crouching jaguar, part of a large block that may have been an altar, a column with a were-jaguar (part human, part feline) engraved on it, and a small carved spiderlike creature. About 500 feet south of this alignment of objects was another were-jaguar with snarling mouth and cleft head, the Olmec rain god. It was buried, appropriately enough, near an elaborate stone drainage system, and located with a magnetometer, the same sort of instrument used to detect buried objects in the Nigerian site of Taruga described in Chapter 11.

The site has also yielded seven of the monuments which have become closely associated with the Olmec. Indeed, they amount to Olmec trademarks—colossal, grim-visaged stone heads which loom up to nine feet high, weigh eighteen tons on the average and, because of their stark and rugged style, look even bigger and more massive than they are.

The most elaborate and astonishing artifact of all may be the mesa itself. It is one of many bulges and blisters in the earth, where the land is being pushed up by expanding salt domes deep underneath, oil-rich geological formations which have brought well-digging rigs, red-light districts and other new developments

Colossal heads from 1200-1900 B.C., and figure, excavated at San Lorenzo, Mexico

Courtesy of Michael Coe, Yale University

Olmec-style relief carving at Chalcatzingo, Mexican central highlands:
"rain god" seated in cavern under rain clouds and rain drops

Courtesy of Daniel C. Grove, University of Illinois, Urbana

to Olmec territory. Prehistoric workers reshaped the mesa in ac-
cordance with a master plan. They piled as much as twenty-five
feet of fill over parts of it, and created a series of ridges and
ravines which Coe originally mistook for natural erosion gullies.
He now suggests that they may have been building, and never
finished, a giant effigy, perhaps a bird-god with a wingspread of
about a mile, flying east.

All this, the monuments and the effigy, seems rather grandiose
for what was little more than an oversized village. Part of the
explanation may be found in another north-south alignment consisting of a mound placed between two long courtyards. The
mound, once a stepped platform or pyramid, probably supported
a thatched-roof temple about the size of San José Mogote's first
public building, hardly a prepossessing structure in itself. But
its position was highly significant. Located at the village's very
center, it represented a holy spot, the center of the contemporary
Olmec world.

That world extended outside the high mesa into surrounding areas. San Lorenzo was a ceremonial center, a small-scale rural Mecca, probably serving people from dozens of villages and hamlets within a radius of perhaps thirty miles or so. They came for "Saturday night" spectacles, the awe and the excitement and the rituals. They also came to work. The basalt for the colossal heads and other monuments had been traced to mountain quarries fifty miles away, and it may have required the labor, perhaps forced, of more than a thousand men to mine and shape blocks of stone weighing many tons, float them on rafts to the mesa area, pull them up the slopes and set them in place.

Such projects demanded power, purpose, religious feeling and, certainly, the existence of planners and people of status. But not the most elaborate sort of status. One is reminded of the art created in early African settlements, and of the missionary who came and saw and scorned the people's "shabby little temples" and the king's "house . . . weather-boarded with grass thatch." The community had not arrived at a stage where leaders lived in splendor, isolated from the rest of the population.

Similar communities arose beyond the San Lorenzo countryside. The Olmec heartland, a crescent-shaped region along the Gulf, may have included half a dozen or more ceremonial centers, some forever lost in the jungles and some perhaps to be discovered by people in search of oil. One of the centers, La Venta, near the coast about sixty miles northeast of San Lorenzo, was located on an island in a swamp. It has yielded elaborately carved stelae, miniature figures made of jade, serpentine and granite, and a large mosaic representing a were-jaguar mask. The site's central area featured an earthen mound 100 feet high facing a stepped pyramid across a long plaza, the whole complex oriented about eight degrees west of north.

So there it was, writ large and clear, monumental evidence that something was crystallizing throughout the Olmec region. Small groups of men and women were thinking in a highly systematic, disciplined way. They were comparing notes, putting together a mass of accumulating facts about repeating phenomena, seasonal cycles and long-term cycles involving the motions of planets and stars. During the course of seeking and finding order, recurrences, they developed the first religion and the first art style in Mesoamerica.

At least this is the way it looks from a twentieth-century perspective. The notions of "religion" and "art style" come straight out of history, out of modern times and a modern world in which art and religion can be separate and conflicting things. That was unthinkable for the Olmec, just as it is unthinkable for us to put things back together again and merge art and religion, and science, too, into a single way of looking at the universe. From their standpoint, it was all one. Coe believes that they may have had calendars and star charts to keep track of cycles and the passing of time, and special ceremonies, some repeated at intervals of half a century or more. They probably had a system of numbers, and may have discovered the compass a millennium or more before the Chinese. Recent studies suggest that a highly polished bar of iron-rich hematite found at San Lorenzo and dating to some time before 1000 B.C. could have been used as a compass needle (although one skeptic asks: "Why did such a fundamental discovery get lost again for all the rest of Mesoamerican history?").

Why did the Olmec often orient their public buildings and spaces on a line just west of north, probably pointing to a star or constellation? At one level it indicates the importance of precise and appropriate placement in their carefully worked out scheme of things. At a deeper level it is part of the ancient vision which finds security, predictability, in linking human affairs with regular movements of celestial bodies.

Marks of a Mesoamerican world view, a Mesoamerican cosmology which may be rooted in early Olmec thinking, have been found beyond the heartland along the Gulf, in a region extending more than 800 miles from east to west. At the foot of three rugged basalt hills jutting out of a volcanic plain near the westernmost end of the region lies Chalcatzingo, a growing center when San Lorenzo was at its height from 1200 B.C. to 900 B.C. Only about 200 people lived at the site itself, but David Grove of the University of Illinois has excavated a ceremonial section, a platform fifteen feet high, with a ball court and pyramids and not far off a cemetery and an altar with human sacrifices. It served settlements over a wide area.

The artistic showplace of the site lies part way up one of the hills, at the foot of a cliff. A winding path rises to a complicated scene carved in relief on a large boulder, three rain clouds above

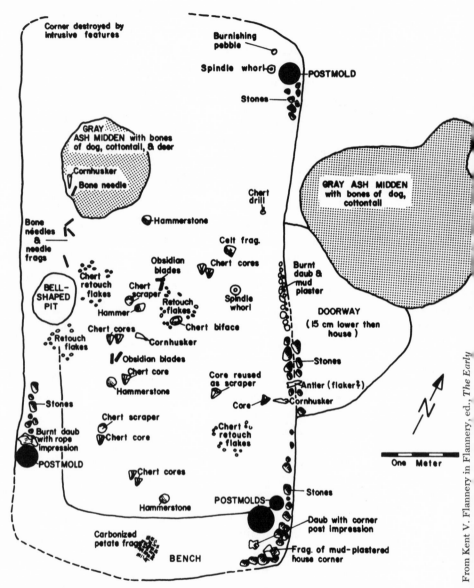

Early Mesoamerican house: plan of house (above), Valley of Oaxaca, 900 B.C.; men's and women's work areas (right)

From Kent V. Flannery in Flannery, ed., *The Early*

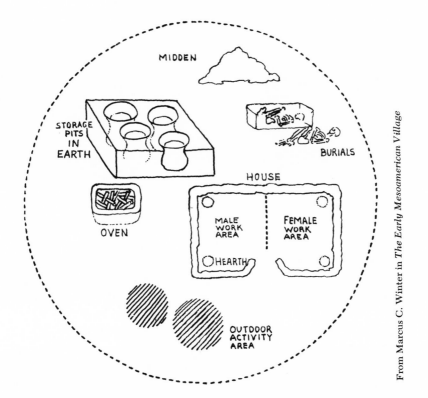

MIDDEN

STORAGE
PITS
IN
EARTH

BURIALS

HOUSE

OVEN

MALE
WORK
AREA

FEMALE
WORK
AREA

HEARTH

OUTDOOR
ACTIVITY
AREA

From Marcus C. Winter in *The Early Mesoamerican Village*

a niche or cave mouth with smoke or incense spiraling out and, seated inside, a dominant figure wearing a high and fancy head-dress—all done in unmistakable Olmec style (see page 337). Eight other similar reliefs and Olmec-style figurines and pottery have been discovered at Chalcatzingo.

Olmec-style objects turned up during the same period in the Valley of Oaxaca. It was the time of the small public buildings on the holy spot at San José Mogote, now a village covering about forty acres and more than twenty times bigger than the valley's next biggest settlement. In addition to the temple, the village included stepped, stone-faced terraces and stairways leading to public buildings on top, at least one of the buildings aligned eight degrees west of north. It also included houses with a living-floor pattern that continues among some people living in Mesoamerica today, to the left as one enters, a man's working area including such tools as projectile points and heavy-duty

Drawings by Nanette Pyne, University of Washington. After Joralemon

Olmec motifs on Oaxaca pottery (right); abstracted from fire-serpent and were-jaguar deities (left); Nanette Pyne says, "probably the rough equivalent of Christian painters drawing simply the cross instead of the whole Crucifixion scene"

scrapers, and to the right, a women's working area (grinding tools, needles, spindle whorls, cooking equipment).

Nanette Pyne of the University of Washington has analyzed the distribution of nearly 600 pottery samples bearing incised and gouged-out Olmec motifs. Houses which were clustered into separate residential units tended to have pottery with the same motifs. Two motifs predominated among the samples, a were-jaguar and a so-called fire-serpent, perhaps representing the mythical ancestors of two major descent groups. Pyne suggests that between 1200 B.C. and 900 B.C. the fire-serpent group ranked higher on the social scale. At least their homes contained greater proportions of exotic prestige materials.

This investigation and a number of others point to a special influence of the people from the Gulf. Although we are light-years from understanding why, the Olmec had a notable head start in art, in the creation of stone sculptures and other objects. The implication is that they may also have made early contributions to a religion, a cult and a way of thinking that became established throughout Mesoamerica.

There is a connection between imposing an order on human affairs, building a society, and imposing an order on the universe. The undertakings reinforce each other, providing a basis for self-confidence and inspiration and action. The massing of people brings a need for more symbols as well as more food, rare objects as well as rare individuals. The Olmec were involved in the exchange of gifts with other people as part of the effort to maintain good relationships.

One of the items they received from San José Mogote has been identified as the result of a thorough surface survey—walking over the site, picking up everything from sherds to stone chips, and noting what items are concentrated where. "We found an interesting area of about five acres near the eastern edge of the site," Flannery notes, "with a disproportionately high concentration of mica, green quartz, mussel shells from the Coast, pearl oysters and magnetite and related iron ores. The ore fragments were particularly dense in one cornfield which yielded more than 600 pieces."

Excavations in the field revealed areas where Zapotec workers, part-time farmers and part-time craftsmen, lived and specialized in grinding and polishing iron minerals. They made thumbnail-sized reflecting elements or "mirrors," artificial jewels of a sort, probably worn as pendants, and inlaid in masks and figurines. A study of Mesoamerican exchange networks by Jane Wheeler Pires-Ferreira of George Washington University indicates that some of the mirrors may have been made for the Olmec. This possibility is based on chemical analyses which show that ores from local Oaxaca deposits went to villages as much as 200 miles away, and on the findings in San Lorenzo of mirrors identical to those produced in San José Mogote.

The Pires-Ferreira study points to a complex of exchange networks involving the Olmec, the people of Oaxaca, and peoples in villages from the Valley of Mexico to central Guatemala. Iron ore was only one of the materials exchanged, the major item by far being obsidian. Other items included pottery, jade, turtle-shell drums, stingray spines and shark teeth for blood-letting rituals, and conch-shell trumpets. Such trumpets are still used in a number of Oaxaca villages today to summon men to communal work projects or emergency meetings, like the one held not long ago to run an unpopular and highly unholy priest out of town. The blowing of a conch trumpet, earnestly but slightly off-key, also marked the opening of a recent anthropological conference in Washington, D.C.

In a special study of the obsidian trade at San Lorenzo, Robert Cobean of Harvard, Coe and their associates show that, as the center reached its height, there was an increase in the amount of the material used and in the number of sources tapped. They compare what happened there with a system evolved in Oceania: "The Olmec must have participated in a trade network with peoples who supplied them with obsidian and other exotic materials. This may have been a ritual exchange system along the lines of the famous kula ring of the Trobriand Islands."

In this system the Olmec moved as elites, sophisticated individuals among less sophisticated "country cousins." According to Flannery, a somewhat similar situation may have existed during the late eighteenth and nineteenth centuries among the Northwest Coast Indians, specifically between the coastal and inland Indians of southeastern Alaska. The Tlingit lived on the coast in densely settled villages, based their subsistence on abundant salmon catches, and boasted chiefs and nobles who accumulated wealth in the form of furs, blankets, slaves, and other valuable goods. The "somewhat humbler" inlanders supplied the furs, and over the course of time attempted to become as much like their high-class neighbors as possible.

They became socially conscious, too. One inland group adopted a version of the Tlingit language, a Tlingit-type society complete with nobles and commoners and slaves, and Tlingit myths and songs involving coastal animals they had never seen. They even divided themselves into two descent groups, the Wolf and Crow clans, imitating the Tlingits' dual Wolf-Raven totem systems. Something like this may have occurred among people coming into contact with the Olmec. The appearance of the fire-serpent motif in some Oaxaca households and the were-jaguar motif in others looks suspiciously like a Mesoamerican two-clan, two-totem system shared with, and perhaps adopted from, the Olmec.

Something more than imitation was taking place. In general people do not go in for social climbing unless they are in some basic sense ripe for it. The Oaxacans, and the Alaskan inlanders, had probably acquired a social momentum of their own, including a budding elite, chiefs and followers, borrowing some of the customs and institutions of outsiders. And, a frequent development, recent elites may find that they have at least as much in common with longer-established elites from the outside as with their own people.

Very little is known about the origins of the Olmec. They may have evolved on the spot, that is, it may all have been a regional Gulf Coast development. Another theory is that they came from across the Mesoamerican isthmus on the Pacific coast, from places among the mangrove swamps and sluggish rivers and tropical forests around the border between Mexico and Guatemala. Gareth Lowe of Brigham Young University is among the hardy few who have braved this countryside, reputed to be even hotter, muggier and more insect-ridden than the Gulf lowlands. Coe has also dug there with his wife Sophie and, on another occasion, with Flannery.

Some impressive sites exist in the Pacific coast lowlands. Lowe found a small ceremonial center in a setting of tropical lagoons and fishing stations. It had platform mounds, numerous grinding stones, and unusual figurines depicting human beings, animals and weird imaginary creatures. There was distinctive pottery, mainly flat-bottomed open bowls and globular narrow-mouth jars, probably for steaming tamales, burnished and cord-marked and often decorated with red sparkling specks and iridescent paint. The people who made this pottery may have been the ancestors of the Olmec. It appeared not only in the Pacific region but also in San Lorenzo itself, two or three centuries before the development of Olmec traditions and Olmec-style art.

The traditions and the art outlived San Lorenzo. The center collapsed around 900 B.C. with the wholesale, systematic mutilation of monuments. Altars and stelae were smashed, heads knocked off the kneeling ballplayer and crouching jaguar and other statues, groove marks and pits ground into the colossal heads. Coe regards the destruction as an uprising against oppressive authority, and compares it the to 1956 toppling of the giant statue of Stalin in Budapest by Hungarian revolutionaries, perhaps a rebellion from within.

A parallel action occurred in Hawaii early in November 1819 at a great feast held to herald the overthrow of the gods, the abolition of an ancient religion and its taboos. Next day people under the direction of a "rebel" priest began destroying idols and temples (an event followed a few months later, interestingly enough, by the arrival from the United States of the good ship *Thaddeus,* bearing the first Christian missionaries). Destroying idols was also a common practice when one chief defeated another, and a similar situation may have accounted for the fall of San Lorenzo.

After 900 B.C., La Venta apparently became the major center in the Gulf Coast region. But things were never the same again. The complex of exchange systems was modified following the upheaval at San Lorenzo. Some networks broke down entirely. Oaxaca may also have seen a shift in the power structure, on a small scale and for a limited time only, as pottery with the Olmec fire-serpent motif became less common and more people turned to were-jaguar pottery. Soon there was a decline in all Olmec motifs and figurines, and an end to the making of iron-ore mirrors. Similar developments elsewhere indicate a general shift from what Pires-Ferreira calls "the long-distance exchange of sumptuary goods among elites" to a more regional system emphasizing local bureaucrats and local consolidation and control.

The change is reflected in art styles. Tatiana Proskouriakoff of the Carnegie Institution of Washington points out that the colossal heads and other San Lorenzo sculptures stress the individual, the figure and its qualities. "Images are overwhelmingly concerned with a heroic presentation of man and his affinity to the jaguar, a beast embodying the virtues of valor and nobility." The full-round sculptures contrast with low-relief carvings on stelae, which are the unique products of La Venta art—and which focus on elaborate headdresses and garments and high-status objects rather than on the figure itself.

In these changes Proskouriakoff sees a decline in leadership by charismatic individuals or big men, and the growth toward a system with its primary focus on office and the marks of office and positions in a hierarchy. Art as well as politics reflects the shift toward tighter organization. In a rough sense, the managers were taking over from the nobles.

15

High Society in Mesoamerica

*Monte Alban's 2,300 terraces/ Conquest records
in stone/ The New World's first writing/
The increasing distance between elites and
commoners/ The rise of the Maya/ The pyramids
of Tikal/ Settlement patterns in the jungle/
Hierarchies and hieroglyphs/ The Maya of the
twentieth century/ Power and ceremony in
the Valley of Mexico/ The cave under the Pyramid
of the Sun/ Planning and empire*

EVIDENCE of early large-scale settlements and of early conquests comes from San José Mogote and an important find made there during the summer of 1975. Carved in low relief on a large stone slab lying on the ground is a man, nearly life-sized and naked and eyes closed—a "danzante" or dancer, so-called because such figures are often depicted in unusual, stylized positions which were originally interpreted as dancing positions. But they are probably captives rather than dancers, naked as a mark of humiliation and dead because of the closed eyes.

The newly found danzante sculpture dates to about 600 B.C., when the Olmec were definitely on the decline. La Venta, like San Lorenzo before it, was passing its peak, its colossal heads and

Courtesy of Joyce Marcus, University of Michigan. Based on L. Sejourne, *El Universo de Quetzalcoatl*, Mexico City: Fonde de Cultura Económica, 1962

Danzantes: slain or sacrificed captive on stone slabs at threshold of public building, new find at San José Mogote, Valley of Oaxaca, Mexico, 600–500 B.C. (above); Monte Alban figures in relief on stone slabs, 500–200 B.C. (below)

other monuments soon to be mutilated and defaced. San José Mogote held a dominant position in the Valley of Oaxaca, erecting large buildings faced with rough-hewn limestone blocks, many weighing a ton or more. The buildings occupied three sides of a central plaza, a glorified version of the old hamlet-village pattern of family houses clustered around a common courtyard.

The entire complex was located on top of a hill overlooking the settlement from a height of fifty feet, a solid symbol of order imposed from above. The only trouble with order is that it has to be kept, generally at the price of bloodshed. The carving of the slain man, presumably the chief of a competing center, was set in place between two of the buildings where people had to walk over the prostrate figure, suggesting none too subtly that it might have been wiser to obey than to fight.

In 600 B.C., San José Mogote was still the valley's largest settlement, boasting the first and probably the only hilltop center. That situation changed within a century or so. There was a population increase throughout the region, in part, perhaps, representing immigrants from other valleys; there was a multiplication of buildings perched on hills, and a multiplication of overseers and elites and centers of control and command. The Zapotec center located on Oaxaca's highest range of hills became one of the first major cities in Mesoamerica. Looming some 1,500 feet high, Monte Alban lies near a natural crossroads, a junction point where the three branches of the Valley of Oaxaca meet. Construction began there around 500 B.C., when, across the Atlantic, Greeks and Persians were at war and Athens would soon fall, and when centralized village complexes appeared in the southwest Sahara.

Work almost certainly proceeded at Monte Alban according to a long-range master plan. It probably involved elites and workers from San José Mogote only ten miles away and elsewhere, individuals with abundant experience in designing and building monumental structures for people in high places. As emphasized in a survey conducted and still being analyzed by Richard Blanton of Purdue University, the project called for a massive top-to-bottom reshaping of the hills. Ravines and erosion gullies had to be filled; extensive areas had to be leveled and terraces constructed on sloping hillsides to provide foundations for roads, homes and public buildings. More than 2,300 terraces have been mapped to date, some large enough for dozens of homes, and the largest and highest of all being the main plaza area of about fifty-five acres, eight times the size of St. Peter's Square at the Vatican. The hills of Monte Alban became a densely packed urban complex. According to Blanton, by 100 B.C. some 5,000 to 10,000 persons were living in an area of about one and a half square miles; half a millennium or so later, when the city was at its peak and covered nearly three square miles, the population may have reached 30,000.

A practical question about this site is where the people got their water. It was the general assumption until recently that menials carried it up from rivers and other sources in the valley, but a number of summers ago during a survey of the southern slopes of Monte Alban below the main plaza, James Neely, working with Blanton at the time, noticed several dark lines running down the hillside. The discovery led to an intensive search.

The lines were strips of extra-dense, extra-lush vegetation growing in the loose water-retaining soils. Such lines often indicate the courses of ancient canals. Neely had seen similar patterns before, at Tehuacan and in the Near East among other places. He soon found a second important feature about two-thirds of the way up the hill—a series of little volcano-shaped limestone cones, deposits marking the locations of defunct "fossil" springs, where waters rich in minerals once bubbled up from the depths. A system of drains, canals and check dams had channeled waters from the springs and from rainfall runoff to terraced fields and reservoirs.

Considerable effort was required to maintain, and to guard, the city and its waterworks. Enemies attacking from the north or west would have had to breach an outer defense wall, a double wall in places and up to thirty feet high, and there is no evidence that they ever did. Inner walls protected certain districts within the city. Vivid signs of conflict and mayhem come from art and architecture at the top, in the main plaza itself.

Excavations there have uncovered some 320 danzantes, low-relief sculptures and fragments of sculptures representing slain persons. Joyce Marcus of the University of Michigan points out that some of the figures are dressed in fancy regalia and may portray high-ranking individuals. The majority, however, seem to have been more humble folk, "probably lesser villagers taken in raids or skirmishes," upon occasion sacrificed and eaten, a custom practiced up to the sixteenth century.

The main plaza includes further evidence of fighting in times past. One building, for reasons unknown, is arrowhead-shaped and points southwest. Set into its walls are records of past subjugations and defeats, forty-odd "conquest slab" sculptures, which, as do some of the danzantes, include samples of the Zapotec Indians' form of writing—the earliest writing in Mesoamerica, dating back to 600 B.C. to 400 B.C. There are some hundred different hieroglyphs, only about twenty-five or thirty of which have been deciphered.

A hieroglyph may combine a number of elements into a compact picture or picture-symbol. The carvings include hieroglyphs representing "hill" or "place," and an upside-down head with closed eye representing "overturned" or "conquered," suggesting records of villages probably forced to pay tribute to Monte Alban. The problem is to deduce the names of the villages from special signs above the hill sign and from headdresses on the inverted heads, by consulting documents listing places in Oaxaca that paid tribute to the Aztecs some four hundred years ago and the Aztec signs for those places.

A center which the Aztecs referred to as "place of the bean" and identified by a picture of a bean may be Etla, a center in the northern arm of the Valley of Oaxaca, or another settlement in the same general area. By a process of matching and cross-checking, Marcus has come up with plausible identifications of some of the place-names on the conquest slabs. Another potentially rich source of hieroglyphic information about military activities at Monte Alban are stelae found in the main plaza.

The city may have arisen as the center of a confederacy, a union of leaders from different parts of Oaxaca. There were probably three groups of leaders, representing the three main branches of the valley, at least that is one possible conclusion from Blanton's observation that the early center consisted of three communities located in three separate areas on the hilltop. He also reports that the areas were "closely spaced but discrete," suggesting that the communities and their leaders were affiliated but independent.

The confederacy controlled people and resources outside as

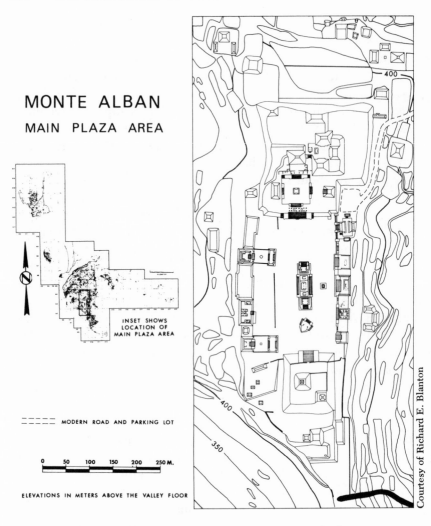

MONTE ALBAN
MAIN PLAZA AREA

INSET SHOWS
LOCATION OF
MAIN PLAZA AREA

- - - - - MODERN ROAD AND PARKING LOT

0   50   100   150   200   250 M.

ELEVATIONS IN METERS ABOVE THE VALLEY FLOOR

Courtesy of Richard E. Blanton

Monte Alban, Valley of Oaxaca: site plan, central plaza; main plaza, looking north (right).

well as inside the valley. The conquest slabs attest to triumphs perhaps involving centers fifty or more miles away. Changes occurred within Oaxaca itself, changes reflected in styles of sculpture. In the beginning there were several local styles, as might be expected among separate and equal groups. Later there tended to be one style, and perhaps one centralized leader or authority. According to Marcus, by about A.D. 400, "the subjugation of politically autonomous sites is complete and . . . becomes more consistent with the dominant style present at the capital, Monte Alban." At its height the city may have controlled an area of 12,000 square miles.

The widening distance between elites and commoners can be seen in the layout of the city. Many so-called public areas were actually private, off-limit areas. Blanton has mapped the major roads, secondary roads and ramps of Monte Alban, as a first step toward a graph or network analysis like that described in Chapter 5 for a center in British Honduras. Preliminary studies point to an increasing tendency to isolate clusters of ceremonial buildings and high-class residences, often located away from major roads. They could be approached only by narrow and easily guarded passageways and gates. The gates may have served to discourage some of the elites from leaving as well as the people from entering; during the later stages of Monte Alban the Zapotec chiefs of outlying villages and towns may have "lived in," by invitation, to be sure, but possibly also as hostages of a sort to keep the peace in their home territories.

The main plaza was also isolated. The stairways of its monumental buildings faced inward. Commoners were probably let in on gala occasions, at least partly to be awed. A secret tunnel running under the plaza suggests some sort of hocus-pocus of sudden appearances and disappearances, special effects and other devices calculated to fool people not in the know. Legerdemain, the art of creating illusion to order, played an early and prominent role in urban politics.

While Monte Alban, the capital of Oaxaca and the Zapotec Indians, was on the rise, major developments were under way some 450 miles to the east. The Maya Indians, centered in the jungles of the Yucatan Peninsula and nearby regions, built more than 100 large towns and cities, only about a dozen of which have been excavated. The rest, including some giants, are buried in roots and underbrush and moss. One important site was so thoroughly hidden that investigators "lost" it after its discovery more than half a century ago, only to rediscover it in 1973, guided by local chicle-gum gatherers. The grandest and best known of Maya cities has been described in these terms:

> Twenty-five hundred or more years ago a group of peoples settled on and about a barely seen hill in the lowland jungles of northern Guatemala. Their descendants were soon to create by almost unfathomable means one of the most astonishing civilizations the world has ever seen. We now know that hill and the surrounding area as Tikal . . . the prime city of the Maya people . . . still asserted by the ruined roof combs of huge white temples rising above an undulating rain forest that ends only at the distant Caribbean Sea.

These are the words of William Coe of the University of Pennsylvania, brother of Michael Coe and director of the Tikal Project. In 1970, he and his associates completed fourteen seasons of excavation and reconstruction. The results will probably fill more than thirty volumes. They mapped about 3,000 temples, plazas, palaces, shrines, terraces and other features, and collected some 100,000 artifacts as well as a conservatively estimated 5 million sherds. (For understandable reasons no one has actually made a count, and the total could be considerably greater.)

The spectacular ruins give only a faint impression of the past. During a recent visit I climbed to the top of a crumbled wall, the stub of what had been a great pyramid, and looked down on Tikal's partly restored ceremonial center. To my right and left, facing each other across a grass-covered plaza, were two temple pyramids fourteen and twelve stories tall—and straight ahead, looking south, the remains of pyramids, of stone-faced terraces, stairways, and buildings with many rooms. Behind the buildings stood a still taller temple pyramid, overgrown with trees and bushes, and rising out of the jungle, in the distance to the southwest and far from one another, two more high lonely temple pyramids.

The jungle dominates this scene today. But in its prime the city dominated. People walked through a patterned, geometric solid-rock world of dark and bright spaces, on paved passages in the

Tikal, Guatemala lowland: 1957, before excavation (above); temple in
ceremonial center (two views); reconstruction in plaster (right, below)

Photographs by William R. Coe, Tikal Project, University Museum, University of Pennsylvania

shadows of the pyramids and towering temples, and out into open paved plazas between limestone walls glaring white in the sun. The colors are gone now, but frescoes and roof combs on the tops of many buildings were once painted red, cream, and probably yellow, blue and green. Traffic moved along causeways, elevated roads leading to parts of the city now isolated from one another by stretches of jungle.

I spent one morning in that jungle, tramping over and around fallen trees, and through underbrush and scores of spider webs. Dennis Puleston of the University of Minnesota served as my guide, which turned out to be fortunate. For one thing, we were following a little-used trail so faint that it was invisible to me and even he, an expert woodsman, had to stop now and then to get his bearings, pick out the places trampled down by old footsteps, and make sure we were not lost.

The jungle conceals a great deal, including most of what made all the grandeur possible. Our trail ran due north of the ceremonial district, near a great hollowed-out area—one of at least half a dozen clay-and-stone-lined reservoirs, each holding millions of gallons of water and supplied by feeder canals up to a mile long. We passed sites where the farmers of Tikal lived, three or four house mounds, most of them almost completely covered by underbrush and located around flat places that had been little plazas. There are about 2,000 such clusters within a mile of the city's center, one for every two to five acres, indicating a dispersed pattern of slash-and-burn gardens.

Every cluster also had a number of bottle-shaped underground chambers hacked out of limestone bedrock, pits which, according to Puleston, were designed primarily for storing the nutritious nuts of the ramon tree, a species of the fig family grown in groves near the houses. As we walked, he explained how he arrived at this conclusion by direct experiment. Using Tikal-style tools such as flint adzes, he dug a Tikal-style pit, put a variety of foods in it, and found that the ramon nut lasted by far the longest, remaining in fine condition for more than a year as compared with the few months for the longest-lasting of the other foods.

After two hours, we came to the main objective of our walk, the overgrown traces of an earthen wall and moat ten feet deep, discovered by accident a decade or so ago and originally mistaken for a canal. The earthworks extends about six miles between two swamps and marks the city's northern border. It was presumably constructed for defense. A similar system marks the southern border. As an indication of how difficult it is to estimate populations of prehistoric cities, Sanders suggests some twenty-five square miles and 20,000 to 25,000 persons for Tikal at its height around A.D. 700 to A.D. 800, while Puleston puts it at forty-five square miles and 65,000 to 80,000 persons. Judging by past tendencies to overestimate, it is generally sound policy to go by the more conservative figures.

The population of the city rose sharply between A.D. 400 and A.D. 800, although the population of the region may not have changed appreciably. People abandoned sites in the Tikal countryside and established new homes within the earthworks. It was a mass streaming into the center, an implosion similar to that which had occurred more than 3,500 years earlier in Uruk and Nippur. Tikal was one of the most spectacular of the hundred-odd known centers in the Maya lowlands. These centers extended over 100,000 square miles and during their peak period housed some 5,000 persons. We do not know when the first settlers came, partly because the jungle obscures so much. In vegetation so thick that temples and palaces may be lost, one cannot expect to find hunter-gatherer camps or the homes of early gardeners. Deposits lying deep below ceremonial buildings, however, indicate that people had built settlements in the lowlands by 2000 B.C.

There were centers in the highlands, too. John Graham and Robert Heizer of the University of California in Berkeley recently found more than fifty stelae at Abaj Takalik, Maya for "standing stones," in southwestern Guatemala. One of them bears the Maya date corresponding to June 3, A.D. 126; another is at least a century or two older. Several of the monuments are done in Olmec style, again raising the question of the nature and extent of Olmec influence on later Mesoamerican cultures.

Populations must have risen swiftly in the highlands and lowlands. According to one theory, a budding-off movement of overflow peoples into the interior led to the founding of many sites, and to ingenious and spectacularly successful methods of farming. In regions where soil may be thin, poorly drained, and flooded during most of the rainy season, people piled earth into long narrow strips and platforms up to six or more feet high, creating ridged or raised fields upon which corn and other crops could

Courtesy of Dennis E. Puleston, University of Minnesota

Tikal: Dennis Puleston digging experimental storage pit

be grown—and which provided food for populations many times larger than could have been supported before the land was modified.

Various types of raised fields have been discovered mainly from aerial photographs, in other parts of Mesoamerica and in South America as well as in the Maya lowlands. Digging at a lowland site, on an island in the Hondo River of northern Belize, Puleston found traces of a deep canal more than 3,000 years old, part of the earliest known raised fields. To investigate the efficiency of the fields, he rebuilt one of them, laying down a foundation of limestone clay and clearing out ancient canals. Soon corn, squash, beans, tomatoes and cotton were growing on the ridges, and a dozen species of edible fish were swimming in the canals, providing manure which could be used to increase soil fertility.

Exchange networks, local and long-distance, influenced the distribution of people, communities, and institutions. In a survey of part of the region which includes Tikal, William Bullard of Harvard University reported a hierarchy of settlements rather reminiscent of the Near Eastern hierarchies. He found a three-level system, the lowest consisting of hamlets of thirty-five to seventy persons living in clusters of houses around central court-yards. The next lowest consisted of minor centers each of which had a single plaza with several public buildings and temple pyra-mids, and supplied ceremonies, marketplaces and other services to ten to fifteen associated hamlets.

At the topmost level in Bullard's survey was the major center with several plazas connected by causeways and carved stelae and ball courts. Each major center serviced perhaps ten to fifteen minor centers in an area of about 100 square miles containing 6,500 to 10,000 persons. Hamlet, minor center, major center—this may represent a three-level hierarchy, an "atomic" or minimal state, according to Wright's definition. The state certainly came with the appearance of a fourth and still higher level made up of supercenters like Tikal, Calakmul to the north, Palenque to the west, and Copan to the south.

Further details about settlement patterns have come from studies of Maya writing, which seems to have been developed from Zapotec writing and, like Zapotec writing, served to record political events. It was a mixed system of 800 symbols, mainly "ideographs" or realistic pictures with abstract meanings (for example, the picture of a frog representing "birth") as well as pictographs (where the picture means what it depicts), phonetic elements and other devices. Some of the symbols, including per-haps the earliest, represent grotesque faces and may be derived from masks used in the dance. Some years ago Heinrich Berlin of Mexico City was studying carved inscriptions associated with figures surrounding a stone coffin found in an underground crypt at Palenque and noted that the inscriptions ended with the same hieroglyph. In every case, the hieroglyph included a superfix with two elements inscribed above the central portion, ⊞ and ⊕ —and a prefix which looks something like seeds or drops of water. ⊡

Berlin speculated that the figures around the coffin were rela-tives of the buried individual, presumably all born in the same community, and that the composite symbol was the name or "emblem glyph" of Palenque. Going further than that, he studied inscriptions from other important centers in search of other emblem glyphs or place-names, pictographs containing versions of the same superfix and prefix. The following are some of the symbols he identified, plus the Calakmul symbol identified by Marcus:

Palenque   Tikal   Copan   Piedras Negras   Calakmul

Marcus recently examined thousands of hieroglyphs on some 1,500 monuments from different sites. She found at least 100 emblem glyphs, and discovered a neat relationship among some of them, a hierarchy of cross references. Inscriptions at super-centers refer to other supercenters, but not to major centers. In A.D. 731 the Palenque emblem glyph is found on Tikal monuments, and vice versa.

Also there were six major centers between fifteen and twenty miles from Calakmul, and none of their inscriptions mentions Tikal or any other supercenter except Calakmul itself. They were dealing predominantly with that supercenter, holding subordinate positions in its service zone. Moreover, as Flannery had pointed out in a previous analysis, the major centers were arranged in a hexagonal pattern around Calakmul, a central place distribution like that found in the Uruk countryside and the Suisiana Plain.

Combined emblem-glyph and map studies suggested broadly similar relationships all the way down the hierarchy to minor-center and hamlet levels, and indicate the powerful influence of service and exchange in determining site locations. As far as the Maya shift to a state structure is concerned—the shift from three to four and more administrative or hierarchical levels—Marcus has traced the event to a specific period, A.D. 514 to A.D. 534.

As in the Near East and elsewhere, a hierarchy of places implies a hierarchy of people, a notion also supported by research on Maya writing. At one time most investigators did not look to graven inscriptions for this sort of insight, believing hieroglyphic records to be concerned in the main with vaguely mystical matters, revelations and prophecies analogous to those of the sixteenth-century French astrologer Nostradamus. Some fifteen years ago, however, Tatiana Proskouriakoff demonstrated how much solid information could be extracted from the records.

The way into an understanding of the writing of the Maya

people, and of their general view of things, is time—specific numbers and dates based on what Wheatley has called "the most complex and accurate of early calendrical systems." Their calendar included two cycles. One, the so-called Sacred Round, consisted of 260 days each of which had its own omens and deity, and was used for ceremonial purposes only—to make prophecies, select the best days for doing business, and generally to propitiate the gods. Coe has described it as "a kind of perpetual fortune-telling machine guiding the destinies of the Maya and of all the peoples of Mexico."

There was also a secular cycle, a solar year, for mundane events. It consisted of eighteen 20-day months; the extra five days had no names and represented a period of bad luck. Maya astronomers conceived of the world as a place of great cycles, universal creations and destructions and re-creations repeated at intervals of about 5,000 years. The current universe came into being in 3114 B.C. (and, according to one theory, is scheduled for annihilation on December 24, 2011), and all dates were measured from that beginning.

Proskouriakoff studied thirty-five dated Piedras Negras monuments spanning the period from about A.D. 600 to A.D. 800, arranging them in order from oldest to most recent. She noted that seven monuments had carved "ascension motifs," richly dressed figures seated in raised niches with ladders and footprints leading up to them, presumably representing the coming of seven successive rulers. She also noted, at or near the beginning of the inscriptions following each figure, a date always associated with a characteristic inauguration glyph. On the basis of such observations and examinations of sculpted figures, she deduced reigns lasting from five to forty-seven years, and suggested the possibility of hereditary rule by dynastic succession.

Her pioneer study has been followed by a number of others, one of the most recent focusing on Tikal. Christopher Jones of the University of Pennsylvania has analyzed dated inscriptions on bones found in a tomb, stelae, altars and lintels, horizontal wooden supports over doorways. The inscriptions involve three inaugural glyphs and the lives of the three individuals who ruled the Tikal zone, and perhaps considerably more territory, one after the other between A.D. 680 and A.D. 790, during the city's heyday.

Combining evidence from the inscription with archeological

evidence, much of it obtained firsthand during his own excavations at Tikal, Jones presents a tentative picture of these three rulers. Inscriptions concerned with Ruler A indicate that he came from the west in the direction of Piedras Negras and Palenque, mourned the death of a person close to him, reigned for more than half a century, and was probably buried in the fourteen-story temple pyramid of the ceremonial center. Also, he "presided over a renaissance of sorts." He was responsible for the first known carved monuments to be built in more than a century, following a period of political instability, which, incidentally, Clemency Coggins of Harvard University has deduced from a study of painting and drawing styles.

Judging by his inscriptions and monuments, Ruler B comes through as a bit of an egomaniac, and somewhat cruder than Ruler A. He mentions himself more often in long passages apparently describing his own accomplishments, traces his ancestry back much further, perhaps to the Olmec, and generally seems rather less concerned with the business of governing. He built more monuments to himself, and his tomb is believed to be in one of the two lonely temple pyramids located away from the main center, the largest tower of all rising more than twenty-one stories. "Its massive heaviness" contrasts with Ruler A's tower, which is "light rather than ponderous, elevating rather than elevated, and, most of all, beautiful." Ruler C, a less creative individual, continued the I-can-top-that tradition, erecting "bigger but not different" monuments to himself.

So research further documents the tendency of power to build up and keep building up, to feed on itself. One result, in past Tikal jungles as well as in the highlands of New Guinea and industrial countries today, has always been a lower living standard for those lower down in the hierarchy. It shows up in the fossil record. William Haviland of the University of Vermont finds that the skeletons of well-off males buried in elaborate tombs averaged about six feet in length, nearly five inches taller than those of sixty-two males buried in humbler household settings and probably living shorter, less healthy lives.

Burials also show that individuals found it increasingly difficult to attain the top levels of Maya society. Part of an analysis by William Rathje of the University of Arizona deals with graves excavated at Uaxactun, a site twelve miles and a five-hour walk north of Tikal. Before A.D. 600, the site's center consisted of three small pyramid temples where a select group of adult males, men who had accumulated sufficient wealth and prestige in outlying rural areas, were buried with jade and other rich grave goods. After A.D. 600, elites were no longer drawn from the countryside. They live in. Places appeared at the center and rich burials included women, children and young adults as well as mature males, implying control by a family or a few families, which could "perpetuate themselves without drawing upon outside . . . populations." As society became increasingly closed, the center became increasingly private and shut off, a pattern noted at Monte Alban and at other Maya sites.

Research on the Maya includes intensive and continuing studies of present-day Maya-speaking descendants of the people who built Tikal and other cities. Under way ever since 1957 in the municipality of Zinacantan in southeastern Mexico, these studies have enlisted the efforts of more than 100 field workers, directed by Evon Vogt of Harvard. Their findings make it possible to appreciate continuities as well as discontinuities, what endures as well as what fades.

Certain similarities exist between ancient and modern settlement patterns. The municipality includes a political-religious center of about 400 persons with a town hall, federal school, jail, and three Catholic churches. Ritual here is an almost continuous round of fiestas and processions. According to Vogt, "there are few days in the year when some ceremony is not being performed, and usually several ceremonial sequences are going on simultaneously." The community, known as Zinacantan Center, serves fifteen hamlets in the surrounding countryside, and may be regarded as roughly the equivalent of an ancient major ceremonial center.

The comparison may be valid at a more fundamental level. In Zinacantan, as in all present-day Maya communities, priestly officials are recruited from the outlying hamlets. They are well-to-do peasants who saved enough money from corn farming to afford a number of years at the ceremonial center, carrying out expensive and prestigious functions. This arrangement is something like that implied in Rathje's analysis of early burials at Uaxactun,

suggesting that Zinacantan may represent the situation that prevailed before the coming of the Establishment in the form of a
full-time elite.

The past still lives. Direction and notions of place and position
had special significance for the ancestors of modern Maya. Studies
of hieroglyphs and art motifs indicate that east, the direction of
sunrise and birth and resurrection, was highly favored in ceremonies, and it still is. Ritual meals in Zinacantan must be served
on traditional rectangular tables with the long dimension oriented
east-west and the highest-ranking individuals seated at the eastern
end. Also, the current belief that February's last five days are
"very bad" may trace back to the five-day, bad-luck period at the
end of the ancient 360-day solar year.

These and many other beliefs, and the entire world view that
goes with them, represented a pattern that extended far beyond
Maya territory, a broad Mesoamerican pattern. Another part of
the pattern was taking shape more than 600 miles west of the
Tikal jungles, in the Valley of Mexico, a plain nearly a mile and
a half high and surrounded by hills to the north and mountains
to the east, west and south. Waters flowing down from the mountains formed 400-square-mile Lake Texcoco in the plain, and
opening on the northeast shore of the lakeshore was a little side
valley where Teotihuacan, the largest of all early centers,
appeared.

Much of what is known about its evolution comes from René
Millon of the University of Rochester and his associates, who
mapped Teotihuacan in detail, and from Sanders, Blanton and
Jeffrey Parsons of the University of Michigan, who together with
their associates spent half a dozen summers surveying the entire
Valley of Mexico and mapping more than 2,000 sites. The earliest
settlements at the site of the city-to-be appeared around 400 B.C.,
when Monte Alban was a century or two old and had already
attained appreciable proportions. There were a few hundred
people living in a cluster of three hamlets and a small village.

Newcomers were attracted, among other reasons because the
area offered a river fed by eighty permanent springs and prospects of good farming. During the next two or three centuries the
village and hamlets merged into a single community of perhaps
10,000 individuals, becoming the second largest town in the
Valley of Mexico—and, of course, competing with the first largest

town, Cuicuilco, some forty miles to the southwest with about twice as many people. The competition apparently broke out into open warfare. Many people abandoned settlements on the valley floor, moved into safer places on the tops of hills, creating a no-man's-land between the two towns. The conflict was finally resolved but, according to Parsons, not entirely as a result of superiority on the battlefield. Teotihuacan seems to have been winning, but it received a timely and violent assist from the gods. Its population reached the 20,000 level sometime around the birth of Christ, when a volcano erupted near Cuicuilco, burying the already declining center under lava. (The ruins of its main temple lie within present-day Mexico City, not far from the 1968 Olympic Village.)

So catastrophe played a role at a crucial stage in Teotihuacan's rise. It was followed by a spectacular bursting inward or implosion like that which occurred some three millenniums previously at Uruk. People streamed in by the thousands, not always perhaps of their own free will, until ninety percent of the entire population of the side valley lived in the city. The center expanded from about 50,000 persons in A.D. 100 to at least 125,000 persons by A.D. 500. According to Millon, it not only increased in population, but became a great deal more compact, as well. The A.D. 100 layout was an urban sprawl. The city was spread out relatively thin, covering ten to eleven square miles or so. That area contracted to some eight square miles of much more concentrated construction by A.D. 500, an increase in density from some 3,000 to 5,000 to more than 15,000 persons per square mile.

The great center represents a brand-new type of New World city, part of the difference being a matter of layout and scale. A foot-by-foot survey of the entire site and its surroundings, conducted by investigators under the direction of Millon, has produced two giant maps, each about 100 square feet in area and reproduced in 147 separate sections in a single volume. One of the maps indicates land contours and the positions of more than 4,500 plazas, temples, houses and other architectural units dated to about A.D. 600 when the city was at its height. The other shows building plans and streets.

Teotihuacan was designed according to a block or grid plan. Its north-south axis, an avenue wider than a ten-lane superhighway and now known as the Street of the Dead, extended for two miles

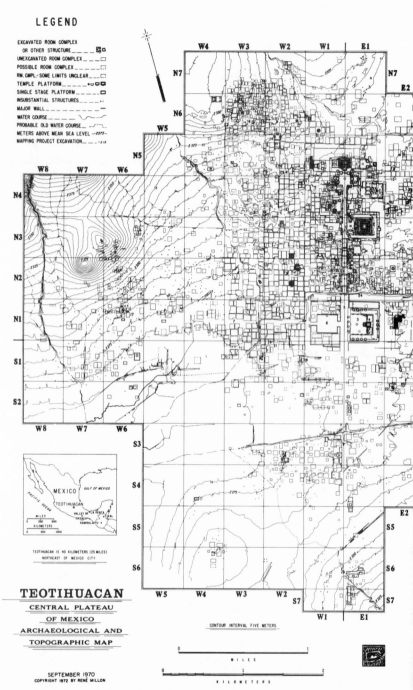

LEGEND

EXCAVATED ROOM COMPLEX
OR OTHER STRUCTURE
UNEXCAVATED ROOM COMPLEX
POSSIBLE ROOM COMPLEX
RM. CMPL.- SOME LIMITS UNCLEAR
TEMPLE PLATFORM
SINGLE STAGE PLATFORM
INSUBSTANTIAL STRUCTURES
MAJOR WALL
WATER COURSE
PROBABLE OLD WATER COURSE
METERS ABOVE MEAN SEA LEVEL
MAPPING PROJECT EXCAVATION

MEXICO
GULF OF MEXICO
PACIFIC OCEAN
TEOTIHUACAN
VALLEY OF LA VENTA
OAXACA
MILES
KILOMETERS
KAMINALJUYU

TEOTIHUACAN IS 40 KILOMETERS (25 MILES)
NORTHEAST OF MEXICO CITY

TEOTIHUACAN

CENTRAL PLATEAU
OF MEXICO
ARCHAEOLOGICAL AND
TOPOGRAPHIC MAP

SEPTEMBER 1970
COPYRIGHT 1972 BY RENÉ MILLON

CONTOUR INTERVAL FIVE METERS

MILES

KILOMETERS

Teotihuacán, north of Mexico City, central area: master map

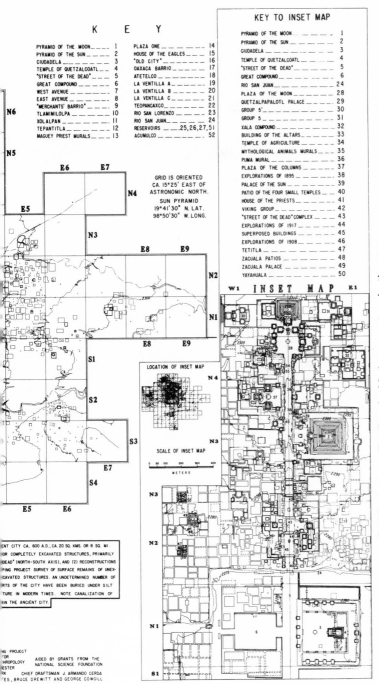

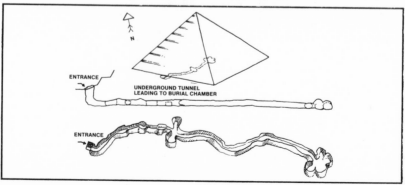

past monumental buildings—and the city's sacred and secular core lay where it intersected the east-west axis. Religious and political affairs were probably conducted in the so-called Citadel, a reconstructed area of nearly forty acres with fifteen small pyramids, palaces and administrative buildings, and the six-terraced Temple of Quetzalcoatl, the feathered-serpent god. An even larger area, the main marketplace, may have been located directly opposite this complex.

An early sacred place, perhaps the earliest in the city, lies hidden under the largest and most imposing structure on the Street of the Dead, under the 200-foot Pyramid of the Sun. The buried site was discovered by accident one evening after all the tourists had left. A guard sweeping up at the foot of the massive monument, in an area that had been walked over and surveyed many times, noticed a depression in the ground. It resembled a hole filled with rubble.

Excavations revealed a flight of steps leading into a deep pit, and to a basalt "tube," a natural channel formed a million years ago in molten lava. The tube ran more than 100 yards under the center of the pyramid, and ended in a chamber which stone workers had shaped into a four-leaf-clover pattern, possibly symbolizing the sacred center and four quarters of the underworld. The cave was almost certainly a holy spot where prehistoric peoples conducted secret rites centuries before the Pyramid of the Sun was built, during Teotihuacan's village days.

The city had a touch of Venice, a system of branching waterways, with artificially straightened portions of its main river and tributary streams as well as interconnecting canals. The network probably extended to Lake Texcoco ten miles away, and may have carried a variety of dugout canoes—plain workaday canoes loaded with food, pottery and other products, and grand "Rolls Royce" canoes for the elite and visiting dignitaries. Traffic and the general pace of things picked up during major religious holidays when the city's population may have doubled as people came in from the entire Valley of Mexico and beyond.

Residential districts have at least as much to tell us about the unusual qualities of Teotihuacan as its more spectacular cere-

Teotihuacan: Street of the Dead, looking south, Pyramid of the Sun, upper left; Pyramid of the Sun, steps to top; tunnel with cloverleaf-shaped cave under Pyramid of the Sun

monial districts. Millon's maps show 2,000 to 2,500 apartment compounds, dwelling units made of plastered volcanic rock and ranging from dingy rooms for the lowliest inhabitants to patio complexes with elaborately painted murals for the elite. At least 500 of these compounds housed groups of 50 to 100 craftsmen, specializing in precious stones, pottery, figurines, and objects of slate, obsidian and basalt—and indicating something special about social organization in the Valley of Mexico.

Monte Alban has a number of workshops, some associated with elite residence-temple areas, but most products apparently came from the outside, from craftsmen in villages scattered throughout the Valley of Oaxaca. A similar situation probably existed in Tikal, where heavy concentrations of woodworking tools, tools for breaking and carving stone, sherds and other remains, suggest localized workshop areas dispersed up to five or more miles from the ceremonial center. In the Valley of Mexico, however, almost everything seems to have been drawn together inside Teotihuacan itself, marking a new intensity of central control, the creation of what Bray identifies as the New World's earliest city-state "superpower."

Reaching that status can be regarded as a two-stage process. During the first stage, until about the birth of Christ, Teotihuacan became a city and important ceremonial center, mainly because it had well-watered lands and could support rising populations. Something more was required to bring about the second-stage spurt to superpower dimensions, and that is where trade came in as a major contributing force—notably trade in obsidian, one of the most valued materials in Mesoamerica. Unlike most materials, the volcanic glass met a double demand, widely used for everyday working purposes and for ceremonies, for knives and other sharp-edged items as well as elaborate show pieces.

Teotihuacan was strategically located. It had access to two abundant sources of obsidian, a gray variety from deposits seven miles away and, about forty-five miles away, a rare and beautiful green variety mined from deep vertical shafts. Research by Michael Spence of the University of Western Ontario, one of Millon's associates in the mapping of Teotihuacan, shows that up to the end of the first growth stage most of the material was used locally, involving only about a dozen workshops located in one district, and probably representing one group of closely related families.

At the city's peak 350 of its 500 workshops were obsidian workshops, and a large proportion of the products—projectile points, scrapers, knives, figurines, strange animallike forms, pierced ornamental disks—went to communities outside the Valley of Mexico and as far away as the Maya lowlands. The need for skilled workers was much greater than could be met within family circles, suggesting that apartment compounds housing up to 100 obsidian workers were organized on an occupational rather than a strictly kinship basis.

The obsidian business, which probably called on the efforts of a quarter to a third of the working force, occupied a crucial position in an elaborate and snowballing process. As population and demand soared, it became too big for amateurs and the little man. The number of within-the-city home workshops declined, and so did the number of workshops outside the city. Mines were probably closely guarded, restricted to persons with official passes. "Caravans" of human carriers made scheduled trips into the steep gorges where nearby deposits were located, and returned with tons of obsidian on their backs. With all this trade and much more, there was certainly a need for detailed records. Yet Teotihuacan, the first superpower in the New World, may also have been the first superpower anywhere to establish itself without inventing writing. At least no firm evidence for writing has been discovered.

Control became tighter and tighter, abroad as well as at home. It extended some 650 miles southeast to an ancient community in the Guatemala highlands. Kaminaljuyu had become a major ceremonial and trade center by 400 B.C. and probably a good deal earlier, complete with sculptures and monumental architecture. Commercial rather than cultural interests drew people from the Valley of Mexico to this center, which happened to be located near a hill of obsidian, one of the richest sources in Mesoamerica.

Kaminaljuyu enjoyed a construction boom starting around A.D. 500. A new twenty-acre central area appeared with temples and ball courts and perhaps elite residences, all done in what Sanders describes as "a slavish imitation of the Teotihuacan style," including characteristic stepped pyramids and the use of plastered volcanic rock. The Teotihuacanos had come to stay, gently but firmly. The fact that their buildings were limited to the central area and the absence of any signs of fighting indicate that they got what they wanted by peaceful methods, sending in emissaries to organize trade and diplomatic relations, and to see to it that things remained organized.

They launched far more ambitious plans in an effort to control Tikal and perhaps the entire Maya lowlands, which depended on Kaminaljuyu as a major source of obsidian. Three Teotihuacan-style platforms have been uncovered in Tikal, and paintings on pottery found in elite tombs depict Teotihuacan temples and warriors. Coggins has evidence that a trade emissary, probably the son of high-born Teotihuacan-Kaminaljuyu parents, married the daughter of a Tikal king and later became king himself. If this marriage was part of an attempted political takeover, it failed; Tikal and other lowland cities remained Maya cities.

In making its move toward dominion and empire, however, Teotihuacan brought the Valley of Mexico into a far-flung Meso-american system concerned with more than obsidian. The city included a Oaxaca district, marked by concentrations of Oaxaca pottery and a tomb with a Monte Alban-style stela, and the discovery of further relationships among early centers can be expected within the next few years. The widespread ties connecting people and their institutions will be better understood as investigators focus increasingly on broad central-place patterns involving regions as well as sites.

16

Survival and Religion in the Andes

*Nomads of the mountains/ Domesticating beans
and guinea pigs and camelids/ High pastures
and low gardens/ Freeze-drying tubers/ High-altitude
patterns of survival/ The spread of the Chavín
cult/ Llama and people caravans/ Settling down along
the coast/ Archeology in the jungle/ The "archipelagoes" of the Andes/ Tiahuanaco, the city
in the clouds/ Insights from village archives/ Mysterious
patterns in the sand/ Origins in Ecuador*

W<small>HEN</small> we fly over the peaks and snows and 12,000-foot plateaus and deep valleys of the Andes, looking down on mile after mile of high isolated wilderness, it is hard to realize that people were here too, long ago and in force. But signs of their presence can be seen from the air along much of the world's longest mountain chain, extending some 4,500 miles from Colombia and Venezuela to Cape Horn—and particularly along the northernmost third of the chain, a ribbon of land including coastal plains to the west and to the east the edges of Amazonian jungles. There are terraces high and low, on steep and rugged slopes, built-up areas where soil and water were trapped to grow crops. There are also the ruins of roads and great monuments and cities in some of the most unlikely places on earth.

377

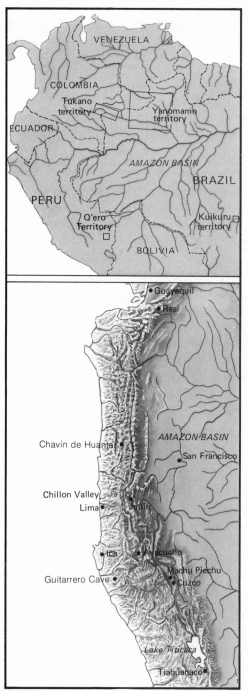

Vantage Art, Inc.

Enduring in mountain
wildernesses: the Andes,
where people survived by
exploiting food resources in
a variety of zones, living and
working at heights from
about a mile to three miles,
with some of the greatest
ceremonial centers and cities
at the highest levels; rivers,
fed by rains and melting
snow, flowed down from the
mountains to nourish coastal
lands to the west and tropical
lands in the Amazon Basin
to the east

Peruvian Andes

The original South Americans were nomads from the north, moving down from Mesoamerica and through the funnel of Panama. Thomas Lynch of Cornell University found and excavated one of their oldest known sites, the Guitarrero Cave in the Andes of northern Peru, located in territory that has seen many geological upheavals in times past. In fact, the cave faces snow-topped Mount Huascaran, more than ten miles away across a valley, where in 1971 an earthquake-triggered avalanche buried a city and 50,000 persons under millions of tons of slush and mud. (Lynch had left the region three months before.)

The cave's first inhabitants arrived around 9500 B.C. and were hunter-gatherers. Still hunter-gatherers two thousand years later, they were beginning to supplement their diet with cultivated plants, the earliest yet discovered in the New World. Among plant remains sieved from deep deposits are about thirty speci-

Courtesy of Thomas Lynch, Cornell University

Guitarrero Cave, Andes: views from cave mouth (left); excavating living floor (above)

mens of the common bean, some spherical, some kidney-shaped, and all fully domesticated. Wild beans are small, tan or gray, often with dark specks; the Guitarrero beans are larger, generally dark all over, and never speckled. Deposits also yielded lima beans, which, judging by their size and shape, were also fully domesticated.

These finds point to the early emergence of a distinctive high Andean pattern, a unique and basic life-style that was to influence the shaping of far more complex societies. The Guitarrero Cave served as a base camp, but did not provide permanent, year-round housing. A mere mile and a half above sea level, relatively low down for people adapted to the Andes, its surroundings offered little by way of subsistence during the dry five-month summer. At that stage the cave dwellers, perhaps ten to fifteen persons, may have moved about 500 feet lower into the nearest river valley, to grow their beans and exploit ample wild species.

People also used much higher lands during the dry season,

climbing almost to the snow lines of the highest peaks, to places so high that breathing is difficult for the unadapted and fires may sputter out in low-oxygen atmospheres. Some 1,500 feet above the cave Lynch found a site with unusually large quantities of chipped stone debris, a camp-workshop where hunters, some of them perhaps from Guitarrero families, stopped to make projectile points and other tools. They were heading for still loftier terrain, grazing grounds for deer and for camelids, the untamed ancestors of alpacas and llamas, in valleys watered by melting glaciers at altitudes of 15,000 to 16,000 feet. Similar living patterns are found in other regions. MacNeish reports prehistoric seasonal movements between the high valley of Ayacucho about 200 miles southeast of Lima. Part of the story here as elsewhere is a slow but steady increase in population from a band made up of an estimated two dozen hunter-gatherers to ten larger bands and a population of 500 by 5000 B.C. or so. Barbara Pickersgill of the University of Reading in England lists some plants that were probably domesticated at about this time: remains of squash, gourds, peppers and amaranth seeds.

Among the domesticated animals were dogs, which, according to Elizabeth Wing of the Florida State Museum, "reached the Andean area fully domesticated in very early times, so early in fact that they may have accompanied the first human migration into South America." The earliest native animal to be tamed was the guinea pig, identified by a size increase of about a third, as deduced by Wing from bones found on Ayacucho living-floors dating back to 7000 B.C.—and still raised today for food, sacrifices, healing ceremonies, and other purposes.

First steps toward the taming of camelids, the beginnings of herd management which led to llama and alpaca breeds, were apparently under way two millenniums later. This is the conclusion of Wing and of Jane Pires-Ferreira, Edgardo Pires-Ferreira, and Peter Kaulicke in an analysis recently completed at the National University of San Marcos in Lima. The San Marcos investigators suggest that a major center of camelid domestication was the Junin plateau region, more than two and a half miles high with lakes, ponds, marshes, rivers and abundant year-round pastures.

Survival depended on moving at just the right times and moving frequently. For some families, it still does. The Q'ero Indians live in a region described by one investigator as "the end of the world." Reaching their home territories requires a two-to-four-day walk some fifty-five miles due east of the ancient Inca capital of Cuzco, over zigzagging mountain paths that must be traveled by foot or horseback, through a magnificent and remote land of glaciers, of passes high in the clouds, and valleys at all levels down to the edges of tropical jungles.

Their life-style was first studied about a generation ago by Oscar Nunez del Prado of the University of Cuzco and his associates and, more recently, by Steven Webster of the University of Auckland in New Zealand. The Q'ero still "commute" between their low and lofty dwelling places. The places they call home are stone-and-thatch houses in hamlets at altitudes of 13,000 to more than 14,000 feet, which approaches the upper physiological limit for permanent settlement. (The record is about 17,500 feet, the level of a United States–owned mining camp in the Peruvian Andes, and beyond that even the hardiest and most acclimated individuals cannot endure.)

The Indians live so high because they have to be near their most valued possessions—alpacas whose long silky hair, in raw form or woven into fine fabrics, represents their major exchange item and source of wealth and prestige. Adapted to swamps and feeding on rough high-plateau plants, the animals need almost constant tending with frequent moves from pasture to pasture. They provide small quantities of meat in addition to wool as do llamas, although llamas can graze with less care at lower levels and may serve as beasts of burden, as well.

For most of their food the people must farm lands half a mile or more below their highest hamlets. The menfolk are at home less than half of the time, and often the whole family descends to lower-level houses to cultivate several dozen varieties of potatoes and other tubers, leaving only an elder or a woman or a child to look after the herds. Corn, squashes, peppers, manioc and other warm-climate foods grow at the lowest levels of all, more than a mile and a half below the potatoes, on the eastern slopes of the Andes.

There is nothing quite like the Andean way of life anywhere else in the world. Webster notes the hazards of getting from the potato zone to the corn-squash zone, and the problems encountered upon arrival: "The trip involves . . . precipitous trails in mud and dense vegetation, and confrontation of feared supernaturals which dwell in the jungle. Crop attrition is high, primarily through loss to bears, wild boars and parrots." A Q'ero farmer may leave home at four o'clock on a bitter cold tundra morning and be in hot humid country by early afternoon. The uphill trip back may come several weeks later and take two or three days.

The largest Q'ero "settlements" are deserted most of the time. At 11,000 feet, about halfway between their highest pastures and lowest gardens, is a village of forty-two large houses used from time to time by families farming in the immediate neighborhood, and by travelers seeking rest or refuge from storms. The village comes alive on special occasions. It serves as a ceremonial center where people take time out from their chores and climbing, and come together for fiestas and religious rituals.

This up-and-down way of life—John Murra of Cornell University calls it "verticality"—provides a model of what may have been going on in prehistoric times. People apparently had little choice. There was simply no place for all seasons, no single level that provided all the food needed for survival. As long as only a few hundred people were involved, a few hamlets, families had to keep on the move in an arduous, energy-consuming round of ascents and descents. It was a delicately balanced situation, and many things happened to upset the balance.

Declining populations with too few workers to carry the load resulted in the wiping out of entire communities. A population increase, on the other hand, even a small and slow increase, could accelerate the coming of larger and more complex social systems. According to Peter Jensen of San Jose State University and Robert Kautz of Hamilton College, that is just what happened in some areas. There were people enough so that families could spend more and more time together at one level, exchanging their products for the products of other families, often their relatives, at other levels. That means less moving, reduced energy requirements, and the release of a spiralling, self-amplifying process toward still higher populations.

The process gathered momentum between 4000 B.C. and 2000 B.C. It affected some important subsistence strategies, notably among Andean Indians committed to farming in high regions where temperatures sank to zero or below, 200 to 300 or more nights per year. They turned rigorous climates to their own advantage by developing effective ways of freeze-drying potatoes, something, by the way, which Germany tried but could not achieve during World War I. Exposing the tubers to the night's heavy frosts, trampling on them to crush out the water, and then drying them in the tropical sun, produced a nourishing food that could be stored for years.

Andean terrain above 10,000 feet has an incredibly crumpled, broken-up quality. It is a world of many little valleys and within the valleys hollows and pockets, a patchwork of plants in browns and greens and blues and a wide variety of textures. Murra describes what this implies in terms of survival today:

Every few hundred feet there is a new microenvironment and, as you go up, the pockets are compressed and become narrower and narrower, more and more shallow. Every few hundred feet you are confronted with different problems, new soil and waters of different chemical compositions—and in every one of these zones you have to domesticate different varieties of tubers and other crops and find new ways of making a living.

Hailstorms often hover over a single "target" and shatter the crops here, while zones only a few hundred feet higher or lower remain unscathed. Survival under such conditions calls for spreading the risks, the objective being to allow for highly localized hailstorms, tuber-destroying epidemics and other catastrophes. Having small plots in as many different zones as possible is one way to spread the risk. The poor, meaning most of the people, marry for more than romance. They know the zones where they have few plots or none at all, and must take that into account when selecting mates.

Controlling more people demanded new strategies, traveling farther to places beyond one's own part of the highlands, to other communities in the highlands and below. That had been going on at an increasing rate for a long time, but the most dramatic signs of the reaching-out have been found at Chavín de Huantar, a

site perched two miles high on the eastern slopes of the Peruvian
Andes, described by John Rowe of the University of California
as "one of the most remarkable surviving monuments of American
antiquity."

Chavín was an important regional center. Excavations of its
temple area reveal plazas, terraces, raised platforms, pyramids,
interconnecting stairways and ramps—and, inside the buildings,
a honeycomb system of dead-end alcoves and galleries supported
by beams of solid stone. Set upright at the center of a lower
gallery in the oldest part of the temple and dating back perhaps
to 1200 B.C. stands a fifteen-foot shaft of carved white granite
depicting a chief deity of the times.

He makes an imposing figure with anaconda snakes for hair,
and the mouth of a cayman (a crocodile-like reptile native to the
Amazon Basin) with huge upper canines and turned-up corners.
The expression on his face has been variously interpreted, an ex-
ample of the fact that experts often disagree, particularly when it
comes to interpreting art forms and symbols. Rowe calls him "the
Smiling God," while Luis Lumbreras of the National Museum of
Archeology in Lima has another reaction: "It is more probably a
'Cruel God' since . . . the treatment of the mouth suggests the
threatening snarl of a wild beast."

This and later deities became widely known. Starting around
1000 B.C., distinctive Chavín-style pottery and Chavín-style sculptures crammed with fantastically ordered sets of religious symbols
representing an ordered universe and social hierarchy began
turning up in other communities. Within half a millennium they
appeared all over the central Andes, from coast to jungle edge,
some 700 miles from Ica in the south almost to the border of
Ecuador in the north. Thomas Patterson of Temple University
sees parallels between the spread of the Chavín cult and the
spread of Christianity during the three centuries following the
death of Christ.

In both cases the apparatus, the physical conditions, which
made the process possible, existed beforehand, ready-made as it
were. Patterson emphasizes that early Christianity "spread from
Palestine along ancient pre-Roman trade routes . . . around the
Mediterranean and in the Near East," and that there were probably also ancient trade routes in the Andes. In the Andes as in

regions surrounding Palestine, the routes led to other centers with temples of their own and specialists in the conduct of local rituals, a network of places where potential converts could come and hear new ideas.

Apparently it was another case of crowds and conflict, this time in an Andean setting. Here as elsewhere intensive land use, less moving about and more settling down, and the growing of more food brought increases in population. That, in turn, brought a demand for still more food, and for more tightly organized ways of getting the food and establishing law and order. The institutional basis for all this involved a blend of art, religion and commerce.

At the root of the problem was the same need that drives societies today, the need for food and security. Caravans of llamas came down from the mountains, bringing obsidian, dry-frozen tubers, meat, and alpaca wool to the lowlands and climbing back laden with quantities of dried fish, manioc, squash and other produce. People caravans were also used, perhaps primarily for the fast delivery of perishable and breakable goods, since llamas tend to go at their own pace and rest and feed when they feel like it. According to Murra, "to the Andean elite, the llama appeared clearly inferior to human beings—who could be made to carry more and farther and in collaboration with one another, and who were more sensitive to fulfilling the requirements of ideology, as well as to the whip."

Above all, food has to keep coming in regularly, according to set and reliable schedules. Good relationships were essential all around, friendships and cliques among traders and the organizers of trade, gifts and bonuses and marriage alliances. So dealings in such luxury items as shells, gold and other metals, cotton, alpaca wool and cocoa became a vital built-in part of the entire exchange system—with highland leaders putting extra effort into the production of fine Chavín-style pottery and textiles designed for ceremonial use and prestige and high exchange value.

In a sense religion itself became a major export. The spread of the Chavín cult established deep ties with people at a distance. It also created a demand for ritual goods manufactured in the highlands. Rathje believes that a somewhat similar emphasis on ritual and trade may help account for the rise of Tikal as a major ceremonial center. Chavín's location is a clue to its central role. Today among the Q'ero the largest settlements lie on high passes where people must travel back and forth on their way from valley to valley. Chavín lay at the junction of two rivers and trails to still higher lands, the jungle and the Pacific coast. The Chavín religion may have been introduced systematically into new regions. A coastal site about 150 miles south of Lima has yielded huge painted textiles woven in the north which illustrate Chavín cosmology in considerable detail. Lathrap suggests that the textiles were textbooks of a sort, that they "could well have served the purpose of teaching Chavín catechism to the heathens."

Not all the pressure came from the highlands, however. The coastal desert of central Peru may seem a most unlikely place for social advancement. It has not rained there since 1925, and the climate was not much different in prehistoric times. But there were oases fed by runoff waters spilling down from the Andes. A map of the coastline has a kind of fringed look. It shows a system of more than fifty rivers and fifty little valleys, most of them parallel and regularly spaced about twenty-five to thirty miles apart.

Studies in one of the valleys, the Chillon River region just north of Lima, indicate that the living was easy for thousands of years. By 5000 B.C. or earlier, hunter-gatherers had established a basic seasonal round, subsisting mainly on fish, shellfish and other coastal fare during the summer. During the winter they moved ten to fifteen miles inland to meadows on the slopes of low Andean foothills, where condensed moisture from thick fogs rolling in from the Pacific made the desert green with wild grasses and tubers. The foothills provided the game, including deer and other animals moving down from the highlands to graze on the plants.

That shuttle pattern began changing during the same period which saw changes in the highlands, and for the same reason. Patterson reports that the number and size of sites in the Chillon Valley increased between 3000 B.C. and 2300 B.C., representing an estimated population increase of from 50 to 100 persons to 500 or more. Many of them may have been newcomers from the Lurin Valley to the south, where seacoast and foothills are only a few miles apart so that people could exploit both zones without moving. In fact, they had settled down two millenniums earlier, establishing an all-year-round village and a source of overflow populations.

Then there may have been a population chain reaction, or "epidemic." Perhaps settling down in the Lurin Valley sent excess families into the Chillon Valley, among other places, where the natives responded in the usual way—by settling down themselves. They cultivated fields of corn, squash, beans and other domesticated plants, most imported from highland farmers with whom they had been exchanging shells and other items for thousands of years. By 1000 B.C., when Chavín-style art began to spread, the Chillon Valley had irrigation, ceremonial-trade centers, and a booming population of some 10,000 persons. Similar developments were under way all along the central Peruvian coast.

Chavín, the Chavín cult, was part of an expanding Andean world. That world included tropics as well as coasts and highlands, the least explored and most difficult to explore of all Andean zones, dense jungles lost in mists on the high steep eastern slopes of the mountains, and merging at the bottom into humid Amazonian rain forests. The first hunter-gatherers in South America knew such terrain. Having already encountered extensive stretches of jungle on their way from the north, they almost certainly ventured into the interior, although the great majority of their sites vanished without trace.

Settling down could have come early in the jungle, particularly along the main tributary rivers of the Amazon River. Some time ago Carneiro left New York City to study a village of 145 Kuikuru Indians in central Brazil, in the very heart of Amazonia. They were living near a large lake and river, and had been for nearly a century. Subsisting mainly on fish, on manioc (eighty to eighty-five percent of their diet) and other garden plants, they did hardly any hunting.

Carneiro came back to the village last year, a generation after his first visit. The people remembered and welcomed him, and a man who had been an infant in the old days turned out to be his most valuable informant. People are now eating somewhat less manioc, still their dietary staple, and somewhat more fish. The population has risen from 145 to 160. As Chagnon has discovered among the Yąnomamö to the north, above a certain level conflict tends to rise with the addition of each new member. In this case the difference was enough to split the group into two villages. The reason given for the split: an increase in witchcraft.

Similar forces were at work in prehistoric times. According to Lathrap, early population increases, a result of the melting of glaciers and rising seas, probably produced the same sort of pressures that arose in the Near East and Southeast Asia. Waters crept inland along the deeply incised inner valley of the Amazon, drowning all of the river's lower valley, a distance of about 1,000 miles from the present mouth, and reducing the best lands for hunting and fishing by more than half. The flooding occurred 10,000 to 15,000 years ago, and for that period in the jungle we have no archeological evidence. But at sites around the little Shipibo Indian village of San Francisco, located near Pucallpa at the eastern foot of the Andes on an ox-bow lake where land-locked dolphins play, Lathrap has found pottery and evidence of agriculture dating to 2000 B.C. and earlier. The tempering material added to the clay included ground-up sherds from still earlier types of pottery, and there are miles of extensive and as yet unexplored sites along earlier courses of the river.

This is only a small part of the accumulating body of evidence which indicates that jungle people contributed to social evolution in South America, and to the ideas and world view represented in Chavín. The most elaborate monument at the highland center, a richly decorated obelisk found by the Peruvian archeologist Julio Tello, depicts among many other things a deified conch shell and a spiny oyster from the coast of Ecuador and a cayman deity from the jungles—symbolizing an underlying cultural unity in the Andean world. Except for the marine shells, all the symbols on the obelisk are Amazonian. This suggests that the great jungle contributed heavily to the shaping of Andean society, a point which Lathrap stresses.

Chavín was in its prime around 700 B.C. or so. After that there are signs of increasing local independence. Local art styles increased, marked by the telltale settlement pattern already noted in Mexico's Oaxaca Valley and other places, the appearance in many villages of fortified hilltop sites. This was a period of "decadence" and breakdown from the standpoint of Chavín leaders, but from a longer-range standpoint it represented a prelude to wider and far more complex organizations.

From a rubbing by John H. Rowe, University of California, Berkeley, of carving on the Tello Obelisk. Drawings reproduced by permission from his "Form and Meaning in Chavín art," *Peruvian Archaeology, selected readings*, Peek Publications, Mountain View, 1967

Chavín de Huantar, Peru: art, including tropical-zone symbols, Tello Obelisk

A number of spectacular sites arose in the highlands. The ruins of the world's highest prehistoric city, Tiahuanaco, lie near Lake Titicaca in a narrow Bolivian valley at an altitude of 13,000 feet, where people depended heavily on dry-frozen tubers for subsistence. The site covers more than 700 acres and includes a sunken temple, walls of neatly cut and fitted stones, stelae and stairways, massive statues in sandstone, and a lone richly carved gateway.

The feeling of lost grandeur in this site in a high desolate setting has inspired some outlandish fantasies. One of the most recent and widely publicized, apparently offered in all seriousness, attributes the building of the city to web-fingered creatures arriving long ago in a golden spaceship "from the stars." There are other far-out notions, all of them examples of pseudoscience at its most flagrant, and all sharing the conviction that since local Andean Indians were too backward to create such striking monuments, it must have been the work of superior outsiders.

Tiahuanaco reflects native not alien traditions, ancient ways of coping with Andean environments. It marks a stage in the process which presumably began with Q'ero-style families moving up and down between different subsistence zones, and—as populations increased—resulted in less moving, more permanently settled communities, and exchange systems involving caravans of people and llamas. The next stage featured a higher order of organization, the transition from exchange among more or less equal communities to exchange dominated by and directed primarily toward meeting the demands of a single center.

More than a decade ago in a large highland village Murra came across papers in the house of a peasant, the keeper of local archives, and found records of many legal disputes which started during the early fifteenth century. Some of the disputes, which concerned rights to corn fields in a lower zone nearly two days away, fields which the village had controlled in days before the coming of the Inca, were not settled until four hundred years later. Others were never settled. Information from such records, as well as from folktales and legends and the reports of Spanish

Tiahuanaco, Bolivia: heads on wall of underground temple (right, above); monolithic figure, probably a god (right, below)

Reprinted from Lumbreras: *The Peoples and Cultures of Ancient Peru:* Smithsonian Institution Press, Washington, D.C.; second printing 1976, by permission of Smithsonian Institution Press.

Photo by Pedro Rojas Ponce

officials and missionaries, yields a preliminary picture of complex Andean society as it existed when the Spaniards arrived and for some time before that.

It was a core or center with colonies at a number of higher and lower levels, a pattern that differs from the common colonial pattern. Usually the center exercises control not only over its outposts and outliers and subcenters, but over all the lands in between, where only friends and citizens are free to pass.

The Andean in-between lands are wild and often exceedingly difficult to get at, and thus they were not brought under such complete control. They were more like the high seas, where it takes a special effort merely to guard major trade routes; communities at varying distances from the center were more like islands. Murra speaks of "archipelagoes," groups of islands, in analyzing social structures in the Andes.

One archipelago was functioning as recently as the 1560s in the highlands of central Peru, with a core area of more than forty villages and 12,000 to 15,000 persons working under the control of elites in ceremonial-trade centers. Outside the core area at distances up to four or five days away were at least four outlying islands—higher communities for salt and herds, and lower communities for cotton, timber, cocoa leaf, peppers, wild honey.

A much larger archipelago existed during the same period more than 550 miles to the southeast near Lake Titicaca. Its core area, where as many as 100,000 persons may have lived at pasture land altitudes of nearly 13,000 feet, controlled resources coming in from some dozen island communities. One community occupied pastures about half a mile higher, and the rest were located down the western slopes of the Andes, all the way to the Pacific coast for fertilizer, cocoa leaf, fish and shells—and twenty-five roadless days away down the eastern slopes into tropical forests.

Travel is often dangerous in the mountains, as it is at sea. Murra was once caught in a blizzard so severe that his tent collapsed from the weight of the snow. People have been lost trying to find shelter from storms. Even in fine weather, in labyrinths of crisscrossing valleys and gullies, a wrong turn could lead deep into uncharted wilderness, a risk somewhat abated by traditional markers of cairns or piles of stones. And travelers always faced the threat of "pirates" who might raid and plunder island communities or ambush caravans at narrow passes. Archipelagoes endured only as long as there were men ready to defend them.

The big question, of course, is to what extent reconstructions of sixteenth-century societies apply to earlier societies—and the general answer is that they seem to apply rather well. The tendency to keep on living as your ancestors lived has been particularly strong in remote Andean regions. They remained relatively unchanged until recent times. "Massive and very real continuities exist between what happened in the Andes during the pre-European period and what is happening there today," Murra stresses. "The language, religion, land tenure—I am more and more impressed with the reality of these continuities, and ask new questions of the old material with more confidence."

The Inca empire, "the land of the four quarters," which lasted from 1430 to 1532, can be regarded as a superarchipelago, an archipelago of archipelagoes. Through a network of highways, cities and forts Cuzco elites controlled scores of island communities up to forty and more days away. There were special colonies for purposes other than subsistence—for soldiers, metal workers, potters, and stone masons as well as all-female barracks for the weaving of cloth, the great Andean prestige and power item. The empire extended some 2,700 miles from northern Ecuador to central Chile and northwestern Argentina, included an estimated 6,000,000 persons and, having reached such dinosaurian proportions, may well have been ripe for collapse even without the able assistance of Spaniards. There were many rebellions in pre-European times.

Societies organized along similar lines almost certainly existed a millennium before the Inca. That was when Tiahuanaco reached its peak, as the capital of an empire two to three times larger than the sixteenth-century archipelago also centered near Lake Titicaca. Thousands of acres of ridged or raised fields have been found along the lake's western shores, some no longer any good for agriculture because of accumulations of plant-poisoning salts. Another empire arose to the southeast during Tiahuanaco times. Across two ridges from the mouth of one of Ayacucho's largest caves lie the ruins of Huari, a city which covered more than 500 acres, housing more than 30,000 persons. It may have been the center of an archipelago-type organization.

An Inca center: Machu Picchu, Peruvian Andes

Photos by Pedro Rojas Ponce

During the same period people were making mysterious marks near Nazca, on the sands of coastal deserts to the southwest of Huari—lines extending five miles and more, patterns made by scraping away "desert pavement" stones, huge spirals and flowers, and a menagerie of mammoth animal representations, including a monkey and a spider. These patterns, like the ruins of Tiahuanaco itself, have been interpreted as the works of beings from interstellar space and elsewhere. The real explanation, if and when we find it, may well be sufficiently intriguing without resorting to science fiction.

Going back another 1,200 years into the past, what can be said about still older centers like Chavín? Were they prearchipelagoes, evolutionary steps on the way toward, but still short of full-fledged island systems? Neither these nor any other complex systems can function without a widespread popular religion. It often helps if people who work hard and give away ninety-plus percent of what they produce feel that it is all going to gods or to elites acting as representatives of gods. Chavín leaders certainly invented a powerful basis for such beliefs. The ancient Andean lowly were convinced that in return for what they gave they received the gift of fertility, their own fertility and that of their lands. In the early seventeenth century, long after the arrival of Spaniards and the destruction of the great archipelagoes, the great temples, and their priesthoods, some peasants were still cultivating special plots of land in secret, growing food not for themselves to eat, but for their gods.

There were beginnings before Chavín, some in the Andean region, and some in the region between the Andes and Mesoamerica which has seen little systematic archeology. Recent studies in this intermediate zone reveal significant developments in art and ritual. During the first season of a long-term excavation program of a site called Real Alto near the Pacific Ocean about eighty miles west of Guayaquil, Ecuador, Lathrap and his associate Jorge Marcos found 60 to 100 large oval-shaped houses built around a long rectangular plaza. Two clay-covered platforms face each other across the center of the plaza. One platform apparently supported a communal house where the menfolk gathered to participate in rituals and other festive activities.

Amid the refuse tossed into nearby pits were fragments of

Real Alto, Ecuador: reconstructed perspective of town where approximately 1500 people lived in 3000 B.C.

pottery mugs like those widely used today by tropical forest groups such as the Shipibo Indians of San Francisco village during beer-drinking bouts, which are, and probably were, often preludes to strictly controlled, tension-relieving ritual fights. On the other platform across the plaza are the remains of a burial in a stone-lined cist with repeated human sacrifices and a charnel house, a place for storing the bones of honored ancestors. Human bones mixed with animal bones in kitchen trash heaps indicate that cannibalism was practiced. "Trophy heads were common, indicating warfare and head-hunting," Lathrap adds. "The many human finger and toe bones scattered all over the village site may have been keepsakes from the ancestors stored in the charnel house."

The community had an early start. More than a thousand people lived in Real Alto, and they built their plaza-platform complex between 2300 B.C. and 2000 B.C. This is the earliest known ceremonial center in the New World, and Lathrap believes that developments in the intermediate zones influenced the shaping of later Chavín and Olmec cultures to the south and north. However, monumental architecture and major ceremonial centers remained at a modest level in the intermediate zone. The forces which brought about such things, which led to the clustering of people into larger and larger groups, were not operating at full strength, and explaining that is as challenging as explaining the appearance of major centers elsewhere.

Those forces were at large outside the intermediate zone, and in widely separated regions. Chavín arose in response to selective pressures. It met needs for more effective controls, new ways of maintaining—or, better yet, creating—law and order. The same needs seem to have become urgent at about the same time among people living more than 2,000 miles away. The period from about 1200 B.C. to 600 B.C. saw what Gordon Willey of Harvard has called "startling florescences," the rise of Olmec as well as Chavín art styles.

17

The City to the North, The Prehistory of Complex Societies in the United States

Villages and irrigation in the Southwest/ The first
pueblos/ The macaw and raven totems/ Pueblo
Bonito, a "high rise" community/ Hunter-gatherers
of the eastern woodlands/ The mound builders
in the midwest/ Graveyard evidence for the coming
of elites/ The Hopewell cult/ Cahokia, the city
on the Mississippi/ Ceremony and sacrifice/
The similarity between ancient and
modern farming strategies

THE entire North American continent, more than eight million square miles from the Mexican border to the Arctic Circle, produced just one prehistoric city. Known as Cahokia, its remains lie in the grass-roots heartland of the Middle West, in Mark Twain country near the Mississippi River and six miles due east of St. Louis. It could be a major national monument, as impressive as Tikal or Teotihuacan. But there is little reconstruction going on and nothing much to see, only a few mounds that look like natural hills.

Things were different in the past, without the trappings of our times, the interstate highways, drive-in movies, supermarkets and gas stations, motels and honky-tonks and hamburger joints. Eight centuries ago, in another America about the time of the signing of the Magna Carta, there was an earthen pyramid ten stories high, by far the largest pyramid ever built in the United States and the third largest in the New World (after Teotihuacan's Pyramid of the Sun, and a still larger structure in nearby Cholula).

At the front of the steep side of the pyramid, down and past three terraces, was a forty-acre plaza, and half a mile away across the plaza, two more large mounds. Beyond the mounds a stockade of heavy logs swept around to your right and left, enclosing the center's ceremonial district, a densely settled area of thatched-roof structures, temples and administrative buildings and elite residences on raised platforms, and hundreds of little houses where commoners lived. And beyond the stockade, extending in all directions to low hills in the distance, were more mounds, more homes, lakes and creeks and fields.

No comparable settlement, nothing even approaching this scale, existed within 1,300 miles. The next largest settlements had two dozen mounds at most; Cahokia had more than a hundred. It had about 30,000 inhabitants, and no other city in the United States reached that level until New York made it about six centuries later. The emergence of Cahokia raises some difficult questions, questions of continental dimensions. Why did it appear there, and at that time? Most intriguing, why did the rest of the continent remain empty of cities?

Change came very slowly north of the Rio Grande, more slowly than in Mesoamerica or the Andes. People moved down from Bering Strait regions along corridors between glaciers to the west coast, and on into "rain shadow" lands of the Great Plains, deserts, arid and semiarid grasslands, and prairies swept by winds from the Pacific, which had lost much of their moisture in heavy snowfalls over the Rockies. They kept moving east, out of the rain shadows and across the prairies and the Mississippi into woodlands so wide and unbroken that, according to a saying from pioneer days, "a squirrel could go from New York to Tennessee without touching ground." A recent series of carbon-14 dates indicates that Indians had reached Pennsylvania and probably spread along much of the east coast, 13,000 or more years ago.

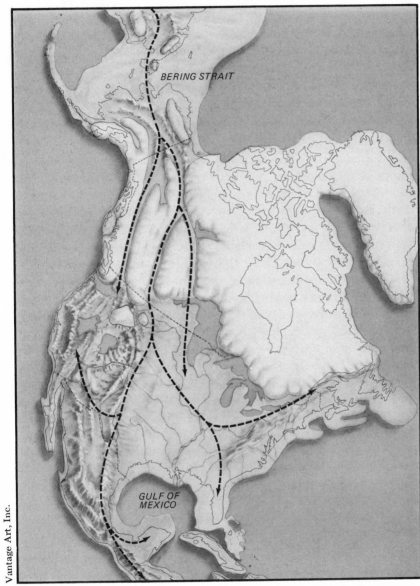

Vantage Art, Inc.

Through glacial corridors: ice sheet regions of Alaska, from which North America's aboriginal pioneers migrated south along the Pacific coast, inland to deserts and prairie grasslands in the rain shadow of the Rocky Mountains, and east through wide forests to the Atlantic coast, reached 13,000 or more years ago

They found ample resources practically everywhere, enough to live by hunting and gathering for thousands of years. There was an extraordinary abundance of big game west of the Mississippi on the Great Plains, for example. Even early and extensive extinctions made little difference. Mastodons, horses, mammoths and other big-game species—which had been in trouble during the preceding million years, long before man arrived—had vanished by 7000 B.C. or so. Huge herds of bison, deer and other animals continued to provide dependable supplies of meat.

Subsistence first presented a major problem on the margins of the plains. In the Southwest climates became drier and accomplished something hundreds of generations of stampeding and mass killing could not accomplish—sharp reductions in bison herds and their eventual disappearance. Newcomers may have aggravated the problem. According to Michael Glassow of the University of California, Santa Barbara, overflow populations from flourishing sites along the California coast may have been coming into the region. Sites show up increasingly on foothills and mesas as well as lowlands, a sign that people were foraging more intensively over a wider range of environments. Between 2000 B.C. and 500 B.C. they began using domesticated plants, notably corn as indicated by the finding of cobs, some no more than an inch long, like those unearthed in Mexico's Tehuacan Valley.

Still, it was a nomadic hunter-gatherer existence. One subsistence pattern of the times emerges from evidence gathered at the Jemez Cave, located near a mineral spring in the foothills of the Rockies in northern New Mexico. According to Richard Ford of the University of Michigan, everything points to warm-weather living: traces of ripe pumpkin as well as corn, no storage pits, and shallow hearths dug into sand and gravel instead of the stone-lined variety designed to throw off more heat.

The cave was used in late summer and early fall. That seems to have been a good time of the year to live off the land, as indicated by remains of pinon nuts, prickly pear cactus and other wild plants, and several species of mammals including deer, antelopes, mountain sheep and cottontail rabbits. Ford suggests that the Jemez people, like the sheep and deer, wintered at lower altitudes, and during the spring followed their migratory prey to grazing lands higher in the mountains, stopping on the way in the cave area to plant corn and pumpkins for summer harvesting.

Settling down was well under way from about A.D 100 to A.D. 300, the span indicated by a cluster of carbon-14 dates recorded at the Snaketown site about 350 miles to the southwest, in an Arizona desert valley on the outskirts of Phoenix. By that time villagers had developed a system of irrigation ditches fed by a wide shallow canal tapping waters from the Gila River more than a mile away, and cultivated plants, with corn as the staple, were providing a major part of their diet, perhaps fifty percent or more. They had cleared a large public space, probably a ceremonial plaza or dance ground.

But large-scale settlements well beyond the village level were still more than a millennium away. They did not appear until at least 12,000 to 13,000 years after people first moved into the Southwest, and about 3,000 years after the introduction of corn and other domesticated plants. When they did appear, it was

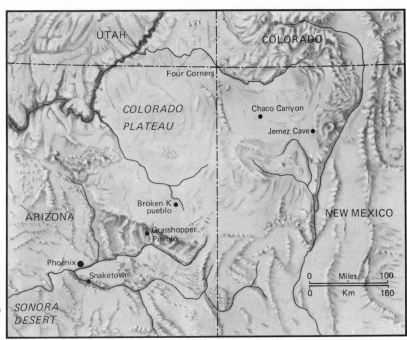

Pueblo territory, the American Southwest: the first clustered house-room complexes characteristic of communal living in the Four Corners region where Utah, New Mexico, Colorado and Arizona meet

United States Department of the Interior, National Park Service

"Swallow nest" cliff pueblos at Mesa Verde National Park, southwest
Colorado: 181 rooms and 19 kivas or ceremonial rooms in long house

in a form uniquely adapted to semiarid conditions and increasing
population. The Indians of the Southwest developed special crops
including varieties of corn that could be planted deep, nearer low
desert water tables. (Galinat reports that plants descended from
these varieties are being grown today "with some success" in
drought-stricken areas of northern Africa.) In their pueblo complexes they developed a kind of module architecture, a system of
standardized stone-plaster-adobe room units which could be
added, singly or in blocks, to existing buildings upon demand.

Starting around A.D. 900 they built hundreds of pueblos, at
first mainly in the Four Corners region where Arizona, Colorado,
New Mexico and Utah meet, and later in surrounding regions.
Some of their largest and most imposing structures arose along
river banks, on desert floors in the shadows of mesa walls, or built
into high overhanging cliffsides like the swallows' nests house
clusters at Mesa Verde, often in places which could only be
reached by ladders or steep paths with steps cut into rock. There

were also many smaller settlements. To get at some of them you clamber down into canyons, jumping from rock to rock along dried-out streambeds and past occasional rattlesnakes, and then up to ruins on ledges half-hidden by pinon and juniper trees.

One of the less spectacular pueblos has furnished some of the most interesting information. In pioneer research conducted during the 1960s, research based on an approach and methods widely used since then, James Hill of the University of California at Los Angeles demonstrated how facts about kinship and social organization can be extracted from analyses of artifacts. His site, located on the Broken K Ranch near the town of Snowflake in east central Arizona, consists of some hundred rooms built in blocks around a plaza; it was occupied from about A.D. 1150 to A.D. 1275.

Most of the rooms at Broken K, like most of the rooms at other sites, fit into one of three categories: large rooms averaging about 100 square feet, small rooms about half as large, and special underground rooms with entrances through the roof, air-vents, wall niches, and a table or platform. The pueblos of present-day Hopi and Zuni Indians have similar units designed for living, storage, and ceremony respectively, and the same functions probably existed in prehistoric times.

To test this assumption, Hill predicted that certain artifacts should go with different types of rooms, and then checked his predictions with actual findings. If the large rooms were indeed living rooms where a wide variety of domestic activities were carried out, they should contain more different kinds of artifacts than the other rooms. This turned out to be the case. The site yielded twenty-two different kinds of artifacts and twenty-one of them were found in the large rooms, as compared with nine kinds in the special rooms and only three in the small rooms.

Hill had a good batting average. He made fifteen predictions about what items should be found in the three types of rooms, and confirmed twelve of them. Two were partly confirmed, and one turned out to be wrong—that if the small units were storerooms, they should contain an extra-high proportion of large decorated pottery jars, which are generally used for storage in present-day pueblos. The rooms included open bowls primarily, although the significance of this finding is not understood.

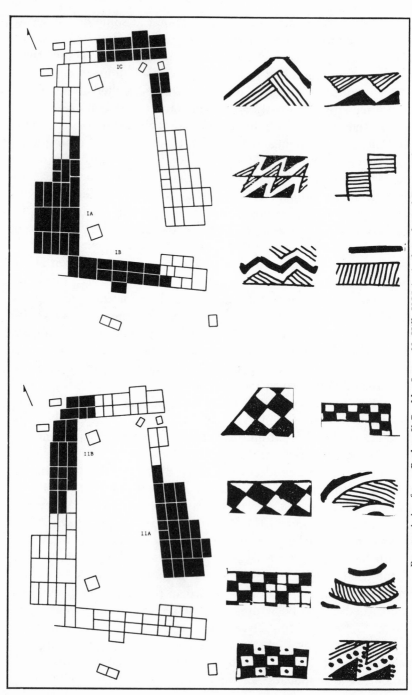

A more detailed analysis of pottery sherds picked up from the floors of the large rooms reveals something about living patterns at Broken K. Certain painted designs tend to appear together, and tend to be found in certain room blocks. One set of half a dozen designs, including chevron, sawtooth and zigzag patterns, occurs mainly on pottery made by people living in one group of forty-four rooms. Other designs occur mainly on pottery from another group of thirty-seven rooms. These and further differences suggest that the settlement was made up of two major groups or family lines.

The analysis can be carried a step or two further. In many present-day pueblos the husband moves in with his wife's family. Hill infers that a similar tradition prevailed in the past, partly on the ground that women make, and probably made, most of the pottery, and pottery designs may be handed down from generation to generation. The argument remains to be proved, and so do other arguments aimed at deducing residential traditions after marriage from studies of artifacts.

But success would bring handsome payoffs. The traditions may reflect tensions among different peoples and ways of surviving in unstable times. In a study comparing a group of societies Melvin and Carol Ember report that two conditions favor husbands living with their wives' families: (1) when men are occupied in warfare with outsiders, and (2) when the absence of men compels women to contribute at least as much as men to subsistence, and often a good deal more. The situation is reversed when the fighting involves groups within the same tribe, in which case wives tend to join their husbands' families.

Insights along such lines call for more detailed and extensive research, research designed to learn more about the evolution of pueblos. New information is coming from University of Arizona studies at a much larger ruin, the Grasshopper Pueblo on the Fort Apache Indian Reservation, about fifty miles southwest of Broken K. Work there is in its fifteenth consecutive season, with five sea-

Broken K. Pueblo, east of Snowflake, Arizona: two clusters of pottery designs found in two residence units—two family lines?

sons to go, by which time investigators hope to have excavated a fifth of the site.

The region, a transition zone between the Sonora Desert and the Colorado Plateau, has not been widely explored. Its first pueblos appeared around A.D. 900, a few small villages of perhaps fifty individuals each. The next three centuries saw a steady rise in population to about 100 villages, also small and fairly evenly distributed, a total of perhaps 5,000 individuals. Then the same number of individuals, or a few more, suddenly clustered together to form fewer and large communities, a phenomenon somewhat reminiscent of the implosions that occurred at Uruk and Teotihuacan, although on a much smaller scale. The number of settlements dropped from 100 to about 30 between A.D. 1200 and A.D. 1250 and, during the next generation or so, to about a dozen.

Climate had a great deal to do with the change. Tree-ring records show a trend from relatively wide annual growth rings which represent years of good rainfall to narrower rings indicating drier years. A twenty-year drought throughout the Southwest produced food scarcities at many sites, and at the same time lowered water levels in previously swampy areas, opening up once unfavorable terrain for corn fields.

Working the new lands demanded a new coming together of people. They had to pool their efforts to control water supplies. Rainfall was reduced, but it often came in the form of violent thunderstorms. Cloudbursts released as much as an inch of rain within an hour, and a high proportion of that generally fell within five minutes. Reducing damage from flash floods and conserving water required drainage systems, terraces, reservoirs and other public works. The drought started in A.D. 1275, and that date marks the beginning of Grasshopper as well as the abandonment of Broken K.

Investigations at the site have led to an elaborate deductive game known as "cornering." A pueblo room built from scratch in a previously unoccupied area has four bonded corners; that is, its walls actually intersect in a structure of interlacing bricks. Abutted corners, places where two walls simply meet without intersecting, appear later when new rooms are tacked on module fashion to the original room. Observations of corner types, com-

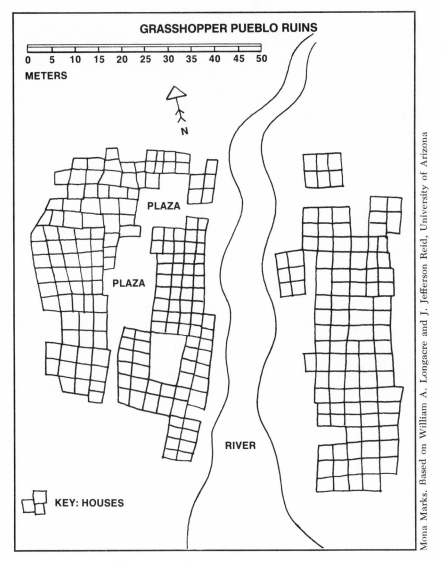

GRASSHOPPER PUEBLO RUINS

0 5 10 15 20 25 30 35 40 45 50
METERS

N

PLAZA

PLAZA

RIVER

KEY: HOUSES

Mona Marks. Based on William A. Longacre and J. Jefferson Reid, University of Arizona

Grasshopper Pueblo: east side-west side, separated by river;
a twenty-year research project

bined with tree-ring dates and other clues, show the order in which rooms were added and the growth of Grasshopper.

According to William Longacre of the University of Arizona, the settlement started with three blocks totalling about thirty rooms on both sides of a stream flowing through the site. On the basis of an estimated 2.8 persons per room, that indicates a pioneer population of about 100. Within half a century after its founding Grasshopper had expanded to nearly 500 rooms, more than 1,000 persons (assuming that about a fourth of the rooms were vacant at any time).

The odds are very much against the possibility of people in such a setting multiplying that fast, and Longacre believes that several groups of newcomers, perhaps as many as 500 to 600 in all, joined the original settlers. Statistical analyses of pottery, yet to be completed, may help check this notion, even indicating where the immigrants came from. Meanwhile there are some interesting hints. Among features excavated on the eastern side of the ruins are extra-large ovens, and charcoal fragments recovered from the ovens consist primarily of pinon wood. The major fuel in the west-side ovens was oak; the people selecting this wood for their fires might have been immigrants from the south, where oak trees are far more common.

Something more than simple immigration was going on, however. A duality, an east-west difference, seems to have existed almost from the beginning. The people who originally settled on the west of the stream added rooms to their two blocks to form a horseshoe-shaped pattern, while people living east of the stream first added rooms in a row to form a linear pattern. Even more intriguing are signs of a difference in symbols. The remains of about a dozen ravens have been found at the site, all but one or two from the eastern side of the pueblo.

The characteristic bird of the west side is the macaw. Fifteen specimens of the long-tailed, bright-feathered parrot have so far been uncovered in this zone, seven of them in the Great Kiva, the site's main ceremonial room. Also at the Great Kiva is an unusual grave, a young boy buried with a macaw on his chest. Perhaps the west-siders had particularly close contacts, trade and otherwise, with people living south of the border in the Mexican highlands 200 or more miles away, the nearest source of the birds.

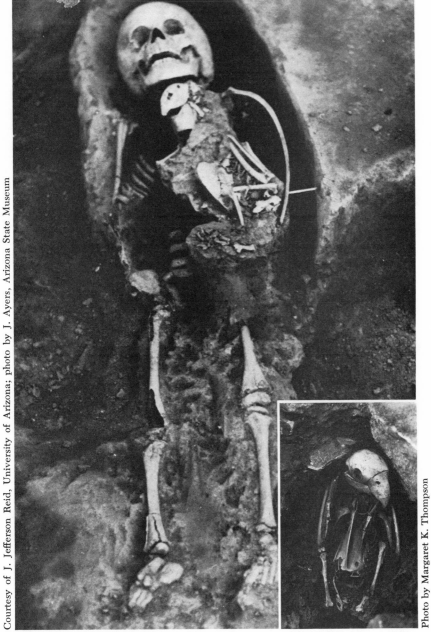

Courtesy of J. Jefferson Reid, University of Arizona; photo by J. Ayers, Arizona State Museum

Photo by Margaret K. Thompson

Grasshopper Pueblo, "clan" symbol of west riverbank people: macaw-and-boy and macaw burials, Apache Indian Reservation, Cibecue, Arizona (see macaw's head under boy's chin)

Chaco Canyon, Pueblo Bonito, northwestern New Mexico: aerial view of ruins that probably housed about 1200 in an 800-room four- or five-story structure; reconstruction, prehistoric "high-rise" apartments (below)

From *Prehistory of North America* by Jesse D. Jennings, 2nd. ed., copyright © 1974 by McGraw-Hill, Inc. Used by permission of McGraw-Hill Book Company

Grasshopper Pueblo may have been divided into two clans, the macaw people and the raven people, tracing their origins to remote mythical ancestors. The same two totemic groups existed until a few decades ago among present-day Zuni pueblo dwellers.

The most highly developed Southwest societies appeared in the Four Corners. New studies point to systems made up of many settlements, and one such system has been found in Chaco Canyon, New Mexico. A ruined pueblo of more than 500 rooms lies up against red sandstone cliffs at about the center of the canyon, not far from two other pueblos, one on the desert floor to the west and one, Pueblo Bonito, a "high-rise apartment" built in the great curve with four or five stories and some 800 rooms. The area includes more than half a dozen other multistory pueblos as well as several hundred small satellite pueblos.

This settlement complex and its 15,000 inhabitants were served by more than 200 miles of roads, the elaborate transport network described in Chapter 5, and discovered with the aid of special electronic equipment designed to detect aerial-photograph features invisible to the naked eye. In analyzing the network, Ebert and Hitchcock prepared a simplified map indicating major roadways, the places they passed through, and where they intersected. They used an engineering formula designed to measure the "connectivity" of the interstate highway system in the present-day United States, the proportion of settlements linked to one another by direct routes, measured on a scale from 0 to 1.

Chaco Canyon ranks low on this scale, with a score of only 0.1645. Its roads, like today's superhighways, were not built to serve the needs of the hinterlands. They tended to run in straight lines from major center to major center, bypassing lesser in-between settlements, a pattern ideally suited for the mass transport, by human carriers in the prehistoric case, of stone, timber, firewood, hides, food and other bulk goods. Some roads lead out of the canyon entirely, linking its centers to other centers associated with distant road systems perhaps hundreds of miles away.

The extent of the Chaco network is something of a puzzle. Keeping densely clustered populations provided with food and other resources certainly implies a degree of central control, organized supply schedules, and people with power. Yet Pueblo Bonito and other large settlements have yielded little evidence for the existence of elites, such as extra-large rooms with extra-high concentrations of fancy pottery and other luxury goods. This situation may reflect a big-man type of local authority. Perhaps the leaders were self-made men rather than members of high-ranking families, individuals who attained power by achievement rather than inheritance, and hence had less chance to accumulate wealth over a number of generations.

The difference may be difficult to prove archeologically. Enduring central place features showing an established hierarchy of settlements might provide arguments for power by inheritance. So might studies of grave goods, although no large cemeteries have yet been found in the canyon. Big men often take their most highly prized possessions with them into the afterlife, but inheritors of power generally tend to pass on valuable status symbols to their heirs. As mentioned in Chapter 4, burials of infants and children with luxury items may also be a sign of inherited status.

Such problems are currently the concern of William Judge of the University of New Mexico's Chaco Center. His task is to complete an intensive study of the canyon by 1980, when National Park Service funds are slated to run out. That highlights the problem of selecting where to dig, since only a fraction of available sites can be excavated.

Judge has already decided to focus on Pueblo Alto, the settlement on the mesa, because it lies at a hub in the transport network, a place where a number of major roads come together. He has also used statistical sampling techniques to decide which Pueblo Alto areas to excavate and, within those areas, which rooms, his objective being to obtain, in a limited period, as much information as possible about Chaco and its relationships to other pueblo complexes in the Four Corners and beyond.

If prehistory had not been interrupted, if Europeans had never arrived, the Southwest might have seen the rise of pueblo metropolises, systems of row apartments, close-packed Pueblo Bonitos based on agriculture and large-scale irrigation. And what about developments in the Northwest, along the Pacific coast? The salmon-fishing Tlingit mentioned in Chapter 14 were just one of the tribes which evolved complex societies and impressive works of art, without any agriculture at all—and which, given time and rising populations, might have produced a chain of maritime cities from Alaska to California.

Judging by the record, however, cities and states with a full measure of central control would probably have appeared earliest outside the wide rain shadow of the Rockies. Although Cahokia vanished centuries before Columbus, other systems were taking shape in the million square miles of virgin forests east of the Mississippi River, in the south and in the Ohio, Illinois and Tennessee valleys. The same broad patterns of living occurred in this wilderness as in the Southwest. More than 10,000 years of hunting-gathering passed before the development of large all-year-round settlements and agriculture.

As an example of how subsistence strategies shifted to meet changing conditions, Howard Winters of New York University cites what happened in prehistoric Illinois, one of the most intensively studied midwestern states. Game flourished in lands amply watered by runoff from glaciers which loomed not far away, covering practically all of Canada and much of the Great Lakes region. Hunters pitched camp along streams opening on prairie "peninsulas," long narrow stretches of open grassland extending into and merging with the forests. They went after ducks and other migratory wildfowl whose flyways ended in wide, shallow seasonal lakes and, when the opportunity arose, bagged an occasional bear-sized beaver. Recent finds suggest that their main prey was another big-game species. Herds of elk numbered several hundred individuals and represented a far more dependable source of meat, until about 700 B.C. By that time the glaciers had retreated, the elks migrated north into Wisconsin, and the Indians moved away from prairie-forest edges into large river valleys.

Sites gradually became larger, a sign of rising populations. There was also heavier traffic along the network of natural waterways that laced the forests, a sharp increase in large flint gouges suitable for making dugout canoes, and an appreciable thinning-out of sites upstream, beyond regions that could be reached by canoe. Deer provided a major share of the meat. A fivefold increase in the number of grinding tools suggests more intensive use of plant foods.

Evidence for this sort of diet has been found at the Koster site

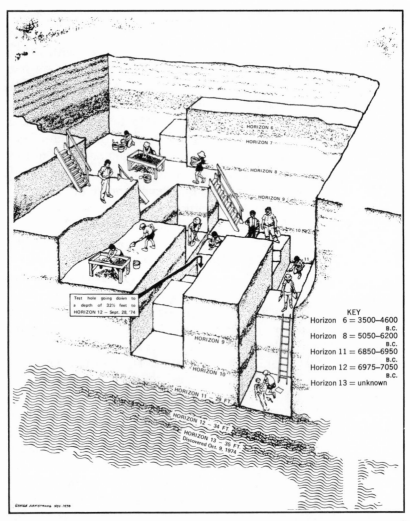

Koster at Kampsville: southern Illinois site excavation with dates determined by radiocarbon

Drawing by George Armstrong, 1974, Northwestern University Archeological Program

north of St. Louis. Microscopic examination of plant fragments extracted by floating-off methods from soil samples shows that nuts were a staple, with a special emphasis on hickory nuts. There are burials in one corner; five large postholes in an arc, possibly the remains of a thatched house; and "lenses" or overlapping layers of bright red-orange soil marking areas used repeatedly for fires. All of which dates back to about 6400 B.C. and, in the words of Gail Houart of Northwestern University, represents "a highly structured settlement pattern, a very stable life style."

That pattern, based chiefly on deer and wild plant foods, endured at Koster and elsewhere for 4,000 to 5,000 years. It began changing either because of a sudden relaxation of infanticide and other population-control measures or else, and more likely, because of a gradual filling-up of woodland territories. In any case, people turned increasingly to farming. They had probably been doing some gardening all along, so that when the pinch came it was in the main a matter of applying more intensively and on a larger scale such familiar techniques as weeding and fencing off selected plots.

Patty Jo Watson of Washington University, St. Louis, has found traces of some of their earliest crops in Salts Cave in central Kentucky, part of the world's longest cave system which includes Mammoth Cave and a maze of about 200 miles of charted passages. (Speleologists are finding new passages at a rate of a mile every month or two.) Starting four thousand years ago, local Indians camped in the Salts entrance chamber, lit cane and weed-stalk torches, and penetrated deep into the cave to obtain gypsum and other minerals. We know what they ate from their garbage dumps, hearths, and well-preserved fecal deposits.

According to Richard Yarnell of the University of North Carolina, the prehistoric explorers of Salts Cave harvested many wild species such as strawberries, blueberries, grapes, and large quantities of hickory nuts. In addition, they were cultivating two plants native to North America, sunflowers and members of the aster family known as sumpweed, both distinguished by seeds somewhat larger than the seeds of wild varieties. The natural range for sumpweed lies most west of Kentucky, indicating that the plant may have been brought in deliberately.

The earliest known domesticated plants in North America were not native plants and were probably not eaten. Using flotation methods to separate plant fragments from soil samples (see Chapter 8), Watson found traces of squash, originally domesticated in Mesoamerica, at two sites some fifty miles west of Mammoth Cave on the big bend of the Green River—in levels carbon-dated at about 2500 B.C. She suggests that the squash, a woody

Courtesy of Cave Research Foundation; photo by James W. Dyer

Salts Cave entrance, Mummy Valley, Mammouth Cave National Park,
Kentucky: investigators, dressed in shorts only, "impersonating"
prehistoric Indian explorers and miners

and not particularly palatable variety, was grown primarily for
its tough shells which served as containers and perhaps as rattles
in ceremonial dances. Edible squash may have come a millennium or more later. It has been identified in Salts Cave, and in
Winters' Riverton site in southeastern Illinois, together with the

remains of chenopod or goosefoot-family plants, which may also have been domesticated.

People under steady and mounting subsistence pressure turned increasingly to marginal, second-line foods, devoting more time to the daily food quest. Enormous shell middens or refuse heaps in Kentucky and Tennessee testify to the large-scale exploitation of mussels and other shellfish, and 100 pounds of such fare represents a great deal more effort than 100 pounds of venison, the yield from one good-sized deer. Another sign of the times was deeper penetration into second-line places, retreating into remote parts of the waterways network, way up along the smallest streams and secondary creeks.

At the same time sites in richer lands tended to become bigger and more complicated. From about 1000 B.C. on, and particularly during the period from 100 B.C. to A.D. 500, mounds appeared by the tens of thousands throughout the eastern woodlands, the largest measuring several hundred feet long and about forty feet

Serpentine Mound, Hopewell culture, Adams County, Ohio

Courtesy of the Museum of the American Indian, Heye Foundation

high. In later days European settlers were to be duly impressed, so much so that they came up with a wild variety of theories.

Most settlers attributed the mounds to outsiders such as Celts, Vikings, Phoenicians, or Romans. Ezra Stiles, an eighteenth-century president of Yale, argued for Canaanite refugees driven out of Israel by Joshua's armies, and checked the idea with his friend Benjamin Franklin. Franklin disagreed and suggested Spaniards instead, specifically De Soto's men. About the only thing that the theorists had in common was the conviction that the mound builders were white men, not natives, and certainly not the "savages" whose lands were in the process of being seized. In fact, the red man was believed to have wiped out the mound builders.

There was no need to look so far afield. As in the case of the grand ruins at Tiahuanaco in the high Andes, the builders turned out to be native Americans—so-called Hopewell Indians, named after a farmer who lived near Zanesville in southern Ohio and whose land included one of their major prehistoric centers. Southern Ohio and Illinois make up the Hopewell heartland, the region where most of their earliest and largest sites are located.

They buried their dead in the mounds, and burial patterns imply a great deal about how they lived. Joseph Tainter of the University of New Mexico has studied more than 500 burials excavated in two groups of mounds on the western bluffs of the Illinois River Valley. His analysis revealed six echelons or rank levels. Members of Rank No. 6, the lowliest of the low, were simply placed in holes on the edges of the mounds and covered with dirt. People in Rank No. 5, making up more than half the population, rated excavated rectangular graves, but little else. At the top of the hierarchy, Rank No. 1 individuals were buried at the center of the mounds in the largest tombs, complete with log walls and earthen ramps and with the most and best of everything. In the uppermost ranks infants were buried in the same style as adults, indicating that high status was inherited.

Hopewell mounds have yielded rich grave goods: ornaments cut out of mica and sheet copper, copper ear spools and breastplates and headdresses, ceremonial knives and spearheads of obsidian, grizzly bear teeth, marine shells, pottery and pottery figurines, stone effigy pipes with elaborately carved bowls. All of

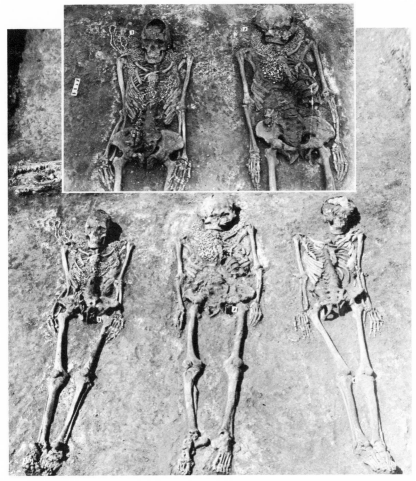

Courtesy of Illinois State Museum; reproduction by written permission only
Hopewell-type burial, Dickson site, near Peoria, Illinois, with enlargement showing status burial

which is evidence of a far-flung exchange network of raw materials and finished products. The shells came from the Gulf Coast more than 600 miles away, most of the copper from "nuggets" weighing from a few pounds to many tons in Lake Superior deposits at about the same distance, the obsidian from Yellowstone Park, and the bear teeth from the Rockies some 1,300 miles away.

The raw materials were worked mainly in the heartland region. Houart and Struever suggest that the Hopewell site itself, a center of 130 acres and more than two dozen mounds, may have specialized in turning out obsidian artifacts (more than 300 pounds of waste obsidian chips being found in a single mound) and bear-tooth ornaments as well as certain types of copper bracelets and ear spools. Other centers concentrated on the manufacture of effigy pipes and other objects. Such artifacts have been found over a wide area outside the heartland, from Minnesota to Florida and from Kansas to Virginia, usually of course in the graves of high-status individuals.

More than a decade ago Joseph Caldwell of the Illinois State Museum emphasized that the Hopewell presence was basically a funerary presence. It was unmistakable as far as grave goods, burial practices and presumed burial ceremonies were concerned. Apparently that presence did not affect the affairs of the living. Marked regional styles existed among secular objects, artifacts associated with daily subsistence activities, such as ordinary projectile points and pottery made for cooking and storage.

Distinctive Hopewell artifacts were probably gifts symbolizing and promoting solidarity among the elite. What seems to have spread together with the artifacts was a set of beliefs about death and the world of the dead. Caldwell speaks of a Hopewell cult which in certain ways resembled the Chavín and Olmec cults of the Andes and Mesoamerica, respectively. It arose when people were gathering into larger groups, before the coming of cities when ceremony and high status were evolving as central features of social control.

The Hopewell world began coming apart after A.D. 500, perhaps because of population stress. People settled increasingly in marginal places along the upper reaches of tributary streams and creeks—and they were not eating as well. Della Cook's bone studies at Indiana University reveal reduced childhood growth rates and a drop in life expectancy. Fewer luxury goods were produced. Winters points out that decorated pottery practically vanished. Exchange networks crumbled; apparently supplies of obsidian from the Rockies were completely cut off. The appearance of more fortified hilltop sites, and more marks of violent deaths on skeletons found in burial mounds around A.D. 700 to A.D. 800, suggest increased fighting for scarce land and other resources.

What followed was a new way of adapting to changing circumstances, a new culture which is known as the Mississippian and whose most dramatic expression was Cahokia. An example of developments taking place at the same time in many parts of the eastern woodlands, the center appeared in a setting of confluences, meeting places of continental and local waters. It arose a few miles downstream from one of North America's great crossroads, where the Missouri River flowing from sources in the Rockies pours into the Mississippi, in a fertile floodplain valley known as the American Bottom.

It had its own network of little waterways fed by runoff from high limestone bluffs to the east. Most of its settlements, more than a dozen and all of them hamlets, lay near or on the top of the bluffs. But significant changes were under way in A.D. 800, out on the floodplain, in a cluster of five hamlets located near a local confluence where two creeks came together on their way to the Mississippi. People here, like their ancestors long before, were engaged in traditional hunting and gathering, exploiting deer, fish, migratory birds, nuts and many wild plants. Their daily diet also included a new staple. After being introduced into the woodlands nearly a thousand years earlier, perhaps as a ceremonial food or delicacy, corn was finally coming into large-scale production, as it was in the Southwest at about the same time.

A transformation took place during the next two or three centuries. Instead of a few settlements, all of them small, there were many settlements and at least three size levels. The number of communities jumped from a dozen to forty-nine: forty-two villages, five small towns, and two large towns, one of them Cahokia which occupied the region formerly occupied by the five-hamlet cluster. Its giant pyramid, known as Monks Mound, rose on the site of one of the hamlets.

By A.D. 1200, the number of communities was about the same, but a new level had been added to the hierarchy. Cahokia, a bustling city now at its peak, was in a class by itself. In its complex of communities were four large towns, five small towns and forty-three villages. The population of the American Bottom had increased nearly a hundred times, with perhaps 50,000 persons, 30,000 of them living in Cahokia.

The scale of ceremony expanded correspondingly. Imagine a

Cahokia, only prehistoric North American city: inner urban area within two-and-a-half stockade of city of six-and-a-half square miles with more than 100 mounds, as it must have looked about 1150 A.D.

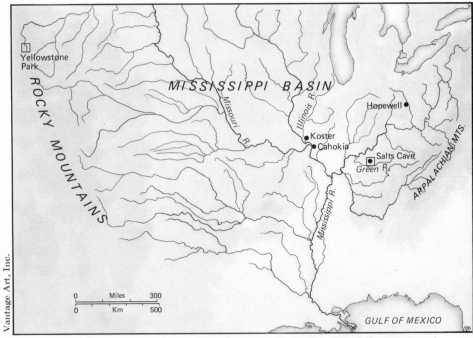

Mississippi Basin, a center at the meeting of waters: one of the continent's
great crossroads, six miles due east of St. Louis, where about a thousand years
ago North America's only prehistoric city, Cahokia, arose. It was located
strategically near the junction of natural prehistoric water "turnpikes," the
Mississippi and Missouri, forming trade networks from the Rockies to the
Appalachian Mountains and into the Mississippi

midsummer dawn on top of Monks Mound where the Great Sun,
the paramount chief of Cahokia, appears in full regalia, feathered
headdress and cape of shell beads. He turns to the east to greet
his celestial brother, the rising sun, falls to his knees, and emits
three high, piercing, howling cries. Echoing cries come from the
crowd on the plaza below, and then a silence. An annual renewal,
a kind of resurrection, is about to begin.

All the fires in all the city's huts and elite residences and shrines
have been extinguished, all but one—the eternal flame which
burns in the temple on the pyramid. Now a tattooed warrior,
bearing embers from the temple in a bowl, walks slowly down
ramps and stairs to a great cross of logs in the center of the plaza,
lights a fire under the logs. The crowd roars as flames leap into
the air. Throughout the valley hearths will glow again, lit with

embers from the burning cross. Once again the Great Sun has replenished the life of the community, bringing fresh fire down from the heavens for the benefit of his people.

This sort of ritual is believed to have marked the opening of annual harvest festivals. The description is based on historical records, eyewitness accounts of ceremonies practiced during the seventeenth and eighteenth centuries by Indians whose religion probably resembled that of the Cahokians. Archeology provides evidence of other ceremonies. In a long low mound south of the main plaza known simply as No. 72, Melvin Fowler of the University of Wisconsin in Milwaukee found the remains of an important person, perhaps a Great Sun, laid to rest on a platform with some 20,000 shell beads and, nearby, a cache of some 800 arrowheads and sheets of mica and copper. He did not die alone. Among those buried with him were more than fifty young women, sacrificed and arranged in neat rows.

There are further glimpses of life in the city. Excavators have found traces of a "woodhenge" or ceremonial "sun circle" with large wooden posts instead of the upright stones of England's Stonehenge. A concentration of seashell debris and little flint drills not far from Monks Mound may have been a bead-making workshop. The great stockade surrounding the central district may represent a defense against raiders from the outside, or an internal barrier of a sort, a symbol of status and isolation separating increasingly powerful elites from local commoners.

Many problems remain, but it may already be too late to solve some of them. Charles Bareis of the University of Illinois has lived a good part of his archeological life trying to ward off bulldozers, protecting the area from people more interested in profits than prehistory. On one occasion, after foiling a real estate venture, he had to contend with a farmer who would have gained from the deal: "He came at me with fists clenched, ready to swing—a tough, hard-working man of the soil, difficult to argue with. He didn't speak to me again for two to three years."

It has often been a losing fight. More than half the site's 100-odd mounds have been destroyed, and many smaller sites have vanished completely.

The Cahokia countryside included twin multimound communities six and seven miles to the south, one on either side of the

Ancient man-made Monks Mound: Cahokia, between Collinsville, Illinois, and East St. Louis, rising more than 100 feet on a 14-acre base, now surrounded by suburban stores

Mississippi where East St. Louis and St. Louis are today. These settlements, like the twin districts of Uruk in the Near East, may have served as "toll booths," controlling traffic along the river. Other satellite communities lay at about the same distance to the north and south, and James Porter of Loyola University of Chicago, who has been thinking in terms of central place theory and regional settlement patterns, believes that a search might reveal a similarly located community to the east.

He sees Cahokia as the hub of a highly organized trade network. Some luxury materials like copper, mica and selected arrowhead flints came from great distances, as in Hopewell days, but not in such great quantities. Winters points out that one good Hopewell mound contained more sheet copper from Lake Superior than entire Cahokia-time sites, and suggests a greater focus on less glamorous regional resources, something like the change which followed the decline of long-distance Olmec trade in Mesoamerica.

The city may have controlled the manufacture of stone hoes made from a tough variety of chert obtained at a quarry about 100 miles to the south—and used to cultivate floodplain soils and forest areas cleared by slash-and-burn methods. It may also have controlled trade in salt which became more important as the proportion of meat in the diet decreased and the proportion of domesticated crops increased. (Corn, for example, contains only about one-nineteenth as much salt as an equal weight of beef.)

Cahokia's power depended on food resources close at hand, in its own backyard—and on the organization required to exploit those resources and support rising populations. The basic problem in the American Bottom, as in the totally different setting of the Andes, was to spread the risks of crop failure due to unpredictable weather and soil conditions. Farmers still living in the area had to cope with precisely the same problem as recently as forty years ago.

William Chmurny of the State University of New York College at Potsdam interviewed fourteen retired American Bottom farmers, and reports that the ones who failed and ultimately lost everything "tried to beat the system." They shared two characteristics: (1) they worked one and only one farm, gambling that a particular area would pay off handsomely if they could just find a way of predicting rainfall and temperature patterns; and (2) none of them had relatives in other areas. The successful farmers made strategic arrangements with kinfolk in different parts of the floodplain and in eastern uplands—and thereby increased the odds that growing conditions would be favorable on at least one farm.

According to Chmurny, Cahokia may have appeared in response to similar conditions. In the beginning perhaps, say around A.D. 800, individual farmers may have insured adequate crop yields by kinship ties, sharing lands in different parts of the valley with their relatives. But that system could not have lasted long, because within a century or so work was already under way on Monks Mound, a strong hint that higher levels of organization were evolving to cope with localized uncertainty and to distribute corn and other resources throughout a region already containing thousands of persons.

The need for centralized authority arose locally in the American

Bottom. On the other hand, outsiders made important contributions. A variety of beliefs and art motifs and architectural styles, including temple-topped pyramids around central plazas, came from Mesoamerica along with corn itself and other crops. By Cahokia's take-off period around A.D. 900, Teotihuacan and Tikal were in various stages of collapse. The connection, if any, between these events has not been established. But the up-and-coming elites of Cahokia and other budding woodland centers may have learned a thing or two about controlling resources and people from their more experienced but fading counterparts to the south.

18

People under Pressure, the Search for Security

Reshaping wildernesses and the high cost of survival/ Supply-and-demand spirals/ Spreading the risks/ Giving, kinship and the struggle to maintain peace/ Artificial trade networks among the Yąnomamö/ "A preoccupation with death"/ Evolving elites in the New Guinea highlands/ The expand-or-perish principle/ Ecology and religion in Colombian rain forests/ The city as the supreme artifact

T HE emergence of agriculture and cities and states, the emergence of power, took place in many parts of the world. Styles in subsistence, art and religion were regional, local, but everywhere the same basic process was under way. It was a revolution, a burst of change. After ages of hunting-gathering, ages of enduring tradition, people managed to transform their world within 10,000 years.

Food scarcities, the threat of total famine and extinction, triggered this explosion of culture. Food scarcities, of course, were nothing new. The new element was *Homo sapiens,* a species so different that its appearance amounted to a new kind of evolution. All other species had responded to similar crises essentially by

433

adapting to the world as they found it. Humans did that, too. But when that was no longer enough, they began changing the world. They "cheated" by reworking the wilderness to suit their own purposes, and multiplied faster than ever. They broke the rules of the game. It remains to be seen whether or not they will get away with it.

The objective, the necessity, was to establish a kind of home base that had existed before only on rare occasions, if at all—an all-year-round place, a place to come back to every night of the year. Instead of moving away seasonally or permanently when natural abundances started declining, people settled down and focused their energies on modifying the countryside. They established new environments, compact areas where things were concentrated and close at hand, lands which provided within restricted boundaries everything that far wider stretches of good hunting-gathering territory had provided, and more.

At first it was mainly a matter of doing what had been done in earlier times, only on a somewhat larger scale and more intensively, relying more on species previously used as dietary supplements. Man-made plant communities appeared, the early gardens of the Near East and the Thailand lowlands and Mesoamerica and New Guinea with varieties of plants in single plots, distributed over wide areas under natural wilderness conditions.

The plants grew wild or nearly wild. Some of their predators were being held at bay. Birds and insects could not be completely controlled, but fences helped keep out goats, deer, pigs and other wild animals. Weeding removed unwanted plants that competed for sunlight and the nourishment in the soil. Sometimes, as among the Paiute Indians and Australian aborigines, water was brought in from a distance along specially dug irrigation ditches. Many plants grew where only a few had grown before. A single acre yielded as much food as twenty or more earlier acres.

People survived, but at a price. In a sense, they succeeded too well, as evolution took an unexpected turn. Instead of dying off in droves, they reproduced at an accelerating rate, an ironic development considering that population pressure was one of the major reasons for settling down originally. Man's prehistoric ancestors could never have foreseen that settling down would boost birthrates. Investigators studying the relationship between fat and fertility are just on the verge of understanding the phenomenon today. It was the beginning of a strange spiral of supply and demand, a continuing race between increasing land productivity and booming population, between more food and more mouths to feed.

In a better balanced world a garden of one's own, a plot of land with plants and some livestock, might represent the height of security and self-sufficiency. But not in the face of that supply-and-demand spiral, and not in the face of a host of new uncertainties. In many respects the settled life was less dependable than a life based entirely on mobility and hunter-gathering. It was more of a gamble. Men and women had to calculate the odds and beat the odds, devising insurance schemes in case of failures.

In the Andes people could not count on any single plot to keep them alive. They spread the risks, locating plots of land at as many different altitudes and in as many different environments as possible. That greatly increased the chances of obtaining some food somewhere. The same policy guided American Bottom farmers living along the Mississippi during the 1930s and probably the Indians who lived in the same area a thousand years before, the builders of Cahokia. Diversifying subsistence investments was one lesson settlers everywhere must have learned very early in the game.

They were wrestling with an old and basic problem, now several orders of magnitude more complicated than ever before—how to obtain enough food for everyone day after day, season after season, year after year. Essentially this is establishing order out of disorder, achieving a measure of stability amid wild fluctuations and booms and busts. The world is a highly unpredictable place, and all subsistence strategies have evolved as part of the effort to make it as predictable as possible, ideally 100-percent predictable.

That means living with, anticipating and allowing for, the possibility of disaster. In one branch of the Valley of Oaxaca an average of some 5.5 inches of rain falls during June, the best month for planting (about one-fourth of the average total for the year). But farmers live on actual rains not on averages, and over a forty-year period June rainfalls ranged from less than half an inch to nearly ten inches—and for all the "systems" and forecasting schemes, you might as well toss a coin. There is no repeating pattern on which to base predictions.

The only thing to do is be ready and on the spot at the right time. Rain may come during meals in Oaxaca, or during fiestas or church. Whenever it comes, all the able-bodied men in the villages are off to the fields on their bicycles. They may spend hours in the downpour opening sluice gates or channels in small stone or brush dams, allowing just enough water to spread over their fields, then damming up the channels so that farmers waiting at their dams further downstream can have their turns at the water.

Crops fail frequently today, perhaps one out of every five or so; they probably failed at least as frequently in prehistoric times. The list of hazards included plagues of insects, plant diseases, and declining soil fertility as well as floods and droughts and, no less devastating, the raids of outsiders. There was a special premium on a level of planning sufficiently sophisticated to forestall disaster. The population of any settlement represents an unceasing and completely predictable demand for food. The farmlands that supply the food are rather less predictable. The goal has always been to create certainty out of uncertainty, to arrange a steady flow of food from fields that are fallible.

People were being domesticated along with their plants and animals. They had to live more than ever before in a world of futures, establishing and sticking to schedules. There were times for clearing land, planting, weeding, harvesting, times even for enjoying leisure—as the emphasis shifted away from feasts and dances coming on the spur of the moment, perhaps when foragers returned to camp with a fine antelope or baskets full of wild fruit, to regular celebrations marking the rainy season or harvest time. Communicating with spirits and gods became a matter of schedules, with fewer spontaneous and more "calendric" or seasonal rituals.

Settlers had no choice but to plan wisely or fail and, as indicated by abandoned "ghost" settlements, many of them did fail. Their only way of making it in the long run, their only effective form of insurance, was to exploit a variety of environments and resources. They had to work hard and steadily in their fields, and not just to meet their own day-to-day dietary requirements. They had to produce more food than they could consume immediately, building up large surpluses to tide them over the winter and, if possible, to allow for the occasional bad year of crop failures and low yields. When it worked, this was a solution to uncertainty; reliable systems had been created out of unreliable units.

The solution carried with it a tendency to expand, to extend boundaries and controls. Survival demanded wider, regional thinking, beyond one's own fields and storage pits, beyond the collective fields and storage pits of one's neighbors and nearest of kin and, increasingly as populations rose, beyond one's village and neighboring villages. Whatever people believed about themselves, whatever their illusions of independence, the hard fact is that they could not endure on their own. So, for the sake of security, life became more and more complicated everywhere, in the Uruk countryside and North China's nuclear area at the bend of the Yellow River and the Four Corners region of the American Southwest.

The first settlers moving into hitherto unsettled territory built their villages and managed to stay together for a number of generations until rising population levels made life too close for comfort. Then the budding-off process started. A few families moved to another part of the valley, not far away because of kinship ties. A cluster of half a dozen villages arose, each with its public space and public building, each perhaps taking its turn in rotation as host for special holidays and ceremonies, and each under subsistence pressure to extend its area of control. At some take-off point the pattern changed from a cluster of separate and equal settlements to a cluster with one large and growing settlement marking the beginning of complexity and centralized control.

Many such beginnings must have been cut short. Even with the best of planning, subsistence systems collapsed from time to time. Life proceeded always in the shadow of catastrophe. There were other sources of disorder. Controlling lands and resources meant controlling people and, upon occasion, people can be as unpredictable as crops. Conflict tends to rise among contemporary hunter-gatherers in the process of becoming farmers, for example, among the Australian aborigines and other tribes. Doubtless it was the same in prehistoric times. Living close together in large groups and permanent villages ran counter to the old formula for avoiding fights: stay small and, when trouble threatens, move away.

New formulas had to be found. Peace was never a natural state; it had to be made and kept. It took considerable effort, at least as much as the daily chores involved in cultivating the land and taking care of domesticated herds. As a product of millions of years of small-band existence, man had to work hard to adapt to conditions no longer favorable to small bands. He had to learn to curb deep-rooted forces which worked for increasing conflict and violence in large groups. That meant building on past customs, traditions designed to help maintain peace and goodwill. At the hunter-gatherer level gift-giving relieved tensions within the band. Judging by current practices, a valued possession like a decorated pouch or a fine knife had a double, positive-negative quality. It was treasured, but not for long because ownership aroused guilt. The possessor usually gave it away to avoid becoming the object of envy and resentment.

Giving was just as important in relationships among bands, to insure a warm welcome elsewhere when it became advisable to move away. Wiesner's study of exchange networks in the Kalahari, "paths for things," documents the importance of gifts in creating a secure world. Because men and women gave continually, and were raised to give from the first few months of life on, they had credit in the form of goodwill among bands scattered over hundreds of square miles. The Trobriand Islanders' kula ring and the potlatches of the Northwest Coast Indians are far more elaborate and ostentatious systems that evolved later among selected groups.

Kinship itself was part of the intensive effort to be close to other people, to be friends and to be welcomed instead of attacked. In some cases it was widened to include those who were not blood relatives, but with whom one shared food and other goods. They became blood relatives by consensus, in all but fact. They were considered members of the family in the most literal sense. Marriage and sexual intercourse was forbidden by the strictest of incest taboos.

Thomas Harding of the University of California in Santa Barbara cites one of the most moving examples of this ethic in action.

He quotes a New Guinea tribal elder discussing what the breakdown of such a system may mean. When sharing comes to an end, so does kinship—and so do the taboos: "When we ask people for help and they do not come, and when we don't help them, we are no longer of one blood. Our children may marry."

Nothing better illustrates man's genius for adapting, for making the custom fit the need, than his unremitting efforts to combat or counteract conflict. The earliest associations and secret societies and fraternities which went beyond blood brotherhood arose as part of that effort. So did artificial trading networks in which each village specialized in making a product that could easily have been made anywhere throughout a wide region. Other villages specialized in other products which could also have been made anywhere. The sole purpose was to have something to trade. Trade established mutual needs and goodwill.

Among the Yąnomamö of southern Venezuela and northern Brazil vine hammocks can be obtained only in one village, bamboo arrowheads in another, and so on, even though there are vines and bamboo plants everywhere. Similar systems have appeared among tribes in the Pacific islands and other regions. People try persistently to eliminate conflict, never discouraged by failure, and after conflict flares up, they are ready with a variety of procedures for keeping it within bounds. The record is full of graded rituals, everything from bloodless confrontations and threat displays and individualized stylized fights calculated to permit some minor spilling of blood, to skirmishes which stop as soon as a few people are injured or killed. The objective is always to contain violence short of all-out war.

Peace, in short, is man-made. It is an artifact, and one of the most fragile of artifacts. The struggle to achieve peace continues today as in the past among all primitive tribes, partly at a conscious and partly at an unconscious level. The Yąnomamö do not realize exactly what they are doing or why. According to Chagnon, they know that their trading networks may upon occasion promote friendly feelings and forestall fighting. But they do not understand that the networks are essentially artificial, that there is no "practical" reason for different villages to specialize in different products, that is, no reason based on unusual skills or favored access to scarce raw materials.

UNESCO/Domonique Roger

Symbol of divine kingship: Abu Simbel statues in the Great Temple on new site, Nubian desert, Egypt, moved in UNESCO-led campaign against Aswan Dam flooding

When a network breaks up, as it always does sooner or later, new networks and new alliances are formed. People can adjust quickly to new political realities. The members of one village mysteriously "forget" how to make their special product and, just as mysteriously, acquire a talent for producing something else. They see nothing strange or inconsistent about this, regarding it as a natural and logical way of getting things done. They have blind spots marking the presence of traditions, rituals that have become essential.

So studies of contemporary and recent societies hint at earlier changes which are difficult to detect unequivocally in the archeological record. The appearance of sites on hilltops and defense walls and earthworks indicates that the scale of conflict escalated along with population density and community size. It remains to be proved that gift-giving, more inclusive kinship systems, and artificial trade networks were part of the effort to maintain peace, although the circumstantial evidence seems good.

The combination of increasing tensions and the need for long-range planning conspired to bring about the passing of another basic feature of the hunting-gathering life style—the old, established tradition of equality among members of the band. The small size of bands hardly encouraged the rise of leaders; after all, there were not many people to lead. Apparently the pressure for status had always existed, however. The story of Lee's Kalahari Christmas shows that the practice of putting down pride and people with big ideas was founded on long and bitter experience.

That was hunter-gatherer wisdom, the wisdom of men and women who enjoyed a relatively stable life by keeping on the move, and who wanted to preserve that way of life. It had no place in the new and rather less reliable world of permanent settlements, or in transition times from hunting-gathering to farming and cities and states. Equality disappeared with the coming of increasingly elaborate controls, with discipline and schedules and moves to reduce fighting.

After a long egalitarian past when people were simply people, equals among equals, and when the weight of tradition worked to keep men from becoming too big—after all that, processes were at last released which ushered in big men, and big men with a vengeance. An early sign of the change came more than 4,000 years ago in Sumer, when scribes placed an asterisklike mark before the names of some of their kings, the cuneiform symbol for "star" or "heaven." That mark represented man as god; he could rise no further.

Of all divine kings, none attained a status higher than the pharaoh in Egypt. "His very physical presence was treated as that of a god," comments Eric Uphill of the University of London, "his throne being literally set up in a shrine like those of the principal deities in the great temples. He was so encompassed about with divinity that it is almost impossible today to understand what this entailed."

Every object he touched was deemed sacred, everywhere he sat must be placed at a higher level upon a dais, thus commanding the place where others stood. . . . His every action was recorded in detail and minute observation, being carved and painted with infinite labor and care upon the walls of temples and palaces. . . . His likeness was copied and made known to millions of subjects and neighboring peoples by such a quantity of statuary and figures, named articles and commemorative objects, as to make the work of modern publicity agents look puerile.

There were changes, too, in notions about what and how much a man should possess. After a hunter-gatherer tradition of feeling ashamed to own a beautiful ornament, so much so that you gave it away quickly to ease your conscience, it became appropriate for some people to accumulate considerable wealth, the more the better, and display it for all to see. They were often buried with their treasures, in low earthen tombs like Mound No. 72 at Cahokia or soaring towers and pyramids like those in the Valley of the Nile and the jungles of Guatemala and Cambodia, a custom which has supported looters ever since. People in high places also accumulated generous shares of real estate. A typical settlement, arranged during the mid-nineteenth century in the Hawaiian Islands, distributed 2,000,000 acres to the king, another 2,000,000 acres to 245 chiefs, and 29,600 acres to some 11,000 common folk.

Another break with the past involved the ultimate in life-and-death powers over people, the nature and scale of human sacrifice. The practice occurred among hunter-gatherers seeking to preserve the harmony of things, to deal with trouble or the threat of trouble. On at least one occasion Australian aborigines settled a dispute over territory by the ritual killing of women; suspected witches and sorcerers were sometimes put to death when game became scarce, or someone fell ill or died.

High status brought sacrifice on a regular, mass-production basis. Bareis, speaking of Cahokia, refers to extensive sacrifice as "a preoccupation with death, and the hereafter." When a leader died, many individuals might be buried with him, including his relatives, especially his wives and daughters (as in the Death Pit at Ur), lesser chiefs and officials, servants, and so on. It was considered a duty and a privilege to be sacrificed on such occasions. According to tradition and historical records, victims went gladly to their deaths, and it may well be that most of them behaved as they were reared to behave. Archeology, however, suggests that some objected. Investigators excavating Cahokia's Mound No. 72 found the remains of one man sprawled out, face down, as if he had put up a fight, while a royal tomb in China contained the skeleton of a man who apparently resisted being buried alive and had to be chained down.

The passing of a paramount chief or kin called for sacrifice on the grandest scale, involving as many as several hundred victims. It was a precarious time, all the more so if he was regarded as divine and had to be replaced by someone previously ranking as a mere mortal. Early emerging societies which depended heavily on an absolute leader were particularly vulnerable when succession was at stake, when elite factions competed for the vacancy at the top. Sacrificing the trusted advisors and high-ranking officials of a deceased leader may have been a way of reducing the competition, something like killing off the Cabinet and the Executive Branch when the President dies. Sacrificing his wives and daughters would eliminate a source of future competitors, sons of royal blood.

As a spectacular and bloody display of power, human sacrifice was part of the process that gave rise to spectacles of all sorts, and to the architecture that went with the spectacles. The effort to control people, rooted in efforts to control new man-made environments, had a strong tendency to go out of control itself. Palaces and ceremonial buildings, what one investigator has called "the ruling machine," tended to become bigger and grander, as if those in power were less and less sure of themselves—and were shouting their names louder and louder.

When Tikal was in its prime, over a period of more than a century, three successive rulers outdid one another by building larger tombs and monuments to themselves. This process has always been self-amplifying and self-defeating in the long run. But it was probably the best that people could do in prehistoric times, in the first stages of learning to devise effective social controls. It created a new human breed, elites who rule by hereditary and sometimes divine right—and who, as studies of excavated skeletal remains demonstrate, lived healthier and longer lives than commoners.

A similar process is unfolding today in certain developing countries. Peter Gorlin of Columbia University found that elites or the forerunners of elites are beginning to appear in the Sepik River region of northern New Guinea. The precipitating forces can be traced back more than thirty years, to a time when no formal status differences existed among people living in the region. There were mounting pressures, however. Populations had reached the point where groups were already starting to bud-off and expand into less densely settled lands to the west.

That was the traditional solution, the old moving-away formula. If it had continued, the rise of status would have been delayed here, as it had been delayed for thousands and thousands of years among prehistoric hunter-gatherers throughout the world. But the crisis would have come sooner or later. In this case, it came sooner, because Australian authorities intervened. They decided to confine tribal groups within fixed boundaries— and thereby established, unconsciously as in the past, a set of conditions favoring the emergence of classes.

A typical course of events, a typical adaptation, is taking place in the village of Nungwaigo. Although population growth is slowing down, it is not slowing equally among all the people. With food and territory limited, those clans that own the most land, the "founding fathers" or original settlers of the village, had a big advantage to start with and it has been increasing ever since. Today they enjoy the best of everything, more food and better health than their less affluent neighbors, more surviving children. Since clan membership is hereditary, privilege and status differences tend to be perpetuated generation after generation. Gorlin believes that the New Guinea picture represents "stratification in its earliest form," a model for the rise of elites in prehistoric times.

Wherever elites appeared they tended to withdraw further and further from lesser folk. They associated predominantly with one another, and in many cases turned increasingly to outside elites. Their isolation is seen in the increasing isolation of their ceremonial centers. These inner precincts within cities may start as large communal plazas, as at Monte Alban and Uaxactun, and ultimately become no-trespassing places open to the public on special occasions only. Privacy expressed in changing architectural patterns becomes an index of the widening gap between elites and the rest of the people.

Elites established closer contacts with their counterparts in other communities, often over great distances. Status involved far-flung networks. The movement of people back and forth along northern and southern routes across the Iranian Plateau is seen in the discovery in Syria, Sumer, and the Indus Valley of carved stone bowls made in Yahya near the eastern end of the Persian Gulf. Pottery, statues and other artifacts mark their travels in many different regions—across the Sahara, along Pacific sea lanes in Polynesia and Andean mountain passes, through the jungles of Mesoamerica and the Amazon Basin. Cuneiform tablets from the Susiana Plain turn up in distant places, most recently at Shahr-i Sokhta more than 750 miles away. Architectural features developed in Uruk are uncovered during excavations at Hierakonpolis on the Nile. Neither distance nor difficult terrain blocked communications among elites and their representatives.

This reaching-out, this moving over barriers beyond familiar borders and horizons into new lands, was a development as compelling as space exploration is in our time. It was adventure, and much more than that. It reflected the seach for security at the highest level, in the face of increasing complexity and severe threats to security. Something like it had occurred in the very same areas much earlier and on a much smaller scale, wherever one village became the biggest in a cluster of villages and dominated an entire region, as Uruk dominated the Uruk countryside.

A similar expand-or-perish principle was at work in a far wider setting. Described in terms of long-distance trade and trade routes and the exchange of gifts among elites, it had at its core something more basic, a part-conscious and part-unconscious search for stability. Armed men and messengers and missionaries moved along the same routes as traders. People were trying to insure their future, to spread the risks as they had always done, to provide for and organize growing populations—to achieve order by creating goodwill or else by conquest.

A process had come full circle. It started with the loss or severe reduction of mobility among hunting-gathering bands that had long been highly mobile, and ended with a new kind of mobility involving expansion from a central home base or heartland. The in-between period saw consolidation at local and regional levels, the development of increasingly elaborate control mechanisms. From the beginning people stopped moving because circumstances, such as other people already established in the most desir-

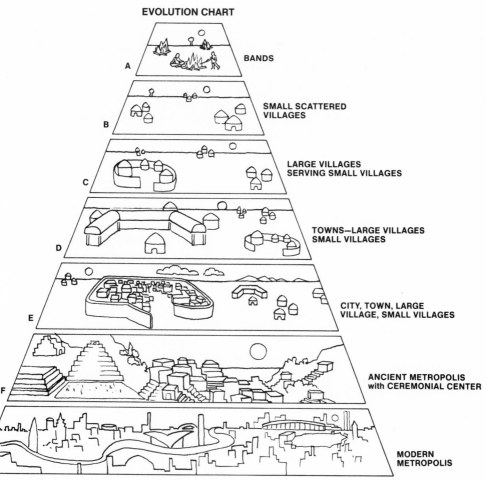

EVOLUTION CHART

A   BANDS

B   SMALL SCATTERED VILLAGES

C   LARGE VILLAGES SERVING SMALL VILLAGES

D   TOWNS—LARGE VILLAGES SMALL VILLAGES

E   CITY, TOWN, LARGE VILLAGE, SMALL VILLAGES

F   ANCIENT METROPOLIS with CEREMONIAL CENTER

MODERN METROPOLIS

An organic process, symbolic representation: from band to village to metropolis (A through G)

able hunting-gathering areas, forced them to stop moving. They had no place to go.

Being hemmed in, compelled to stay put as in the case of the Sepik River people in New Guinea, was a key factor in triggering early social change. Carneiro believes it played a major role in the evolution of the state itself. He emphasizes that the environment, the lay of the land, restricted mobility in many regions, giving rise to pristine states, in the valleys of the Tigris-Euphrates, Nile and Indus rivers as well as the highlands of Mexico and in the mountain and coastal valleys of Peru: "They are all areas of circumscribed agricultural land. Each of them is set off by mountains, seas, or deserts, and these . . . features sharply delimit the area that simple farming people could occupy and cultivate."

It is within these natural "traps" that the drama of social complexity unfolded. Driven by population pressure, the chief reason for farming the lands in the first place, each village struggled with a double problem: controlling conflict among its own members, and living in harmony with neighboring villages. The struggle was partly successful, as people followed their leaders, made alliances, traded with one another, exchanged gifts. Such measures might have worked, or at least worked for longer periods, if population had only leveled off. As it was, however, conflict broke out frequently and on a larger and larger scale—first village against village and then, after one village had conquered the rest and unified its valley, valley against valley and on to wider battles and unifications.

According to Carneiro, people can hem other people in as effectively as oceans or deserts or mountains. Families living in the central parts of a territory, for example, cannot move away when tension approaches the bursting point. Surrounded by settlements, they must stand their ground and fight. Such confining conditions operating over longer periods may have contributed to the rise of complex societies and states in North China, the Maya lowlands and other regions where geographical barriers present less of a problem.

Other forces seemed to draw people closer and closer together. A packing effect often came into play during the culminating stage in the growth of cities, an implosion stage marked by a streaming inward of immigrants from surrounding villages and towns. Within a few centuries, starting around 3000 B.C., Uruk expanded from 250 to 1,000 acres, until its walled-off area included an estimated two-thirds of the entire Uruk countryside population. Monte Alban's population tripled between 100 B.C. and A.D. 400, while its area barely doubled, as some 30,000 persons settled on hillside terraces. Teotihuacan holds the record for packing: its area decreased from about ten to eight square miles between A.D. 100 and A.D. 500, as its numbers soared from 50,000 to at least 125,000 persons.

This was a common phenomenon. In a study of the origins of cities Wheatley discusses the shift from dispersed to compact populations, and speculates that it occurred in "a high proportion, possibly all" of early urban communities. It signified a growing sophistication in the technology of control. Societies were trying to cover themselves, to protect themselves, against all eventualities and all uncertainties by encompassing wider and wider regions. That meant bringing in people to carry food and supplies, to build, oversee, fight, and fill higher positions in the social hierarchy. Expansion into new terrain called for contraction, a general tightening-up of things, at the center.

The heart of the city, the center of the center, included the religious apparatus of the ruling machine, the greatest tombs and temples and monuments. Belief fulfilled many functions and operated at many levels. One of its most important functions was to provide detailed and consistent reasons and rules for doing what had to be done, a basis for decisions which were too urgent to be postponed, involving situations too complex for analysis. It represented an ideology of order and necessity.

To cite a present-day example, Tukano Indians living in the vast Amazonian rain forests of southeastern Colombia have long been first-rate conservationists, for religious rather than scientific or ecological reasons. Gerardo Reichel-Dolmatoff of the Institute of Colombian Anthropology in Bogota shows in considerable detail how beautifully their views about cosmic origins and man's place in the scheme of things fit in with the demands of the land. They believe that the sun or Sun Father created the universe and everything in it including man and a Master of Game Animals, a "jealous guardian" responsible for the fertility and multiplication of all species, such as deer, tapir, and peccary.

A man must obey the Master's rules. He must refrain from sexual intercourse for at least a day before going hunting, and have no erotic dreams. None of the women or girls living in his communal house, which may contain four to eight families, can be menstruating before the hunt. Only when these and other conditions are met can he proceed to take emetics to cleanse his stomach, bathe in the river, paint his face, use various amulets and aromatic herbs, and go through a number of further rituals —all of which effectively discourages overkill by limiting hunting times and by demanding special forethought and preparation. They are all only part of a still larger complex including rituals designed to limit human birthrates. The Tsembaga of the New Guinea highlands practice other rituals with the same aims and the same results, achieving a balance with nature, what Rappaport calls "a ritually regulated ecosystem."

Such systems confront us glaringly with complexities upon complexities. The workings of even relatively simple societies like those of the Tsembaga and Tukano are enormously complicated, so complicated that even after the most intensive studies, we understand them in part only. It is a far more formidable task to investigate the far more complex workings of even early states, which are at least several orders of magnitude simpler than today's industrial states.

The religions of early states incorporated new subsystems of belief, new rituals, reflecting changes in survival patterns. People living closer to the hunting-gathering style of life than we do, people working the land in ways their ancestors never did, needed to know why their work was necessary—and sheer necessity was not, and has never been, a sufficient explanation. Among other things, they asked why the times had changed, why they were staying in one place and working so hard and giving the best to those who already had the best.

The general answer was that man existed to serve gods, through his rulers, who acted as intermediaries and often as gods in their own right. His work represented a small price to pay considering what he received in return—good health and good crops and numerous offspring, some form of life after death and, above all, security in the assurance that he was living in an orderly society and universe. The daily grind, the daily rhythm of discipline and rationing and schedules, the keeping track of seasons and commercial transactions, all fostered increasing concern with time and the universe, expressed vividly in the elaborate calendar-cosmology of the Maya. People saw themselves as intimately involved in the repeating, predictable motions of the enduring sun and moon and stars, and by the association achieved a measure of order and harmony.

At times, of course, belief apparently clashed with the way things actually worked out. Bloch discusses the contrast in his study of the rise of the state in Madagascar during the late eighteenth and nineteenth centuries. According to accepted dogma, the right to power was widely distributed. About half the free people in the island state were supposed to be members of the ruling class, endowed by birth with varying degrees of divinity in the form of "an intangible and mystical essence," a natural force which assured good fortune to all and the continuation of life itself. As their due for possessing this essence, for being born to the purple, they received food and other gifts in abundance from those ranking lower in the hierarchy, mainly the other half of the people.

This view of Madagascan society was sheer illusion, sheer fiction. Bloch shows that it operated "by hiding the brutishly extortionate reality of the traditional . . . power." In effect, it denied the very presence of what was most obvious to observers looking in from the outside. There was not and had never been a large and inclusive ruling class. The "gifts" were forced gifts, and most of them flowed all the way to the top to a tyrannical few, a handful of despots.

Exploitation undoubtedly existed in the earliest states, exploitation as blatant as that in Madagascar. Religions often sanctioned activities which must seem distinctly on the unholy side, and on occasion elites as well as commoners may have had some second thoughts about the system. But most of the time most of the people probably did not see it that way. Their conduct of everyday affairs was flawed, not their religion. According to Wheatley, "for the ancients, who conceived the natural world as an extension of their personalities . . . only the sacred was real"—and their cities represented the supreme embodiment of this point of view. Or Nietzsche: "We have art in order not to die of the truth."

The planned city was the supreme artifact. It arose as a created topography, a precise geometric pattern imposed by edict on an unpatterned landscape. It arose in a carefully selected and magical place, a holy spot described in an ancient Chinese text as "the place where earth and sky meet, where the four seasons merge, where wind and rain are gathered in, and where yin and yang are in harmony." The text speaks for all early cities and all early aspirations.

The city asserted symmetry from its grid system of intersecting and parallel streets, often with the main avenue running north-south, and palace built on the holy spot, to its artificial hills with towers on top and open plazas and everything enclosed snug within high impregnable walls. It asserted order and immortality, or a yearning for order and immortality, because there were always doubts and the fear of chaos at the core of things.

19

Understanding Society, Man's Struggle for Perspective

*Why cities die/ Declining soil fertility in Sumer/
Possible food shortages in the Valley of
Mexico/ The limits of control/ The problem of
overseas influences/ The downgrading of women
and the emergence of contempt/ Sexism among settled
Bushmen/ The "Yellow Peril" and systems theory/
The strengths and weaknesses of hierarchies/
Checks and balances and magic numbers/ Laws of
social evolution/ The impact of writing/
Creating secure man-made environments*

BURIED in the jungle surrounding Tikal, not far from the partly restored ruins of its main ceremonial district, not far from the great walls and pyramids and engraved stones, lie signs of a sudden abandonment. Investigators, Puleston and Blanton among them, surveyed a fourteen-mile sample strip of tangled undergrowth, locating nearly 300 small house-plaza sites. They dug test trenches at some ninety of the sites and found that all but one or two had been deserted by about A.D. 950.

Tikal was at its height between A.D. 700 and A.D. 800, so the center must have collapsed within two centuries or so. Within that brief span it somehow managed to decline from one of the Maya's proudest cities to a lonely place of perhaps no more than

1,000 persons, a relic population living among neglected monuments commemorating half-remembered ancestors. Furthermore, the same period saw the abandonment of centers throughout the Maya lowlands, where an estimated total of 5,000,000 persons had lived.

All early cities suffered a similar fate, although not always so swiftly. Collapse came at a different pace in the Indus Valley. The long straight streets and side-alley mazes and hallways of Mohenjo-daro were largely deserted by 1750 B.C., about half a millennium after its founding. "The city was already slowly dying before its ultimate end," writes Wheeler. "Houses mounting gradually upon the ruins of their predecessors or on artificial platforms in the endeavor to out-top the floods, were increasingly shoddy in construction, increasingly carved up into warrens for swarming lower-grade population.... The city, to judge from excavated areas, was becoming a slum."

At about the same time Uruk and other Sumerian cities to the west dwindled to villages, and Egypt was enduring its "great humiliation," its first collapse (although the final collapse of its empire did not occur for another 1,200 years). In China, Anyang and the Shang dynasty came to an end between 1100 B.C. and 1000 B.C. Teotihuacan seems to have fallen suddenly some time after A.D. 800. Cahokia's population dropped from perhaps 30,000 to fewer than 5,000 persons between 1300 and 1400, and all traces of the city had vanished some three centuries later when French explorers came and saw nothing but grass-covered mounds which they mistook for hills.

Explaining such matters is only one of a number of important problems which remain unsolved. There are questions about beginnings as well as endings, about which early states were actually "pristine" in the sense of having arisen primarily as a result of local or regional conditions—and which, if any, received crucial assists from still earlier states. Some investigators are convinced that contacts existed between the Old and New Worlds far earlier than is generally believed. They are also convinced, and this is a distinct and quite separate issue, that the contacts had a major influence on the course of social evolution in the New World.

Many of the tensions of our own times had their origins in prehistory. Hierarchies, which seem always to have been essential for organizing people on a large scale, apparently encouraged exclusions and discriminations from the top down, perhaps the most widespread and baffling involving the lowly status of women. Studies of times past can be expected to help account for the forces that keep people apart as well as the forces that bring them together. At the most ambitious level, the search is for nothing less than the underlying laws of hierarchy and state formation. Prospects for the discovery of such laws are good, because considerable research has gone into an analysis of the things which states have in common, basic similarities in the evolution of states everywhere. Differences, accounting for example for Chinese art styles and cosmologies as contrasted to the art styles and cosmologies of, say, the Egyptians or Maya, remain a puzzle.

Social evolution, the passing of old states and the emergence of new ones, is a continuing challenge. Many possible causes have been offered for the collapse of ancient societies: barbarians from the outside, rebels from within, a loss of moral fiber, epidemics, overpopulation, deteriorating climate, and crop failures. The problem in any particular case is to establish, preferably by direct proof rather than speculation, the combination of causes involved. Explaining why a relatively simple society went into eclipse long ago may prove less of a problem than explaining the fate of more recent and far more complicated societies—there is a great deal yet to learn about the passing of the British Empire.

A creeping disease of the soil almost certainly contributed to the decline of Sumer's city-states more than 3,500 years ago, and represents a widespread threat today. I passed signs of the condition during my drive through the Iraqi countryside en route to Uruk. Scattered among once-fertile fields on both sides of the road were patches of white, crusty deposits of salts washed off Turkish mountain slopes in headwater regions of the Tigris and Euphrates rivers more than 600 miles away—and carried into the fields along irrigation canals.

Similar patches, dead places on the land, may form wherever people practice large-scale irrigation over long periods. Salts remain in the ground when water evaporates and, especially when drainage is poor, accumulate decade after decade. Plants

Courtesy of William M. Denevan, University of Wisconsin, Madison
Salt deposits in ridged fields: Lake Titicaca's dying lands, Bolivia

cannot flourish. High salt concentrations interfere with the ability of roots to absorb water and nutrients from the soil. This problem may have plagued high Andean societies, as indicated by salt deposits on prehistoric ridged fields along Lake Titicaca. It currently confronts engineers in Egypt's Aswan Dam region, in the lower reaches of the Indus Valley, and, to a lesser extent, in the western United States where salt deposits are reducing crop yields by an estimated twenty percent.

Adams notes that salt deposits afflicted ancient Sumer. Cuneiform archives written in 2100 B.C. describe the appearance of telltale white patches in fields that were salt-free some three centuries earlier. Another sign of increasing trouble comes from counts of the number of cereal-grain impressions on the clay of excavated pottery vessels. Barley is considerably more resistant to high salt levels than wheat, and wheat and barley grains are about equally represented in impressions from vessels dating to 3500 B.C. The balance shifted thereafter. Farmers seem to have been growing more and more barley and less and less wheat, a strategy presumably dictated by a steady rise in salt levels. Barley production soared to eighty-three percent of the total by about 2500 B.C., and to ninety-eight percent by 2100 B.C. Some four hundred years later all the clay impressions were impressions of barley grains. Even with the shift, overall crop yields during this period fell from about thirty to ten bushels per acre. Such conditions were enough to reverse population flow into the cities of Sumer and force families to scatter into the hinterlands.

The Sumerian evidence is as good as any we have. No single cause can explain any complex phenomenon, but in most other regions there is less to go on, little more than plausible arguments and equally plausible counterarguments. Other cities may well have been abandoned because of food shortages resulting mainly from salty soils or from any one of a number of other causes. Wheeler speculates that the people of Mohenjo-daro "were wearing out their landscape." They may have turned their fertile valley into a dust bowl by cutting down trees and other vegetation and exposing the soil to eroding rains.

Population pressure can be as devastating as dying lands. There is some suspicion that toward the end Teotihuacan, for all the abundance of its countryside, was starting to feel the strain of rising numbers. Sanders estimates that if corn furnished about sixty percent of calorie requirements, probably a conservative figure for a food staple, the average Teotihuacano consumed some twelve ounces a day (mostly in the form of tortillas which, judging by the remains of numerous clay griddles, were as popular then as now). Assuming a population of 125,000, also on the conservative side, that came to a daily citywide supply of nearly 94,000 pounds of corn.

Local farmers could have met the city's needs, that is, farmers living within a radius of ten to fifteen miles. But the system may have been approaching its limits. Since the Valley of Mexico had no beasts of burden, corn and everything else had to be brought in on people's backs, and it must have taken a small army of carriers and organizers to keep storehouses filled. The city probably played host to tens of thousands of visitors on ceremonial occasions, as its own population continued to climb toward the 200,000 level. The result need not have been a dramatic breakdown, but simply temporary scarcities and a general drop in the quality of goods and services, the usual marks of a system beginning to come apart at the seams.

Fragments of evidence are tantalizing hints, the equivalent of a few incomplete sentences torn from the last chapter of a murder mystery. The center of the city of Teotihuacan was in trouble during the eighth century A.D., the period of its collapse. A major fire destroyed many buildings and, significantly, the burned-out section was never rebuilt. It remained in ruins as a reminder that something important, something more than masonry had fallen into disuse.

The collapse of the earliest cities was seldom the consequence of local failures alone. As part of a regional network, each center had to cope with forces acting at a distance, outside the massive walls and natural barriers which seemed to separate it from lesser settlements. Its range of control was usually limited, to a radius of 50 to 100 miles at most. Beyond that, success or failure depended on events it could not control, the fortunes of people concentrated in the centers of other networks, the establishment of new patterns of power and trade among other elites.

Cities vanish, but not people. As Cahokia declined, flourishing mound-and-plaza complexes were built elsewhere in the eastern woodlands, in Georgia, West Virginia, Ohio, Kansas, and Missouri. New cities and trade routes appeared to the north after the abandonment of Tikal and other Maya lowland cities. There were always new centers elsewhere, new states, ready to carry on when the old ones faded. Also, as indicated by trade routes between the Near East and the Indus Valley and beyond, distance was no barrier to communications linking remote centers and regional networks.

Did these links extend across the oceans? Did people in boats cross from the Old World to the New World, either by Atlantic or Pacific sea routes, two thousand or more years before Columbus? Some investigators who believe that these questions have already been answered in the affirmative offer proof positive for theories which, to put them in the best possible light, are only slightly less outlandish than the tallest of tall tales about extraterrestrial beings building cities in the Andes. Among recent examples is the claim that voyagers from Egypt, sent by Rameses III, landed on the Gulf of Mexico coast around 1200 B.C. and founded the Olmec culture.

The case for or against transoceanic contact will be decided on the basis of research of a more scientific sort, like that of Paul

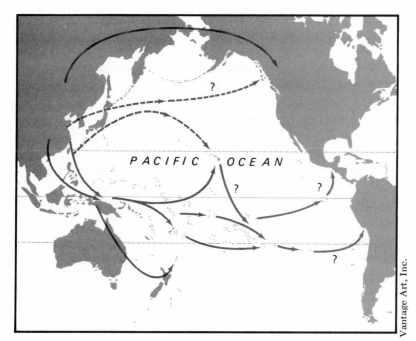

Trans-Pacific contacts: Unsettled questions—did voyagers from India, China, Southeast Asia and other Old World lands cross the Pacific 1500 or more years before the time of Columbus? If so, did they have a major effect on the rise of art, elites and city-states in the New World?

Tolstoy of the City University of New York. He points to the close resemblance between certain types of beaters which prehistoric people on opposite sides of the Pacific used to make cloth from the bark of selected trees. A study of some 400 beaters from Mesoamerica and more than 200 from Southeast Asia reveals a group with a number of shared features, including heads made of flat rectangular stones with grooves along the edges for hafting and distinctive patterns of deep and shallow grooves on the striking surfaces.

There is more to the story. Tolstoy had compiled a list of seventy characteristics of bark-cloth manufacture as practiced until recently in Mesoamerica, such as soaking the bark before beating, boiling with ashes, adding lime to the water, drying on a plank in the sun, and ways of dyeing and rolling up the finished cloth; and fifty of these characteristics are also found in Southeast Asia in a process involving use of the same kinds of beater. Taking

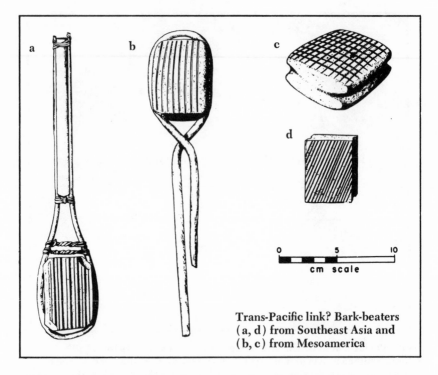

Trans-Pacific link? Bark-beaters
(a, d) from Southeast Asia and
(b, c) from Mesoamerica

all the evidence together, he argues that people of Mesoamerica, probably in Mexico and regions to the south, learned how to make bark cloth from Pacific voyagers around 1000 B.C., that the process originated much earlier in Southeast Asia, probably in Java and Celebes and neighboring islands.

The search for further parallels continues. David Kelley of the University of Calgary has assembled an enormous amount of detail bearing on ancient calendars and cosmologies, on concepts concerning time and the universe, in Europe and Asia and Meso-america. To cite only one example, more than 2,000 years ago, the Hindus had a concept of four world ages, perhaps borrowed from the Greeks, four intervals in human history marked by catastrophic endings. They associated the first world age with white, the second with yellow or red, the third with red or yellow, and the fourth with black. About a millennium and a half later the Aztecs also had four world ages associated with the destruc-tion by flood, wind, fire and earthquake of white-haired, yellow-haired, red-haired and black-haired people.

Kelley has come across a great many other intriguing similarities—the same animals associated with early Indian and Mesoamerican calendar days, the same sequences of sounds associated with sequences of numbers and written symbols, and observations suggesting that the layout of Teotihuacan is related to the layout of early Indian cities. He believes that no earlier than the second century B.C. people from the east sailed across the Pacific, landed in Mesoamerica, and influenced the shaping of the Mesoamerican calendar and other cosmological ideas.

Coincidence, sheer chance, is not to be rejected out of hand and utterly in accounting for such facts. It is a major factor in all unexplained similarities and identities. People throughout the world were observing, pondering about what they observed, associating day and night and the seasons with life cycles, and speculating about the meaning of repeating changes and the future. They were shaping elaborate views of the universe, religions, symbol systems. The enormous number of ideas and observations, and permutations of ideas and observations, was enough to guarantee many identical associations of colors and other features in different lands.

Coincidence can account for only some of the findings of Tolstoy, Kelley and others. Certainly communications existed between east and west, Egypt and Greece and India and China. Also, considering the outstanding navigational skills of the South Sea islanders, people were capable of sailing all the way across the Pacific. Even in the absence of transoceanic contact, people with similar mental powers and similar ways of thinking may have evolved some similar ideas and symbols although, as Kelley emphasizes, no one has demonstrated "some facet of thought linkage which would make this kind of result plausible." One thing is clear: the knowledge to decide among alternative explanations is lacking. My own inclination, my prejudice until proved right or wrong, is to choose a combination of coincidence and similar thought processes in accounting for the facts.

Whatever the outcome, there is no evidence that newcomers took over from the natives in prehistoric times, no evidence of anything comparable to what the Europeans did to the American Indians from the sixteenth century on. If earlier voyagers made Atlantic or Pacific crossings to Mesoamerica or South America, and survived to tell the tale, they did little if anything to interrupt or accelerate the course of local evolution. Representatives of the Old World may have arrived on the scene, but what happened in the New World can be explained without them.

Change came in all lands, wherever people settled down. Of all hunter-gatherer traditions, the tradition of equality declined most swiftly and with the most drastic effect on human relations. The rise of elites was related to the increasing complexity of life. The gap between a privileged few and their lowly brethren reflected an increasing need for leaders and organizers, and then as now room at the top was limited.

The widening gap between the sexes, the appearance of contempt for women and for women's work, is less easily understood. Why did the religions of the Maya and other peoples associate women, the sex that gives birth, with pollution, the setting sun, and death? What purposes could that attitude possibly have served? Such questions put the evolutionary perspective to the test. They demand a specific kind of explanation, an adaptive explanation based on the assumption that every major development somehow promotes the survival of the species. The downgrading of women is not easy to fathom in such terms.

Draper has had a rare opportunity to see the beginnings of the process in the Kalahari Desert. She reports that among Bushman hunter-gatherer bands equality between the sexes seems to be the general rule from the very beginning. Adults do not treat little girls differently from little boys, punishment is rare, and all children grow up in a highly permissive atmosphere. Any basic differences in the behavior of the sexes, any characteristic male or female traits which are independent of upbringing, should be evident under such conditions, and they are.

Girls tend to stay closer to home base. In more than 300 spot observations made over a period of fourteen months Draper noted that on the average about three-quarters of the girls but only half the boys were within the camp circle. Among children who had wandered out of sight and earshot boys outnumbered girls two to one. Girls also tended to join groups of adults more readily than boys, spend more time in actual physical contact with other individuals, and participate less in children's play groups.

These differences do not matter very much when it comes to getting along together, either in childhood or later on. Draper is impressed with "the relaxed and egalitarian relationship between men and women," a relationship which endures as long as the Bushmen remain hunter-gatherers, and no longer. She has observed the undermining of that relationship which occurs when Bushmen settle down and become farmers. The very act of taking root in one place creates a new type of status. Work which might formerly be done by members of either sex somehow becomes inferior work, women's work (and for children, who are also downgraded).

In a hunter-gatherer context women usually go after water, especially when the source is relatively close, say, within a mile or so. Boys often share the work, and when greater distances are involved, men join the ranks of regular water-fetchers. Men usually do the hunting and the women the gathering, but not always. Men may collect mongongo nuts, a food staple, with or without their wives and daughters, and women may come home with meat, particularly small game. Attitudes toward who does what are informal and flexible. When the need arises, members of either sex may take on some of the other's duties without making a big fuss about it.

All this changes among Bushmen who have recently turned to farming. There is more work to be done, and more work that can be done by children. Children are recruited at ages when they would still be playing in a hunter-gatherer setting, and sexual differences often determine the work they do. Girls who tend to stay near home base close to adults usually help take care of younger children and do a wide variety of household chores, while boys who wander more freely usually do work outside the village, such as tending herds and keeping goats and monkeys out of gardens.

"Here we can see the emergence of a familiar pattern in the division of labor by sex," Draper summarizes. "The rule is females inside and males outside, females doing many tasks and under the pressure of more or less continuous supervision—males doing fewer tasks which generally last longer and with less supervision by adults." The problem is not that some differences exist and are taken advantage of. The problem is not the emergence of a particular type of division of labor, but the emergence of contempt.

For the first time pride and dignity become extremely important when there is work to be done. Among the Bushmen, a man is likely to scorn water-fetching as unworthy of his maleness, and boys are quick to take the cue from their fathers. Much flexibility has gone out of life; work is increasingly segregated along sex lines. The trend is away from the one-group atmosphere of the hunter-gatherer band toward a society of subgroups of women, men, girls and boys—always, it seems, to the detriment of females. Similar tendencies have been noted, although not observed systematically, among recently settled Eskimos and Australian aborigines.

Contemporary and prehistoric conditions are never strictly comparable. Hunter-gatherers are settling down because their way of life cannot survive in a world of tourism, conservation laws, and national boundaries that may not be crossed in going after game. The hunter-gatherers of times past settled down for quite different reasons. In both cases, however, people resisted change and changed under stress. The modern situation may serve as a tentative model of earlier developments.

The shift to farming may have been more of a blow to the male than to the female of the species. Taming the male, making him part of a group, is an old and continuing problem in primate evolution. Agriculture confronted him with a kind of technological unemployment, a loss of status and self-esteem. With increasing reliance on domesticated animals, hunting became less and less necessary, and dwindled as a source of prestige. Perhaps men found new sources of prestige in "the most dangerous game," preying more on other men and specializing in power struggles and violence, organized and otherwise. Some sort of connection apparently existed between men's fighting and women's status. Fighting favored the notion of woman as property, as booty, and that automatically put her in a demeaning position.

Such forces were probably at work in the early days. Understanding the origins and uses of sexism demands further research. A study by Nan Rothschild of New York University suggests what archeology can contribute. One phase of her work, records of funerals in the midwestern United States between 500 B.C. and

A.D. 1500 with an analysis of grave goods from nearly 2,500 burials, shows that sexism tends to increase with social complexity.

Studies of history as well as prehistory would help explain why the status of women is higher in Southeast Asia, especially in Java and Bali, than in any other part of the world. Men and women dress very much the same, have the same slender body build and delicate features, share in cooking and taking care of children, enjoy equal inheritance rights, and worship hermaphroditic or bisexual gods. Although the fact that the whole family must work hard together in rice fields has something to do with the curious state of affairs in Southeast Asia, it cannot be a determining factor because families in places such as India also work hard together, and women occupy a lowly position there. No one, surprisingly, seems to be interested in exploring the situation.

The shaping of early society demands analysis of the most intensive sort. The archeological record speaks of simple beginnings, holy spots in small villages and grounds set apart for ceremony. Increasingly elaborate settlements culminated in cities and city centers where the monuments were concentrated, and where rising elites competed with one another, and sometimes with the gods themselves, for high places and absolute authority.

The custom had been to view the passing scene, the course of events, in terms of power and glory, storybook heroes and grand ambitions and manifest destinies. Investigators are seeking to get at the organizing principles behind the melodrama which, it turns out, apply to a good many things besides societies. The human brain is also organized in hierarchies. It is not a single organ but a collection of interconnected subbrains arranged one on top of the other like images carved on a totem pole, nerve centers controlling the simplest reflexes at the bottom and centers involved in the highest thought processes at the top.

Businesses are organized along similar lines, with the president of the firm emphasizing his lofty position by occupying offices on the top floor. Engineers can use the same basic principles of control by hierarchies in designing a wide variety of computer-directed machines and machine systems, everything from electronic pilots for ships and airplanes to self-guilding missiles and automatic or "robot" factories run by a few men at control panels.

The science, the mathematics, of complex organizations was born during the early days of World War II. It appeared in the form of a document stamped TOP SECRET and nicknamed the "Yellow Peril," because it came in a bright yellow cover—and included abstruse equations which only its author, Norbert Wiener of the Massachusetts Institute of Technology, and other professional mathematicians (and not all of them), could understand. One of Wiener's colleagues at the Institute translated the report into somewhat simpler language for investigators unversed in higher mathematics.

The central ideas of the Yellow Peril, now incorporated into so-called general systems theory, are just beginning to find a place in studies of complex societies. In a preliminary analysis Flannery discusses a number of features evolving hierarchies such as "promotion," the rise of an institution or office to a higher level. He points out that something of this sort may have occurred in early Sumer where at one time temple precincts included residences which later developed into larger and more impressive palaces, suggesting the emergence of kings from "some kind of priest-manager role." The evolution of public buildings in the Valley of Oaxaca may represent a similar process.

Hierarchies also have weaknesses, tendencies to break down. Although they normally operate to keep things on an even keel, balancing supply and demand, sometimes too many middlemen and not enough information cause trouble. If an official in charge of one of the major farming zones outside a city finds that the farmers under his control are failing to meet grain quotas, he will order a general step-up in production, just enough to make up for the deficit. Suppose his message is unduly delayed so that underproduction continues longer than he expected. In that case, he will have to send a second message ordering a further increase. Now suppose that someone higher up in the hierarchy has not been informed of these decisions and, anticipating an influx of visitors for a forthcoming ceremony, also orders more grain.

The net effect of the messages may be appreciable overproduction. If there are further delays between messages intended to compensate for the situation, if signals continue to cross out one another, production may swing in the opposite direction, resulting in grain shortages. Such fluctuations have not been picked up in the archeological record, although it might be interesting to try. But they represent a typical "disease" of hierarchies. They occur in modern cities and may well have occurred in Uruk or Mohenjo-daro or Teotihuacan. At a higher and more complex level, an analogous failure may account for the building of bigger and bigger monuments by successive rulers at Tikal.

Survival depends on effective checks and balances. All complex systems with purposes, self-adjusting machines and individuals as well as societies, have certain built-in standards and behave accordingly. For an automatic ship's pilot it may be a true-north compass setting, and the device has elements designed to measure deviations from that heading and flash error-correcting signals to engines which move the rudder. Special sense organs in the body operate in very much the same way to keep the temperature close to 98.6 degrees Fahrenheit, blood sugar levels at 80 to 120 milligrams per 100 cubic centimeters, heartbeat rates at about 70 per minute, and so on.

Societies have similar standards, or canonical values. That may be the significance of the magic numbers which investigators call attention to from time to time, such as 25 as the number of individuals in a hunter-gatherer band, about 100 or so for early villages, 500 for a hunter-gatherer tribe, 1,000 for the stage at which a village begins to need policing. None of these numbers are hard and fast. Actual values may vary widely, but they do tend to hover around these levels.

Elizabeth Colson of the University of California in Berkeley notes that members of the Gwembe Tonga tribe of Zambia generally maintained close relationships with about two to twelve persons, and even limited their caring as far as departed ancestors were concerned: "From eight to fifteen shades seemed sufficient for the purposes of any living individual, and the rest were relegated to the forgotten dead." At the other end of the scale, Sanders and Paul Baker of Pennsylvania State University point out that village tribes, associations of villages, sharing common customs and a common language and territory, included as many as 5,000 or 6,000 persons, another rough limit beyond which splitting either occurred, or was prevented from occurring by the creation of a central authority made up of a chief and people ready to carry out his orders.

Chiefdoms were capable of unifying far larger populations, 10,000 to perhaps 15,000 or more persons without too much trouble. But from that critical point on, splitting tendencies became stronger and stronger. Observations in the South Seas and among the American Indians indicate that chiefdoms of up to 50,000 persons existed, but lasted only a generation or two at best. Such situations gave rise to new orders of control, a stage in which stability depended on an acknowledged chief among chiefs, an absolute ruler and his cohorts, the coming of the Establishment.

Renfrew suggests some territorial magic numbers. He speaks of "early state modules" in the Maya lowlands, Sumer, Greece, and other regions, units which include the countryside around centers like Uruk and Tikal and generally average about 1,500 square kilometers. According to his analysis of the evidence, about a dozen modules are included in "many early civilizations before subsequent unification," although in some cases there may be considerably more.

In a unique approach Johnson focuses on the evolution of hierarchies. He assumes that people are confronted with the task of coordinating and acting on information from a number of different sources, say, groups involved in farming, crafts, trade, fighting and so on—also that the information comes through clear, that the system always runs smoothly in the sense of coordinating the activities of all groups, and that the amount of information increases at a uniform rate (as a consequence of increasing population or increasing complexity or both).

These and a few other simple assumptions serve as the basis for a theoretical model of "the development of decision-making organizations." The model generates certain numbers. It suggests specific levels of complexity at which major changes may occur. As complexity increases and with it the number of activities and information sources, administering an organization becomes more and more difficult. As far as reducing work loads is concerned, it first becomes profitable to create a new level of organization, an elementary hierarchy, when the number of groups increases to six. The model also implies that a hierarchy operates most efficiently when those at one level are administering the next lower-level activities of two or three to a maximum of six groups, with three or four groups as an average.

These hypothetical values may be related to certain real-world observations. Psychological tests indicate that on the average an administrator can coordinate about four different activities, with a range of perhaps three to seven. This may help explain the stability of states like the Yoruba states in West Africa with its five provinces administered by a king at the capital. Revolt seems to be more common among states with nine or more provinces, while just before Monte Alban collapsed its rulers were trying to control thirteen territorial units. Playing the numbers game is always risky, but it is fascinating nonetheless—and Johnson and other investigators are in the early stages of developing a theory of hierarchy formation.

There is a search for related laws applying to the growth of states. Rathje has used general systems theory to interpret the changes through time, the "trajectory," of Maya culture. Translated into social terms, the theory asserts that as a community's population increases, its complexity increases at a disproportionately high or exponential rate. Thus, every doubling of the population produces what amounts to a quadrupling of information and decisions, a quadrupling of complexity. Stresses build up as a result, and steps must be taken to reduce them and keep the system operating.

Rathje suggests how such steps, predicted by theory, may be traced in the actual archeological record. For more than a thousand years control was an elaborate and costly business, in the hands of an elite minority. Tremendous effort went into building ceremonial centers like the one at Tikal, impressive not only for their massiveness, but also for the skill and art that went into their shaping—stones neatly cut and fitted together and carved, sculptures in stone and stucco, distinctive stone arches.

Things changed after A.D. 1200. The city of Mayapán near the northern tip of Mexico's Yucatan Peninsula had a relatively small main temple, and its monuments were not put together with as much care as previously. Instead of quarrying fresh stones people reused old stones, did not bother to fit them precisely, and covered the masonry with thick layers of plaster. In the words of one excavator, "there seems to be little striving for permanence,

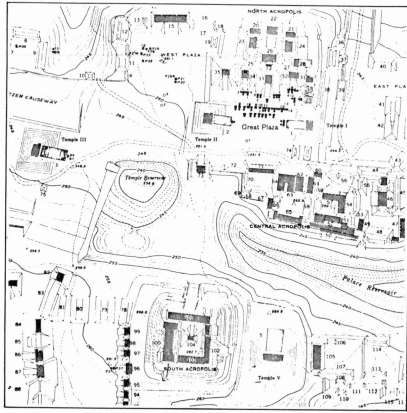

From William L. Rathje, University of Arizona, "The Last Tango in Mayapan," in *Ancient Civilization and Trade*, ed. Jeremy A. Sabloff and C. C. Lamberg-Karlovsky, School of American Advanced Seminar Series, University of New Mexico Press, Albuquerque, 1975

Reaction against regimentation: centralized ceremonial district, in an early city, Tikal (above); local shrines for private worship in a later city, Mayapán (right)

just window dressing and false fronts," all of which has been interpreted as a sign of decadence.

One man's decadence, however, may be another man's renaissance. Less effort was being spent on the care and feeding of elites and more on the rest of the population, on such things as wider distribution of wealth and higher standards of living. The use of old stones in new buildings can be regarded as a form of conservation or recycling. Workers constructed houses with

Many small structures, such as 105, 106, 107 (here, black), usually in center of plazas, were probably shrines; large building in center, a temple

mortar-and-beam or thatched roofs instead of roofs supported by stone arches. Pottery was made increasingly for mass markets. It had standardized shapes and designs, and was turned out on a standardized mass-production basis, which tends to confirm the notion that more people were sharing "middle class" material benefits.

The final stage in the growth of Maya society may have been a reaction to too much standardizing, too much regimentation. Two signs of the change are an increase in the number of local shrines, in the words of Proskouriakoff, an "intensive development of private ceremonial," and an interesting modification of mass-production methods—pottery and figurines still manufactured in quantity, but now with interchangeable parts, allowing people to assemble a wide variety of forms and designs. Rathje believes that the shift from almost total control by elites to more material wealth for more people to increased local variety and autonomy may represent a pattern that holds for other societies. He notes that the pyramids of Egypt, like the Maya temples and monuments, also tended to decrease in size and quality of workmanship.

Many elites have come and gone since the founding of the earliest states. But the first elites had a special aura, a special degree of power and divinity, simply because they were the first, and the shock of their passing must also have been something special. Modern society is still very much under the influence of pomp and circumstance and ritual, yet it is difficult to imagine how utterly the early elites and the rest of the populace must have been committed.

Everything they knew and believed, the full force of ancestral authority and tradition, came to a glowing white-heat focus in ceremony. What began with a shaman performing in a trance among people around camp fires culminated in spectacles conducted by high priests and their cohorts from platforms elevated above the multitude. There was singing and chanting, words said over and over again, recited in singsong metrical patterns with punctuating rhymes at the ends of lines. Music, setting the pace in the background and echoing and rising to crescendos and climaxes, reinforced the beat. Dancers with masks kept time to the words and the music as they acted out the roles of gods and heroes. Spectators moved with the rhythms and chanted ritual responses.

The skies, too, were involved. Paramount chiefs and kings frequently associated themselves with celestial bodies, as sons or brothers of the sun, and in something more than a merely figurative sense. As gods on earth, leaders had the authority to influence the risings and settings of the sun itself. Perhaps not everyone accepted given dogma. Archeology can tell us only a little about the depth and prevalence of ancient faith. But, then as now, many of the people must have believed what they were supposed to believe.

All the elaborate mechanisms of ceremony must have had a combined impact comparable to that envisioned by Eric Havelock of Yale University for the early days of Greece: "They represented a mobilization of the resources of the unconscious to assist the conscious. . . . The audience found enjoyment and relaxation as they were themselves partly hypnotized by the response to a series of rhythmic patterns, verbal, vocal, instrumental and physical, all set in motion together and all consonant in their effect." People swept up in a mass display, a chorus of communications, were ripe for inspiration and instruction and awe as well as pleasure.

Ritual on such a scale operated primarily to glorify, and preserve, the accumulated wisdom of times past. Ordinary conversation, word-of-mouth communication from person to person in everyday "prose," would never have worked. As indicated by studies of rumor and gossip, people tend to embellish and distort what they have heard until messages currently circulating bear little resemblance to what was said originally. Only periodical high-pressure bombardment of the senses, a flooding of the mind, could insure that tradition would remain intact generation after generation.

Tradition embodied everything worth remembering: myth and history, what to believe, how to behave and whom to obey, the virtues and ethics and loyalties of daily life. Probably it also embodied certain technical knowledge. The songs of people in the Carolines and other Pacific islands included detailed sailing directions as well as legends about ancestors and ancestral voyages, and information about many other practical matters may have passed by song and ritual from experts to novices. Ceremony was the only effective way of learning the contents of what Havelock calls "the tribal encyclopedia," a body of knowledge "imprinted upon the brain of the community"—that is, until the invention of writing.

Writing brought major changes into a world where tradition had always been imparted by repetition and rhyme. It changed the nature of ceremony, and thereby the nature of thinking itself. It may have arisen for the most practical and mundane of reasons in most regions, as in Sumer and the Susiana Plain, at a critical stage when memory alone could no longer cope with the details

a la momu senje so.
The first man who was sent

1925

Courtesy of Sylvia Scribner and Michael Cole, Rockefeller University

The invention of writing: a nineteenth-century Vai script from Liberia, from a history book written by a man in Diyak, Cape Mount County

of increasingly numerous and complicated transactions involving supplies of food and other goods, or with the prevention and control of large-scale cheating. Writing was soon used to record a wide range of activities from the accomplishments of kings and communications with deceased ancestors to epics, laws, and methods of healing.

A unity had been shattered. Religion and schooling and entertainment and the arts, all that had once been included together exclusively in ceremony, now began to acquire separate lives. They were becoming specialties, separate fields of endeavor. A new level of analysis was born. It was one thing to be swayed and aroused in great public gatherings, and something rather different to sit alone and read what had been said, in private and without passion and pageantry. In the words of Jack Goody of Cambridge University, this is the distinction "between wild and domesticated thinking."

A rare opportunity to observe thought in the actual process of being domesticated has arisen in West Africa, where Sylvia Scribner and Michael Cole of Rockefeller University in New York are studying the impact of a syllabic script invented from scratch between 1825 and 1850 by the Vai people of Liberia. They are studying documents discovered in a back-country village which are written in that script—and which provide hints of how the early days of writing may have affected thought and behavior.

Working with Goody, Scribner and Cole analyzed a set of family records that reveal one man's fascination with dates, names and intervals of time. The record keeper noted when he married his first wife, when he divorced her, when she died, the time elapsed since the marriage and between their divorce and her death, and so on. He asked himself the sort of detailed and "thought up" questions which he would never have asked in such quantity (or answered) if he had not entered the facts in his books. "He sets about manipulating the figures in ways which are not immediately called for by the situation," the investigators point out, "but which remind one of the kind of operation children are constantly called upon to perform in school—numbers games for their own sake."

He kept dues records for some 450 members of a religious organization over a period of twenty years, listing payments by sex, clan, town, and phonetic similarities in names. One notable effect of the records has been to form categories like "member" independent of his or her personality or attendance at meetings, based entirely on such criteria as dues paid or owing. The very act of writing down names and numbers generates innovation. It permits new ways of organizing information, stimulates experiments with codes and indexes, and suggests new kinds of transactions. Analogous experiments were probably conducted in prehistoric times. Some of the tablets unearthed at Uruk in 3500 B.C. also contain lists that apparently had no practical value, lists of trees and animals and gods and fish.

This sort of activity was the beginning of research. Making lists, describing and classifying things, is the first step in the establishment of a science. The deepest insights come afterward. To extract from the seeing of many different kinds of trees the notion of "tree," and later the notion of "plant" and still later "living thing" or "species," is a process of increasing abstraction and generality. It involves the creation of new kinds of hierarchy, hierarchies of successively higher and more inclusive categories, all in the good cause of learning more about the world and man's place in it.

Writing spurred analysis and inquiry. It played a major part in the continuing search for realities behind rhetoric, in creating a way of thinking and responding different from that created by the half-hypnotic forces of mass ceremony. Like the city and the state, this also was something new under the sun. The great problem was always, and still is, to break away from patterns of repeating conflict, of insults and face-savings and victories and defeats—and to devise man-made environments as secure and abundant as the best of the old and all-but-vanished natural environments of hunter-gatherer times.

Bibliography

CHAPTER 1

Eisenberg, John F., "The Social Organization of Mammals," *Handbuch der Zoologie*, vol. 10 (7), 1965.
Holling, C. S. and Goldberg, M. A., "Ecology of Planning," *Journal of the American Institute of Planning*, July 1971.
Levine, Norman D. et al., *Human Ecology*, North Scituate, Mass.: Duxbury Press, 1975.
Pfeiffer, John E., *The Emergence of Man*, New York: Harper & Row, 1972.
Rappaport, Roy A., *Pigs for the Ancestors*, New Haven: Yale University Press, 1967.
————, "The Flow of Energy in an Agricultural Society," *Scientific American*, September 1971.
Sahlins, Marshall D., *Tribesmen*, Englewood Cliffs, N.J.: Prentice-Hall, 1968.

CHAPTER 2

Bicchieri, M. G., (ed.), *Hunters and Gatherers Today*, New York: Holt, Rinehart and Winston, 1972.
Gould, Richard A., *Yiwara: Foragers of the Australian Desert*, New York: Scribner, 1969.
Isaac, Glynn L., Leakey, Richard E. F., and Behrensmeyer, Anna K., "Archaeological Traces of Early Hominid Activities, East of Lake Rudolf, Kenya," *Science*, 17 September 1971.
Klein, Richard G., "Ice-Age Hunters of the Ukraine," *Scientific American*, June 1974.
Lee, Richard Borshay, "Eating Christmas in the Kalahari," *Natural History*, December 1969.
———— and DeVore, Irven, *Man the Hunter*, Chicago: Aldine, 1968.
Pfeiffer, John E., "Man the Hunter," *Horizon*, Spring 1971.
Solecki, Ralph S., "Shanidar IV, A Neanderthal Flower Burial in Northern Iraq," *Science*, 28 November 1975.

Teleki, Geza, *The Predatory Behavior of Wild Chimpanzees*, Lewisburg, Pa.: Bucknell University Press, 1973.

———, "The Omnivorous Chimpanzee," *Scientific American*, January 1973.

Thomas, Elizabeth Marshall, *The Harmless People*, New York: Knopf, 1959.

Ucko, Peter and Rosenfeld, Andrée, *Palaeolithic Cave Art*, London: Weidenfeld and Nicolson, 1967.

Van Lawick-Goodall, Jane, *In the Shadow of Man*, Boston: Houghton Mifflin, 1971.

Wobst, H. Martin, "Stylistic Behavior and Information Exchange," Museum of Anthropology, *Anthropological Papers*, No. 61, Ann Arbor: University of Michigan, 1976.

CHAPTER 3

Allan, William, "Ecology, Techniques and Settlement Patterns," in *Man, Settlement and Urbanism*, Cambridge, Mass.: Schenkman, 1972.

Binford, Lewis R., "Post-Pleistocene Adaptations," in *New Perspectives in Archeology*, Chicago: Aldine, 1968.

Boserup, Ester, *The Conditions of Agricultural Growth*, Chicago: Aldine, 1965.

Braidwood, R. J., *Prehistoric Men*, 8th ed., Glenview, Ill.: Scott, Foresman, 1975.

CLIMAP Project Members, "The Surface of the Ice-Age Earth," *Science*, 19 March 1976.

Flannery, Kent V., "The Origins of Agriculture," *Annual Review of Anthropology*, vol. 2, 1973.

Frisch, R. E., "Critical Weight at Menarche, Initiation of the Adolescent Growth Spurt, and Control of Puberty," in *Control of Puberty*, New York: John Wiley, 1974.

Harris, David R., "Alternate Pathways Towards Agriculture," in *Origins of Agriculture*, Chicago: Aldine, 1966.

———, "Settling Down: An Evolutionary Model for the Transformation of Mobile Bands Into Sedentary Communities," in *The Evolution of Social Systems*, London: Duckworth, 1976.

Higgs, E. S., (ed.), *Papers in Economic Prehistory*, New York: Cambridge University Press, 1972.

———, *Palaeoeconomy*, New York: Cambridge University Press, 1974.

——— and Jarman, M. A., "The Origins of Agriculture: A Reconsideration," *American Antiquity*, March 1969.

Howell, Nancy, "Toward a Uniformitarian Theory of Human Paleodemography," *Journal of Human Evolution*, vol. 5, p. 25, 1976.

Pfeiffer, John E., "The First Food Crisis," *Horizon*, Autumn 1975.

———, "A Note on the Problem of Basic Causes," in *Origins of African Plant Domestication*, Chicago: Aldine, 1976.

Sahlins, Marshall D., *Stone Age Economics*, Chicago: Aldine, 1972.

Scudder, Thayer, "Gathering Among African Woodland Savannah Cultivators," Institute for African Studies, University of Zambia, 1971.

Smith, Philip E. L., "Changes in Population Pressure in Archaeological Explanation," *World Archaeology*, June 1972.

——, *Food Production and Its Consequences*, Menlo Park, California: Cummings, 1976.

Struever, Stuart, (ed.), *Prehistoric Agriculture*, New York: Natural History Press, 1971.

Ucko, P. J. and Dimbleby, G. W., (eds.), *The Domestication and Exploitation of Plants and Animals*, Chicago: Aldine, 1969.

CHAPTER 4

Adams, Robert McC., *The Evolution of Urban Society*, Chicago: Aldine, 1966.

Chagnon, Napoleon A., *Yąnomamö, The Fierce People*, New York: Holt, Rinehart and Winston, 1968.

——, *Studying the Yąnomamö*, New York: Holt, Rinehart and Winston, 1974.

Crumley, Carole L., "Toward a Locational Definition of State Systems of Settlement," *American Anthropologist*, March 1976.

Flannery, Kent V., "The Cultural Evolution of Civilizations," *Annual Review of Ecology and Systematics*, vol. 3, 1972.

Peebles, Christopher S., "Moundville and Surrounding Sites: Some Structural Considerations for Mortuary Practices," *Memoirs of the Society for American Archaeology 25*, 1971.

—— and Kus, Susan M., "Some Archaeological Correlates of Ranked Societies," in *The Emergence of the Mississippian*, Albuquerque, N.M.: University of New Mexico Press. In press.

Pfeiffer, John E., "How Man Invented Cities," *Horizon*, Autumn 1972.

Ucko, Peter J., Tringham Ruth, and Dimbleby, G. W., *Man, Settlement and Urbanism*, Cambridge, Mass.: Schenkman, 1972.

Wheatley, Paul, *The Pivot of the Four Quarters*, Chicago: Aldine, 1971.

Wright, Henry T. and Johnson, Gregory A., "Population, Exchange and Early State Formation in Southwestern Iran," *American Anthropologist*, June 1975.

CHAPTER 5

Binford, Lewis R., "Hatchery West: Site Definition—Surface Distribution of Cultural Items," in *An Archaeological Perspective*, New York: Seminar Press, 1972.

Cook, Della C., "Pathologic States and Disease Process in Illinois Woodland Populations: An Epidemiologic Approach," doctoral dissertation, University of Chicago, 1976.

Drew, Isabella Milling; Perkins, Dexter; and Daly, Patricia, "Prehistoric Domestication of Animals: Effects on Bone Structure," *Science*, 22 January 1971.

Ebert, James I. and Hitchcock, Robert K., "Chaco Canyon's Mysterious Highways," *Horizon*, Autumn 1975.

Friedrich, Margaret Hardin, "Design Structure and Social Interaction: Archaeological Implications of an Ethnographic Analysis," *American Antiquity*, August 1970.

Hammond, Norman, "The Planning of a Maya Ceremonial Center," *Scientific American*, May 1972.

Hill, James N., "Individual Variability in Ceramics, and the Study of Prehistoric Social Organization," in *The Individual in Prehistory: An Approach to the Past*, New York: Academic Press, 1976.

Hole, Frank; Flannery, Kent V.; and Neely, James A., "Prehistory and Human Ecology of the Deh Luran Plain," *Memoirs of the Museum of Anthropology*, University of Michigan, No. 1, 1969.

Reed, Charles A., "Animal Domestication in the Prehistoric Near East," *Science*, 19 December 1959.

——— and Palmer, Harris A., "A Late Quaternary Goat in North America?" *Zeitschrift fur Saugetierkunde*," vol. 29, p. 372, 1964.

——— and Schaffer, William H., "How to Tell the Sheep from the Goats," *Field Museum Bulletin*, March 1972.

Skinner, G. William, "Marketing and Social Structure in Rural China," Parts I and II, *Journal of Asian Studies*, vol. 24, pp. 3–43, 195–228, 1975–6.

Zeder, Melinda A., "Discrimination Between the Bones of Caprines from Different Ecosystems in the Near East: With the Use of Osteological Microstructure and Chemical Composition," B.A. thesis, Museum of Anthropology, University of Michigan, 1976.

CHAPTER 6

Cambel, Halet and Braidwood, Robert J., "An Early Farming Village in Turkey," *Scientific American*, March 1970.

Flannery, Kent V., "The Ecology of Early Food Production in Mesopotamia," *Science*, 12 March 1965.

———, "The Origins of the Village as a Settlement Type in Mesoamerica and the Near East: A Comparative Study," in *Man, Settlement and Urbanism*, Cambridge, Mass.: Schenkman, 1972.

Harlan, Jack R., "A Wild Wheat Harvest in Turkey," *Archaeology*, June 1967.

Mellaart, James, "A Neolithic City in Turkey," *Scientific American*, April 1964.

Oates, Joan, "The Background and Development of Early Farming Communities in Mesopotamia and the Zagros," *Proceedings of the Prehistoric Society*, 1973.

Renfrew, Jane M., *Palaeoethnobotany*, New York: Columbia University Press, 1973.

Saxon, Earl C., "Prehistoric Economies of the Israeli and Algerian Littorals," doctoral dissertation, Jesus College, Cambridge, 1976.

Smith, Philip E. L., "Ganj Dareh Tepe," *Iran*, XIII, 1975.

—— and Young, T. Cuyler Jr., "The Evolution of Early Agriculture and Culture in Greater Mesopotamia: A Trial Model," in *Population Growth: Anthropological Implications*, Cambridge, Mass.: M.I.T. Press, 1972.

Vita-Finzi, C. and Higgs, E. S., "Prehistoric Economy in the Mount Carmel Area of Palestine: Site Catchment Analysis," *Proceedings of the Prehistoric Society for 1970*.

Watson, Patty Jo, "Clues to Iranian Prehistory in Modern Village Life," *Expedition*, Spring 1966.

Zohary, Daniel, "The Progenitors of Wheat and Barley in Relation to Domestication and Agricultural Dispersal in the Old World," in *The Domestication and Exploitation of Plants and Animals*, London: Duckworth, 1969.

CHAPTER 7

Adams, Robert McC., *Land Behind Baghdad*, Chicago: University of Chicago Press, 1965.

——, "Patterns of Urbanization in Early Southern Mesopotamia," in *Man, Settlement and Urbanism*, Cambridge, Mass.: Schenkman, 1972.

——, "The Mesopotamian Social Landscape: A View From the Frontier," in *Reconstructing Complex Societies*, Supplement to the Bulletin of the American Schools of Oriental Research, No. 20, 1975.

—— and Nissen, Hans J., *The Uruk Countryside*, Chicago: University of Chicago Press, 1972.

DeCardi, Beatrice, "The British Archaeological Expedition to Qatar 1973–4," *Antiquity*, September 1974.

Gibson, McGuire, "Population Shift and the Rise of Mesopotamian Civilization," in *The Explanation of Cultural Change: Models in Prehistory*, London: Duckworth, 1972.

——, "Violation of Fallow and Engineered Disaster in Mesopotamian Civilization," in *Irrigation's Impact on Society*, Tucson: University of Arizona Press, 1973.

Johnson, Gregory A., "Locational Analysis and the Investigation of Uruk Local Exchange Systems," in *Ancient Civilization and Trade*, Albuquerque, N.M.: University of New Mexico Press, 1975.

Nissen, Hans J., "The City Wall of Uruk," in *The Explanation of Cultural Change: Models in Prehistory*, London: Duckworth, 1972.

Oates, Joan, "Prehistory in Northeastern Arabia," *Antiquity*, March 1976.

Wright, Henry T., "The Administration of Rural Production in an Early Mesopotamian Town," Museum of Anthropology, *Anthropological Papers*, No. 38, Ann Arbor: University of Michigan, 1969.

CHAPTER 8

Barth, Fredrik, *Nomads of South Persia,* Boston: Little, Brown, 1961.

Beale, Thomas W., "Early Trade in Highland Iran: A View from a Source Area," *World Archaeology,* October 1973.

Cronin, Vincent, *The Last Migration,* London: Rupert Hart-Davis, 1957.

Dixon, J. E.; Caan, J. B.; and Renfrew, Colin, "Obsidian and the Origins of Trade," *Scientific American,* March 1968.

Hole, Frank, "Excavation of Tepe Tula'i," *Proceedings of the III'd Annual Symposium on Archaeology in Iran,* November 1974.

Johnson, Gregory Alan, "Local Exchange and Early State Development in Southwestern Iran," Museum of Anthropology, *Anthropological Papers,* No. 51, Ann Arbor: University of Michigan, 1973.

———, "Early State Organization in Southwestern Iran: Preliminary Field Report," *Proceedings of the IVth Annual Symposium on Archaeological Research in Iran,* November 1975.

Lamberg-Karlovsky, C. C., "Trade Mechanisms in Indus-Mesopotamian Interrelations," *Journal of the American Oriental Society,* April–June 1972.

———, "Third Millennium Models of Exchange and Modes of Production," in *Ancient Civilization and Trade,* Albuquerque, N.M.: University of New Mexico Press, 1975.

——— and Lamberg-Karlovsky, Martha, "An Early City in Iran," *Scientific American,* June 1971.

Lattimore, Owen, *Inner Asian Frontiers of China,* Boston: Beacon, 1962.

Lees, Susan H. and Bates, Daniel G., "The Origins of Specialized Nomadic Pastoralism: A Systemic Model," *American Antiquity,* April 1974.

Lisitsina, G. N., "The Earliest Irrigation in Turkmenia," *Antiquity,* December 1969.

Masson, V. M., "Altin-depe and the Bull Cult," *Antiquity,* March 1976.

——— and Sarianidi, V. I., *Central Asia,* New York: Praeger, 1972.

Sumner, William, "Excavations at Malyan, 1971–2," *Iran,* XII, 1974.

Tosi, Maurizio, "The Early Urban Revolution and Settlement Pattern in the Indo-European Borderland," in *The Explanation of Cultural Change: Models in Prehistory,* London: Duckworth, 1972.

——— and Piperno, Marcello, "Lithic Technology Behind the Ancient Lapis Lazuli Trade," *Expedition,* February 1973.

Weiss, Harvey and Young, T. Cuyler Jr., "The Merchants of Susa," *Iran,* XIII, 1975.

CHAPTER 9

Allchin, Bridget and Raymond, *The Birth of Indian Civilization,* Baltimore, Md.: Penguin Books, 1968.

Clauson, Gerard and Chadwick, John, "The Indus Script Deciphered?" *Antiquity,* September 1969.

Dales, George F., "Excavations at Balakot, Pakistan, 1973," *Journal of Field Archaeology*, vol. 1, 1974.

Fairservis, Walter A. Jr., "The Origin, Character and Decline of an Early Civilization," *American Museum of Natural History Novitates*, No. 2302, October 20, 1967.

——, *The Roots of Ancient India*, New York: Macmillan, 1971.

Masson, V. M., "Prehistoric Settlement Patterns in Soviet Central Asia," in *The Explanation of Cultural Change: Models in Prehistory*, London: Duckworth, 1972.

Mughal, Mohammad Rafique, "The Early Harappan Period in the Greater Indus Valley and Northern Baluchistan," doctoral dissertation, University of Pennsylvania, 1970.

——, "New Evidence of the Early Harappan Culture From Jalilpur, Pakistan," *Archaeology*, vol. 27, 1974.

Possehl, Gregory L., "Lothal: A Gateway Settlement of the Harappan Civilization," in *Studies in the Paleoecology of South Asia*, Ithaca, N.Y.: Cornell University Press, 1976.

——, "Variation and Change in the Indus Civilization," doctoral dissertation, University of Chicago, 1974.

——, ed., "Papers on the Indus Civilization," Dehli, India: Oriental Publishers, 1977.

Singh, Gurdip, "The Indus Valley Culture," *Archaeology and Physical Anthropology in Oceania*, July 1971.

Wheeler, Sir Mortimer, *The Indus Civilization*, 3rd ed., New York: Cambridge University Press, 1968.

CHAPTER 10

Bayard, Donn T., "Non Nok Tha: The 1968 Excavation," *University of Otago Studies in Prehistoric Anthropology 4*, 1971.

——, "An Early Indigenous Bronze Technology in Northeastern Thailand: Its Implications for the Prehistory of East Asia," in *The Diffusion of Material Culture*, Canberra: Australian National University Press. In press.

Bronson, Bennet and Dales, George F., "Excavations at Chansen, Thailand, 1968 and 1969: A Preliminary Report," *Asian Perspectives*, vol. XV, 1973.

Chang, Kwang-chih, *The Archaeology of Ancient China*, New Haven, Conn.: Yale University Press, 1968.

——, "The Beginnings of Agriculture in the Far East," *Antiquity*, vol. LXIV, p. 175, 1970.

——, "Man and Land in Central Taiwan: The First Two Years of an Interdisciplinary Project," *Journal of Field Archaeology*, vol. 1, no. 3/4, 1974.

——, "Urbanism and the King in Ancient China," *World Archaeology*, June 1974.

Gorman, Chester F., "Hoabinhian: A Pebble-Tool Complex with Early Plant Associations in Southeast Asia," *Science,* 14 February 1969.

——, "The Hoabinhian and After: Subsistence Patterns in Southeast Asia During the Late Pleistocene and Early Recent Period," *World Archaeology,* February 1971.

——, "*A Priori* Models and Thai Prehistory: A Reconsideration of the Beginnings of Agriculture in Southeastern Asia," in *Origins of Agriculture,* Chicago: Aldine, 1976.

Ho, Ping-ti, "The Loess and the Origin of Chinese Agriculture," *American Historical Review,* October 1969.

——, *The Cradle of the East,* Chicago: University of Chicago Press, 1975.

Honan, William H., "The Case of the Hot Pots: An Archaeological Thriller," *New York Times Magazine,* 8 June 1975.

Hutterer, Karl L., "An Evolutionary Approach to the Southeast Asian Cultural Sequence," *Current Anthropology,* June 1976.

Li, Hui-Lin, "The Origin of Cultivated Plants in Southeast Asia," *Economic Botany,* January–March 1970.

Ng, Ronald C. Y., "Population Explosion on the North Thai Hills," *Geographical Magazine,* January 1971.

Solheim, Wilhelm G. II, "Southeast Asia and the West," *Science,* 25 August 1967.

——, "Early Man in Southeast Asia," *Expedition,* Spring 1972.

——, "An Earlier Agricultural Revolution," *Scientific American,* April 1972.

Treistman, Judith M., *The Prehistory of China,* New York: Natural History Press, 1972.

Wheatley, Paul, "Archaeology and the Chinese City," *World Archaeology,* October 1970.

——, *The Pivot of the Four Quarters,* Chicago: Aldine, 1971.

——, "The Earliest Cities in Indianized Southeast Asia," paper presented at London Colloquy on early Southeast Asia, September 1973.

CHAPTER 11

Achebe, Chinua, *Things Fall Apart,* Greenwich, Conn.: Fawcett, 1959.

Bisson, Michael S., "Copper Currency in Central Africa: The Archaeological Evidence," *World Archaeology,* February 1975.

Bloch, Maurice, "The Disconnection Between Power and Rank as a Process: An Outline of the Development of Kingdoms in Central Madagascar," in *The Evolution of Social Systems,* London: Duckworth, 1976.

Charney, J.; Stone, P. H.; and Quick, W. J., "Drought in the Sahara: A Biogeophysical Feedback Mechanism," *Science,* 7 February 1975.

Clark, J. Desmond, "A Re-Examination of the Evidence for Agricultural Origins in the Nile Valley," *Proceedings of the Prehistoric Society,* vol. XXXVII, part II, December 1971.

————, "Mobility and Settlement Patterns in Sub-Saharan Africa: A Comparison of Late Prehistoric Hunter-Gatherers and Early Agricultural Occupation Units," in *Man, Settlement and Urbanism,* Cambridge, Mass.: Schenkman, 1972.

————, "Prehistoric Populations and Pressures Favoring Plant Domestication in Africa," in *Origins of African Plant Domestication,* Chicago: Aldine, 1976.

Davidson, Basil, *A History of West Africa to the Nineteenth Century,* New York: Anchor, 1966.

————, *African Kingdoms,* New York: Time-Life Books, 1971.

Fagg, Bernard, "Recent Work in West Africa: New Light on the Nok Culture," *World Archaeology,* June 1969.

Hoffman, Michael A., "City of the Hawk," *Expedition,* Spring 1976.

————, *Egypt Before the Pharaohs—The Prehistoric Foundations of Egyptian Civilization,* New York: Knopf, 1977.

Klein, Richard G., "Environment and Subsistence of Prehistoric Man in the Southern Cape Province, South Africa," *World Archaeology,* February 1974.

Kottak, Conrad P., "Cultural Adaptation, Kinship, and Descent in Madagascar," *Southwestern Journal of Anthropology,* Summer 1971.

————, "Ecological Variables in the Origin and Evolution of African States: The Buganda Example," *Comparative Studies in Society and History,* June 1972.

Munson, Patrick J., "Archaeological Data on the Origins of Cultivation in the Southwest Sahara and Its Implications for West Africa," in *Origins of African Plant Domestication,* Chicago: Aldine, 1976.

Netting, Robert McC., *Hill Farmers of Nigeria,* Seattle: University of Washington Press, 1968.

————, *Ecosystems in Process: A Comparative Study of Change in Two West African Societies,* National Museums of Canada, Bulletin 20, November 1969.

Oliver, Roland and Fagan, Brian M., *Africa in the Iron Age,* London: Cambridge University Press, 1975.

Posnansky, Merrick, "Bantu Genesis—Archaeological Reflexions," *Journal of African History,* vol. IX, p. 1, 1968.

————, "Aspects of Early West African Trade," *World Archaeology,* October 1973.

Saxon, Earl C., "Prehistoric Economies of the Israeli and Algerian Littorals," doctoral dissertation, Jesus College, Cambridge, 1976.

Shaw, Thurstan, "Archaeology in Nigeria," *Antiquity,* vol. XLIII, p. 187, 1969.

————, "Africa in Prehistory: Leader or Laggard?" *Journal of African History,* vol. XII, p. 143, 1971.

————, "Early Crops in Africa: A Review of Evidence," in *Origins of African Plant Domestication,* Chicago: Aldine, 1976.

Smith, Philip E. L., "Stone Age Man on the Nile," *Scientific American,* August 1976.

Wendorf, Fred, "The Use of Ground Grain During the Late Paleolithic of the Lower Nile Valley, Egypt," in *Origins of African Plant Domestication*, Chicago: Aldine, 1976.

———, Said, R., and Schild, R., "Egyptian Prehistory: Some New Concepts," *Science*, vol. 169, p. 1161, 1970.

Wheatley, Paul, "The Significance of Traditional Yoruba Urbanism," *Comparative Studies in Society and History*, October 1970.

Wilson, John A., *The Culture of Ancient Egypt*, Chicago: University of Chicago Press, 1951.

CHAPTER 12

Ammerman, A. J. and Cavalli-Sforza, L. L., "Measuring the Rate of Spread of Early Farming in Europe," *Man*, December 1971.

Berciu, Dumitru, *Romania*, New York: Praeger, 1967.

Chadwick, John, "Life in Mycenaean Greece," *Scientific American*, October 1972.

Crumley, Carole L., "Celtic Social Structure: The Generation of Archaeologically Testable Hypotheses From Literary Evidence," Museum of Anthropology, *Anthropological Papers*, No. 54, Ann Arbor: University of Michigan, 1974.

Evans, John D., "Neolithic Knossos; The Growth of a Settlement," *Proceedings of the Prehistoric Society*, vol. XXXVII, part II, December 1971.

Fleming, Andrew, "Tombs for the Living," *Man*, June 1973.

Fox, Sir Cyril, *The Personality of Britain*, Cardiff: National Museum of Wales, 1959.

Jacobsen, Thomas W., "17,000 Years of Greek Prehistory," *Scientific American*, June 1976.

Norton-Taylor, Duncan, *The Celts*, New York: Time-Life Books, 1974.

Piggott, Stuart, *Ancient Europe*, Chicago: Aldine, 1965.

Renfrew, Colin, "Monuments, Mobilization and Social Organization in Neolithic Wessex," in *The Explanation of Culture Change: Models in Prehistory*, London: Duckworth, 1972.

———, *The Emergence of Civilization: The Cyclades and the Aegean in the Third Millennium B.C.*, New York: Harper & Row, 1973.

———, *Before Civilization*, New York: Knopf, 1973.

———, *Beyond a Subsistence Economy: The Evolution of Social Organization in Prehistoric Europe*, Boston: M.I.T. Press, 1975.

———, "Acculturation and Continuity in Atlantic Europe," *Dissertationes Archaelogicae Gandenses*, Vol. XVI, 1976.

Rodden, Robert J., "An Early Neolithic Village in Greece," *Scientific American*, January 1965.

Rowlett, Ralph M., "The Iron Age North of the Alps," *Science*, 12 July 1968.

Soudsky, Bohumil and Pavlu, Ivan, "The Linear Pottery Culture Settlement

Patterns of Central Europe," in *Man, Settlement and Urbanism*, Cambridge, Mass.: Schenkman, 1972.

Tringham, Ruth, *Hunters, Fishers and Farmers of Eastern Europe, 6000–3000 B.C.*, London: Hutchinson University Library, 1971.

Wailes, Bernard, "The Origins of Settled Farming in Temperate Europe," in *Indo-European and Indo-Europeans*, Philadelphia, Pa.: University of Pennsylvania Press, 1970.

CHAPTER 13

Allen, Harry, "The Bagundji of the Darling Basin: Cereal Gatherers in an Uncertain Environment," *World Archaeology*, February 1974.

Allen, Jim, "The First Decade in New Guinea Archaeology," *Antiquity*, September 1972.

Bellwood, Peter, "Fortifications and Economy in Prehistoric New Zealand," *Proceedings of the Prehistoric Society*, July 1971.

———, "The Prehistory of Oceania," *Current Anthropology*, March 1975.

Cassels, Richard, "Locational Analysis of Prehistoric Settlement in New Zealand," *Mankind*, vol. 8, p. 212, 1972.

———, "Human Ecology in the Prehistoric Waikato," *Journal of the Polynesian Society*, June 1972.

Cordy, Ross H., "Cultural Adaptation and Evolution in Hawaii: A Suggested New Sequence," *Journal of the Polynesian Society*, June 1974.

———, "Complex Rank Cultural Systems in the Hawaiian Islands: Suggested Explanations for Their Origins," *Archaeology and Physical Anthropology in Oceania*, July 1974.

Ember, Carol R. and Ember, Melvin, *Anthropology*, New York: Appleton-Century-Crofts, 1973.

Gladwin, Thomas, *East Is a Big Bird: Navigation and Logic on Puluwat Atoll*, Cambridge, Mass.: Harvard University Press, 1970.

Golson, Jack, "The Pacific Islands and Their Prehistoric Inhabitants," in *Man in the Pacific Islands*, Oxford: Clarendon Press, 1972.

———, "Both Sides of the Wallace Line: New Guinea, Australia, Island Melanesia, and Asian Prehistory," in *Early Chinese Art and Its Possible Influence in the Pacific Basin*, New York: Intercultural Arts Press, 1972.

———, "The Making of the New Guinea Highlands," in *The Melanesian Environment: Change and Development*, Canberra: Australian National University Press, 1976.

———, "No Room at the Top: Agricultural Intensification in the New Guinea Highlands," in *Sunda and Sahul: Prehistoric Studies in Island Southeast Asia, Melanesia, and Australia*," London: Academic Press, 1976.

——— and Hughes, P. J., "The Appearance of Plant and Animal Domestication in New Guinea," paper prepared for the Ninth Congress of the International Union of Pre- and Protohistoric Sciences, Nice, September 1976.

Green, R. C., "Sites With Lapita Pottery: Importing and Voyaging," *Mankind*, December 1974.

———, "New Sites with Lapita Pottery and Their Implications for an Understanding of the Settlement of the Western Pacific," paper prepared for the Ninth Congress of the International Union of Pre- and Protohistoric Sciences, Nice, September 1976.

Harris, David R., "Subsistence Strategies Across Torres Strait," in *Sunda and Sahul: Prehistoric Studies in Island Southeast Asia, Melanesia and Australia*, London: Academic Press, 1976.

Hutterer, Karl L., "The Evolution of Philippine Lowland Societies," *Mankind*, vol. 9, p. 287, 1974.

Lewis, David, *We, The Navigators*, Canberra: Australian National University Press, 1973.

Matthiessen, Peter, *Under the Mountain Wall*, New York: Viking, 1962.

Sahlins, Marshall D., *Tribesmen*, Englewood Cliffs, N.J.: Prentice-Hall, 1968.

Sorenson, E. Richard, "Socio-Ecological Change Among the Fore of New Guinea," *Current Anthropology*, June–October 1972.

Tainter, Joe, "The Social Correlates of Mortuary Patterning at Kaloko, North Konoa, Hawaii," *Archaeology and Physical Anthropology in Oceania*, April 1973.

Webb, M. C., "The Abolition of the Taboo System in Hawaii," *Journal of the Polynesian Society*, March 1965.

White, Peter; Crook, K.A.W.; and Buxton, B. P., "Kosipe: A Late Pleistocene Site in the Papuan Highlands," *Proceedings of the Prehistoric Society*, vol. XXXVI, 1970.

CHAPTER 14

Bada, Jeffrey L. and Helfman, Patricia Masters, "Amino Acid Racemization Dating of Fossil Bones," *World Archaeology*, October 1975.

Beadle, George W., "The Mystery of Maize," *Field Museum Bulletin*, November 1972.

Bray, Warwick, "From Foraging to Farming in Early Mexico," in *Hunters, Gatherers and First Farmers Beyond Europe: An Archaeological Survey*, Leicester, England: Leicester University Press, 1976.

Carlson, John B., "Lodestone Compass: Chinese or Olmec Primacy?" *Science*, 5 September 1975.

Cobean, Robert H. et al., "Obsidian Trade at San Lorenzo Tenochtitlan, Mexico," *Science*, 12 November 1971.

Coe, M. D., *America's First Civilization: Discovering the Olmec*, New York: American Heritage, 1968.

———, "San Lorenzo and the Olmec Civilization," in *Dumbarton Oaks Conference on the Olmec*, Washington, D.C., 1968.

Flannery, Kent V. et al., "Farming Systems and Political Growth in Ancient Oaxaca," *Science*, 27 October 1967.

————, "The Olmec and the Valley of Oaxaca: A Model for Inter-Regional Interaction in Formative Times," in *Dumbarton Oaks Conference on the Olmec,* Washington, D.C., 1968.

————, "The Origins of the Village as a Settlement Type in Mesoamerica and the Near East: A Comparative Study," in *Man, Settlement and Urbanism,* Cambridge, Mass.: Schenkman, 1972.

————, (ed.), *The Early Mesoamerican Village,* New York: Academic Press, 1976.

———— and Marcus, Joyce, "The Evolution of the Public Building in Formative Oaxaca," in *Cultural Change and Continuity,* New York: Academic Press, 1976.

———— and Schoenwetter, James, "Climate and Man in Formative Oaxaca," *Archaeology,* April 1970.

Galinat, Walton C., "The Origin of Maize," *Annual Review of Genetics,* vol. 5, 1971.

Grove, David C., "Chalcatzingo, Morelos, Mexico: A Reappraisal of the Olmec Rock Carvings," *American Antiquity,* October 1968.

————, "The Highland Olmec Manifestation: A Consideration of What It Is and Isn't," in *Mesoamerican Archaeology: New Approaches,* Austin: University of Texas Press, 1974.

————, et al., "Settlement and Cultural Development at Chalcatzingo," *Science,* 18 June 1976.

Heizer, Robert F., "New Observations on La Venta," in *Dumbarton Oaks Conference on the Olmec,* Washington, D.C., 1968.

Kirkby, Anne V., "The Use of Land and Water Resources in the Past and Present Valley of Oaxaca, Mexico," *Memoirs of the Museum of Anthropology,* University of Michigan, No. 5, 1973.

Lees, Susan H., "Sociopolitical Aspects of Canal Irrigation in the Valley of Oaxaca," *Memoirs of the Museum of Anthropology,* University of Michigan, No. 6, 1973.

MacNeish, Richard S., "Food Production and Village Life in the Tehuacan Valley, Mexico," *Archaeology,* October 1971.

————, "Ancient Mesoamerican Civilization," *Science,* 7 February 1974.

————, *The Prehistory of the Tehuacan Valley: The Dawn of Civilization,* vol. 6, Austin: University of Texas Press, 1976.

Patterson, Thomas C., *America's Past: A New World Archaeology,* Glenview, Ill.: Scott, Foresman, 1973.

Pickersgill, Barbara, "Agricultural Origins in the Americas: Independence or Interdependence," paper presented at Institute of Archaeology, London, 25 March 1975.

Pires-Ferreira, Jane W., "Formative Mesoamerican Exchange Networks With Special Reference to the Valley of Oaxaca," *Memoirs of the Museum of Anthropology,* University of Michigan, No. 7, 1975.

Proskouriakoff, Tatiana, "Olmec and Maya Art: Problems of Their Stylistic Relation," in *Dumbarton Oaks Conference on the Olmec,* Washington, D.C., 1968.

Rainer, Berger, "Advances and Results in Radiocarbon Dating: Early Man in

America," *World Archaeology*, October 1975.

Swanson, Earl H.; Bray, Warwick; and Farrington, Ian, *The New World*, London: Elsevier-Phaidon, 1976.

CHAPTER 15

Blanton, Richard E., "Prehispanic Adaptation in the Ixtapalapa Region, Mexico," *Science*, 24 March 1972.

———, "The Origins of Monte Alban," in *Cultural Change and Continuity*, New York: Academic Press, 1976.

Bray, Warwick, "The City State in Central Mexico at the Time of the Spanish Conquest," *Journal of Latin American Studies*, vol. 4, p. 161, 1973.

Bullard, W. R. Jr., "Maya Settlement Pattern in Northeastern Peten, Guatemala," *American Antiquity*, vol. 25, p. 355, 1960.

Coe, Michael D., *The Maya*, New York: Praeger, 1966.

———, "Death and the Ancient Maya," in *Death and the Afterlife in Pre-Columbian America*, Dumbarton Oaks Research Library and Collections, Washington, D.C., 1975.

Coe, William R., "Tikal, Guatemala, and Emergent Maya Civilization," *Science*, 19 March 1965.

———, *Tikal: A Handbook of the Ancient Maya Ruins*, Philadelphia: University of Pennsylvania, 1967.

Coggins, Clemency Chase, "Painting and Drawing Styles at Tikal: An Historical Iconographic Reconstruction," doctoral dissertation, Harvard University, 1975.

Cowgill, George L., "Quantitative Studies of Urbanization at Teotihuacan," in *Mesoamerican Archaeology: New Approaches*, Austin: University of Texas Press, 1974.

Flannery, Kent V., "The Cultural Evolution of Civilization," *Annual Review of Ecology and Systematics*, vol. 3, 1972.

——— and Marcus Joyce, "Formative Oaxaca and the Zapotec Cosmos," *American Scientist*, July 1976.

Hammond, Norman, "The Distribution of Late Classic Maya Major Ceremonial Centres in the Central Area," in *Mesoamerican Archaeology: New Approaches*, Austin: University of Texas Press, 1974.

Haviland, W. A., "Stature at Tikal, Guatemala: Implications for Ancient Maya Demography and Social Organization," *American Antiquity*, vol. 32, p. 316, 1967.

———, "Tikal, Guatemala, and Mesoamerican Urbanism," *World Archaeology*, October 1970.

Jones, Christopher, "Inauguration Dates of Three Late Classic Rulers of Tikal, Guatemala," *American Antiquity*. In press.

Marcus, Joyce, "Territorial Organization of the Lowland Classic Maya," *Science*, 1 June 1973.

———, "The Origins of Mesoamerican Writing," *Annual Review of Anthropology*, vol. 5, 1976.

————, "The Iconography of Militarism at Monte Alban and Neighboring Sites in the Valley of Oaxaca," in *The Origins of Religious Art and Iconography in Preclassic Mesoamerica*," Latin American Center University of California at Los Angeles, 1976.

Millon, Clara, "Painting, Writing, and Polity in Teotihuacan, Mexico," *American Antiquity*, July 1973.

Millon, René, "Teotihuacan," *Scientific American*, June 1967.

————, "Teotihuacan: Completion of Map of Giant Ancient City in the Valley of Mexico," *Science*, 4 December 1970.

————, "The Study of Urbanism at Teotihuacan, Mexico," in *Mesoamerican Archaeology: New Approaches*, Austin: University of Texas Press, 1974.

Neely, James A., "Prehistoric Domestic Water Supplies and Irrigation Systems at Monte Alban, Oaxaca, Mexico," paper presented at 37th Annual Meeting of the Society for American Archaeology, Miami, May 1972.

Parsons, Jeffrey R., "Teotihuacan, Mexico, and Its Impact on Regional Demography," *Science*, 22 November 1968.

————, "The Development of a Prehistoric Complex Society: A Regional Perspective from the Valley of Mexico," *Journal of Field Archaeology*, vol. 1, 1974.

Pfeiffer, John, "The Life and Death of a Great City," *Horizon*, Winter 1974.

Proskouriakoff, Tatiana, "Historical Implications of a Pattern of Dates at Piedras Negras, Guatemala," *American Antiquity*, vol. 25, p. 454, 1960.

————, "The Lords of the Maya Realm," *Expedition*, vol. 4, p. 14, 1961.

Puleston, Dennis E., "An Experimental Approach to the Function of Classic Maya Chultuns," *American Antiquity*, July 1971.

————, "Intersite Areas in the Vicinity of Tikal and Uaxactun," in *Mesoamerican Archaeology: New Approaches*, Austin: University of Texas Press, 1974.

————, "The Art and Archaeology of Hydraulic Agriculture in the Maya Lowlands," in *Social Process in Maya Prehistory: Studies in Memory of Sir Eric Thompson*, New York: Academic Press, 1976.

———— and Puleston, Olga Stavrakis, "An Ecological Approach to the Origins of Maya Civilization," *Archaeology*, October 1971.

Pyne, Nanette M., "The Fire-Serpent and Were-Jaguar in Formative Oaxaca: A Contingency Table Analysis," in *The Early Mesoamerican Village*, New York: Academic Press, 1976.

Rensberger, Boyce, "New Finds Suggest Mayas Originated in the Highlands," *New York Times*, 11 April 1976.

Sabloff, Jeremy A. et al., "Trade and Power in Post-classic Yucatan: Initial Observations," in *Mesoamerican Archaeology: New Approaches*, Austin: University of Texas Press, 1974.

———— and Rathje, William L., "The Rise of a Maya Merchant Class," *Scientific American*, October 1975.

Sanders, William T., "The Cultural Ecology of the Lowland Maya: A Reevaluation," in *The Classic Maya Collapse*, Albuquerque: University of New Mexico Press, 1973.

Siemens, Alfred H. and Puleston, Dennis E., "Ridged Fields and Associated Features in Southern Campeche: New Perspectives on the Lowland Maya," *American Antiquity*, April 1972.

Spence, Michael W., "The Obsidian Industry of Teotihuacan," *American Antiquity*, October 1967.

———, "The Development of the Classic Period Teotihuacan Obsidian Production System," paper presented at Annual Meeting of the Society for American Archaeology, San Francisco, May 1973.

Turner, B. L. II, "Prehistoric Intensive Agriculture in the Maya Lowlands," *Science*, 12 July 1974.

Vogt, Evon Z., *Zinacantan: A Maya Community in the Highlands of Chiapas*, Cambridge, Mass.: Harvard University Press, 1969.

Weaver, Muriel Porter, *The Aztecs, Maya, and Their Predecessors*, New York: Seminar Press, 1972.

Winter, Marcus C., "Residential Patterns at Monte Alban, Oaxaca, Mexico," *Science*, 13 December 1974.

CHAPTER 16

Browman, David L., "Pastoral Nomadism in the Andes," *Current Anthropology*, June 1974.

Cohen, Mark N., "Population Pressure and the Origins of Agriculture: An Archaeological Example from the Coast of Peru," in *Advances in Andean Archaeology*, Chicago: Aldine, 1976.

Denevan, William M., "Aboriginal Drained-Field Cultivation in the Americas," *Science*, 14 August 1970.

Gross, Daniel R., "Protein Capture and Cultural Development in the Amazon Basin," *American Anthropologist*, September 1975.

Jensen, Peter M. and Kautz, Robert R., "Preceramic Transhumance and Andean Food Production," *Economic Botany*, January–March 1974.

Kaplan, L.; Lynch, Thomas F.; and Smith, E. E. Jr., "Early Cultivated Beans (*Phaseolus vulgaris*) From an Intermontane Peruvian Valley," *Science*, 5 January 1973.

Lathrap, Donald W., *The Upper Amazon*, New York: Praeger, 1970.

———, "The Tropical Forest and the Cultural Context of Chavín," in *Dumbarton Oaks Conference on Chavín*, Dumbarton Oaks Research Library and Collections, Washington, D.C., 1971.

———, "Gifts of the Cayman: Some Thoughts on the Subsistence Basis of Chavín," in *Variation in Anthropology*, Urbana, Ill.: Illinois Archaeological Survey, 1973.

———, "The Antiquity and Importance of Long-Distance Trade Relationships in the Moist Tropics of the Pre-Columbian South America," *World Archaeology*, October 1973.

———, "The Origins of Mesoamerican Civilization as Viewed from Northern South America," paper presented at 2nd Symposium on Mesoamerican Archaeology, Cambridge, August 1976.

————, "Our Father the Cayman, Our Mother the Gourd: Spinden Revisited, or a Unitary Model for the Emergence of Agriculture in the New World," in *Origins of Agriculture*, Chicago: Aldine, 1976.

————, Marcos, Jorge, and Zeidler, James, "Real Alto: An Ancient Ecuadorian Ceremonial Center?" *Archaeology*, April 1977.

Lumbreras, Luis G., *The Peoples and Cultures of Ancient Peru*, New York: George Braziller, 1974.

Lynch, Thomas F., "Preceramic Transhumance in the Callejon de Huaylas, Peru," *American Antiquity*, April 1971.

————, "The Antiquity of Man in South America," *Quaternary Research*, vol. 4, p. 356, 1974.

MacNeish, Richard S.; Berger, R.; and Protsch, Reiner, "Megafauna and Man from Ayacucho, Highlands Peru," *Science*, 22 May 1970.

————, Patterson, Thomas C. and Browman, David L., *The Central Peruvian Prehistoric Interaction Sphere*, Andover, Mass.: Peabody Foundation for Archaeology, 1975.

Menzel, Dorothy, "The Inca Occupation of the South Coast of Peru," *Southwestern Journal of Anthropology*, Summer 1959.

————, "Style and Time in the Middle Horizon," in *Peruvian Archaeology: Selected Readings*, Palo Alto, Calif.: Peek Publications, 1967.

Moseley, M. Edward, "Subsistence and Demography: An Example of Interaction from Prehistoric Peru," *Southwestern Journal of Anthropology*, Spring 1972.

Murra, John V., "The Economic Organization of the Inca State," doctoral dissertation, University of Chicago, 1956.

————, "Cloth and Its Functions in the Inca State," *American Anthropologist*, August 1962.

————, "Herds and Herders in the Inca State," in *Man, Culture and Animals*, Washington, D.C.: American Association for the Advancement of Science, 1965.

————, "An Aymara Kingdom in 1567," *Ethnohistory*, Spring 1968.

————, "Current Research and Prospects in Andean Ethnohistory," *Latin American Research Review*, Spring 1970.

———— and Morris, Craig, "Dynastic Oral Tradition, Administrative Records, and Archaeology in the Andes," *World Archaeology*, February 1976.

Parsons, James J. and Denevan, William M., "Pre-Columbian Ridged Fields," *Scientific American*, July 1967.

Patterson, Thomas C., "Central Peru: Its Population and Economy," *Archaeology*, October 1971.

————, "Chavín: An Interpretation of Its Spread and Influence," in *Dumbarton Oaks Conference on Chavín*, Dumbarton Oaks Research Library and Collections, Washington, D.C., 1971.

Pearsall, Deborah M., "Evidence of Maize from Real Alto, Ecuador: Preliminary Results of Opal Phytolith Analysis," paper presented at the 41st Annual Meeting of the Society for American Archaeology, St. Louis, May 1976.

Pires-Ferreira, Jane Wheeler; Pires-Ferreira, Edgardo; and Kaulicke, Peter, "Preceramic Animal Utilization in the Central Peruvian Andes with Particular Reference to Uchcumachay Cave and the Puna of Junin," paper presented at the 41st Annual Meeting of the Society for American Archaeology, St. Louis, May 1976.

Rowe, John Howland, "Form and Meaning in Chavin Art," in *Peruvian Archaeology: Selected Readings*, Palo Alto, Calif.: Peek Publications, 1967.

Willey, Gordon R., "The Early Great Art Styles and the Rise of Pre-Columbian Civilizations," *American Anthropologist*, February 1962.

Wing, Elizabeth, "Animal Domestication in the Andes," paper presented at the XII International Congress of Prehistoric and Protohistoric Sciences, Chicago, 1973.

CHAPTER 17

Bannister, Bryant and Robinson, William J., "Tree-Ring Dating in Archaeology," *World Archaeology*, October 1975.

Brown, James A., "Spiro Art and Its Mortuary Contexts," in *Death and the Afterlife in Pre-Columbian America*, Dumbarton Oaks Research Library and Collections, Washington, D.C., 1975.

Caldwell, Joseph R., "Interaction Spheres in Prehistory," in *Hopewellian Studies*, Springfield, Ill.: Illinois State Museum, 1964.

Chmurny, William Wayne, "The Ecology of the Middle Mississippian Occupation of the American Bottom." In press.

Dragoo, Don W., "Some Aspects of Eastern North American Prehistory: A Review 1975," *American Antiquity*, January 1976.

Ebert, James I. and Hitchcock, Robert K., "Spatial Inference and the Archaeology of Complex Societies," paper prepared for Conference on Formal Methods for the Analysis of Regional Social Structure, Santa Fe, New Mexico, October 1973.

Ember, Melvin and Ember, Carol R., "The Conditions Favoring Matrilocal Versus Patrilocal Residence," *American Anthropologist*, June 1971.

Ford, Richard I., "Northeastern Archeology: Past and Future Directions," *Annual Review of Anthropology*, vol. 3, 1974.

————, "Re-excavation of Jemez Cave, New Mexico, *Awanyu*, Archaeological Society of New Mexico, September 1, 1975.

Fowler, Melvin L., "A Pre-Columbian Urban Center on the Mississippi," *Scientific American*, August 1975.

Fritts, Harold C., "Tree Rings and Climate," *Scientific American*, May 1972.

Haury, Emil W., *The Hohokam: Desert Farmers and Craftsmen*, Tucson: University of Arizona Press, 1976.

Hill, James N., "A Prehistoric Community in Eastern Arizona," *Southwestern Journal of Anthropology*, Spring 1966.

————, *Broken K. Pueblo: Prehistoric Social Organization in the American Southwest*, Tucson: University of Arizona Press, 1970.

Houart, Gail L., "Koster: A Stratified Archaic Site in the Illinois Valley," Springfield, Ill.: Illinois State Museum, Reports of Investigations No. 22, 1971.

Longacre, William A., "Current Directions in Southwestern Archaeology," *Annual Review of Anthropology*, vol. 2, 1973.

———, "Population Dynamics at the Grasshopper Pueblo, Arizona," *American Antiquity*, April 1975.

Osborne, Douglas, "Solving the Riddles of Wetherill Mesa," *National Geographic*, February 1964.

———, "Slow Exodus from Mesa Verde," *Natural History*, January 1976.

Pfeiffer, John, "America's First City," *Horizon*, Spring 1974.

———, *Indian City on the Mississippi*, New York: Time-Life Nature/Science Annual, 1974.

Prufer, Olaf H., "The Hopewell Cult," *Scientific American*, December 1964.

Schwartz, Douglas W., "Prehistoric Man in Mammoth Cave," *Scientific American*, July 1960.

Struever, Stuart and Houart, Gail L., "An Analysis of the Hopewell Interaction Sphere," in *Social Exchange and Interaction*, Museum of Anthropology, *Anthropological Papers*, No. 46, Ann Arbor: University of Michigan, 1972.

——— and Vickery, Kent D., "The Beginnings of Cultivation in the Midwest-Riverine Area of the United States," *American Anthropologist*, October 1973.

Stuart, George E., "Who Were the Mound Builders?" *National Geographic*, December 1972.

Watson, Patty Jo, "The Prehistory of Salts Cave, Kentucky," Springfield, Ill.: Illinois State Museum, Reports of Investigations No. 16, 1969.

———, "Archeology of the Mammoth Cave Area," New York: Academic Press, 1974.

Winters, Howard D., *The Riverton Culture*, Springfield, Ill.: Illinois State Museum, 1969.

CHAPTER 18

Bloch, Maurice, "The Disconnection Between Power and Rank as a Process: An Outline of the Development of Kingdoms in Central Madagascar," in *The Revolution of Social Systems*, London: Duckworth, 1976.

Carneiro, Robert L., "A Theory of the Origin of the State," *Science*, 21 August 1970.

Chagnon, Napoleon A., *Studying the Yąnomamö*, New York: Holt, Rinehart and Winston, 1974.

Gorlin, Peter, "Medical Variation and the Origin of Social Stratification: A New Guinea Case," *Human Ecology*, October 1976.

Harding, Thomas G., "Money, Kinship and Change in a New Guinea Economy," *Southwestern Journal of Anthropology*, Autumn 1967.

Rappaport, Roy A., "Ritual Regulation of Environmental Relationships

Among a New Guinea People," in *Environment and Cultural Behavior,* New York: Natural History Press, 1969.

Reichel-Dolmatoff, Gerardo, *Amazonian Cosmos,* Chicago: University of Chicago Press, 1971.

———, "Cosmology as Ecological Analysis: A View from the Rain Forest," *Man.* In press.

Uphill, Eric, "The Concept of the Egyptian Palace as a 'Ruling Machine,'" in *Man, Settlement and Urbanism,* Cambridge, Mass.: Schenkman, 1972.

CHAPTER 19

Beer, Stafford, *Brain of the Firm,* New York: Herder and Herder, 1972.

Cole, M. and Goody, Jack, "Writing and Formal Operations in Misila," *Africa.* In press.

Culbert, T. Patrick, *The Classic Maya Collapse,* Albuquerque: University of New Mexico Press, 1973.

Dales, George F., "The Decline of the Harappans," *Scientific American,* May 1966.

Draper, Patricia, "Socialization for Sex Role Among Kung Bushmen Children," paper presented at the Annual Meeting of the American Association for the Advancement of Science, Philadelphia, December 1971.

———, "Kung Women: Contrasts in Sexual Egalitarianism in Foraging and Sedentary Contexts," in *Toward an Anthropology of Women,* Lexington, Mass.: Xerox Publishing Company, 1972.

Flannery, Kent V., "The Cultural Evolution of Civilizations," *Annual Review of Ecology and Systematics,* vol. 3, 1972.

Goody, Jack, "Evolution and Communication: The Domestication of the Savage Mind," *British Journal of Sociology,* March 1973.

Jacobsen, Thorkild and Adams, Robert M., "Salt and Silt in Ancient Mesopotamian Agriculture," *Science,* 21 November 1958.

Johnson, Gregory A., "Information Sources and the Development of Decision-Making Organizations," paper presented to a Conference on Social Differentiation and Interaction at the State University of New York, Binghamton, April 1976.

Kelley, David H., "Eurasian Evidence and the Maya Calendar Correlation Problem," in *Mesoamerican Archaeology: New Approaches,* Austin: University of Texas Press, 1974.

Kolata, Gina Bari, "Kung Hunter-Gatherers: Feminism, Diet, and Birth Control," *Science,* 13 September 1974.

Pfeiffer, John, "The Life and Death of a Great City," *Horizon,* Winter 1974.

Possehl, Gregory L., "The Mohenjo-daro Floods: A Reply," *American Anthropologist,* February 1967.

———, "The End of a State and the Continuity of a Tradition: A Discussion of the Late Harappan." In press.

Rathje, William L., "The Last Tango in Mayapán: A Tentative Trajectory of Production-Distribution Systems," in *Ancient Civilization and Trade*, Albuquerque: University of New Mexico Press, 1975.

Renfrew, Colin, "Trade as Action at a Distance: Questions of Integration and Communication," in *Ancient Civilization and Trade*, Albuquerque: University of New Mexico Press, 1975.

Rothschild, Nan A., "Sex, Graves and Status," paper presented at the Annual Meeting of the American Anthropological Association, New Orleans, November 1973.

Sabloff, Jeremy and Rathje, William L., "The Rise of a Maya Merchant Class," *Scientific American*, October 1975.

Tolstoy, Paul, "Cultural Parallels Between Southeast Asia and Mesoamerica in the Manufacture of Bark Cloth," *Transactions of the New York Academy of Sciences*, April 1963.

Willey, Gordon R., "The Classic Maya Hiatus: A Rehearsal for the Collapse?" in *Mesoamerican Archaeology: New Approaches*, Austin: University of Texas Press, 1974.

Index